THE LONG SHADOW OF WORLD WAR II

The Legacy of the War and its Impact on Political
and Military Thinking since 1945

MATTHIAS STROHN

CASEMATE
academic

Oxford & Philadelphia

Published in Great Britain and the United States of America in 2021 by
CASEMATE PUBLISHERS
The Old Music Hall, 106–108 Cowley Road, Oxford OX4 1JE, UK
and
1950 Lawrence Road, Havertown, PA 19083, USA

Hardback Edition: ISBN 978-1-95271-502-0
Digital Edition: ISBN 978-1-95271-503-7

A CIP record for this book is available from the British Library

Printed and bound in the United Kingdom by TJ Books

Typeset by Lapiz Digital Services.

For a complete list of Casemate titles, please contact:

CASEMATE PUBLISHERS (US)
Telephone (610) 853-9131
Fax (610) 853-9146
Email: casemate@casematepublishers.com
www.casematepublishers.com

CASEMATE PUBLISHERS (UK)
Telephone (01865) 241249
Email: casemate-uk@casematepublishers.co.uk
www.casematepublishers.co.uk

Front cover images: (top) Brandenburg Gate seen through a barbed-wire barrier erected by the East Berlin Police. (NARA)
(bottom) Putin at the Victory Parade in Red Square, Moscow, marking the 74th anniversary of victory in World War II. (Kremlin)

Contents

Editor's Acknowledgements

The idea for the book developed out of a number of lectures that I gave to the British Foreign, Commonwealth and Development Office, and to different audiences from the British and the German armies. My first expression of gratitude therefore has to go to these institutions and the individuals that made these presentations possible. In particular, I would like to thank the Chief of the General Staff, General Sir Mark Carleton-Smith, Tara Finn (FCDO), and Michael Orr (Honourable Artillery Company). The intent of the lectures was to provide background knowledge to strategic decision makers, and the discussions I had helped me to structure a book that would be both useful for this particular audience and informative for the general reader. This raison d'être meant that some tough decisions had to be made when deciding what to include in this book and what to leave out. I hope that you, the reader, will approve of the selection of countries in the anthology that you hold in your hands.

I am grateful to the British Army and its commitment to the Centre for Historical Analysis and Conflict Research (CHACR), the Army's internal strategic think tank, that gave me the opportunity to produce this book. I am indebted to the CHACR team and the director, Major-General (retired) Dr Andrew Sharpe. The entire CHACR team was at some stage or other involved in the project and the collegiate, friendly and research-driven atmosphere at CHACR has most definitely helped me when I was putting this book together.

Without the authors that contributed to the book, this opus would simply not have seen the light of day. They made my job as editor a pure joy; their dedication to the project, the quality of the writings and the ability to stick to sometimes rather tight timelines meant that the entire project developed and progressed smoothly and without any difficulty.

I would like to thank Casemate Publishers and the team that has worked with me on this project, in particular Ruth Sheppard and Isobel Fulton. I have worked with the team on many projects and their professionalism has always impressed me.

The book is dedicated to the soldiers of all nations who fought honourably in World War II believing, rightly or wrongly, that they were fighting for good and just causes. And to Wilhelm, Maximilian and Jacob; may they live in a time without war and the upheavals that their great-grandparents had to endure.

Matthias Strohn
Camberley 2021

CHACR

The Centre for Historical Analysis and Conflict Research (CHACR) is a 'think-tank' based in Robertson House, the former British Army Staff College, in Camberley. It was established on behalf of the British Army in 2016 to help to strengthen the conceptual component of fighting power and to offer independent and objective views to inform future force development. It is designed to appraise the Army of wider thinking in order to challenge convention and inform strategic decision-making. It is not, therefore, a vehicle to portray the Army's own thinking; on the contrary, it is a vehicle to bring varied views together to stimulate the Army's thinking.

List of Contributors

Pavel K. Baev is Research Professor at the Peace Research Institute, Oslo (PRIO); he is also Senior Non-Resident Fellow at the Center for the United States and Europe (CUSE) at the Brookings Institutions, Washington DC; Senior Associate Researcher at the Institut Francais des Relations Internationales (IFRI), Paris; and Senior Associate Research Fellow at the Italian Institute for International Political Studies (ISPI, Milan). After graduating from the Moscow State University (MA in Political Geography, 1979), he worked in a research institute in the USSR Defence Ministry, received PhD in International Relations from the USA & Canada Institute, USSR Academy of Sciences (1988), and then worked in the Institute of Europe, Moscow, before joining PRIO in October 1992. His research on Russia's policy in the Middle East is supported by the Norwegian Foreign Ministry; other research interests include the transformation of the Russian military; the energy and security dimensions of the Russian-European relations; Russia's Arctic policy; Russia–China partnership; and post-Soviet conflict management in the Caucasus and the greater Caspian area. His weekly column appears in *Eurasia Daily Monitor* (http://www.jamestown.org/programs/edm).

Jonathan Boff is Reader in the History of Warfare at the University of Birmingham, where he has taught since 2011. He specialises in the history of the two world wars. His most recent book, *Haig's Enemy: Crown Prince Rupprecht and Germany's War on the Western Front, 1914–18*, was published in 2018. It was selected as British Army Military Book of the Year 2019, and was joint winner of the Tomlinson Prize for the best book on World War I. His previous book, *Winning and Losing on the Western Front: The British Third Army and the Defeat of Germany in 1918* (2012) was short-listed for the Templer Medal and for the British Army Book of the Year award. His current research centres on the political, social and cultural history of money in wartime, and on the nature of strategy. He was educated at Merton College, Oxford and the Department of War Studies, King's College London, and spent 20 years working in finance before returning to academia. He serves on the council of the National Army Museum, has worked as a historical consultant with the British Army, the US Military, and the BBC, and is a Fellow of the Royal Historical Society.

Kerry Brown is Professor of Chinese Studies and Director of the Lau China Institute at King's College London. He is an Associate of the Asia Pacific Programme at Chatham House, London, an adjunct of the Australia New Zealand School of Government in Melbourne, and the co-editor of the *Journal of Current Chinese Affairs*, run from the German Institute for Global Affairs in Hamburg. From 2012 to 2015 he was Professor of Chinese Politics and Director of the China Studies Centre at the University of Sydney, Australia. Prior to this he worked at Chatham House from 2006 to 2012, as Senior Fellow and then Head of the Asia Programme. From 1998 to 2005 he worked at the British Foreign and Commonwealth Office, as First Secretary at the British Embassy in Beijing, and then as Head of the Indonesia, Philippine and East Timor Section. He lived in the Inner Mongolia region of China from 1994 to 1996. Professor Brown directed the Europe China Research and Advice Network (ECRAN) giving policy advice to the European External Action Service between 2011 and 2014. He is the author of 20 books on modern China.

James S. Corum holds a MA from Brown, M. Litt. from Oxford, and a PhD from Queen's University, Canada. He is the author of nine military history books and editor and co-author of five more. His most recent books are *The Second World War and the Baltic States*, editor and co-author (2014), *Mitigating Disinformation Campaigns Against Air Power*, editor and co-author (2017) and *The Legion Condor* (2020). He has authored more than 70 major book chapters and journal articles on military history, counterinsurgency, and Baltic military history. From 1991 to 2004 he was Professor at the USAF School of Advanced Air and Space Studies. In 2005 he was elected to a fellowship at All Souls College, Oxford University and also held a Levershulme fellowship in the Department of International Politics at Oxford. From 2005 to 2008 he was Associate Professor at the US Army Command and General Staff College, Ft. Leavenworth, Kansas. From 2009 to 2014 he was dean of the Baltic Defence College in Tartu Estonia. The Baltic Defence College offers staff college and advanced military courses to officers from the Baltic countries and Eastern Europe. From 2014 to 2019 he was head of the MA Programme in Terrorism and Security at Salford University, UK. He is a retired lieutenant colonel in the US Army Reserves with his last assignment serving in Iraq in 2004.

Lothar Höbelt is Associate Professor of Modern History and Lecturer at the Military Academy in Wiener Neustadt, a member of the Editorial Advisory Board of *War in History* and has published extensively on the Habsburg Monarchy, World War I and the post-war politics of Austria. He lives with his family in Bohemia.

Jan Hoffenaar is Head, Research Department of the Netherlands Institute of Military History (MOD) in The Hague, and Professor in Military History at Utrecht

University. He specialises in the political and military aspects of the Cold War, in 'East' as well as in 'West', and in Dutch military history. He has published many books and articles on these subjects, including (with Dieter Krüger, eds) *Warfare in the Central Sector 1948–1968* (2012). He is a member of the Executive Board of the International Commission of Military History, president of the editorial board of *Militaire geschiedenis van Nederland* (Military History of the Netherlands), a series of six volumes on Dutch military history in Europe and overseas (since 1500) (which will also be published in English), and president of the international scientific board of the large research project on 'Independence, decolonization, Violence and War in Indonesia, 1945–1950'.

Paul Latawski is Senior Lecturer in the Department of War Studies, Royal Military Academy Sandhurst. Before coming to RMAS he lectured at the School of Slavonic and East European Studies (SSEES), University of London where he was also an Honorary Visiting Fellow. He was also an Associate Fellow at the Royal United Services Institute for Defence Studies (RUSI), London. In 2012 he was made a Senior Research Fellow in Modern War Studies with the Humanities Research Institute, University of Buckingham. He completed his PhD at Indiana University USA specialising in Central and Eastern Europe with an emphasis on modern Poland. His official research work includes post-1945 British contingency operations, the changing character of armed conflict and the historical evolution of British Army doctrine. His area studies specialist research includes the operational history of the Polish Armed Forces in the west and Polish resistance to occupation 1939–45.

Michael S. Neiberg is Professor of History and Chair of War Studies at the United States Army War College in Carlisle, Pennsylvania. His published work specialises on World Wars I and II in global context. *The Wall Street Journal* named his *Dance of the Furies: Europe and the Outbreak of World War I* one of the five best books ever written about that war. In 2016 his *Path to War* was published, a history of American responses to the Great War in Europe, 1914–1917 and in 2017 his *Concise History of the Treaty of Versailles*. In 2017 he was awarded the Médaille d'Or du Rayonnement Culturel from La Renaissance Française, an organization founded by French President Raymond Poincaré in 1915 to keep French culture alive during World War I.

Ali Parchami is Senior Lecturer in the Department of Defence and International Affairs at the Royal Military Academy Sandhurst. He received his BA, MPhil and DPhil from the University of Oxford and, between 2004 and 2007, was Stipendiary Lecturer at Exeter College, Oxford. His research interests encompass the fields of history, international relations and regional studies – with particular emphasis on Roman antiquity and strategic developments in the contemporary Middle East. This broad interdisciplinary interest is reflected in his publication record, which includes the monograph *Hegemonic Peace and Empire: The Pax Romana, Britannica and Americana* and peer-reviewed articles in imperial and commonwealth history, contemporary politics and Middle East journals. His latest projects focus on Sino-Iranian collaboration, Iran's expeditionary operations in the Middle East, and the evolution of the Islamic Republic's 'cascade strategy'.

Niels Bo Poulsen is Director of Institute for Military History, Culture and Military Theory at the Royal Danish Defence College, Copenhagen (since 2008). Prior to that he worked for ten years in the Danish Ministry of Foreign Affairs. He has an MA in History and East European Studies from Copenhagen University in 1996 and holds a PhD degree on a dissertation on the Soviet Investigation of Nazi War Crimes from Copenhagen University in 2005. He is the author of a substantial number of books and articles on the two world wars, Russian military history and war veterans. Currently Dr. Poulsen is heading a project on the Danish armed forces' international missions since 1990. He is also editor of the section on military history of the forthcoming *Springer Handbook of Military Sciences*.

Richard Reid is Professor of African History in the Faculty of History and a Fellow of St Cross College at the University of Oxford. His work has focused particularly on the history of political culture, historical consciousness, warfare and militarism in Africa, notably eastern and northeast Africa, including Eritrea, Ethiopia, Uganda and Tanzania. He is the author of a number of books, including *A History of Modern Uganda* (2017) and *Warfare in African History* (2012), while a revised third edition of his *History of Modern Africa: from 1800 to the present* appeared in 2019. A former editor of the *Journal of African History*, most recently he has written a first-hand account of the social, political, and cultural impact of conflict in the Horn, *Shallow Graves: a memoir of the Ethiopia-Eritrea war* (2020).

Andrew Sharpe has commanded on operations in every rank from second lieutenant to brigadier during 34 years of military service. He also had a rich and varied career of staff appointments, notably including involvement in national and international strategic and campaign planning, and in training and education, including time as the Director of the Higher Command and Staff Course and as Deputy Commandant of the Staff College. His final appointment, as a major general, was as director of the MoD's independent think tank the DCDC. For three years he ran the Chief of Defence Staff's strategic advisory panel. Since leaving the army, he has led a varied business, mentoring, speaking, writing and consultancy career, and is also the Director of the British Army's Centre for Historical Analysis and Conflict Research. He holds visiting fellowships at Exeter University and Kings College London, and a PhD in strategic leadership from Trinity College, Cambridge.

Olivier Schmitt is Professor (with special responsibilities) at the Center for War Studies, University of Southern Denmark. He is currently director of research and studies at the French Institute for Higher National Defense Studies (IHEDN). His research focuses on multinational military operations, transatlantic security, contemporary warfare and French defence policy. His recent books include *Allies that Count. Junior Partners in Coalition Warfare* (2018) and *French Defence Policy since the End of the Cold War* (2021, with Alice Pannier).

Matthias Strohn, MSt (Oxon), DPhil (Oxon), FRHistS, is Head of Historical Analysis at the Centre for Historical Analysis and Conflict Research, the British Army's strategic think tank, Visiting Professor of Military Studies at the University of Buckingham, and a member of the academic faculty at the Royal Military Academy Sandhurst. Matthias was educated at the universities of Münster (Germany) and Oxford. He holds a commission in the German Army and is a member of the military attaché reserve, having served on the defence attaché staffs in London, Paris and Madrid. Prior to this, he served as Military History Instructor at the German Staff College in Hamburg. He deployed to Iraq (with the British Army) and Afghanistan (with both the British Army and the German Bundeswehr). Matthias has published widely on 20th-century German and European military history; he has authored and edited 17 books and numerous articles.

Introduction: Why World War II Still Matters in the 21st Century

Matthias Strohn

World War II has always been present in my family. I remember that, as a small boy, I listened with naïve fascination to my father telling me about our family's experiences in those days. How one family member was badly injured in North Africa by a British strafing aircraft and died as a consequence of the injuries only a few years after the war. I would ask my grandfather about his experience in an anti-aircraft unit and wondered why he did not want to talk about it. My father told me that my grandfather had never spoken about the war with one exception, when he said to him that a comrade had been executed by the SS during the withdrawal from France. Even today, every day, I look at my grandfather's picture that hangs on the wall in my study next to his Iron Cross. I listened to my grandmother's stories about her work in the German air force headquarters close to Berlin; she told me about Hermann Göring, whom she had met several times, and how she just managed to escape as the Soviets were closing in on Berlin. My other grandmother told me about the mixed feelings she had when the Americans arrived in her small village in 1945. I learned about my family's expulsion from their homelands in Pomerania and the Sudetenland and how they settled in Westphalia. In a childish and naïve way, I was fascinated by the stories they told – and the ones they hesitated to tell. My first real taste of the hardships of war occurred when we visited yet another family member. He was in constant agony, because of Soviet shrapnel that was still in his body. In my immature way I told him that I was fascinated by war and, to my surprise, he said that war was horrible. He then showed me his scars and it made me shudder. When I was 14, I tried on the uniform that had been given to one of our family members when he returned from Soviet captivity long after the war had finished; the fact that the uniform was too tight for me, a slim boy, has left a lasting impression on me. When I visited the German war cemetery at Stalingrad about ten years ago, to pay my respects to a family member whose name is on the wall of the missing soldiers of the battle, I had grown up and understood what influence the war has had on myself, our family, and countries and societies.

I was therefore astonished, when, a few years ago, I watched a play put on by a primary school in England. The theme was the Battle of Britain. Primary school children were dressed up as Spitfires and Messerschmitts. The play also included a 6-year-old representing Churchill and, naturally, Hitler was there as well. Seeing a small boy marching up and down the stage and shouting English words in a fake German accent was comical. Or was it? I asked the parents afterwards what they thought of the play. Everybody had enjoyed it, with two exceptions. One was me; as I already said, I was astonished. Another one was a non-British mother whose father had served in the Special Forces of his country. She was appalled. 'Do they not know what war is and how terrible World War II was?', she asked me. Naturally, you cannot expect a full debate of historical events when putting on a primary school play, but the scene, and even more the reactions of the audience, were revealing. It was obvious that there was a disconnect here, and it seemed to play out along the lines of national memory and remembrance of the war. This is not to say that everybody in a country holds the same views with regards to historical events, but 'national views' and stereotypes do exist and they shape mainstream thinking. It would have been hard trying to convince the audience that such a show looked plainly weird to international onlookers, in particular those whose national identity and memory have been shaped by the consequences of World War II far more drastically than those of the British population.

Of course, there are reasons why it seemed appropriate to some to stage such a play in a primary school in Britain. The country had fought on the 'right' side in this war. The perception that in 1940 Britain stood alone against a seemingly almighty Germany is as wrong as it is widespread in the UK (and is re-enforced constantly by TV productions and popular history books). It was Britain's 'finest hour' as we are constantly reminded – although this implies that everything that had come before and came afterwards was 'less fine'. All this only enhances the general view that this is a war worth remembering. A poll conducted by YouGov in 2015 shows this clearly.[1] People in the US, France, Germany, Denmark, Sweden, Finland, Norway and the UK were asked 'who did most to win the war?' With the exception of the UK and Norway, people in all countries overwhelmingly said that it was the US. In the UK, 50% of the people asked said that the UK deserved the prize for the most important belligerent in bringing the war to a successful end. This view was only shared by 7% in the US and Germany. The Soviet Union did not get a lot of votes, with the exception of the former enemies: 27% in Germany and 24% in Finland thought that the Soviet Union contributed most to winning the war. The people in Russia were not asked, but, undoubtedly, they would have had a very different view. During a battlefield tour to Kursk in Russia, the local guide told the participants only a few years ago that it was the Soviet Union alone which had defeated the Nazi beast, and that the western Allies had done nothing to support the Soviet Union. From a western point of view, this is simply untrue and, as always, the truth is more grey than black and white. And yet, we should not laugh at this rather simplistic view. The fact that in the YouGov poll the British identified the UK as the main contributor to victory mirrors the national perception of the Russian guide in Kursk.

Now, we could simply turn the page and say that these things do not matter anymore to people in the 21st century. However, this is not so. Periods of turmoil, upheaval and change are the times that we remember from history. Take the French Revolution, for example. We all learn about it in school. Who has ever learned about the so-called 'Vormärz', the period between the end of the reign of Napoleon in 1815 and the revolutions of 1848? Probably not many people, because this was a 'boring' and uneventful period for most Europeans nations. And yet, I know in which period I would have preferred to live. No event is more upsetting and drastically life changing than a 'total' war, which impacts upon entire nations and their people, be they military or civilian. World War II was arguably the most 'total' war the world has ever seen. And yet, the experiences are different at an individual level, and they also differ from nation to nation. It is, really, too abstract to talk of 'national' experiences. The war of a Spitfire pilot in Britain was fundamentally different from that of a coal miner in the north of England. And German women enduring the bombing raids had different stories to tell than the soldiers on the Eastern Front. And yet, a degree of 'nationalisation' in the memory and remembrance of war is visible in all countries. Too diverse are the kaleidoscopic individual experiences to remember them all at an official level. And so, the individual experience is moulded into an accepted national memory. The signs of these are everywhere. If you, the reader, want to get a good understanding of this, visit some military cemeteries on the Western Front. The differences in appearance, and thus messaging, are striking. The British cemeteries are clean, somewhat heroic and, through individual graves, emphasise the individualism of the Anglo-Saxon world. All of these attributes are even more strikingly obvious in American cemeteries. French cemeteries, with the simple designs of the crosses for all the graves and the inscription 'mort pour la France' embody the values of the French revolution of *liberté*, *égalité* and *fraternité*. German cemeteries have a sombre and somewhat dark feeling to them, which, some would argue, mirrors the soul of German romanticism. More often than not, in German war cemeteries you also find people buried together rather than in individual graves. There were simple reasons for this; the former enemy countries were often unwilling to hand over large plots of land to the Germans for graveyards, so space was scare. However, it is also an embodiment of 'Kameradschaft', a term that is only insufficiently translated by comradeship.[2]

History is not an exact science. You can draw different conclusions from the same event. This interpretation happens through specific lenses and the analysis can also act as an external reference framework. Wulf Kansteiner has argued that:

> Memory studies offer an opportunity to acknowledge that historical representations are negotiated, selective, present-oriented, and relative, while at the same time insisting that the experiences they reflect cannot be manipulated at will.[3]

Often, the result of these negotiated representations is the creation of myths which legitimise and popularise not only historical deeds and actions, but also impact upon our individual and our nations' views and actions today.[4] We could also follow Napoleon, who is supposed to have expressed this view more drastically by allegedly stating that 'history is a set of lies agreed upon'. The way we choose and interpret these 'lies' often says more about our current times than the events themselves. As the philosopher Friedrich Nietzsche said, the real purpose of the study and knowledge of history is to serve the present and the future.[5] This not only allows for, but demands constant re-interpretation of historical events within the changing social and political contexts in time. This should happen, as the Roman author Tacitus said 'sine ira et studio'[6] (without anger and passion) so that the historian can present the facts 'wie es eigentlich gewesen'[7] (how it really happened), as the German historian Leopold von Ranke argued. The realisation that we are all biased by our social backgrounds and histories is the first step towards an 'objective' understanding of history. However, we can see tensions developing the moment we combine this academic ideal with the realities of using history to establish or support a framework for actions today. These are important factors and not some that are only of value for the inhabitants of the academic ivory tower. As Hal Brands and Jeremi Suri have argued in relation to US foreign policy (and this is by no means restricted to this country, but happens everywhere across the globe):

> [American officials] have used history to gain perspective on the world and its challenges; to impose familiarity on novel and perplexing issues; to channel the perceived verities of the past in grappling with the uncertainties of the future; or simply to frame and market their policies in an appealing fashion.[8]

In a standard textbook of international relations, it is argued that strategic culture, which determines state behaviour in the international arena, can be described as a combination of national historical experience, aspirations for responsible behaviour in national terms, the civic culture of this state, and the predominant way of life with which its citizens identify.[9] Again, history and the interpretation of history take centre stage. The historian Margaret MacMillan summed up this debate by stating that '… history – an understanding, whether accurate or inaccurate, of the past – is omnipresent in foreign politics.'[10] The concept could easily be widened to capture not only foreign, but also domestic politics (and policies), too.

To prove this point, we just need to look at the rhetoric that some countries have used in recent times. To show that the statements above are by no means restricted to the US, one could, for instance, turn to the UK. Wartime rhetoric has seen a recent revival. It seemed to have diminished when British newspapers stopped linking every

Germany versus England football match to World War II. Headlines like that of the *Daily Mirror* prior to a match between the two countries ('Achtung! Surrender. For you Fritz, ze Euro 96 Championship is over'[11]) gave way to more objective reporting. This was most probably also helped by the abysmal performance of the German national football team in recent years, which led to the *Sun*'s headline of 'Schadenfreude' when it reported that Germany had been kicked out of the 2018 World Cup.[12] In the last few years, war-time rhetoric and the clear recollection of the war in general, and World War II in particular, could be observed again in Britain in many areas, for instance in the current 'fight' against COVID-19. The approval of the vaccine has been called a 'weapon in our armoury' against the virus.[13] Brexit offers a particularly clear link to the first half of the 20th century. As the historian and commentator Sir Max Hastings wrote:

> World War II still dominates British self-image. As a historian of the conflict, I am sometimes driven to despair by my fellow-countrymen's determination to preserve nationalistic myths about it, rather than to acknowledge harsh realities … Many British people, at the onset of this year of our Lord 2021, still sincerely suppose that, because we were on the winning side in 1918 and 1945, while most Continental nations were humiliated or shamed, we are superior beings.[14]

This is a strong statement, but it goes a long way to explaining the developments that we have seen since the Brexit referendum and which have left the rest of Europe (at least) in utter astonishment.

If history was an exact science with no room for these 'lies' that Napoleon talked about to develop and change, then we would only need one book for every event in history. Just a quick glance at the shelves in any bookshop tells you that things are more complex. We are constantly re-assessing our histories through our contemporary lenses. And this means that history in general, and World War II in particular, matter. Despite the fact that the war ended 75 years ago, it is still with us. It continues to shape peoples' – and thus states' – perceptions and actions in the national and international arenas. This influence can be clearly visible, and it can also be present subconsciously. It is said that traumatic psychological experiences can be passed on for generations, and World War II probably caused more traumatic experiences than any other conflict the world has ever seen, be it among the soldiers who fought, the populations in the bombed-out cities or the inmates of the concentration camps.[15] A paper published by the World Bank in 2020 even argues that the countries that had lost a high number of people in World War II have lost less people in the current COVID-19 pandemic.[16] The argument is that the big shockwaves that the war experience sent through these societies have induced stronger societal responses for adaptation and protection from future big shocks. The paper argues that there exists 'a positive correlation between past war experiences and contemporary participation in collective actions and community groups'[17], and 'that war-exposed individuals have higher resilience to shocks and increased perception of uncertainty and uncontrollability of the environment'.[18]

Despite 75 years of distance to the events, and despite a seemingly endless output of historical research, the differences remain. The diverse legacies of the war and the different interpretations of the conflict will remain with us for a long time, even though the protagonists have all but left us. If you want to understand the world of today, you need to understand history. This applies to all history, and, in particular, it applies to the cataclysmic events that threw the world into turmoil and whose ripple effects we still feel and experience today. No event did this more in recent history than World War II. We simply cannot make sense of the modern world that surrounds us if we do not understand our own and other nations' interpretations of history. Only if we understand the frames of reference of our friends, allies and adversaries can we make sense of peoples' and nations' actions. This also means that we should start this process by analysing our own nations. Only this will make it possible to really understand ourselves and others in the 21st century, a prerequisite for sensible policy, strategy and action in both the national and international arenas. The aim of this book is to contribute to this process.

Notes

1   https://yougov.co.uk/topics/politics/articles-reports/2015/05/01/Britain-America-disagree-who-did-more-beat-nazis (accessed 27 October 2020).

2   For a much broader discussion of these questions of memory, see Wolfgang Schivelbusch, *The Culture of Defeat. On National Trauma, Mourning, and Recovery* (London: Granta Books, 2001).

3   Wulf Kansteiner, 'Finding Meaning in Memory: A Methodological Critique of Collective Memory Studies', *History and Theory*, Vol. 41, No. 2 (2002): 195. I am grateful to Niels Bo Poulsen, whose early draft of his chapter in this book provided me with food for thought and some references for the second part of this introduction.

4   See, on this general matter, Cyril Buffet and Beatrice Heuser (eds), *Haunted by History. Myths in International Relations* (New York and Oxford: Berghahn Books, 1998).

5   Friedrich Nietzsche, 'Vom Nutzen und Nachteil der Historie für das Leben', in idem, *Unzeitgemäße Betrachtungen* (Frankfurt a. M.: Insel Verlag, 1981),120. The essay quoted here was first published in 1874.

6   Tacitus, *Annales*, 1.1.

7   Leopold von Ranke, *Geschichten der romanischen und germanischen Völker von 1494 bis 1514* (Leipzig: Bäntsch, 1824), VII.

8   Hal Brands and Jeremi Suri (eds), *The Power of the Past. History and Statecraft* (Washington: Brooking Institution Press, 2016), 2.

9   John Bailys et al., *Strategy in the Contemporary World: An Introduction to Strategic Studies* (Oxford: OUP, 2007), 86.

10 Margaret MacMillan, *Dangerous Games: The Uses and Abuses of History* (London: Profile Books, 2009), 8.

11 *Daily Mirror*, 24 June 1996.

12 *The Sun*, 28 June 2018.

13 These words were used by the UK's Vaccine Deployment Minister Nadhim Zahawi in an interview with the BBC on 9 January 2021; see https://www.bbc.co.uk/news/av/uk-politics-55593102 (accessed 9 January 2021).

14 Max Hastings, 'How Delusions About World War II Fed Brexit Mania', *Bloomberg Opinion*, 3 January 2021, https://www.bloomberg.com/opinion/articles/2021-01-03/max-hastings-how-delusions-about-world-war-ii-fed-brexit-mania (accessed 9 January 2021).

15 See, for instance, https://www.dw.com/de/wie-der-zweite-weltkrieg-das-leben-von-kriegskindern-und-kriegsenkeln-prägt/a-53226023 (accessed 16 November 2020); and https://www.dw.com/de/kriegsenkel-die-geerbte-last-des-krieges/a-17051101 (accessed 20 November 2020). The technical term adopted for the generations that are indirectly affected by the war through the traumas of their parents and grandparents is 'Kriegsenkel' or 'grand-children of the war', a rather fitting description. Sabine Bode, *Kriegsenkel: Die Erben der vergessenen Generation* (Stuttgart: Klett-Cotta, 2013) (first edition 2009) provides insightful examples of how the trauma of the war has impacted upon German families.

16 Michael Lokshin, Vladimir Kolchin, Martin Ravallion, 'Scarred but Wiser: World War 2's COVID Legacy' (World Bank Group Policy Research Working Paper 9481), Washington D.C., 2020, https://openknowledge.worldbank.org/bitstream/handle/10986/34836/Scarred-but-Wiser-World-War-2s-COVID-Legacy.pdf?sequence=1&isAllowed=y (accessed 9 January 2021).

17 Lokshin, Kolchin, and Ravallion, 'Scarred but Wiser: World War 2's COVID Legacy', 7.

18 Ibid., 8.

CHAPTER I

Misusing Victory: How Russia Has Struggled with the Legacy of the Great Patriotic War

Pavel K. Baev[1]

Introduction

The 75th anniversary of victory in the Great Patriotic War (GPW) was celebrated in Russia with great fanfare – and with a fierce political campaign against 'distortions of history'. In fact, one of the typically Russian distortions is the separation of the GPW, which started with the German attack on 22 June 1941 and ended with the capitulation signed in Berlin on 9 May 1945 (which actually happened on 8 May, while the Berlin garrison surrendered on 2 May), from the total historic phenomenon of World War II. The battles in the Asia-Pacific theatre are essentially bracketed out because the USSR remained faithful to the April 1941 Neutrality Pact with Japan, which was only denounced in April 1945. The three-week campaign launched on 9 August 1945 (which happened to be the day of US atomic bombing of Nagasaki) is treated as a particular episode, and its conclusion has never been properly celebrated not least because Russia still doesn't have a formal peace treaty with Japan.[2]

The persistent proposition on separating the GPW from WWII is underpinned and shaped by the desire to bracket out the early stage of the latter when Stalin's USSR was to all intents and purposes a key ally to Hitler's Germany and worked on the mutually agreed plan for dividing Europe into the two spheres of exclusive control, ideologically incompatible as they were. This desire becomes clear in President Vladimir Putin's article on the causes and 'real lessons' of WWII, which was supposed to establish an inviolable official interpretation of the role of the USSR and, by extension, Russia as its successor-state.[3] The finality of this interpretation is asserted by the new amendment to Russia's constitution, which prescribes to the state the task of defending the 'historical truth'.[4] The mainstream media duly engaged in a well-funded campaign against 'falsifications' of the newly-minted truth, but many Russian historians and analysts have expressed concerns about the straightforward exploitation of history for current and dubious political purposes.[5]

Putin is certainly not inventing any new historical narrative and his slightly updated recycling of the Soviet discourse (minus the 'leading role' of the Communist Party) is aimed at tapping into the reservoir of memories, feelings and even trauma, which remains deep even 75 years after the momentous event. This lasting impact of the increasingly distant experience in mobilization of all state resources toward a clearly understood goal is a complex phenomenon that deserves attention not only from historians but also from analysts of the present-day risks related to Russia's new confrontation with the west, and this chapter aims at examining the relevance of lessons of WWII for the choices Russia is currently making. It starts with assessing the role of history-shaped means and methods in the contemporary policy-making in Moscow, then proceeds to evaluating briefly the utilization of war memories for consolidating the social base of Putin's regime, and then gives greater attention to the influence of the WWII-centric thinking on the fast-moving transformation of Russian strategic culture.

Old war as a continuation of new politics

Russian foreign policy actions centred on upholding the memory of the GPW may often seem to European politicians and public to be not only exaggerated but also counter productive. The angry reaction in Moscow to the removal of the statue of Marshal Ivan Konev in Prague did considerable damage to Russia's relations with the Czech Republic.[6] The intensity of propaganda offensive was such that it was indeed possible to believe in a special operation involving poisoning several Czech officials, a story soon exposed as fake.[7] In the 2007 case of the removal of the Bronze Soldier monument in Tallinn, Russia's furious overreaction was clearly an attempt to put pressure on Estonia, but the demarches against the Czech Republic did not seem to serve any rational political purpose.[8] This apparent emotional outburst was, however, a part of a carefully prepared, wider political plan.

The publication of Putin's article with its strong emphasis on rejecting any 'falsifications' of WWII historical records needed a fresh point, to which his defensive stance could be linked. It was the September 2019 resolution of the European Parliament on the 80th anniversary of the start of the war that provided for Putin the initial impetus, but by summer 2020, that controversy had become stale, and the Kremlin decided that Prague makes a perfect target, which turned out to be an embarrassing blunder.[9] Leaving the propaganda mishap aside, it is not that difficult to establish that Putin's laborious and at places dubious (particularly regarding pinning the blame on Poland) re-examinations of causes of WWII lead to the seemingly sensible initiative on conveying the summit of the five victorious powers.[10]

The argument about the enduring responsibility of Russia, China, France, the UK and the USA for shaping global governance might appear old-fashioned and at odds not only with the new role of Germany and Japan, but also with the desire for greater prominence strongly expressed by Brazil, India, and South Africa, which Russia generally supports in the BRICS format. There is more, nevertheless, to Putin's initiative than just an attempt to compensate for the humiliating exclusion from the G7 club. What he seeks to achieve, besides a place at the high table, which Russia has no right to claim on the strength of its stagnating economy or on its meagre contribution to global governance, is an arrangement resembling the deal negotiated by Josef Stalin at the 1945 conferences in Yalta and Potsdam with US presidents Franklin D. Roosevelt and Harry S. Truman, and British prime ministers Winston Churchill and Clement Attlee.[11]

The imagined 'New Yalta' model has two key elements, building on the re-interpreted legacy of WWII. The first one is the primacy of state sovereignty, which in the Russian understanding means the right of ruling regime to execute domestic affairs as it sees fit, without any external interference regarding suppression of freedoms or violations of human rights. In the world order as seen in the Kremlin, only a few powers possess real sovereignty (and the issues in the EU caused by delegation of authority to the Brussel bureaucracy are eagerly amplified), and Russia must guard its privileges whatever international commitments it has taken. Another power with full sovereignty – and with views on its meaning remarkably close to Russian – is China, which sternly rejects Western 'interference' in its policies in Xinjian and Hong Kong, with full support from Moscow.[12] It was indeed unthinkable for the western leaders to question Stalin's GULAG system, but as some thoughtful Russian analysts point out, the unique historical circumstances in 1945 determined that moment of revival of old westphalian rules, which is irreproducible.[13]

The second element is the proposition that the few powers that possess full sovereignty are also entitled to their 'spheres of influence' where they carry and execute responsibility for maintaining stability and order. This idea certainly pre-dates the Yalta deal, but what matters for the Kremlin is the clearly established and still valid precedent of western consent for establishing effective control over the Eastern Europe by the USSR.[14] The limits of these spheres are certainly not carved in stone, and Russia's intervention in Syria, for that matter, is definitely a step beyond its extended boundaries, aimed primarily at asserting its readiness and capacity to manage conflicts. In real terms, this capacity is actually far from certain, and while there is no shortage of 'theoretical' reasoning on the imperative need for Russia to consolidate its influence in the Eurasian post-Soviet geopolitical space, many sober voices point to the plain reality of shortage of 'hard' and 'soft' power resources.[15] Since the annexation of Crimea in 2014, it has been the Russian aggression against Ukraine that constituted the main test for the 'sphere of influence' proposition, but the August 2020 revolution in Belarus has set a new and probably more impactful one, and Putin's performance together with Alexander Lukashenko at the opening of the monument at the site of the 1942–1943 Rzhev battle signified the importance of legacy of the GPW for the uneasy relations between the two autocrats.[16]

Overall, the persistent attempts to instrumentalise the legacy of WWII for advancing the status-maximising agenda of Russian foreign policy are mostly unsuccessful, particularly in Europe. Moscow has managed to escalate tensions in relations with the three Baltic States and Poland, offend historical sensitivities in Finland, reduce goodwill feelings in Norway and deplete the propensity to show 'understanding' (the term *Putinversteher* has become a bad word in international discourse) in Germany, inter alia. The idea of a 'New Yalta' is increasingly recognised as a challenge to European security.

Exploiting victory for regime glorification

The lack of success in using the reinvented 'lessons' of WWII in Russia's foreign policy is directly connected with the diminishing returns on the massive investments into exploiting the great victory for the purpose of regime consolidation in domestic policy. The question about the significance and the meaning of the war memories for the Russian society is hugely complex and painfully sensitive, and so can be addressed here only insofar as its impact on the current political and strategic matters is concerned. It is apparent, however, that this impact is significantly different from the desired results of the centrally directed efforts.

The celebration of the 70th anniversary of victory in 2015 happened in the context of annexation of Crimea, which saw strong condemnation in the west, but also a massive upsurge of 'patriotic' (though, in essence, distinctly jingoist) enthusiasm in Russia. Planning for the 75th anniversary in 2020, Putin aimed at reproducing that momentum, knowing that public support for the 'return' of Crimea remained broad and solid, and assuming that the joy could be reignited by propaganda means.[17] The carefully orchestrated mobilization of political base was then supposed to be used for producing overwhelming approval for the package of amendments to the constitution, which appeared to be rather bric-a-brac when first proposed by Putin – as a big surprise – in the January address to the Federal Assembly, but then made perfect sense when an amendment making it possible for him to stand in the 2024 presidential elections was introduced.[18] The public vote (which was not formally defined as a referendum) was scheduled for 22 April, just 15 days before the pompous Victory Day parade, but the COVID-19 epidemic derailed that smart schedule.

The spread of COVID-19 had been ignored and denied up to the end of March 2020, but since mid-April the acceleration of the infection in Moscow gained such force that holding any public event became out of the question and a lockdown had to be enforced, so the parade was rescheduled for 24 June (which was the day the parade was staged in 1945), and the vote for 1 July. The delay was more than an unfortunate technicality; the attempt to generate a strong wave of support for consolidating the autocratic regime essentially failed. A propaganda campaign employing the techniques that are described in modern Russian language as 'victory-craze' (*pobedobesiye*) was resolutely out of tune with public worries about the consequences of the epidemic.[19] It became apparent even to usually fanfare-responsive audiences that glorification of victory was a means for justifying priority resource allocation toward military build-up, while the underfunding of the severely stressed health care system was aggravated by the new economic contraction.[20]

The desired result in the vote on amending the constitution was achieved only by resorting to gross falsifications, which were apparent not only to experts but also to great many voters who abstained from partaking in the dubious plebiscite.[21] Perhaps the most convincing proof of the public discontent aggravated by Putin's stubborn implementation of his political project was produced in Khabarovsk, where the abrupt arrest of popular governor Sergei Furgal triggered a long series of street protests.[22] Putin's transparent attempts to utilise the memories of the common purpose in gaining victory in the GPW for ensuring success of his plan for extending the grasp on power indefinitely (as in the abovementioned ceremony of inaugurating the Rzhev memorial together with Lukashenko) did not hit the right note with the populace. In fact, his claim on ownership of the supreme triumph achieved by the USSR inevitably puts him into the same box (if not on the same level) with Josef Stalin, who remains remarkably popular with traditionalists and 'patriots' of various persuasions, but is also a symbol of brutal repressions and a sad reminder about inglorious ends of autocratic rulers.[23]

One particular message resonating with the experiences of the GPW is the Kremlin's appeal to the 'common people' to unite and stand together against the threat of external aggression, which is allegedly again looming in the situation of a new and irreducible confrontation between Russia and the west. Putin may be more subtle in describing this threat than Lukashenko, who claimed that NATO tanks were moving to Belarus borders in order to support the illegitimate protests.[24] The Russian leader focuses more on sanctions, assuming that his audiences feel their direct impact, but public opinion has been gradually shifting in the direction of downplaying the western threat, and the impact of the COVID-19 pandemic has strengthened this shift.[25] The traditional propaganda theme of presenting Russia as a 'besieged fortress' is getting stale and tiresome, and as one sharp mainstream analyst argues, the propensity of the leadership to believe in own propaganda could deliver it into a 'bunker' rather than to ensure the mobilization of the garrison of the imagined 'fortress'.[26]

Overall, the effectiveness of the well-funded policy of consolidating mass support for Putin's regime by exploiting the memories of the GPW is clearly diminishing. The occasion for re-energising these memories on the 75th anniversary of the victory has passed without any useful results, and further attempts to play on the legacy of common determined effort and painful sacrifices could be counter-productive.

Lasting influences and innovative interpretations in the strategic culture

Russian strategic culture is a complex phenomenon, which is deeply rooted in the Soviet legacy and fast transforming in the course of the new confrontation with the west. The experiences from the GPW are a major component in the foundation of this seemingly coherent but actually rather eclectic culture, and as the generations that gained those first-hand (of which General Makhmut Gareev was one of the most influential) fade away, new interpretations gain prominence.[27] Different elite groups perform dissimilar roles as 'carriers' and 'guardians' of strategic culture, and for the purpose of this analysis it appears useful to examine how the memories of the GPW influence the relations between the political leadership and the top brass, how they shape decisions regarding the development of the defence-industrial complex and how they interplay with the changes in the professional military culture.[28]

Mastering the military force as the instrument of Putin's policy

The Leninist interpretation of the old Clausewitzean dictum of war as continuation of policy, which was questioned and rejected by Mikhail Gorbachev, is unconditionally embraced by the current Russian leadership, which tends to see the military force as the most reliable instrument of policy, and in many cases – as the instrument of choice. This sets the question about the efficiency of control over the military command by the political rulers, particularly since Putin's proverbial 'inner circle' of loyal courtiers does not include a single person with a military background. This is strikingly similar to Stalin's court, which was reshuffled many times, but invariably had no place for combat-hardened marshals. This is also remarkably different from Brezhnev's informally reduced Politburo, in which Marshal Dmitry Ustinov was a major influence, and Marshal Nikolai Ogarkov had a major say on, for instance, launching the intervention into Afghanistan.[29] Putin revealed that four 'colleagues' were present at the fateful all-night meeting on the Crimean issue, and it is easy to place around that table Sergei Ivanov, the head of his administration, Nikolai Patrushev, the secretary of Security Council, Alexander Bortnikov, the director of the FSB, and Mikhail Fradkov, the head of the FIS, all with KGB background and of about the same age, while loyal minion Prime Minister Dmitri Medvedev and Foreign Minister Sergei Lavrov were most probably left out.[30]

Defence Minister Sergei Shoigu is the only high-level official in Russia with an independent political profile and support base, and despite often accompanying

Putin to vacations, he has never been a member of the Kremlin's 'inner circle' of loyal courtiers. His political career goes back to the early 1990s, and he excels at navigating intrigues and showing deference to the boss. In his role as the commander-in-chief, Putin delights in supervising exercises and presiding over parades, but never wears a uniform (unlike Lukashenko – and against Stalin's tradition), while Shoigu (who has no military background) typically dons tailor-made regimentals. He has eagerly assumed the role of a key defender of 'historical truth' regarding WWII and directs military historians (the institute of military history is now a part of the General Staff Academy) to dominate the discourse in the escalating 'memory wars'; on his initiative, a grandiose military cathedral was erected outside Moscow to commemorate the 75th anniversary of victory.[31]

In the demonstratively problem-free and actually uneasy relations between Putin's Kremlin and Shoigu-led top brass, one particular issue in the legacy of WWII, which has a profound impact on the evolving strategic culture, is the shocking start of the GPW. The German multi-prong assault caught the Soviet numerically superior armies so unprepared that an explanation for the monumental strategic blunder is necessary, and the modern Russian official interpretation is as much at pains to produce it as the Soviet history used to be.[32] The revisionist proposition that the USSR was preparing for an offensive war against Germany, which was severely condemned in the Soviet era, is gradually moving to the mainstream in Russia, but it still leaves unexplained the painful question about the responsibility for missing the huge fact of German preparations for the massive attack.[33] It is clear that Stalin is at fault in completely misreading Hitler's intentions, but it is also apparent that the military command was keen to report only what the feared dictator wanted to hear – and to act accordingly.

That old acrimony translates into the pervasive fear of a sudden attack by a technologically superior adversary, which underpins the strategic preference for preemption and capturing the initiative in the initial phase of confrontation. This preference fits with Putin's inclination to make surprise moves and catch even his henchmen, not to mention opponents, unprepared, but it clashes with his propensity to procrastinate in dynamic crisis situations, which is quite apparent, for that matter, in the decision-making on the turmoil in Belarus.[34] The logical clash between the two propaganda narratives – on the looming threat of NATO invasion and on the deepening discord in Western alliance – resembles the schizophrenic perceptions of alliance with Nazi Germany forged in the division of Poland in September 1939; it also answers the pronounced tendency in the Russian leadership to believe in own propaganda. This co-existence of mutually disagreeable propositions in contemporary Russian strategic culture means that scenarios of an offensive in southern Ukraine or an invasion into Estonia are not figments of alarmist geopolitical imagination but a real threat, which can be effectively deterred.[35]

One highly significant but not properly conceptualised change in Russia's military posture is the departure from the Soviet planning for a protracted large-scale conventional war in the western theatre, envisaged as a replay of the GPW with modern weapon systems. This departure happened mostly by default in the course of implementation of drastic and painful reforms (which were actually never described as a 'reform') in 2008–2012 by Defence Minister Anatoly Serdyukov. He never pretended to be a theorist and quite possibly did not fully understand the implications of the swiftly executed dismantling of the structure of mass mobilization, including hundreds of 'skeleton' regiments, which were supposed to be expanded to full strength when reservists were called in the period of high threat.[36] Serdyukov's replacement with Shoigu in November 2012 was supposed to placate the outrage in the top brass with the severe cuts in the officer corps, and some superficial measures indeed helped in restoring loyalty to the commander-in-chief, as Putin reclaimed this position. The strategic reality of absence of the traditional capacity for mobilising huge human reserves, as it was done after the devastating defeats in 1941, has, however, remained unchanged.

Patching the flaws in the defence-industrial complex

Embarking in late 2011 on a costly effort at modernising the armed forces with the 2020 State Armament Program (SAP), Putin addressed the demand in the high command to prepare for wars of new type (exemplified by the swift US victory in the Second Gulf War), but also referred to the experience of the GPW, which informed that domestic industrial base was capable of producing weapon systems of superior quality. The severe degradation of the Soviet defence-industrial complex in the 1990s, and in the first decade of Putin's era as well, was perceived as reversible with the newly available funding secured by the inflow of petro-revenues. What was striking about that program was its ambition for upgrading the whole arsenal of nuclear and conventional weapons with only marginal contribution from imported western armaments and technologies (like the Mistral-type amphibious assault ships ordered from France), which was informed by reflections on the 'lend-lease' program during the GRW.[37] This import was terminated after the 2014 Russian aggression against Ukraine (which also stopped military-technical cooperation), so the new SAP-2027 program, approved with long delays in December 2017, envisages exclusive reliance on domestic production and maintains the guideline on upgrading all weapon systems, albeit with somewhat reduced funding.[38]

What this guideline fails to take into account is the major difference in scale: the USSR in the mid-1980s had the armed forces of about 5.5 million personnel and maintained massive reserves, while Russia cannot quite reach the target strength of 1,000,000-strong armed forces and has miniscule reserves. This downsizing means that mass production of armaments is practically impossible, so the proposition for designing and building of great many weapon systems in small series is economically inefficient and technologically unfeasible. The persistent political enforcement of this proposition means that the state-owned corporations (reconfigured back to the Soviet organizational model) engage in wasteful activities and prioritise exhibition of prototypes over delivering on orders.[39]

Examples of this structural flaw in military modernization plans abound, and one of the most telling is the production of armoured vehicles, which used to be one of the core strengths of the Soviet defence-industrial complex. The T-34 tank is perhaps the most recognizable symbol of the victory in 1945, and it is still proudly rolling over the Red Square in parades. The new main battle tank T-14 Armata (and the family of combat vehicles on its base) was also demonstrated with great fanfare in the 2015 parade, but it has transpired since that its design is too sophisticated and the price too steep for equipping combat units, so it serves as an expensive show case.[40] Production of some weapon systems, particularly combat aircraft, has been boosted by export, but the Armata series has not found any buyers so far.[41]

A fundamental difference between the Soviet tradition rooted in the GPW experience and the present-day situation is that the defence-industrial complex is by no means the main economic sector, consuming the bulk of resources and enjoying priority funding above every other economic sector. The USSR was essentially a war machine, which Russia is quite obviously not; if anything, it is rather a petro-state with added military superstructure. Oil and gas companies, and specifically Rosneft and Gazprom, are influential political actors, which are not interested at all in re-distribution of their revenues in favour of the defence industries. In the periods of 'plenty' (in terms of oil prices), like at the start of the past decade, when the SAP-2020 was approved, the state can accumulate sufficient budget income for contracting expensive defence projects, but in the spasms of crisis, like in 2014–2016, it has to re-evaluate its expenditures – hence the delay and curtailing of the SAP-2027. The arrival of a new recession in 2020 has necessitated hard bargaining in the OPEC+ format on painful production cuts, and this is certain to undercut profits in the oil-and-gas sector, and necessitate deeper cuts in weapons acquisition than the modest 5% that the Ministry of Finance cautiously suggested.[42]

It is not only macro-economic parameters that are of relevance here, but also the business culture, which interplays with the strategic culture in ways unthinkable in the Soviet past. Corruption was certainly a prominent feature of the Soviet way of life (and the looting of occupied Germany was notorious), but it never challenged the dominant militarism.[43] For the old economic elites, the priority of resource allocation toward defence was unquestionable and tapping into that stream of funding for personal gain was reprehensible and highly risky. For the new Russian business elite, including such key figures in Putin's court as Gennady Timchenko or brothers Arkady and Boris Rotenberg, the redistribution of state revenues toward the military and the defence-industrial complex is at best a necessary evil and typically a sad waste. The main exception is Sergei Chemezov, Putin's long-time henchman and the head of the Rostech corporation, which constitutes a key and expanding part of the defence-industrial complex, who has built a no-small fortune from supervising military contracts.[44] The lavish lifestyle of Putin's oligarchs and top bureaucrats exposes the falsity of the discourse on the vital commitment to strengthening the national defence with the habitual references to common sacrifices for the sacred victory.

New capabilities into old mindsets

Russian professional military culture has been evolving fast under the impact of experiences gained in armed conflicts, and in the 30 years of its post-Soviet history, Russia has been involved in rather too many of those. This impact is strengthened as Shoigu (unlike his predecessors Serdyukov and Ivanov) has consistently promoted 'warriors' with real combat experience to the top positions, traditionally occupied with 'parquet generals' who excel at bureaucratic intrigues. Perhaps the key figure personifying this trend is General Valery Gerasimov, who progressed from platoon commander to division commander and saw action in the Second Chechen War before the appointment as the chief of the General Staff in November 2012. Gerasimov may be not the brilliant theoretician as he is sometimes described, but he has certainly eliminated the traditional discord between the General Staff and the Ministry of Defence and commands authority in the officer corps, making sure that Shoigu is also held in high regard.[45]

Lessons from the GPW are taught to Russian officers from day one in their cadet schools to the graduation from the General Staff Academy (typically, a colonel spends a third of his career in education before the compulsory retirement at 55 years). The most basic of these lessons is that the Russian army must have both superior numbers and qualitative edge in key weapon systems; for that matter, the mass production of combat aircraft of inferior types in the late 1930s is recognised as a major cause of the devastating defeat of Stalin's air force in the first weeks of war.[46] The reality of much reduced numbers (and dismantled mobilization base) is clashing with this imperative, so the fact that the USSR deployed a grouping of forces amounting to 450,000 troops for the unresisted occupation of Estonia, Latvia and Lithuania in 1940, while Russia presently cannot possibly concentrate a third of such force, is carefully omitted. Putin finds it necessary to argue that the annexation of the Baltic States was perfectly legitimate in the European relations of the early phase of WWII.[47]

The fear of facing qualitatively superior weapon systems was focused since the NATO air war against Yugoslavia in 1999 on the threat of long-range cruise missiles, and later on massive use of strike drones. The response to this acutely perceived threat was two-fold: to build effective defences and to develop own strike capabilities. In the first track, long-range surface-to-air missile systems S-400 in combination with the shorter-range Pantsir-SM systems are supposed to effectuate protective 'bubbles' around high-value targets, for instance, the Khmeimim airbase in Syria. On the second track, the deployment of 3M-54 Kalibr cruise missiles on naval platforms, as well as in standard containers and in combination with land-based Iskander missiles, is supposed to close the gap with the US strike capabilities, and the Syrian war provided a perfect theatre for testing this new instruments of policy.[48] Shoigu and Gerasimov place great emphasis on learning the lessons from the Syrian war both in military academies and by rotating hundreds of officers through the command and advisory positions there, so that this limited and *sui generis* intervention comes close in the influence on the transformation of strategic culture to the everlasting importance of the GPW, while many other wars, from Afghanistan to Georgia to Donbass are carefully bracketed out.[49]

Syria provides a focus for developing a set of propositions in the Russian military thinking that is often described as 'hybrid warfare', even if this notion is used in Russian discourse only for describing hostile activities of the west.[50] These propositions prescribe combining indirect use of military force with various cyber-attacks, propaganda offensives, economic pressure and export of corruption, which may appear innovatively post-modern, but in fact they involve re-learning some old lessons, leaving the joy of directing tank battles to computer games. For that matter, the script of using quasi-states as proxies for staging well-prepared military provocations goes back to the 1939 clash with Japan in the Mongolian steppes along the Khalkhin-Gol river, and protection of quasi-independent South Ossetia in the 2008 Georgian war was a successful remake, while the farce of helping the pseudo-republics in Donetsk and Luhansk is still exploited for destabilising Ukraine.[51]

A major difference between the WWII-era and modern-day conceptualization of 'hybrid wars' is in the prominence of military means. Despite Josef Stalin's mistrust in and purges of the military elite, the centrality of armed forces was the key premise of his geopolitics, and various unconventional means – from propaganda to the Comintern networks – were employed in support of the big battalions. In the contemporary strategising the role of military force is downplayed and perceived as a core asset providing for deployment and supporting the use of other instruments of projecting power and influence.[52] The problem with this emphasis on non-military means is that most of them have in the short time of the new confrontation proven to be of limited efficiency. Russia's 'soft power' is seriously compromised by the investigations of meddling into the US elections, the ability to 'weaponise' the oil and gas export is diminished as the global energy market becomes over-supplied, and the notorious 'troll factories' cannot possibly help Russia to qualify as a 'Great Cyber-Power'. Putin may much prefer to execute multi-prong 'special operations', but because of a chain of embarrassing failures – from the devastating defeat of a troop of 'Wagner' mercenaries in Syria in February 2018 to the arrest of a group of alleged 'Wagners' in Minsk in July 2020 – his high command has apparently recognised the risks and drawbacks of 'hybrid' means.[53]

One consequence of this rethinking is the greater emphasis on the role of nuclear weapons, which were strongly prioritised already in the SAP-2020, but have received a greatly elevated profile after Putin's 2018 address to the Federal Assembly, in which he, rather unexpectedly, presented a whole range of 'wonder-weapons', so that corrections for their accelerated development had to be inserted in the just approved SAP-2027.[54] In the Russian military leadership, the attitude toward this bombastic nuclearization is rather ambivalent, as the generals see greater need in power-projection capabilities than in hugely expensive strategic submarines. They see the value of nuclear weapons primarily in terminating a conventional conflict on favourable terms according to the loosely interpreted 'escalate-to-deescalate' proposition, which originates in the reflections on the US nuclear strikes on Japan in 1945.[55] The top brass, however, cannot overcome the overstretch of military power from the Arctic to the Kuril islands to Syria and cannot wish the Soviet military machine back into existence, so political reliance on the nuclear arsenal – a unique element of Russia's international profile – is set to stay.

Conclusion

Memories and reflections on WWII and the GPW as its presumably central part generate a strong impact on Russian political thinking, identity construction and strategic culture. Putin's leadership seeks to control and further strengthen this impact by producing a uniform official version of the causes, drivers and outcomes of that global conflict and ostracising all alternative interpretations. This monopolization of the war discourse, however, is seriously overdone, and the attempts to claim ownership of the great victory, which continues to be of great value for the society, are alienating many social groups, which recognise the falsity of prevalent propaganda, and families, which cherish their own memories of sacrifices. The official line may be set firmly in the state media, but the internet in Russia, despite the sustained but ineffectual efforts at censoring, remains mostly free, and it provides platforms for discussions and research in such networks as, for instance, the Free Historical Society (Вольное Историческое Общество), which have greater reach than the officially-sponsored Russian Military Historical Society.[56]

Russian strategic culture struggles with the contradiction between the acclaim of the GPW experiences and the impossibility to reproduce the model of total mobilization. The Soviet economy worked for sustaining and modernising a military machine, and the Russian economy functions in the rent-harvesting and profit-maximisation mode. For the Soviet elites, the priority of building the military might set with the start of WWII had been unquestionable up to Mikhail Gorbachev's *perestroika*, and for the majority of Putin's elites, access to financial flows and self-enrichment are the key motivations. The economic base of the military modernization has deeply shrunk and is further damaged by the unfolding recession, and the political demand for producing every type of modern weapon system clashes with this reality.

In the Russian professional military culture, the lessons of the GPW are held in extremely high regard, and the fast-progressing re-conceptualization of the character and methods of modern wars is informed by the juxtaposition of rich new experiences with these lessons. The top brass, while by no means corruption-free, resents the economic predation of Putin's oligarchs and their lavish life-style, which reveals the falsity of the 'patriotic' discourse on mobilization of efforts for strengthening the national defence. The old fear of a surprise attack, rooted in the shock of 22 June 1941, blends with the new fear of a sudden explosion of mass protests, aggravated by the unrest in Belarus, to produce a strategic mindset that focuses on preemptive strikes, disregards human costs and casualties, and expects escalation of 'hybrid warfare' to a nuclear exchange.

Notes

All online sources were accessed on 11 February 2021.

1   My research on the transformation of Russian strategic culture was supported by the US EUCOM Russia Strategy Initiative (RSI), which is greatly appreciated.
2   In April 2020, Russian State Duma adopted a legislation changing the date of the ending of that war from 2 September to 3 September, primarily in order to adjust to the official celebrations in China. For the official explanation, see Artyom Lokalov & Semyon Ekshut, 'And again September 3', *Rossiiskaya gazeta* (in Russian), 15 April 2020, https://rg.ru/2020/04/15/pochemu-gosduma-izmenila-datu-okonchaniia-vtoroj-mirovoj-vojny.html. One useful comment is Anna Borshchevskaya, 'Japan's false hopes of courting Russia', *The American Interest*, 24 June 2020, https://www.the-american-interest.com/2020/06/24/japans-false-hopes-of-courting-russia/.
3   Putin declared his intention to write this article in December 2019, and published it, rather unexpectedly, in a US journal of questionable repute; see Vladimir Putin, 'The real lessons of the 75th anniversary of World War II', *The National Interest*, 18 June 2020, https://nationalinterest.org/feature/vladimir-putin-real-lessons-75th-anniversary-world-war-ii-162982. The Russian version (under a more historically correct title) appeared the next day on the Kremlin website; see Vladimir Putin '75 years of Great Victory: common responsibility before history and future', *Kremlin.ru* (in Russian), 19 June 2020, http://kremlin.ru/events/president/news/63527.
4   This amendment was proposed by Putin in his address to the Federal Assembly on 15 January 2020, and it was approved as a part of big package by the national vote on 1 July; for a critical scrutiny, see Toomas Alatalu, 'Putin continues victory campaigns to defend historical truth using the constitution', *Diplomaatia*, ICDS, 27 August 2020, https://icds.ee/en/putin-continues-victory-campaigns-to-defend-historical-truth-using-the-constitution/.
5   On the funding for the official line, see Dmitri Grinkevich, Natalya Portyakova, Aleksei Ramm 'The rescued world will know: Finance Ministry grants money for the fight against fakes', *Izvestiya* (in Russian), 22 July 2020, https://iz.ru/1038288/dmitrii-grinkevich-nataliia-por-tiakova-aleksei-ramm/uznaet-mir-spasennyi-minfin-dast-dengi-na-borbu-s-feikami-o-voine. Reflections on Putin's essay are Igor Pushkarev, "It is a claim for reshaping the world', interview with Ivan Kurilla, *Znak.ru* (in Russian), 19 June 2020, https://www.znak.com/2020-06-19/chto_putin_hotel_skazat_statey_o_vtoroy_mirovoy_voyne_i_o_chem_umolchal; and Stanislav

Kuvaldin, 'A word about war: What Putin decided to convey before the parade', *Snob.ru* (in Russian), 19 June 2020, https://snob.ru/entry/194341/.

6   The role of units of the Russian Liberation Army in supporting the Prague uprising in May 1945 before Kone's tanks arrived is one of the episodes resolutely deleted from Russian history texts; see Amy Mackinnon, 'As Putin's seeks to reinvent history, Russia-Czech relations hit a new low', *Foreign Policy*, 29 April 2020, https://foreignpolicy.com/2020/04/29/russia-czech-republic-relations-new-low-poison-plot/.

7   The origin of the fake was actually an intrigue inside the Russian embassy; see Shaun Walker, 'Czechs expel two Russian diplomats over fake poisoning plot', *The Guardian*, 5 June 2020, https://www.the-guardian.com/world/2020/jun/05/czechs-expel-two-russian-diplomats-over-fake-poisoning-plot.

8   The pressure on Estonia involved one of the first documented cyber-attacks; see Stephanie Maclellan & Naomi O'Leary, 'Doing battle in cyber-space: How an attack on Estonia changed the rules of the game', Centre for International Governance Innovation, 26 October 2017, https://www.cigionline.org/articles/doing-battle-cyberspace-how-attack-estonia-changed-rules-game.

9   One compelling examination of Putin's article in the context of debates in the European Parliament is Philip D. Zelikow, 'A reply to President Putin', *The American Interest*, 31 July 2020, https://www.the-american-interest.com/2020/07/31/a-reply-to-president-putin/.

10   This bottom line is identified in Tom Balmforth & Andrew Osborn, 'Putin uses the WW2 anniversary to push idea of Russian-backed summit to stabilize world', *Reuters*, 19 June 2020, https://www.reuters.com/article/us-russia-putin-article/putin-uses-ww2-anniversary-to-push-idea-of-russian-backed-summit-to-stabilise-world-idUSKBN23Q24S. See also Pavel Aptekar, 'Presidential history: Putin's article is not a historical research, but a message to the West', *Vedomosti* (in Russian), 20 June 2020, https://www.vedomosti.ru/opinion/articles/2020/06/20/833067-prezidentskaya-istoriya.

11   On the significance of the Yalta model for Putin, see Vladimir Frolov, 'Entrenchment strategy: Foreign policy dimension of Putin's article', *Republic.ru* (in Russian), 22 June 2020, https://republic.ru/posts/97031.

12   One sample of this meeting of minds is an article in the Chinese propaganda outlet; Shan Jie and Yang Sheng, 'China, Russia reaffirm mutual support on core interests, sovereignty', *Global times*, 7 August 2020, https://www.globaltimes.cn/content/1193952.shtml.

13   See Andrei Kortunov, 'The mirages of Westphalia', *Analytics and Commentary*, Russian International Affairs Council, 14 August 2020, https://russiancouncil.ru/en/analytics-and-comments/analytics/the-mirages-of-westphalia/.

14   On the need to reject this precedent, see Steven Pifer, 'Contending with – not accepting – spheres of influence', *Russia Matters*, 5 March 2020, https://www.russiamatters.org/analysis/contending-not-accepting-spheres-influence.

15   For the former, see Dmitri Evstafyev, 'New Yalta of Vladimir Putin: Strategic perspective for Eurasia', *Eurasia Expert* (in Russian), 29 January 2020, https://eurasia.expert/novaya-yalta-vladimira-putina-strategicheskaya-perspektiva-dlya-evrazii/; for the latter, an argument by an influential Russian intellectual is fairly representative, see Victor Erofeev, 'New Yalta is not going to happen, despite Putin's wishes', *Deutsche Welle* (in Russian), 20 June 2020, https://p.dw.com/p/3e41p.

16   Russian media was not shy to point out the sour chemistry between them; see Elena Egorova, 'Lukashenko demanded a 'serious conversation' with Putin in Rzhev', *Moskovsky komsomolets* (in Russian), 30 June 2020, https://www.mk.ru/politics/2020/06/30/lukashenko-potreboval-sereznogo-razgovora-s-putinym-vo-rzheve.html.

17   A reasonably reliable opinion poll from March 2019 showed 58% of respondents expressing strong approval of the annexation and another 28% – conditional approval, while only 3% expressed strong disapproval; the figures not significantly different from 2015. See 'Incorporation of Crimea', *Levada.ru* (in Russian), 1 April 2014, https://www.levada.ru/2019/04/01/prisoedinenie-kryma/.

18 The 'annulment' of his two current presidential terms was a rather awkward political twist; see Tatyana Stanovaya, 'Putin's coup: cunning plan or improvisation?', *Commentary*, Carnegie Moscow Center, 18 March 2020, https://carnegie.ru/commentary/81311.

19 One sharp discussion of these methods is Ivan Belyaev, 'On the plateau of Pobedobesiye: Social networks on the preparations for May 9', *Svoboda.org* (in Russian), 5 May 2020, https://www.svoboda.org/a/30593464.html.

20 Ambivalent feelings, see Ivan Kurilla, 'The weirdest Victory Day in Russian history', *Raam op Rusland*, 11 May 2020, https://www.raamoprusland.nl/dossiers/geschiedschrijving/1598-the-weirdest-victory-day-in-russian-history.

21 The data collected by Russian experts demonstrated an extraordinary scale of fraud, even by Russian political standards; see Alexander Kireev, 'Schrodinger's referendum', *Novaya gazeta* (in Russian), 8 July 2020, https://novayagazeta.ru/articles/2020/07/06/86170-referendum-shredingera.

22 The case was distinctly local, but it gives a good measure of the depth of public disappointment in Putin's leadership; see Andrei Kolesnikov, 'Russia's permanent revolution of dignity', *Commentary*, Carnegie Moscow Center, 31 July 2020, https://carnegie.ru/commentary/82408.

23 On Putin's awkward justification of Stalin's intrigues in the onset of WWII, see Andrei Zubov, 'On the new historic article of Mr Putin', *New Times* (in Russian), 3 July 2020 (https://newtimes.ru/articles/detail/195739).

24 References to the beginning of the GPW were plentiful in his rambling speeches; see for instance, 'Lukashenko warns Europe of consequences if situation in Belarus escalates', *Belta*, 28 August 2020, https://eng.belta.by/president/view/lukashenko-warns-europe-of-consequences-if-situation-in-belarus-escalates-132983-2020/.

25 A reasonably reliable opinion poll at the early stage of the pandemic showed that only 16% of respondents were certain that Russia had reasons to worry about NATO and 12% were certain that there were no such reasons; see 'Attitudes to countries', *Levada.ru* (in Russian), 18 February 2020, https://www.levada.ru/2020/02/18/otnoshenie-k-stranam-6/.

26 See Andrei Kortunov, 'Fortress or bunker?', *Analytics and Comments* (in Russian), Russian International Affairs Council, 13 July 2020, https://russiancouncil.ru/analytics-and-comments/analytics/krepost-ili-bunker/.

27 On Gareev's formulation of lessons of the GPW, see Sergei Pershutkin, 'How the Red Army became invincible', *Nezavisimoe voennoe obozrenie* (in Russian), 17 April 2020, https://nvo.ng.ru/history/2020-04-17/13_1090_gareev.html.

28 My recent in-depth examination of this theme can be found in Pavel K. Baev, 'Transformation of Russian Strategic Culture: Impacts from Local Wars and Global Confrontation', *Russie.Nei.Visions* Report 118, IFRI, June 2020, https://www.ifri.org/en/publications/notes-de-lifri/russieneivisions/transformation-russian-strategic-culture-impacts-local.

29 One useful examination of that decision is Artemy Kalinovsky, 'Decision-making and Soviet war in Afghanistan: From intervention to withdrawal', *Journal of Cold War Studies*, Vol. 11, No. 4 (Fall 2009): 46–73.

30 Putin's account of that session is in fact quite sketchy; see 'Putin reveals secrets of Russia's Crime takeover plot', BBC News, 9 March 2015, https://www.bbc.com/news/world-europe-31796226.

31 For the imagery of the consecration ceremony, with Shoigu center-stage, see 'Russia consecrated grandiose armed forces cathedral', *Moscow Times*, 15 June 2020, https://www.themoscowtimes.com/2020/06/15/russia-inaugurates-grandiose-armed-forces-cathedral-a70567.

32 On the official downplaying of the see Andrei Kolesnikov, 'Hiding the blood trail', *Gazeta.ru* (in Russian), 25 June 2019, https://www.gazeta.ru/comments/column/kolesnikov/12436387.shtml.

33 A prominent historian Mark Solonin finds it much easier to discuss this issue from Kiev; see Leonid Velekhov, 'Hitler just moved ahead of Stalin', *Svoboda.org* (in Russian), 20 June 2020, https://www.svoboda.org/a/30008543.html.

34   At the moment of this writing, the outcome is unclear; see Alexander Baunov, 'Internal geopolitics: Belarus protests and Russian transit', *Commentary* (in Russian), Carnegie Moscow Center, 31 August 2020, https://carnegie.ru/commentary/82606.

35   In the often emotional discussions of this scenario, one sound research is Stephen J. Flanagan, Jan Oberg, et al, 'Deterring Russian aggression in the Baltic States through resilience and resistance', *RAND Research Report* RR-2779-OSD, 2019, https://www.rand.org/pubs/research_reports/RR2779.html.

36   A sharp and insightful examination of these reforms can be found in Alexander Golts, *Military Reform and Militarism in Russia* (Washington DC: Jamestown Foundation, 2018).

37   Revisionist Russian historians challenge the official acknowledgement of insignificant importance of the controversial 'lend-lease' aid; see Boris Sokolov, 'Lend-lease – the arms for Victory: The role of Western aid to the Eastern front', *Svoboda.org* (in Russian), 9 April 2020, https://www.svoboda.org/a/30538060.html.

38   One sound overview of implementation of SAP 2020 and parameters of SAP 2027 is Richard Connelly & Mathieu Boulegue, 'Russia's New State Armament Programme: Implications for the Russian Armed Forces and Military Capabilities to 2027', *RIIA Research Paper*, Chatham House, May 2018, https://www.chathamhouse.org/publication/russia-s-new-state-armament-programme-implications-russian-armed-forces-and-military.

39   On the issues in military modernization, see Pavel Luzin, 'Russia's arms manufacturers are a financial black hole', *Riddle*, 30 January 2020, https://www.ridl.io/en/russia-s-arms-manufacturers-are-a-financial-black-hole/.

40   Brad Howard, 'Russia's futuristic T-14 tank was designed to defeat Western armies, but they are too expensive for Russia', *Business Insider*, 31 July 2018, https://www.businessinsider.com/russias-t-14-tank-made-to-beat-the-west-is-too-expensive-for-russia-2018-7?r=US&IR=T.

41   The lack of interest in China and India has been deeply disappointing for Moscow; see Michael Peck, 'Russia is eager to sell its sophisticated T-14 Armata tank. Will anyone buy it?' *Forbes*, 16 July 2020, https://www.forbes.com/sites/michaelpeck/2020/07/16/russia-is-eager-to-sell-its-armata-tank-will-anyone-buy-it/#36fd1abd6fd1.

42   On the impact of oil production cuts, see Mikhail Krutikhin, 'This is death to the oil industry. Hundreds of thousands of people will lose salaries', *Business Online* (in Russian), 13 April 2020, https://www.business-gazeta.ru/article/464770. On the proposed SAP-2027 curtailing, see Inna Sidorova & Ivan Tkachev, 'Finance Ministry suggests cuts expenditures on the State Armament Program', *RBC* (in Russian), 20 July 2020, https://www.rbc.ru/politics/20/07/2020/5f15a00e9a7947326377dd89.

43   On the scale of that looting, see Martin K. A. Morgan 'Wretched Misconduct of the Red Army', *Warfare History Network*, 23 December 2018, https://warfarehistorynetwork.com/2018/12/23/wretched-misconduct-of-the-red-army/.

44   Alexei Navalny targeted Chemezov in one of his investigations; see 'How the heads of state corporations live', *Navalny.com* (in Russian), 11 October 2018 (https://navalny.com/p/5972/).

45   On Gerasimov's pivotal role, see Michael Kofman, 'Russia's armed forces under Gerasimov, the man without a doctrine', *Riddle*, 1 April 2020, https://www.ridl.io/en/russia-s-armed-forces-under-gerasimov-the-man-without-a-doctrine/. On misreading his conceptual contribution, see Mark Galeotti, 'I am sorry for inventing the 'Gerasimov Doctrine'', *Foreign Policy*, 5 March 2018, https://foreignpolicy.com/2018/03/05/im-sorry-for-creating-the-gerasimov-doctrine/.

46   One useful examination is Scott W. Palmer, *Dictatorship of the Air: Aviation Culture and the Fate of Modern Russia* (Cambridge: Cambridge University Press, 2006).

47   The responses were appropriately scathing; see Una Bergmane 'How Putin is rehabilitating the Nazi-Soviet pact', *Baltic Bulletin*, FPRI, 28 July 2020, https://www.fpri.org/article/2020/07/putin-rehab-nazi-soviet-pact/.

48 One thoughtful evaluation is Roger N. McDermott and Tor Bukkvoll, 'Tools of future war – Russia is entering the precision-strike regime', *Journal of Slavic Military Studies*, Vol. 31, No. 2 (2018): 191–213.

49 On the exaggerated significance of the Syrian experience, see Dmitry Adamsky, 'Russian lessons from the Syrian operation and the culture of military innovation', *Security Insight 47*, George C. Marshall European Center for Security Studies, February 2020, https://www.marshallcenter.org/en/publications/security-insights/russian-lessons-syrian-operation-and-culture-military-innovation.

50 One useful examination of these ideas is Oscar Jonsson, *The Russian Understanding of War: Blurring the Lines Between War and Peace* (Washington DC: Georgetown University Press, 2019).

51 Meticulous critical examination of the official version of the Khalkhin-Gol (Nomonhan) conflict is presented in Vladimir Voronov & Alexander Krushelnitsky, 'Border post that wasn't: Odd way to Khalkhin-Gol', *Svoboda.org* (in Russian), 29 June 2019, https://www.svoboda.org/a/30027606.html.

52 This preference for non-military means is examined in Mark Galeotti, *Russian Political War: Moving Beyond the Hybrid* (London & NY: Routledge, 2019).

53 One sharp evaluation of the 2018 debacle is Kimberly Marten, 'The puzzle of Russian behavior at Deir-al-Zour', *War on the Rocks*, 5 July 2018, https://warontherocks.com/2018/07/the-puzzle-of-russian-behavior-in-deir-al-zour/.

54 My assessments of this new emphasis are in Pavel K. Baev, 'Russian nuclear modernization and Putin's wonder-missiles: Real issues and false posturing', *Russie.Nei.Visions Report 115*, IFRI, August 2019, https://www.ifri.org/en/publications/notes-de-lifri/russieneivisions/russian-nuclear-modernization-and-putins-wonder.

55 One in-depth evaluation of this proposition and other nuclear-related shifts in Russian doctrines is Michael Kofman, Anya Fink, Jeffrey Edmonds, 'Russian Strategy for Escalation Management: Evolution of Key Concepts', *CNA Research Memorandum*, April 2020, https://www.cna.org/CNA_files/PDF/DRM-2019-U-022455-1Rev.pdf.

56 See the website of the Free Historical Society, https://volistob.ru/.

CHAPTER 2

Belated Victory: Poland's Legacy of World War II

P. C. Latawski

World War II began in Europe in the early hours of 1 September 1939 with the German attack on Poland and ended five years and eight months later with Germany's unconditional surrender on 7 May 1945. It was unquestionably one of the largest and most destructive conflicts of the 20th century that had an enduring political, social, economic and security impact across Europe. In 2019, 80 years after the outbreak of World War II, commemoration ceremonies around Europe highlighted the fact that for each country World War II produced a legacy distinctive to each individual country's experience. For Poland, where the war in Europe began, it is a narrative quite different from the celebratory or self-congratulatory tone of other western states who formed part of the victorious allied coalition. On 1 September 2019, Polish President Andrzej Duda gave a speech at a ceremony in Warsaw marking the commemoration of the 80th anniversary of the outbreak of World War II. In it, President Duda suggested a very different legacy for Poland from the war:

> … we were unfortunately not the beneficiaries of that great victory. We found ourselves under a different occupation, this time the Soviet one. So, it can be said that, in a sense, World War II, in the context of its political effects … did not end until 1989. So, it [the war] lasted much longer than in other places in the world. What can we say about the end of war and victory when you do not live in a truly free country, when you do not live in a truly sovereign country, when you do not live in a truly independent country? When you are not completely free.[1]

This narrative of Poland's legacy of World War II is built on two dominant and interconnected strands. The first is that the betrayal perpetrated by Poland's wartime allies resulted in an outcome from the war that did not meet Polish aspirations. The Yalta conference of February 1945 is a totem of this sense of betrayal.[2] The second is that one occupation was exchanged for another. At the core of this idea is the view that the Communist Polish Peoples Republic (Polska Rzeczpospolita Ludowa – PRL) represented an illegitimate state of limited sovereignty imposed by the Soviet Union and thus was tantamount to a new occupation. To understand the roots of the two dominant strands of the narrative of Poland's World War II legacy, it is necessary to put them into the broader framework of Poland's contested statehood and repeated state reconstruction in the 20th century. What is striking about Poland since its re-emergence in the first quarter of the 20th century is the fact that the Polish state has undergone fundamental reconstruction on three occasions – 1918, 1939 and 1989 – as the result of major armed conflict or seismic change to the European political landscape. The first two of these reconstructions are important for understanding Poland's legacy of World War II which is rooted in what preceded the conflict, what happened during it and what followed in its aftermath.

First reconstruction 1918–1939

After 123 years of foreign domination of the Polish lands, World War I produced the international conditions necessary for the re-creation of a Polish state. With Austria-Hungary dissolving into a series of successor states and Germany and Russia defeated and consumed by revolution, the seemingly immovable political obstacles were swept away. In this geopolitical window of opportunity, Poland was reborn. The new Poland, however, fought six wars in three tumultuous years in which its boundaries were defined and the state consolidated between 1918 and 1921. Five of these wars were of a more limited nature: the Polish–Ukrainian conflict in Eastern Galicia (November 1918–July 1919), the Greater Poland Uprising (Powstanie Wielkopolskie) (December 1918–February 1919), the clash with Czechoslovakia over Cieszyn–Těšín (January 1919), the Polish–Lithuanian conflict over Wilno (1919–1920) and the conflict with Germany for control of Silesia (1919–1921). Only one major conflict could be described as an existential threat to Poland and dwarfed all the others in its importance and scale – the Polish–Soviet war. The conflict started in early spring 1919 and lasted until the Treaty of Riga ended the war in March 1921.[3]

In 1918, the visions of two men competed during the Poland's painful emergence. Roman Dmowski, the leader of the National Democratic Party (Narodowa Demokracja), was a nationalist ideologue who did much to shape the modern Polish national identity.[4] He believed the new Poland should be as ethnically Polish as possible and built on a territorial base sufficient to ensure its internal development and ability to stand between Germany and Russia. There was, however, a contradiction between his impulse to create a monocultural Polish state and the boundaries he championed for the new Poland which would include national minorities. His politics had a dark side as Dmowski embraced anti-Semitism. He saw Germany as a more serious danger to Poland and before World War I considered the German threat to be the basis of a *modus vivendi* with Russia.[5] During World War I, Dmowski sought the support of the Entente Powers from London and Paris during the war for his project to rebuild Poland and was the key Polish representative at the Paris Peace conference in 1919.[6]

Opposed to Dmowski was Józef Piłsudski who offered a radically different vision of the new Poland. Piłsudski saw Russia as the principal threat to Polish security. His politics took him to the top of the Polish Socialist Party (Polska Partia Socjalistyczna – PPS). The PPS served as a useful vehicle for his radical politics. He was a man of action and not an ideologue and his party-political affiliation lasted only for as long as he thought that it had utility in his efforts to regain an independent Poland.[7] When Poland gained independence in 1918, he famously told his former PPS colleagues, 'Comrades, I rode on the red-painted tramcar of socialism as far as the stop called Independence, but there I alighted.'[8] He parted company with Austria-Hungary (and Germany) after it became clear that they would not deliver an independent Polish state after 1916. The starting point of his views on the territorial reconstruction of Poland were firmly rooted in the historic pre-partition Polish–Lithuanian Commonwealth (Rzeczpospolita Obojga Narodów, Polskiego i Litewskiego). He sought to cripple Russian power with an ambitious project to bring together the Baltic States, Belarus and Ukraine into a vague and ill-defined federation that Poland would lead.[9] Although Piłsudski was in a better position to pursue his scheme as Poland's undisputed leader at independence, his ambitious aim proved beyond the country's strength. In the end, the Poland that emerged between 1918 and 1923 was neither national enough according to Dmowski's criteria nor did it match Piłsudski's vision of linchpin of a great anti-Russian federation.[10]

With an end to Poland's wars to regain its independence, the country now faced the formidable challenges of state-building. Poland had to integrate territories of three partition zones that all possessed the inherited infrastructure of the three former partitioning powers. Thus, the need to create a new internal economic, social and political order involved not only national development but basic integration. The society and economy were overwhelmingly agrarian with 76% in 1921 and 73% in 1931 living in the countryside.[11] Employment in sectors in 1931 had 61% of the economically active population earning their living in agriculture and forestry with only 19% in mining and industry.[12] Levels of prosperity differed regionally in Poland with the eastern region being the poorest, earning the moniker Polska B (Poland B). Another challenge of integration was that of Poland's extensive national minorities. Because census-taking practices tended to minimise numbers in the national minorities, religious affiliation was the most reliable measure of the size of ethnic groups in Poland. In 1931 the breakdown in Poland's population showed that Poles formed 68.9%, Ukrainians 13.9%, Belorussians 3.1 %, Jews 8.6% and Germans 2.3%.[13] In inter-war Poland, Ukrainians and Belorussians were concentrated in the east, Germans in west with Poland's non-contiguous population Jewish population resident in many regions and urban areas. Although the national minorities had their rights guaranteed by the March 1921 Polish constitution and international treaties and government policy periodically followed liberal policies, no consistent attempt was made to conciliate or assimilate the national minorities. Polish government policy favoured those of Polish nationality and actively suppressed minority activity seen as disloyal to the Polish state.[14] The lack of identification of national minorities to the Polish state and foreign exploitation of their discontent was a source of weakness to inter-war Poland.

The adoption of the March 1921 constitution demonstrated Poland's intent to follow the path of liberal democracy. The democratic institutions of Poland, however, functioned poorly in part because of the lack of previous involvement in self-government when under foreign rule and a political elite lacking in experience in democratic political culture. Moreover, the political rivalries of Dmowski and Piłsudski played an important role in the failure of democratic institutions. At the behest of the Dmowski camp, the March 1921 constitution created a weak executive dependent on parliamentary coalitions that was intended to insure Piłsudski's exclusion from political life.[15] Piłsudski withdrew from public life to bide his time. In May 1926 he launched a coup d'etat that effectively made him the leader of Poland until his death in 1935. Piłsudski exercised a very bespoke political influence on the Polish state and government that was centred on his person.[16] Piłsudski's chosen successor, Marshal Edward Śmigły-Rydz, made few changes to the pattern of government in his four years of tenure before the outbreak of war in 1939.

While Piłsudski's coup d'etat had a deleterious effect on democratic politics in Poland, the impact on the army was to undermine its effectiveness. Ironically, driving his decision to launch the coup d'état was the need to save the Army from the 'degenerating influences' of politicians.[17] The opposite would prove to be the case as some of the most important seeds of military failure in 1939 were sown by Piłsudski's action in May 1926. His approach emphasised the moral component of war fighting and he underestimated the role of technology and material in the conduct of war.[18] He gave preferential treatment to the promotion of officers who served under him in the Polish legions during World War I. As one historian labelled the period 1926 to 1935, it was the 'period of legionary supremacy'.[19] As a group, however, the Polish officers from the legions had the least professional military experience, education and training of any group making up the Polish Army's officer corps. It effectively created a two-tier army of professionally underdeveloped senior officers and more able and professional middle-ranking and junior officers. This would be an important factor in Poland's swift military collapse in 1939.[20]

The favourable geopolitical context that allowed the rebirth of Poland did not persist for long. Germany and the Soviet Union both enjoyed by considerable margins economic and military strength that Poland could not match. Moreover, Poland's larger eastern and western neighbours never fully accepted the legitimacy of the Polish state or the territorial settlement that established the new Poland. Germany was the most openly revisionist in its diplomacy while Soviet intentions were more masked. During the inter-war period, Polish efforts to mitigate the precariousness of its geopolitical position initially rested on both collective defence and collective security arrangements. Collective defence was built on a bilateral treaty with France in 1921 but proved to be an edifice built on foundations of sand. The signature of the Locarno agreement in October 1925 produced mutual guarantees of France's eastern frontier with Germany but not that of Poland's western frontier in effect calling into question the international legitimacy of its border with Germany. With Locarno evaporated any French military credibility or political commitment to its alliance with Poland. The only thing Poland gained from the agreement was further isolation on a geopolitical tightrope.[21]

The great experiment in collective security, the League of Nations, offered even less international security to Poland. Occupying first place in the number of petitions filed and general discussion initiated relating to German minority complaints to the League of Nations, Germany effectively used the League of Nations as a forum to wage incessant propaganda campaigns on alleged ill-treatment of Poland's German minority.[22] In practice, the League of Nations provided Poland with more insecurity by its encouragement of irredentism among the country's German minority. Building security on a regional basis proved no more successful than pan-European attempts. The only formal ally of Poland in the region was Romania (Polish–Romanian treaty March 1921). Poland remained outside the largest inter-war regional grouping – the Little Entente.[23] An alliance with Czechoslovakia, which may have seemed a natural security partnership, remained elusive. Despite a common German threat, a more benign Czechoslovak view of the Soviet Union and a disputed border in Cieszyn (Těšín) proved unbridgeable obstacles in seeking an alliance between Poland and Czechoslovakia.[24]

What resulted was a balancing policy of trying to steer an independent course between Poland's two powerful neighbours of Germany and the Soviet Union. In practical terms, this balancing policy found expression in non-aggression treaties signed with the Soviet Union on 25 January 1932 and with Germany on 26 January 1934. The emergence of the Polish balancing policy in the 1930s of seeking to maintain reasonable relations with both of Poland's powerful neighbours was the result of diminishing options. It represented not so much the unprincipled cavorting with totalitarian regimes as the lack of realistic alternatives given the failure of collective defence, collective security and regional security arrangements for Poland. Poland's isolation was made stark at the time of the Munich agreement and its recovery of Cieszyn (Těšín). Whatever the strength of the Polish case, the action was seen as joining in the dismemberment of Czechoslovakia.

Interwar Poland undoubtedly faced seemingly unresolvable security challenges in the context of its external geopolitical environment and its internal weaknesses as manifested in its failures in democratic governance, its level of economic development and the centrifugal pressure of discontented national minorities. Despite this formidable list of challenges, in its 20 years of independence, the new Poland made enormous strides in state-building by stitching together the infrastructure of state and society, making the three partition zones into a common entity. A generation of Poles only knew life in an independent Poland. For the majority of the Polish population identification with the state was strong, despite its failures and weaknesses. This identification with the idea of the Polish state would see the nation through the cataclysm that was about to be unleashed in September 1939. Moreover, the first reconstruction created a normative expectation that Poland should and would exist as a sovereign and independent state and that it had secured its place in Europe.

Second reconstruction 1939–1989

The outbreak of World War II brought an end to the Poland of the first reconstruction. The defeat of the Polish Army was swift and comprehensive in 1939, taking only 35 days for the German Army to complete the campaign.[25] A little over a fortnight after the German Army crossed the Polish frontier, a Soviet invasion of eastern Poland on 17 September led to the 'fourth partition' of Poland by Germany and the Soviet Union with the Molotov–Ribbentrop Pact of 23 August 1939. Large tracks of Polish territory were either incorporated into Germany or the Soviet Union. Only one part of German-occupied Poland remained as separate entity as a protectorate – the General Government (Generalgouvernement). By eliminating the Polish state from the map of Europe, Germany and the Soviet Union demonstrated their dominant position in determining Poland's future.

Germany and the Soviet Union set into motion what was to be World War II's most brutal occupation. Each was driven by an ideology that sought to extinguish the Polish state and eliminate or remove its population. Whether classified as subhumans (*Untermensch*) by Nazi racial ideology or class enemies by Soviet Marxist-Leninist ideology, the consequences for the Poles ultimately meant oppression, physical obliteration, or deportation from occupied Poland. In practical terms the German and Soviet occupations were indistinguishable from each other between 1939 and 1941.[26] After the onset of the German–Soviet war in June 1941, all of Poland was under German occupation until the Red Army reached Polish territory in 1944. The German and Soviet occupations were an important catalyst to Polish resistance. The result was arguably the most comprehensive civil and military resistance organisation in occupied Europe, which established a virtual underground state. The military wing of the Polish underground state emerged in 1939 and by 1942 evolved into its definitive form as the Home Army (Armia Krajowa – AK).[27]

When war loomed in 1939, there was a last-minute revival of collective defence arrangements with British and French offering military guarantees that soon became mutual defence treaties. Having distant allies did nothing to prevent the Germany's crushing defeat of Poland and the country's subsequent partition between Nazi Germany and the Soviet Union. Despite the failure of the alliance with France and Britain to prevent invasion and occupation, the Polish government reformed in exile in Paris and then in London and pinned its hopes on allied support in the re-establishment of Poland within its pre-war borders. This exile government could claim legitimacy based on a constitutional transfer of government authority abroad and support across the Polish political spectrum with the notable exception of the small and uninfluential Polish Communist Party. Despite its perceived legitimacy, the Polish government-in-exile occupied a precarious position as it was wholly dependent on allied support.[28] The Polish government-in-exile controlled the Home Army and the extensive apparatus of the underground state in occupied Poland and possessed land, air and sea forces fighting abroad under British command. By the end of the war these forces would number 228,000.[29] Polish loyalty to the allied cause and Polish blood spilled in the struggle with the common adversary, however, would not prove enough to restore pre-war Poland.

The Polish wartime alliances with the liberal western democracies failed to restore Poland either within its pre-war boundaries or as a sovereign state. The wartime imperative of collaboration with the Soviet Union in the defeat of Germany and its allies outweighed treaty commitments made to Poland or arguments based on international law. Instead, Britain and the United States co-operated with the Soviet Union in a geopolitical reconstruction of the territorial base of Poland. The Polish state lost large swathes of its eastern territory including the important Polish cities of Lwów (Lviv) and Wilno (Vilnius) and in exchange was given German territory in the west. These changes were endorsed by a series of conferences between Britain, the Soviet Union and the United States held at Tehran (November–December 1943), Yalta (February 1945) and Potsdam (July–August 1945). In particular, the Yalta Conference led to the derecognition of the Polish government-in-exile and the acceptance of the establishment of a communist-dominated provisional government by the western allies in concert with the Soviet Union. For the western powers, the absence of perceived vital interests and the lack of geographical access proved decisive in their policy calculations.[30]

The political *fait accompli* presented to the Polish government-in-exile and its armed forces both at home and abroad became an important element in Poland's legacy of World War II. For the Polish government-in-exile, its armed forces and the wartime Home Army, the fact that Britain and the United States were party to the wartime decisions that reshaped Poland without Polish consent constituted a great betrayal. As for the Soviet Union, its actions in 1939 and after 1943 were those of an adversary and not an ally. The idea of western betrayal of Poland, however, was not limited to a group of embittered emigres, but became part of the national narrative.

The cost of the war to Poland can not only be measured in political and territorial changes. The human and material losses suffered by Poland during World War II were enormous. At the start of the war, Poland's population numbered just over 35 million. By the war's end it had been reduced to just 24 million or a 32% decrease in Poland's population through border changes and deaths.[31] Poland lost six million dead in five years of war which amounted to 17% of its pre-war population. In terms of percentage of pre-war population lost, Poland had the highest losses of any European country.[32] Warsaw epitomised the large material losses of the war. Poland's capital lost 44% of its pre-war buildings with destruction in the city centre comprising 72% of all structures.[33] In human terms, the high loss of life and material destruction represented the most painful legacy of World War II.

By 1944, the Red Army entered Polish territory and began what looked more like an occupation than a 'liberation' of Poland. Creating a 'new geopolitical reality', the Soviet Union provided everything that Poland needed to function as a state enjoying limited sovereignty: a political, social and economic system with the leaders to run it and Soviet bayonets to insure its survival. Soviet power was essential to transform Poland into the image of the Soviet Union as the Polish Communist Party (Komunistyczna Partia Polski – KPP) was too weak and commanded very little measurable political support in the country.[34] Part of the reason for the weakness of Polish communists was that the Soviet leader Joseph Stalin in 1938 purged the KPP and executed the bulk of its leadership then resident in the Soviet Union. The KPP's surviving leaders only did so because they languished in Polish prisons. With the outbreak of war, Stalin allowed the recreation of the communist party in 1942, rebranded as the Polish Workers' Party (Polska Partia Robotnicza – PPR) with its surviving leaders willing instruments of Soviet policy in Poland. Party membership did grow between 1942 and 1947 among workers, poor peasants and opportunists believing 'communist rule as inevitable'.[35] By the end of 1948, after its absorption of the Polish Socialist Party (Polska Partia Socjalistyczna – PPS), the PPR became the Polish United Workers' Party (Polska Zjednoczona Partia Robotnicza – PZPR). The PZPR became the ruling party of what had become a one-party state.

The Polish People's Republic at the end of World War II was moved approximately 150 miles to the west with its territory reduced by 20%.[36] One of the important objectives of Poland's communist rulers was to create a homogenous state shorn of national minorities. In a speech given in May 1945, PPR's leader, Władysław Gomułka, made clear that communist policy was to build Poland on 'national lines and not on multi-national ones'.[37] The creation of a homogenous Polish state could not be achieved without mass population transfers. In the newly acquired western territories mass expulsions took place of 2,750,000 Germans between 1946 and 1949.[38] In the east, Poles from what had been pre-war eastern Poland were moved west from the Soviet Union while just under half a million Ukrainians were sent eastwards to the Soviet Union.[39] Other Ukrainians were internally resettled in small groups in territory recovered from Germany in western Poland. To achieve this resettlement, Operation *Vistula* (*Akcja Wisła*) conducted between April and July

1947 utilised between 17,000 and 21,000 soldiers, internal security troops, militia (police) and security service operatives to eliminate Ukrainian insurgent groups and remove 135,000 to 149,000 Ukrainians from eastern Poland.[40] By the time the territorial and demographic redesign of Poland was completed in the early 1950s, Poland became one of the most homogeneous states in Europe with statistically insignificant residual national minorities.

The reshaping of the country's territory and composition of its population was not the only radical change in the nascent communist PRL. The imposition of Soviet socialism dramatically altered the material development of the country. Following the pattern of the Soviet Union, nationalization of industry occurred and virtually all sectors of the economy were placed under the control of the state. By 1960, 86% of the Polish economy was controlled by the state.[41] Industrial development was based on central planning with an emphasis on heavy industry and this imbalance made standard of living improvements modest with chronic shortages of consumer goods and housing. Land reform and collectivization of agriculture was launched but failed, with most farms uniquely remaining privately owned small holdings.[42] The benefits of 'real socialism' were at best skewed and such modernization as occurred in the PRL was overshadowed by the costly and economically irrational policies of the state-run, centrally planned economy. The Polish economy would throughout the history of the PRL experience a cycle of crises that resulted in stagnation and repeated periods of hardship for the Polish population. Thus, the result of 45 years of communist economic policy was 'the ruin of the economy and the environment, as well as the demoralization of society'.[43]

Such dramatic and fundamental change to Poland was not possible without a communist regime in Poland and a communist regime was not possible without Soviet support. It is not the intention here to examine in detail the process that placed the communists in power in Poland between 1944 and 1948.[44] It is important to note, however, the communist regime faced armed resistance that lasted into the early 1950s. Former members of the Home Army morphed into new organizations such as Freedom and Sovereignty (Wolność i Niezawisłość – WiN) with anti-communist resistance groups having an overall number of between 8,000 and 12,000 during the most intense period of fighting in 1945 and 1946.[45] In early 1946, the Polish communist regime had to deploy from 150,000–180,000 men from the army and other internal security formations in its effort to eliminate anti-communist insurgents.[46] Soviet support, however, was to prove indispensable. From the beginning of the Soviet entry into Polish territory, Soviet internal security forces were engaged in operations against Polish armed resistance and in arresting people in Polish society deemed opponents to the communist regime. The scale of Soviet support was such that in 1944 and 1945 seven 'overstrength' People's Commissariat for Internal Affairs (Naródnyy Komissariát Vnútrennikh – NKVD) divisions operated in Poland in support of the large and growing Polish internal security apparatus.[47] The scale of

Soviet 'fraternal' security assistance was an important illustration of the weakness and lack of popular support for the Polish communists and how dependent they were on Soviet backing to come to power.

Part of the reason for direct Soviet intervention to consolidate the communist regime in Poland was the fact that the Polish armed forces had to be completely rebuilt into something the Soviet Union considered reliable. When the Soviet Union created the first formation of what was to become Polish People's Army (Ludowe Wojsko Polskie – LWP) in May 1943, it needed a reliable leadership cadre. At its creation, the LWP lacked trained Polish officers – a circumstance that was a direct result of Soviet policy. In 1939, approximately 11,000 Polish army officers fell into Soviet hands as prisoners of war. Over 8,000 of these men were held at camps in Kozelsk, Ostashkov and Starobelsk and were executed on the order of the Soviet leadership in May 1940.[48] The surviving 3,000 Polish officers left Soviet territory with the evacuation of Anders Polish Army to the Middle East in 1942. Only a handful of pro-Soviet officers from the pre-war Polish Army chose to work with the Soviet Union.[49] Soviet officers filled the gap. In July 1943 they represented 66% of officers in the Polish Army in the Soviet Union and by the war's end 45% of all officers. Thereafter slowly diminishing, nevertheless a handful of Soviet officers served in the LWP into the late 1960s.[50] The employment of Soviet officers provided the time necessary to build a 'reliable' Polish officer corps. The Soviet Union's reconstruction of the LWP reflected both its doubts that the cadre of the LWP could be fully trusted and a desire to make it a reliable instrument of Soviet interests. During the Cold War there was much western analysis considering the reliability of Warsaw Pact armed forces, much of which focussed on the LWP. The LWP, however, proved a reliable enough instrument of Poland's communist regime in suppression of internal unrest in 1956, 1970 and 1981.[51] Its reliability in an east–west conflict, however, was never put to the test.

Given the weak position of Polish communists at the onset of the PRL, the Polish communist leadership elevated the maintenance of close relations with the Soviet Union to the level of a *raison d'etat*. Indeed, the Polish constitution introduced in 1952 enshrined the idea of permanent friendship with the Soviet Union:

> In its policy the Polish People's Republic shall follow the noble traditions of solidarity with the forces of liberty and progress, shall consolidate friendship and cooperation with the Union of Soviet Socialist Republics and other socialist states.[52]

An important shorthand for the Polish communist regime's dependency on the Soviet Union was the expression 'geopolitical realities'. The geopolitical realities brought together as an integrated whole the PRL's international alignment with the Soviet Union and its Soviet imposed domestic order:

> The permanent and secure place occupied by Poland in the East has presented the Polish nation with a new and previously unknown image of geopolitics. This is the historic process which is currently underway, a process of putting into practice friendly relations of partnership

between Poland and its neighbours, [Soviet Union] something which is only possible within a community of socialist states with a homogenous class basis and political system. That new, absolutely positive and constructive geopolitics is called socialism.[53]

With Poland's western frontier lacking full *de jure* international recognition and the Federal Republic of Germany (West Germany) unwilling to recognise it until 1970, the communist leadership of the PRL maintained that only the Soviet Union could guarantee the country's territorial integrity. Party leaders in Poland were fond of reminding the country's restive population of the need for Soviet support against German revanchism. The threat of German revanchism, however, was something of a chimera and by the 1970s disappeared with Chancellor Willy Brandt's *Ostpolitik* denuding it of any real credibility.

Defence and security policy in the PRL were in practice completely subordinated to the Soviet Union. A bilateral alliance concluded in December 1956 and the multilateral Warsaw Treaty Organization (WTO – May 1955) provided the legal framework of the close integration. The basing of over 60,000 Soviet troops in Poland was a visible guarantee of the PRL's subordination to Soviet security policy.[54] Security integration with the Soviet Union was an externally imposed solution to Poland's security problems and as such took no account of Polish interests. In military terms, Poland would become a nuclear free-fire zone for NATO nuclear weapons in any Soviet-initiated east–west confrontation during the Cold War.[55] The real threat to Polish security came from its fraternal ally to the east. The near interventions of the Soviet Union in the domestic crises of 1956 and 1980–81 demonstrated the PRL's limited room for internal manoeuvre.

Given the dependency on Soviet power, the manifest weakness in public support and perceived lack of legitimacy, it is not surprising that the history of the PRL was one of repeated domestic crisis. Opposition to the regime took many forms including intellectual dissent, working-class discontent and the enduring influence of the Roman Catholic Church which the communist authorities never succeeded in suppressing.[56] The Polish People's Republic experienced what amounted to a cycle of crises with major domestic upheavals in October 1956, December 1970, June 1976 and August 1980–December 1981. This last crisis gave rise to the mass opposition movement Solidarność (Solidarity) which set in motion the eventual end to Poland's communist regime in 1989. The PRL in its 45 years of existence was a state dependent on Soviet power, was only able to exercise limited sovereignty and possessed an externally imposed political, economic and social order. Given the scope of this Soviet external imposition and control, it is hard not to see the PRL as a form of occupation.

Legacy of World War II: Belated victory

Poland's third reconstruction in the 20th century began with the collapse of communism in 1989. By throwing off the constraints of limited sovereignty, Poland was able to reclaim its independence and embarked on a transformation every bit as far-reaching as that of its communist predecessor. Post communism, Poland became a democratic state with a market economy that has pursued a policy of 'return to Europe' that resulted in the country's integration into institutions such as the European Union (EU) in 2004 and the North Atlantic Treaty Organization (NATO) in 1999. The country's economic performance in European terms has been stellar with its per capita GDP increasing eight-fold since 1989.[57] EU membership has anchored Poland economically firmly in the west and has been a major factor in its growing economic strength. What the EU brings economically, membership in NATO matches in defence terms. Poland's security is more assured than at any time in the 20th century. While criticisms have been made in recent years over issues regarding rule of law and threats to democracy in Poland, these do not reflect a deep understanding of Polish politics, law and institutions nor does Polish democracy face a mortal threat.[58] Unlike the previous two reconstructions, the third has not been one born of violent conflict and can be considered from a political perspective a successful exercise in peaceful national self-determination and social and economic development.

Three decades into Poland's successful third reconstruction, it might seem remarkable that the legacy of World War II can still cast such a long shadow. Moreover, recent scholarship that examines 'dominant historical narratives' and 'commemorative practices' promotes a view that legacies are artificial and therefore constructed and not grounded in facts or truth.[59] At the beginning of this chapter the thesis was put forward that the narrative of Poland's legacy of World War II is built on two dominant and interconnected strands. The first of these was the idea of betrayal by Poland's wartime allies and the thwarting of Poland's post-war aspirations. There can be no disputing that the wartime diplomacy and decisions taken by the major western powers in conjunction with the Soviet Union determined the post-war future of Poland. Events can be seen from multiple perspectives, but those who are most directly concerned must articulate the legacies they live with. In a speech before the Council of Europe on 30 January 1990, Prime Minister Tadeusz Mazowiecki stated that 'we also continue to feel reproachful because of Yalta' suggesting a deep-seated national feeling of betrayal and implied distrust of allies.[60] Despite the enduring sense of betrayal, post-communist governments made the forging of new alliances in the form of the EU and NATO central to the country's defence, foreign and security policy. Nevertheless, the consequences of the legacy of betrayal cannot be completely erased. Recent Polish government attempts to get the United States to increase the numbers of its forces based in Poland and the creation by Poland of Territorial Defence Forces (Wojska Obrony Terytorialnej – WOT) suggest that reliability of allies is still an issue. With the former, Poland is seeking more than verbal commitments but tangible capability from its principal ally and with the latter, the country is intending to meet any potential aggression by all national means with or without allies.[61] Clearly the legacy of betrayal still rests on the minds of Poland's political establishment.

The second strand of the narrative is that the communist Polish People's Republic represented an illegitimate state of limited sovereignty and was in fact a de facto Soviet occupation. As prominent Polish historian Wojciech Roszkowski has argued, the end of World War II ended 'one terrible oppression' but marked the 'beginning of another terrible one, which lasted for more than four decades'.[62] This view has been contested by others, such as Adam Michnik, a prominent intellectual opponent of the communist regime, who has maintained that a more nuanced approach is necessary for Polish understanding of the complicated legacy of the PRL which he believes cannot be simply compared to a military occupation.[63] What all sides of the debate can agree is that the PRL was a regime that did not enjoy the support and legitimacy of more than the minority of the Polish population who willingly served it. These differing Polish perspectives form part of a lively *polityka historyczna* (politics of history) debate in Poland, but these issues also have made it into the international arena.[64] Thus, this debate has an interrelated internal and external dimension driven by the desire of the conservative populist Polish Law and Justice Party (Prawo i Sprawiedliwość) when it came to power to shape the direction of national memory and the emergence of a provocative Russian line at the 60th anniversary celebrations of World War II.[65] Indeed, subsequent statements by Russian President Vladimir Putin regarding Polish history appeared to be part of a hostile information campaign to undermine Poland within the western community. One dominant theme of the Russian mendacious line of historical invention has been to blame Poland for the outbreak of World War II. It has prompted a robust Polish official response to counter the view of history promulgated by Russia.[66] More importantly it has prompted a wider international response in the form of a resolution of the European Parliament comprehensively refuting the Russian portrayal of history as false. The resolution went further to suggest that Russia required an honest reappraisal of its past:

> Russia remains the greatest victim of communist totalitarianism and that its development into a democratic state will be impeded as long as the government, the political elite and political propaganda continue to whitewash communist crimes and glorify the Soviet totalitarian regime; [the resolution] calls, therefore, on Russian society to come to terms with its tragic past.[67]

The din of the politicised internal Polish debate over the legacy of the PRL and Russian efforts to weaponize a mendacious view of events of World War II as part of hostile information campaign distract from what is the central point of Poland's legacy of World War II. It was a legacy defined by allied betrayal and the establishment of a Soviet satellite state of limited sovereignty that, for many Poles, was a second prolonged occupation. Therefore, Poland only achieved its belated 'victory' by overturning this wartime legacy in 1989.

Notes

1 Address by President Andrzej Duda, 1 September 2019, https://www.president.pl/en/news/page,11. html, accessed 13 July 2020.

2 Wojciech Roszkowski, *The Shadow of Yalta: A Report* (Warsaw: Warsaw Rising Museum, 2005).

3 Summaries of the rebirth of Poland include: Norman Davies, *God's Playground: A History of Poland Volume II 1795–Present* (Oxford: Clarendon Press, 1981), 378–401 and Janusz Pajewski, *Budowa Drugiej Rzeczypospolitej 1918–1926* (Poznań: Wydawnictwo Poznańskie, 2007), 57–80.

4 Roman Dmowski, *Myśli nowoczesnego Polaka* (Lwów: Towarzystwo Wydawnicze, 1903).

5 Roman Dmowski, *Niemcy, Rosya i kwestya polska* (Lwów: Towarzystwo Wydawnicze, 1908).

6 Roman Wapiński, *Roman Dmowski* (Lublin: Wydawnictwo Lubelskie,1988), 228–288.

7 Piłsudski's has been the subject of a number of important biographies. See: Andrzej Garlicki, *Józef Piłsudski 1867–1935* (Kraków: Wydawnictwo Znak, 2008); Wacław Jędrzejewicz, *Józef Piłsudski 1867–1935: życiorys* (Łomianki: Wydawnictwo LTW, 2008) and Bohdan Urbanowski, *Józef Piłsudski: marzyciel i strateg* (Poznań: Zysk i S-ka Wydawnictwo, 2014).

8 As quoted in Norman Davies, *White Eagle, Red Star: The Polish-Soviet War 1919–20* (London: Orbis Books Ltd., 1983), 63.

9 M. K. Dziewanowski, *Joseph Piłsudski: A European Federalist, 1918–1922* (Stanford: Hoover Institution Press, 1969), 350–352.

10 B. A. Porter, 'Who is a Pole and Where is Poland? Territory and Nation in the Rhetoric of Polish National Democracy Before 1905', *Slavic Review,* Vol. 51, No. 4 (Winter 1992): 639–653; K. Sobczak, 'Koncepcja nie podleglosciowa Jozefa Pilsudskiego', *Wojskowy Przeglad Historyczny* (1989): 61–79 and P. S. Wandycz, 'Poland's Place in Europe in the Concepts of Pilsudski and Dmowski', *East European Politics and Societies,* Vol. 4, No. 3 (Fall 1990): 451–468.

11 Zbigniew Landau and Wojciech Roszkowski, *Polityka Gospodarcza II RP i PRL* (Warszawa: Wydawnictwo Naukowe PWN, 1995), 32.

12 Andrzej Jezierski and Cecylia Leszczyńska, *Historia Gospodarcza Polski* (Warszawa: Wydawnictwo Key text, 1999), 248.

13 Ireneusz Ihnatowicz, Antoni Mączak, Benedykt Zientara and Janusz Żarnowski, *Społeczeństwo Polskie od X do XX wieku* (Warszawa: Wydawnictwo 'Książka i Wiedza, 1996), 632.

14 Marian M. Drozdowski, 'The National Minorities in Poland 1918–1939', *Acta Polnica Historica*, Vol. 22 (1970): 229–233 and Jerzy Tomaszewski, *Mniejszości narodowe w Polsce XX wieku* (Warszawa: Editions Spotkania, 1991), 24–30.

15 Anthony Polonsky, *Politics in Independent Poland 1921–1939: The Crisis of Constitutional Government* (Oxford: Clarendon Press, 1972), 508–510.

16 Ibid., 147–185.

17 Joseph Rothschild, *Piłsudski's Coup d'etat* (New York: Columbia University Press, 1966), 181.

18 Lech Wyszczelski, *Wojsko Piłsudskiego: Wojsko Polskie w latach 1926–1935* (Warszawa: Wydawnictwo Neriton, 2005), 172.

19 Bartosz Kruszyński, *Kariery oficerów w II Rzeczypospolitej* (Poznań: Dom Wydawniczy Rebis, 2011), p. 185.

20 Piotr Stawecki, *Generałowie polscy: Zarys portretu zbiorowego 1772–1945* (Warszawa: Oficyna Wydawnicza, 2010), 89–90.

21 Jon Jacobson, *Locarno Diplomacy: Germany and the West 1925–1929* (Princeton: Princeton University Press, 1972) and Piotr S. Wandycz, *France and Her Eastern Allies* (Minneapolis: The University of Minnesota Press, 1962).

22 Stanisław Sierpowski, 'Mniejszość niemiecka na tle aktywności mniejszościowej ligi narodów', in Wojciech Wrzesiński (ed), *Polska – Polacy – mniejszości narodowe* (Wrocław: Zakład Narodowy im. Ossolińskich, 1992), 77–90.

23 Andrzej Essen, *Polska a Mała Ententa 1920–1934* (Warszawa: Wydawnictwo Naukowe PWN, 1992), 56–58.

24 Piotr S. Wandycz, *Czechoslovak-Polish Confederation and the Great Powers* (Westport: Greenwood Press, 1956), 1–32.

25 Eugeniusz Kozłowski (ed), *Polski czyn zbrojny w II wojnie światowej: Wojna obronna Polski 1939* (Warszawa: Wydawnictwo Ministerstwa Obrony Narodowej, 1979), 282; Adam Sawczyński (ed), *Polskie siły zbrojne w drugiej wojnie światowej, Tom 1, Kampania wrzesniowa 1939, cz. 1, Polityczne i wojskowe polozenie Polski przed wojną* (Londyn: Instytut Historyczny im. Gen. Sikorskiego, 1951), 292 and Stephen J. Zaloga, *Poland 1939: Germany's 'Lightening Strike'* (Oxford: Osprey Publishing, 2002), 23.

26 J. T. Gross, *Polish Society under German Occupation: The Generalgouvernement 1939–1944* (Princeton: Princeton University Press, 1979); J. T. Gross, *Revolution from Abroad: The Soviet Conquest of Poland's Western Ukraine and Western Belorussia* (Princeton: Princeton University Press, 1988); R. C. Lukas, *Forgotton Holocaust: The Poles under German Occupation 1939–1944* (Lexington: The University Press of Kentucky, 1986) and T. Piotrowski, *Poland's Holocaust: Ethnic Strife, Collaboration with Occupying Forces and Genocide in the Second Republic, 1918–1947* (Jefferson, North Carolina: McFarland & Company, Inc., 1998).

27 See: Stefan Korbonski, *The Polish Underground State: A Guide to the Underground, 1939–1945* (New York: Columbia University Press, 1979) and *Polskie Siły Zbrojne w drugiej wojnie światowej Tom III Armia Krajowa* (London: Instytut Historyczny im. Gen. Sikorskiego, 1950).

28 Paul Latawski, 'Polish Exile Armies, 1939–45: Manpower and Military Effectiveness', in Matthew Bennett and Paul Latawski, *Exile Armies* (Basingstoke: Palgrave Macmillan, 2005), 32–33.

29 Andrzej Liebich, *Na obcej ziemi: Polskie Siły Zbrojne 1939–1945* (London: Wydawnictwo Światowego Związku Polaków z Zagranicy, 1947), 44.

30 G. Lundsted, *The American Non-Policy towards Eastern Europe* (Romso: Universitetsforlaget, 1978).

31 Andrzej Wyczański (comp), *Historia Polski w liczbach: Państwo Społeczeństwo* (Warszawa: Główny Urząd Statystyczny, 2003), 364, 369.

32 Franciszek Kubiczek, *Historia Polski w liczbach: Ludność, Terytorium* (Warszawa: Główny Urząd Statystyczny, 1994), 197.

33 K. Romaniuk (ed), *Statistical Year Book of Poland 1947* (Warsaw: Central Statistical Office, 1947), 37, 104.

34 Susanne S. Lotarski, 'The Communist Takeover in Poland', in Thomas T. Hammond (ed), *The Anatomy of Communist Takeovers* (New Haven: Yale University Press, 1971), 339.

35 Ibid., 347.

36 R. H. Osborne, *East-Central Europe: An Introductory Geography* (New York: Praeger, 1967), 229.

37 'Protokół z plenarego posidzenia Komitetu Centralnego [PPR], odbytego w Warszawie w dniach 20-21 maja 1945 r.', in Aleksander Kochański (ed), *Dokumenty do dziejów PRL Zeszyt 1: Protokół obrad KC PPR w maju 1945 roku* (Warszawa: Instytut Studiów Politycznych PAN, 1992), 11.

38 F. E. Hamilton, *Poland's Western and Northern Territories* (Oxford: Oxford University Press, 1975), 12.

39 Eugeniusz Misiło, 'Polska polityka narodowościowa wobec Ukraińców 1944–1947', in Wojciech Wrzesiński (ed), *Polska – Polacy – mniejszości narodowe* (Wrocław: Zakład Narodowy im. Ossolińskich, 1992), 402.

40 Jan Pisuliński, *Akcja specjalna Wisła* (Rzeszów: Libra, 2017), 142, 427.

41 Landau and Roszkowski, *Polityka Gospodarcza II RP i PRL*, 221.

42 Zbigniew Landau and Jerzy Tomaszewski, *The Polish Economy in the Twentieth Century* (London: Croom and Helm, 1985), 187–194, 262–271.

43 Landau and Roszkowski, *Polityka Gospodarcza II RP i PRL*, 221.

44 For a classic account of the establishment of the communist regime in Poland see: Krystyna Kersten, *Narodziny system władzy: Polska 1943–1948* (Poznań: Kantor Wydawniczy SAWW, 1990).

45 Jerzy Ślaski, 'Siły zbrojnego oporu antykomunistycznego w latach 1944–1947', in Andrzej Ajnenkiel (ed), *Wojna domowa czy nowa okupacja?: Polska po roku 1944* (Warszawa: Oficyna Wydawnicza Rytm, 2001), 50.

46 Leszek Grot, 'Działania ludowego Wojska polskiego przeciwko zbrojnemu podziemu w latach 1944–1947', *Wojskowy Przegląd Historyczny*, Vol. XVIII, No. 3 (Lipiec-Wrzesień 1973): 485.

47 Andrzej Chmielarz, 'Działania 64 dywizji Wojsk Wewnętrznych NKWD przeciwko polskiemu podziemiu', in Ajnenkiel (ed), *Wojna domowa czy nowa okupacja?: Polska po roku 1944* (Warszawa: Oficyna Wydawnicza Rytm, 2001), 88–89.

48 See note Chief of NKVD, L. Beria to J. Stalin, March 1940 in Ewa Wosik (ed), *Katyń: Dokumenty Ludobójstwa* (Warszawa: ISP-PAN, 1992), 35–39.

49 See note L. Beria to J. Stalin, 12 March 1942 in Wojciech Materski (ed), *Z archiwów Sowieckich tom II: Armia Polska w ZSRR 1941–1942* (Warszawa: ISP-PAN, 1992), 49–73.

50 Edward Jan Nalepa, *Oficerowe Armii Radzieckiej w Wojsku Polskim 1943–1968* (Warszawa: Wydawnictwo Bellona, 1995), 15–16.

51 Jan B. de Weydenthal, 'Martial Law and the Reliability of the Polish Military', in: Daniel N. Nelson (ed), *Soviet Allies: The Warsaw Pact and the Issue of Reliability* (Boulder: Westview Press, 1984), 229, 245.

52 Chapter 1, Article 6, Paragraph 2 of the Constitution of the Polish People's Republic in *Dziennik Ustaw*, 21 February 1976, No. 7, Item 36.

53 Ignacy Krasicki, 'Poland's Alliances: Historical Significance and Contemporary Importance', *Trybuna Ludu*, 23 September 1988.

54 Mariusz Lesław Krogulski, *Okupacja w imię sojuszu: Armia Radziecka w Polsce 1956–1993* (Warszawa: Wydawnictwo von borowiecky, 2001), 34.

55 Jarosław Pałka, 'The Third World War as Envisaged by Polish Generals at the Turn of the 1950s and the 1960s', *Kwartelnik Historyczny*, Vol. CXXIV, No. 1 (2017): 122–123.

56 See: Timothy Garton Ash, *The Polish Revolution: Solidarity 1980–82* (London: Jonathan Cape, 1983) and Andrzej Friszke, *Opozycja polityczna w PRL 1945–1980* (London: Aneks, 1994).

57 Eglé Fredrikson, 'How Poland's 'Golden Ade' of Economic Growth is Going Unreported', *Euronews*, 25 June 2019, https://www.euronews.com/2019/06/25/how-poland-s-golden-age-of-economic-growth-is-going-unreported-view, accessed 22 July 2020.

58 Sava Jankovic, 'Polish Democracy under Threat?: An Issue of Mere Politics or a Real Danger?', *Baltic Journal of Law and Politics*, Vol. 9, No. 1 (2016): 63–64.

59 For a highly thought-provoking and detailed study on these issues see: Ewa Ochman, *Post-Communist Poland – Contested Pasts and Future Identities* (London: Routledge, 2013), 1.

60 Speech by Tadeusz Mazowiecki to the Council of Europe, 30 January 1990 in Lawrence Freedman (ed), *Europe Transformed: Documents on the End of the Cold War: Key Treaties, Agreements, Statements and Speeches* (London: Tri-Service Press, 1990), 431.

61 'U.S. Military Presence in Poland', *Congressional Research Service*, 2 July 2020 and Remigiusz Żuchowski and Marcin Stachowski, 'Poland's Ministry of Defence Concept for Territorial Defence Forces', *Ante Portas – Studia nad Bezpieczeństwem*, Vol. 2, No. 7 (2016): 109–112.

62 Roszkowski, *The Shadow of Yalta: A Report*, 15.

63 Adam Michnik, *The Trouble with History: Morality, Revolution and Counterrevolution* (New Haven: Yale University Press, 2014), 37.

64 Ochman, *Post-Communist Poland – Contested Pasts and Future Identities*, 22.

65 Ibid., 42–44.

66 Anne Applebaum, 'Putin's Big Lie', *The Atlantic*, 5 January 2020; James Shotter and Agata Majos, 'Polish President Accuses Putin of 'Historical Lie' over Second World War', *Financial Times*, 22 January 2020 and Ben Sixsmith, 'Russia and Poland's War of Words over the Second World War', *The Spectator*, 22 January 2020.

67 Joint Motion for a Resolution on the Importance of European Remembrance for the Future of Europe, European Parliament, 19 September 2019, https://www.europarl.europa.eu/doceo/ document/RC-9-2019-0097_EN.html 4/, accessed 24 July 2020.

CHAPTER 3

'This Must Never Happen Again': The Continuous Presence of World War II in Germany

Matthias Strohn

The shadow of World War II has hung over Germany since the surrender of its armed forces in May 1945, and it will continue to shape German society and politics for many years to come. The mantra of 'never again' has been a potent, and arguably, the most important driver internally and externally. Never again should Germany launch a war, never again should Germany be the breeding ground of extremism and never again should Germany engage in or even stand by when atrocities and persecution of specific groups occur. Germany, its politics, society and military (dis-) engagements in the 21th century cannot be understood without understanding the deep and lasting impact that the war, and the 12 'dark years' of the National Socialist regime, have left on the German soul. It is a scarred soul and these scars will not heal soon – if they will ever heal. In recent years, Germany has been criticised for its cautious steps in the field of foreign and security policies. The voices are getting louder that Germany needs to wake up and smell the coffee: the most powerful economic country in Europe and the country with the fourth largest GDP worldwide cannot hide behind its dark past and needs to be a more active (military) partner in the world. From a non-German view, this is a very valid and logical argument. However, it completely neglects the German perception.

This chapter analyses the painful struggle that the Germans have had to face in coming to terms with their recent history and their responsibility for throwing Europe and the wider world into the abyss of total war, occupation and the Shoa. The chapter will concentrate on the Federal Republic of Germany, from its founding in 1949, and will not deal in detail with the former German Democratic Republic, the GDR, which existed from 1949 until 1990. For ease of writing, this chapter will therefore say 'Germany' when talking about the Federal Republic of Germany. There are several reasons for this restriction. The Federal Republic has regarded itself as the constitutional successor organisation of the German Empire, which collapsed in 1945. It was the far more populous of the two German states that existed during the Cold War (approximately 64 million inhabitants compared to about 16 million in the GDR), and thus shaped a 'German' view and behaviour more than the GDR ever could. Lastly, and perhaps most importantly, the GDR regarded itself as a country that had been founded on principles that stood opposed to and rejected any historical links with the former German Empire and its actions. The fact that it was based on socialist ideals was seen as a reminder of the rejection of the 'old' regimes and elites – perhaps neatly ignoring the strong socialist element that had been part of the National Socialist DNA, the clue is in the name. The GDR was a new state 'resurrected from ruins and facing the future', as the opening lines of its national anthem stated. The historical analysis of the Nazi period and World War II was restricted by ideology, which saw Nazism as the most radical form of the rule of the bourgeoisie and Hitler as the henchman of the capitalist establishment. This meant that, as is often the case, historical analysis was used to shape contemporary thinking and politics.[1] It was stated that the historical analysis of fascism did not deal with a closed chapter of history, but that it 'participates directly in the class struggle of our time, the peoples' fight against imperialism, for peace and socialism.'[2] The GDR did not regard itself as a successor of the German Empire and did not feel responsible for the latter's actions. National Socialists and their ideology did, officially, not linger on in the new state. Naturally, reality turned out somewhat different. In 1954, 27 percent of the members of the socialist party SED had previously been members of the NSDAP and, peaking in the 1980s, the Staatssicherheit, the infamous secret police, kept extensive files on the estimated 6,000 members of the underground neo-Nazi movement in the new German state of workers and peasants.[3]

The political system in Germany has been deeply influenced by the war and Allied occupation. The federal structure was re-established after 1945 (this did, however, not happen in the GDR), but not along old-established territorial boundaries, instead to reflect the new realities of a divided and occupied Germany. The state of Prussia was dissolved in 1947 and has faded into history; attempts to create a 'rump Prussia' in the early 2000s by combining the states of Berlin and Brandenburg came to nothing, not least because of monetary questions. New states were formed, in particular in the areas that had been part of Prussia. North-Rhine Westphalia, the so-called 'hyphen state (in German Nordrhein-Westfalen)' is perhaps the best example, which combines the former Prussian province of Westphalia with the northern part of the former Prussian Rhine province and the territory of Lippe. At the local level, in particular, the influence of the political systems of the occupational forces is still very much visible today and influences, for example, the election of municipal representatives. As a consequence of the lessons of German history, the political system created in 1949 is characterised by a set of check and balances. At the top, the president was turned into not much more than a mere figurehead, a consequence of the alleged disastrous role that President Hindenburg played in Hitler's assumption of power in 1933. The fact that Hindenburg prevented Hitler from becoming chancellor in July 1932, when the NSDAP for the first time became the strongest party in parliament, is often conveniently overlooked. The two chambers of parliament (called Bundestag and Bundesrat) have to work together closely. In the areas of foreign and security policy, the federal government is still the most important player, but it is tightly controlled by parliament, which sets the German governmental system apart from most of its allies. In particular, there is a very strict parliamentary prerogative on all armed military deployments outside of NATO territory. Parliament has to mandate these operations, agree on mandate renewals and decide on the withdrawal of German troops engaged in international missions.[4] It is this tight control which has sometimes causes raised eyebrows amongst international friends and partners, because Germany is seen as a somewhat unreliable military player. It has to be said, though, that so far parliament has never rejected a military engagement when this has been proposed by the government. Due to the tight control over the armed forces, the military is called a 'Parlamentsarmee', the military of parliament, which, in theory, is also supposed to express the strong links between the military and the population. The set-up of the political system is also an expression of the general distrust of the founding fathers of the republic in the democratic and political characteristics of the German people. Konrad Adenauer, the most influential political figure in Germany after the war and the first chancellor of the country, expressed his views quite drastically by stating 'the citizens are incredibly stupid.'[5] Direct political participation is, realistically, limited to elections at the different levels; the hurdles for plebiscites are high and they are not seen as a useful tool for political decision making. In the German understanding, complex political issues cannot be reduced to simple yes or no answers of a plebiscite.

European integration is widely regarded as the only viable option to address the problems of the present and future. It is, however, also the consequence of the analysis of the time from 1933 to 1945. For Germany, as the economic powerhouse in Europe, economic integration is, clearly, of vital importance. In the early years after the war, the integration into the western systems of security and economy was also seen as a lever for establishing the new republic as an important and (semi-independent) player. The debates about this integration were heated in Germany, in particular because an affiliation with the western economic and security systems would cement the partition of Germany. This debate was fuelled by the so-called Stalin note of 1952, in which Stalin offered the unification and neutral status of Germany. It has been debated whether this was a genuine offer, but the German government under Adenauer regarded it as a bluff and an attempt to drive a wedge between Germany and the western powers.[6] It is quite possible that Adenauer's dislike of protestant Prussia – he was a devout Catholic from the Rhine province and had been mayor of Cologne between 1917 and 1933 – also played a role in this process. Adenauer is supposed to have said that 'in Deutz (the part of Cologne on the east bank of the river Rhine) Bolshevism starts' and 'For me, Asia starts in Magdeburg'.[7]

Germany only achieved partial sovereignty in 1955, six years after the founding of the republic. The treaty of Paris, signed on 5 May 1955, ended the occupation that had existed since 1945 and gave the Germans sovereignty over internal and external affairs. This also paved the way for NATO membership. Having said this, the Allies retained certain rights: They were allowed to station troops on German soil, they still were responsible for the status of all of Germany, and they kept control over West Berlin, which, as a consequence, was legally not seen as part of the Federal Republic. This process was also a consequence of the fact that no peace treaty has ever been signed after World War II. The German surrender in May 1945 was only a military capitulation. Full sovereignty was only bestowed upon Germany in 1991 with the ratification of the 'Treaty on the Final Settlement with Respect to Germany' (also known as the 2+4 Treaty). The treaty had been negotiated in 1990 among the two German states and the four former occupation powers, i.e. the Soviet Union, the USA, the United Kingdom and France, and had made German re-unification possible.

However, with regards to European integration, the economic factor is not everything. In the German perspective, only a deep European co-operation can prevent tensions and potential conflict in Europe. The links to the violent past of Europe are omnipresent in this debate in Germany. For instance, in 2017, placards went up in 1,250 German towns and cities. They were put up by the Volksbund Deutsche Kriegsgräberfürsorge, the national organisation that cares for German military cemeteries. The placards depicted a German military cemetery and had, in big letter, the words 'Darum Europe' (Because of this Europe) written over them.[8] As a consequence of its history in the 20th century, Germany regards itself very much as a driver of European integration. It is therefore not astonishing that the EU as an institution has been viewed overwhelmingly favourably by the Germans. In a poll conducted in 2019, 69 percent of Germans held favourable views of the EU, compared with 28 percent who held unfavourable views.[9] Within this context, the mantra of 'never again' has evolved. In 2020, in his speech commemorating the 75th anniversary of the end of World War II in Europe, the German President Frank-Walter Steinmeier stated that:

> 'Never again,' we vowed after the war. But for us Germans in particular, this 'never again' means 'never again alone.' And this sentence is nowhere as true as in Europe. We must keep Europe together. We must think, feel and act as Europeans. If we do not hold Europe together, also during and after this pandemic, then we will have shown ourselves not worthy of 8 May. If Europe fails, the 'never again' also fails.[10]

And this 'never alone' does not stop at the borders of the states of the EU. Despite the long period of deep integration into the western systems, and the often-heard mantra that Germany is looking first and foremost to the west, German unification seems to have changed this perspective a little. Germany has moved back into being a bridge between the west and the east, a position it held over centuries. Economic reasons play a role here and Germany remains highly interested in the Russian market and its export of natural resources, in particular gas. This, however, is only one side of the coin. Germany is well aware of the hardships and the sufferings that World War II brought over the Soviet Union. To provide just one example: the building of the North Stream 2 gas pipeline will provide Germany with increased direct access to the Russian gas market. The decision to build it has been met with fierce criticism, not least from the US and the central European states, through which existing gas pipelines run. So far, Germany has resisted all calls to stop the project. Naturally, economic interests stand in the centre of this venture. But this is not all. In an interview in early February 2021, Steinmeier linked the project to the history of World War II. When asked about the pipeline he stated that:

> For us Germans there is another dimension. We have had an ambivalent history with Russia. There were periods of fruitful partnership, but even more periods of horrible blood-shedding. On 22 June we will see the 80th anniversary of the German invasion of the Soviet Union. More than 20 million people of the former Soviet Union became victims of the war. This does not justify current wrongdoings in Russian politics, but we must not lose sight of the bigger picture.[11]

Another factor that should not underestimated in this process of becoming a bridge is the disillusionment with western state leaders in recent years, in particular with regards to the US and the United Kingdom. A poll conducted in 2019 found that Germans regarded the US under Trump as the biggest threat to world peace, before North Kora, Turkey and Russia.[12] Brexit is widely seen as a very bad decision, both for the UK and the EU.[13] The wide-spread view is that it was brought about by a clique of irresponsible politicians who built their arguments on lies and were able to deceive the electorate. In the German view, this is a stark reminder of Adenauer's statement that the citizens cannot be trusted and that plebiscites are not useful political tools.

Despite this clear direction and the frank analysis of history, accepting the national guilt was a long process. In the years immediately after the war, German cities were destroyed, and the country had to be re-built. Approximately eight million Germans had died and millions of people from the former eastern territories had been expelled from their homes. The integration of these caused immense problems in a war-torn country and was not without difficulties. That this process eventually succeeded is, together with the so-called 'economic wonder' of the 1950s, in the author's view, the biggest achievement of Germany after the war.[14] In addition, most of the Nazi perpetrators were still living among the population. All this meant that there was a limited interest in Germany to address questions of national guilt and responsibility for Nazism and the war. Moreover, after 1949, Germany had to re-establish itself as a state, and for this is had to make use of the old elites. During the debate of German re-armament in the 1950s, Chancellor Konrad Adenauer summed up this conundrum by saying 'NATO will not believe me if I send them 18-year-old generals.' As a consequence, the early years of the post-war period were characterised by a degree of continuity and denial. A 'zero hour' and a complete re-setting of the German society did, in this sense, not exist.[15] In some areas, these continuities were more obvious than in others. The military, obviously, fell into this category, and so did the diplomatic service, which, until recently, had been able to present itself as a clean organisation, unaffected by Nazism.[16] Perhaps the most obvious case of these continuities was that of Hans Globke, who had been involved in developing discriminatory laws against the Jews in the Third Reich. In the early years of the newly founded German state he became the closest adviser of Konrad Adenauer and head of the chancellery office, which cemented his central position in the new democratic system.

The Nuremberg processes against the Nazi leadership, conducted between November 1945 and October 1946, were widely regarded as 'Siegerjustiz' (victor's justice). At this stage it was still too early to make the German population accept its guilt and it took several years until this changed within German mainstream society. A number of key events were of particular importance in this process. The first episode were the so-called Frankfurt Auschwitz trials. In a serial of trials running between December 1963 and August 1965, 22 lower- to mid-level officials were charged under German criminal law for their participation in the extermination of Jews in Auschwitz. This was not the first trial to address these atrocities. In 1947, the senior leadership of the camp, including the former commandant Rudolf Höss, had been trialled by Polish authorities. The Frankfurt Auschwitz trials were different, because this time the accused had to face a German court adhering to German law. The term 'victor's justice' could therefore not be applied. The Hessian state attorney general Fritz Bauer, who led the prosecution, concluded that the trials had been a failure with regards to changing the perception of Nazi atrocities in Germany, mainly because of the way the media had handled the process.[17] And yet, it was the beginning of a journey which has seen its current end point in February 2021 in the persecution of a 100-year-old former guard in the Sachsenhausen concentration camp.

Over the years, societal changes opened eyes more and more, especially among the young generations. In the late 1960s, the so-called student revolution swept across Europe and affected Germany as well. One of the driving factors of this movement was the rejection of the Vietnam War, and this anti-war stance found many supporters in Germany, often linking Vietnam to the German atrocities of World War II. The anti-war movement, partly funded and supported by the GDR to undermine the stability of the west-German state, became an important political movement. The struggle between the war-time generation and the young intensified in this period and perhaps saw its clearest expression in 1968: the young activist Beate Klarsfeld publicly slapped the then-chancellor Kurt Georg Kiesinger in the face to protest against his involvement in the Third Reich – Kiesinger had been a member of the NSDAP since 1933 and had worked in the foreign office's broadcasting department. In the following years, this struggle continued and intensified even more, expressing itself both peacefully and violently. In the 1970s, the left-extremist 'Red Army Fraction' spread terror over Germany, culminating in the so-called 'German autumn' of 1977.[18] That year, the Red Army Faction killed Siegfried Buback, Germany's attorney-general, Jürgen Ponto, the head of the Dresdner Bank and Hanns Martin Schleyer, the president of the German employers association and former member of the SS. 1977 also saw the hijacking of the 'Landshut', a Lufthansa passenger plane, which ended with the storming of the aircraft in Mogadishu by the German special police force GSG 9. The peaceful protests were directed against military aggression and, in particular, the stationing of nuclear armed middle-range Pershing II missiles on German territory as part of the so-called NATO Double-Track decision in 1979. The peace movement (also heavily funded and supported by the GDR) organised a number of demonstrations, of which the 1983 one in Bonn was the biggest with over 500,000 people turning out to demonstrate against 'atomic death'.

If anybody still needed convincing about the atrocities committed by Germans during World War II, the so-called Wehrmacht exhibition opened their eyes.[19] It focussed on the crimes of the Wehrmacht between 1941 and 1944. The exhibition opened in March 1995, travelled to 33 German and Austrian cities and attracted 800,000 visitors. The exhibition was marred by factual inaccuracies and errors, which led to the withdrawal and re-designing of the presented material. A second, updated exhibition was presented to the public in 2001. The exhibition did not really show any new material that had been unknown to the experts, but it presented the public with drastic and clear messages: the war of annihilation had been waged by all organisations of the Nazi state, and no longer could the wider public follow the rather convenient path that the Wehrmacht had fought honourably all the time and that all atrocities had been committed by the 'real' Nazis and organisations such as the SS.

This realisation only increased the widely held belief that military power should not be regarded as a legitimate political tool. It is interesting to see that with the end of the Cold War and the reduction of the direct threats associated with it, this view has only grown in Germany. For the first time in its history, Germany is 'surrounded by friends' as the slogan goes, and the majority of the population rejects the idea that military force can or should be used to achieve political success on the international stage. The first Gulf War saw huge demonstrations in Germany; the main slogan was 'no blood for oil'. Germany did not participate in the Second Gulf War. At the Munich Security Conference held in 2003, Foreign Minister Joschka Fischer from the Green Party rejected the notion of going to war to topple Saddam Hussein. In a famous speech, he addressed the US delegation and stated, 'You have to make the case, and to make the case in a democracy you must be convinced yourself. Excuse me,

I am not convinced, this is my problem.'[20] The military engagement in Afghanistan has remained deeply unpopular in Germany, and the uneasiness only grew when it became apparent that the military would have to fight. The notion of the former defence minister Peter Struck, that 'Germany's security is also being defended at the Hindukush' never convinced the majority of the German population.[21]

And yet, one question remained. Should Germany be grateful to the Allies for having ended Nazism not only in Europe, but in Germany itself, or had the defeat of Germany with the horrendous loss of life and cultural goods, as well as the partition of the country, been too high a price to pay? This was an on-going debate in a society that was still directly scarred by the war. The views in this context clearly changed over time. In May 1985, to commemorate the 40th anniversary of the end of the war, President Richard von Weizsäcker gave a speech in parliament, which is often regarded as one of the most important speeches in post-war Germany. Weizsäcker had served as an officer in the very prestigious Infantry Regiment 9 during the war, and his brother had been killed on the second day of the conflict. He acknowledged the hardships that the end of the war had brought on Germany and its people, but he also said that the end of the war had been a liberation from Nazi oppression. The end of the war, he thus concluded, was ambivalent.[22] In recent years, the development has gathered pace and the dominant view is now that the German surrender in 1945 should be remembered predominantly as an act of liberation. The city of Berlin made 8 May 2020 a bank holiday to commemorate the liberation and the end of Nazism. A good example for the change of mood are the commemorations of the battle of Normandy. When Chancellor Helmut Kohl was invited to join the celebrations of the 40th anniversary in 1984, he said that 'There is no reason for a German chancellor to celebrate when others are marking their victory in a battle in which tens of thousands of Germans were killed.'[23] Ten years later the events remained a sore point. Chancellor Kohl instructed officials what to say about D-Day: 'We don't want to be invited. We say nothing else', and he underlined 'nothing' twice.[24] In 2004, the view had changed. Chancellor Gerhard Schröder accepted the invitation and he called his participation 'hugely symbolic. It means the Second World War is finally over.'[25] A poll conducted found that over 70 percent of Germans supported that view.[26] In this context it is also interesting to note that, over time, the language has changed in Germany when speaking about the dark days of 1933–1945. It is now usual to talk of 'Nazi Germany' and the 'National Socialist Wehrmacht', which immediately creates a gap between the Germany of the past and 'modern' Germany.

A poll conducted in 2019 showed clearly that the younger generations of Germans no longer feel morally responsible for the war and the actions of the National Socialist regime. The poll showed that 63 percent of the population rejected the idea that those born post-war should accept moral responsibility.[27] And yet, as expressed in the poll, the majority of the population also deemed it important that German society analysed and commemorated the events further. Interestingly, this view was particularly prevalent among those Germans with higher education. Amongst those with an academic degree, 80 percent answered the question in this way, while at the other end of the educational spectrum this view was shared by only 46 percent.[28] The poll also showed that it was, in particular, the younger generations which regarded it as important to keep the memory of the Nazi period alive. Perhaps the most powerful expression of this general view is the memorial to the murdered Jews in Europe, which was inaugurated in central Berlin, right next to the Brandenburg Gate, in 2005. Located in the heart of the German capital, it serves as a stark and constant reminder of the importance of history. These findings present us with some interesting facts: German society on the whole does no longer feel a personal responsibility for the war and the Nazi regime, but it accepts a responsibility to ensure that such things never happen again – neither in Germany itself, nor elsewhere in the world. This attitude can sometimes be perceived as a typical German know-it-all approach and is not always well received on the international stage. Taken to the extreme, the so-called 'Auschwitz-club' can be swung in political debate, and those who use it are fully aware that this ends every discussion in Germany. Perhaps the most striking example of this moral approach could be observed in the debates surrounding the deployment of German troops to Kosovo as part of a NATO mission in 1999. This was a heated debate, because it involved the deployment of German combat troops for the first time since 1945, and this into a part of Europe that had seen extensive atrocities under Axis occupation. The foreign minister, Joschka Fischer, made his view clear at an extraordinary party convention of the traditionally anti-military Green Party. He stated that 'Never again war, never again Auschwitz, never again genocide, never again fascism. All this belongs together.' He then went on to explain that if these morally driven policies were fundamental for inner-German discussion, they were also fundamental for foreign policy and the will and determination to stop genocide in Kosovo.[29] Fischer's argument won the debate: on 12 June 1999, as part of operation Joint Guardian, over 6,000 German soldiers, including combat troops, crossed the border into Kosovo.[30]

This general approach presents the German public with some issues – on the whole, the population supports the idea that politics should be based on moral principles that reflect the lessons of World War II, but it shies away from the question of how to ensure that these principles can be implemented globally. The German Armed Forces Centre for Military History and Social Sciences conducts an annual survey on the population's view in the areas of security and defence. The results of the 2019 survey convey the somewhat naïve view of the population.[31] According to the survey, the majority of people support an active foreign and security policy. Having said this, this engagement should be restricted to peaceful and diplomatic means. The ambivalence between policy goals and the means to achieve these is clearly visible in the study. Military operations are only supported by the majority as long as they are restricted to training and stabilisations operations. According to the study, the population does not reject the military as a tool of foreign policy, but is not in favour of the use of force.[32] It remains unclear whether the authors of the study saw the irony in this statement, but it is a clear description of the underdeveloped state of debate on foreign and security issues in Germany.

What does this now mean for the institution that has to cope with these somewhat dichotomous views and understandings, the military? How has the military been shaped by the experience of World War II and how does (and can) it act within the realities of German politics and society? The Bundeswehr was founded in 1955, only ten years after the end of World War II.[33] The step to re-arm was met with severe criticism from the population, which overwhelmingly rejected this move. Too fresh and sore were the wounds that the war – often quite literally – had caused. And yet, against this resistance, the government under Chancellor Adenauer pushed ahead. The politicians saw the Bundeswehr as an important contribution to cementing Germany's position within the western world, and Germany's re-emergence as an equal partner on the world stage. The first 101 volunteers took their oath on 12 November 1955. This was not a random date: it was the 200th birthday of Gerhard von Scharnhorst, one of the great Prussian army reformers of the early 19th century. The idea was that this would show a new spirit of the new German Army: supposed to be gone was the mindless obedience, which allegedly had characterised the German armed forces up to that point. The new Bundeswehr should consist of 'citizens in uniform', who would be full and equal member of both the military and civilian worlds.[34] For instance, for the first time in history, German soldiers were now given the active right to vote. In previous times, this right had been denied to them, because, as the argument used to run, the military serves the state, not parties. A new type of 'social contract' was drawn up in the military as well. The so-called 'innere Führung' (which, literally, means inner leadership) stressed the need to educate a soldier as well as train him. Only a well-educated soldier, who accepted the new structures and realities of democracy, would, so the argument ran, be a successful defender of these values that characterised the new German state. This concept, mainly developed by Wolf Graf von Baudissin, has formed the basis of the Bundeswehr's leadership ethos ever since. It was designed in clear rejection of the perceived realities of the Third Reich and was to ensure that the new Bundeswehr would defend both its fatherland and the democratic institutions. This was also reflected in the new oath that had to be taken: 'I swear (or I vow for conscripts) to loyally serve the Federal Republic of Germany and to defend bravely the right and freedom of the German people.'[35] This was a clear breach with the history of World War II, when the members of the Wehrmacht had had to swear personal allegiance to Adolf Hitler. The new principles of the 'innere Führung' were not always met with enthusiasm. In particular the war generation rejected these ideas and principles, because they feared that they would result in a 'soft' military which would not be able to prevail in modern war. It has also been argued that, for the average soldier, these concepts can also appear too academic and abstract and thus irrelevant for every-day life in the forces.[36]

In line with the rest of the German population, the military was faced with totally new parameters. As the German military historian Sönke Neitzel has argued:

> The Second World War changed everything. The incomprehensible scale of German crimes, millions of dead on the battlefields, a continent in ruins and the stigma of defeat changed the self-perception of the Germans. Terms such as nation, patriotism and fatherland have been tarnished, the relationship to war contaminated. For centuries, war had been a legitimate tool of politics; soldiers existed in order to march into battle for interests of the state. However, after two lost world wars, the Germans had enough. Since then, the years 1939/45 are the reference points for the relationship with war and the military.[37]

And yet, in the early years of the Bundeswehr's existence, the war also offered some positive reference points. The Wehrmacht had fought against the Soviet Union and the experiences at the tactical and operational levels were sought after by the new NATO partners. The perceived military superiority also offered the former (and new) soldiers the space for personal and institutional pride. By concentrating on the military achievements, both the military and society could also shy away from the painful discussion of the Wehrmacht's involvement in atrocities and the extermination of the Jews and other groups. This also meant that the defeats of the second half of the war were not considered in the same way as the astounding victories in the years 1939–41. As Sönke Neitzel has shown, this process was actively supported by the officers of the Bundeswehr that had served as officers in the Wehrmacht.[38] This view was also enhanced by the memoir literature of former officers which hit the bookshelves in the 1950s. The tenor was always the same: the tactically and operationally superior Wehrmacht had been led to defeat by strategically incompetent leaders, in particular Hitler himself.[39]

Naturally, the Wehrmacht's experiences had been those of a conventional war. The realities of the nuclear war age meant that the German military lessons were only relevant as long as the nuclear threshold would not be crossed in a major military conflict. Realistically, this meant that deterrence rather than actual fighting was the main task of the Bundeswehr. Slogans like 'being able to fight in order not to fight' and 'if we fire our weapons we have failed in our task' became increasingly the norm. This also suited the political leadership. The Bundeswehr had, in many respects, been a political project first and foremost; both to integrate the population with the new state, and also to give this state a certain gravitas in the international arena. This set-up continued to work until the end of the Cold War, when the new geopolitical realities demanded a shift in German defence and security. Suddenly, deterrence was no longer needed and military operations, 'out-of-area' (i.e. outside of NATO territory) became the norm. Adjusting to this was a long and painful process for the Bundeswehr.[40] It demanded new military structures, new equipment and, arguably most importantly, a different mind-set. Perhaps the most drastic embodiment of these new times was the factual ending of conscription in 2011. The importance of this step cannot be overestimated for a military that always saw conscription as the natural form of recruiting.[41] In line with the Prussian reformer Scharnhorst, Germany had adopted the idea that 'the citizen is the born defender of his country'. In professional terms, the end of conscriptions was arguably a good thing: the period of conscription had been gradually reduced after the end of the Cold War and, in 2011, stood at a mere 6 months. The majority of young men at the time avoided military service and instead opted for the 'civil service', often in hospitals or care homes. This provided the social service system with a lot of cheap labour, but did nothing to improve the situation of the military. In contrast, the conscripts tied up resources, which could thus not be used in out-of-area operations. Conscripts could not be sent on these operations and, as a consequence, they were seen as a hindrance rather than a benefit within the new geo-strategic situation Germany found itself in after the Cold War. However, in accordance with the political parameters, conscription had ensured that the Bundeswehr kept close ties to the rest of society, and it was also seen as a restraining element in security. If, so the argument ran, the electorate sends its children to the armed forces this would make politicians think twice about using these in a military conflict. In line with German history, this restraint has been valued by the population. The re-election of Chancellor Schröder in 2002 was to a large degree based on his and his government's opposition to a war in Iraq, which dominated campaigning in the run-up to the elections.

And yet, the changed geo-political order and the realities of out-of-area operations meant that war, fighting, killing and dying had become a reality again. Accepting this was very difficult not only for society, but also for the Bundeswehr itself. The watershed was the engagement in Afghanistan, which for the first time saw German soldiers being killed in combat since 1945, but which also showed that the soldiers were able and willing to fight. The uneasiness about this topic can be seen in the memorials that the military erected to commemorate those who were killed in battle or died in accidents during out-of-area operations. One of these is placed within the grounds of the Einsatzführungskommando close to the city of Potsdam. This headquarters is responsible for co-ordinating and commanding the German contingents on operations. The other memorial is placed on the grounds of the Ministry of Defence in Berlin.[42] Initial plans to place a memorial in front of the Reichstag, the seat of German parliament, were not realised. A chance was missed, considering that the Bundeswehr is seen as a 'military of parliament' and parliament has to mandate all military operations. It is also, however, a good expression of the continuing uneasiness that Germans feel with regards to all things military. Sönke Neitzel has provocatively argued that Germany should be more honest. Either use the military, or, alternatively, abolish it (or, at least, abolish the combat arms) if the political will is lacking to use the military in its genuine realm, i.e. war.[43]

The general issues that the German military is facing with regards to its history is also visible in the way traditions are defined and what is deemed worthy to be seen as an official tradition. In the Bundeswehr, this is established in an official decree. During the history of the Bundeswehr, several versions of this decree have existed, which themselves show the interpretation of history within the contexts of their time. In 2018, a new version of the decree was passed.[44] This decree now places the history of the Bundeswehr in the centre of the armed forces tradition. The decree mentions the following areas as being particularly important for the tradition of the Bundeswehr[45]: the protection of the Federal Republic of Germany and its citizens; loyal service in freedom, which binds military action to one's conscience and sets boundaries to obedience; the concept of 'innere Führung' with its ideal of the citizen in uniform; the joint contribution to readiness of the Bundeswehr by the military and civilian work force; the contribution of the Bundeswehr to international crisis management and its ability to prevail on operations and in combat; preserving peace and freedom during the Cold War and its contribution to German re-unification; the heritage of universal conscription; the involvement in international structures and formations of NATO and the European Union; its contribution to reconciliation with former enemies; the successful humanitarian support both in Germany and internationally; and the success of integration within the context of German re-unification. It is astonishing to see that the genuine realm of the armed forces, the conduct of military operations and fighting, appears only half-way down the list and is more or less hidden amongst the other factors. But this re-enforces the idea that the Bundeswehr is, first and foremost, a political project and the fighting force only comes second. Organisations like the Wehrmacht or the Nationale Volksarmee of the GDR are excluded from the tradition of the Bundeswehr. Individual members of these organisation can be added to the canon of tradition, but the decree makes clear that military actions and achievements per se are not enough for this. Instead, the decision has to rest on an evaluation of 'individual guilt' and is dependent on an action which is exemplary and relevant for today, e.g. the participation in the military resistance against Nazism or an outstanding contribution to the build-up of the Bundeswehr after World War II. In all this, the context is important. The political leadership deemed a new decree necessary, because of some alleged neo-Nazi groups forming within the Bundeswehr. In the course of this process, the then-defence minister, Ursula von der Leyen, attested publicly in 2017 that 'the Bundeswehr has an attitude problem and there are clearly leadership weaknesses at several levels.'[46] As a consequence of the suspected right-wing groups within the Bundeswehr, the defence ministry ordered an iconoclasm and ensured that memorabilia of the Wehrmacht had to be removed from all barracks. This even resulted in a picture of Helmut Schmidt being removed from the Bundeswehr university in Hamburg that bears his name. Schmidt, chancellor of Germany between 1974 and 1982, had in his tenure as defence minster founded the Bundeswehr universities. The university removed a picture of Schmidt showing him in his officer's uniform during World War II.

All these developments have scarred the Bundeswehr. It led to a break-down of trust between the military personnel and the ministry of defence, including the then Generalinspekteur, the highest-ranking German officer, who did not speak out publicly to defend his subordinates.[47] As a consequence, most military personnel also now shy away from any dealing with matters of history or tradition, because this is perceived as a mine field in which much can be lost, but not much is to gain.[48] And yet, the Wehrmacht and World War II are, unofficially, still present in the Bundeswehr and, in particular, within the combat arms. The involvement of the Wehrmacht in the crimes of the Nazi regime is seen and understood clearly everywhere, but, for the men and women in uniform, this is often not enough to totally abandon the pure military links to this organisation. It seems that the military personnel are more able to distinguish between military achievement and other factors than the ministry of defence gives them credit for.[49]

Germany has lived under the shadow of the history of World War II for a long time. In some areas, the links to earlier times are weakening as time progresses and the direct memory of this dark period fades and disappears with those who lived through it. Names like Königsberg or Breslau do not mean a lot to most Germans today and, amongst the young generation, many probably do not even know that these were German cities up to 1945. Recently, the author gave a lecture on tradition in the Bundeswehr to a German Army audience. As part of this presentation, a film clip from the 1950s was shown in which the actor spoke with a very distinct East Prussian accent. Not one person in the audience could place this accent directly. To the younger Germans, the battle of Stalingrad often means not much more than the battles of antiquity, and the battle of Normandy is seen through the eyes of Private Ryan and not the Germans who fought and died there in 1944. But this is just one side of the coin. Germany has faced up to its history like probably no other country in the world and too deep runs the understanding of the horrors of the Nazi period and World War II, which Germany unleashed. The responsibility that Germans feel on their shoulders will accompany them for many more years, albeit indirectly. The young generations do not feel responsible for the war anymore, and nor should they. But they understand that 'this must never happen again', and this is, and will remain, the mantra of modern Germany. Everybody who demands a more active German engagement in security and defence needs to understand this; otherwise, Germany and the Germans will disappoint them.

Notes

1 For a general discussion of this see Matthias Strohn's introduction in this book.
2 Dietrich Eichholtz and Kurt Gossweiler (eds), *Faschismusforschung. Positionen, Probleme, Polemik* (Berlin (East): Akademie, 1980), 14. For a concise overview of these issues, see Martin Sabrow, 'Beherrschte Erinnerung und gebundene Wissenschaft. Überlegungen zur DDR-Geschichtsschreibung über die Zeit von 1933 bis 1945', in Christoph Conelißen et al. (eds), *Erinnerungskulturen. Deutschland, Italien und Japan seit 1945* (Frankfurt a. M.: Fischer, 2004), 153–167; and Kurt Pätzold, 'Research on Fascism and Antifascism in the GDR: A Retrospective', in Axel Fair-Schuly and Mario Kessler (eds), *East German Historians Since Reunification. A Discipline Transformed* (Albany: Suny, 2017), 107–124. For the relationship of history and state identity in the GDR, see Marcus Colla, 'The Politics and State Identity in the German Democratic Republic', in Royal Historical Society (ed), *Transactions of the Royal Historical Society*, sixth series, vol. XXIX (Cambridge: Cambridge University Press, 2019), 223–251.
3 Bernd Wagner, 'Vertuschte Gefahr: Die Stasi & Neonazis', *Bundeszentrale für politische Bildung*, 2 January 2018, https://www.bpb.de/geschichte/deutsche-geschichte/stasi/218421/neonazis (accessed 8 February 2021).
4 See, on these themes, Julian Junk and Christopher Daase, 'Germany', in Heiko Biehl et al. (eds), *Strategic Cultures in Europe. Security and Defence Policies Across the Continent* (Wiesbaden: Springer, 2013), 139–152.
5 'Der Bürger ist entsetzlich dumm', *Der Spiegel*, Vol. 15 (2017): 10–17.
6 On the Stalin note, see Rolf Steiniger, *The German Question: the Stalin Note of 1952 and the Problem of Reunification* (New York, Columbia University Press, 1990).
7 These and similar quotes by Adenauer can be found widely in the literature; see, for instance, Manfred Görtemaker, *Geschichte der Bundesrepublik Deutschland. Von der Gründung bis zur Gegenwart* (Munich: Beck, 1999), 90.
8 'Volksbund. Kampagne in über 1200 Städten: Darum Europa! Kriegsgräber ermahnen zum Frieden', 3 July 2017, https://www.netzwerk-ebd.de/nachrichten/vdk-kampagne-in-ueber-1200-staedten-darum-europa-kriegsgraeber-ermahnen-zum-frieden/ (accessed 8 December 2020).
9 Richard Wike et al., 'The European Union', Pew Research Center, 14 October 2019, https://www.pewresearch.org/global/2019/10/14/the-european-union/ (accessed 2021).
10 'Federal President Frank-Walter Steinmeier on the 75th anniversary of the liberation from National Socialism and the end of the Second World War in Europe at the Central Memorial of the Federal Republic of Germany to the Victims of War and Tyranny (Neue Wache) in Berlin', 8 May 2020, https://www.bundespraesident.de/SharedDocs/Downloads/DE/Reden/2020/05/200508-75-Jahre-Ende-WKII-Englisch.pdf?__blob=publicationFile (accessed 10 November 2020).
11 'Federal President Frank-Walter Steinmeier interview with the Rheinische Post', 6 February 2021, https://www.bundespraesident.de/SharedDocs/Reden/DE/Frank-Walter-Steinmeier/Interviews/2021/210206-Interview-Rheinische-Post.html (accessed 9 February 2021).
12 'Sicherheitsreport 2019: Die Deutschen sehen die USA als größte Bedrohung für den Frieden', Centrum für Strategie und Höhere Führung,13 February 2019, https://www.sicherheitsreport.net/wp-content/uploads/PM_Sicherheitsreport_2019.pdf (accessed 8 January 2021).
13 In a poll conducted in 2020, 69 percent of Germans stated that Brexit was 'bad', while only 9 percent regarded it as a 'good' development.
14 On the question of German refugees and the impact of this on German national memory, see Eva Hahn and Hans Henning Hahn, 'Flucht und Vertreibung', in, Etienne François and Hagen Schulze, *Deutsche Erinnerungsorte*, 3 vols., I (Munich: Beck, 2003), 335–351.
15 John Kampfner, *Why the Germans Do it Better. Notes from a Grown-Up Country* (London: Atlantic Books, 2020), 25–26.

16   This view has changed now, not least because of a study that had been commissioned in 2005 by the then foreign minister Joschka Fischer. The study was published as Eckart Conze et al., *Das Amt und die Vergangenheit. Deutsche Diplomaten im Dritten Reich und in der Bundesrepublik* (Munich: Blessing, 2010).

17   Robert Fulford, 'How the Auschwitz Trial failed', *The National Post,* 4 June 2005, http://www.robertfulford.com/2005-06-04-auschwitz.html (accessed 8 January 2021).

18   On this complex matter, see Stefan Aust, *The Baader-Meinhof Complex. The Inside Story of a Phenomenon* (London: The Bodley Head, 1987).

19   For a short overview of the exhibition and the surrounding debates, see Bogdan Musial, 'Der Bildersturm', https://www.bpb.de/geschichte/zeitgeschichte/deutschlandarchiv/53181/die-erste-wehrmachtsausstellung (accessed 10 January 2021).

20   This speech is available at https://www.youtube.com/watch?v=_k_QbpFl7RM (accessed 4 January 2021).

21   Peter Struck's official statement, given on 11 March 2004, can be found at https://www.bundesregierung.de/breg-de/service/bulletin/regierungserklaerung-des-bundesministers-fuer-verteidigung-dr-peter-struck--792688 (accessed 10 February 2021).

22   The speech is available at https://www.youtube.com/watch?v=C3ZAzpk4IbE (accessed 10 February 2021).

23   Ian Traynor, "For us Germans, the war is finally over', *The Guardian,* 4 June 2005, https://www.theguardian.com/world/2004/jun/04/secondworldwar.germany (accessed 6 December 2020).

24   Ibid.

25   Ibid.

26   Ibid.

27   Anne-Kathrin Sonnenberg, 'Die Kriegsschuld der Deutschen und das symbolische Schuldbekenntnis des Bundespräsidenten in Polen', YouGov, 7 November 2019, https://yougov.de/news/2019/11/07/die-kriegsschuld-der-deutschen-und-das-symbolische/ (accessed 15 December 2020).

28   Ibid.

29   The speech can be found at https://www.youtube.com/watch?v=7jsKCOTM4Ms (accessed 14 November 2020).

30   DBwV, 'Vor 20 Jahren: Der Kfor-Einsatz der Bundeswehr beginnt', 6 November 2019, https://www.dbwv.de/aktuelle-themen/blickpunkt/beitrag/vor-20-jahren-der-kfor-einsatz-der-bundeswehr-beginnt/ (accessed 14 December 2020).

31   Markus Steinbrecher et al., 'Sicherheits- und verteidigungspolitisches Meinungsbild in der Bundesrepublik Deutschland. Ergebnisse und Analysen der Bevölkerungsbefragung 2019'. The survey can be found at https://augengeradeaus.net/wp-content/uploads/2019/12/20191217-Bericht-Bevölkerungsumfrage-ZMSBw-2019.pdf (accessed 10 February 2021).

32   Ibid., 5.

33   For a concise overview of the founding of the Bundeswehr, see Agilolf Kesselring and Thorsten Loch, 'Aufstellung der Bundeswehr', https://www.kas.de/en/web/geschichte-der-cdu/calendar-detail/-/content/gruendung-der-bundeswehr (accessed 20 December 2020).

34   For the Bundeswehr's official definition of the concept see 'Das Konzept der Inneren Führung', https://www.bmvg.de/de/themen/verteidigung/innere-fuehrung/das-konzept#:~:text=Die%20Grundsätze%20der%20Inneren%20Führung,Inneren%20Führung%20gibt%20es%20nicht (accessed 10 February 2021).

35   For the development of the oath within the German armed forces, see Militärgeschichtliches Forschungsamt (ed), *Symbole und Zeremoniell in den deutschen Streitkräften vom 18. bis zum 20. Jahrhundert* (Herford: Mittler & Sohn, 1991), 86–106.

36 Sönke Neitzel, *Deutsche Krieger. Vom Kaiserreich zur Berliner Republik- eine Militärgeschichte* (Berlin: Propyläen, 2020), 590.

37 Ibid., 583. Translation of the quote by the author.

38 Sönke Neitzel, 'Von Mythen und Wahrheiten', *Die Bundeswehr. Das Magazin des Deutschen Bundeswehr Verbandes*, November 2020, 10–11.

39 Probably the most famous book in this category is by the former field marshal Erich von Manstein, *Verlorene Siege* (Bonn: Athenaum, 1955).

40 For an overview of this process, see Militärgeschichtliches Forschungsamt (ed), *Grundkurs deutsche Militärgeschichte*, 3 vols, iii, *Die Zeit nach 1945. Armeen im Wandel* (Munich: Oldenbourg, 2008), 326–395.

41 On conscription, see Roland Foerster, *Die Wehrpflicht. Entstehung, Erscheinungsformen und politisch-militärische Wirkung* (Munich: Oldenbourg, 1994).

42 'Das Ehrenmal der Bundeswehr – ein Überblick', https://www.bundeswehr.de/de/ueber-die-bundeswehr/gedenken-tote-bundeswehr/ehrenmal-bundeswehr (accessed 14 February 2021).

43 Neitzel, *Deutsche Krieger*, 597–599.

44 For a discussion of the new decree and the events that led to its publication, see Donald Abenheim und Uwe Hartmann (eds), *Tradition in der Bundeswehr. Zum Erbe des deutschen Soldaten und zur Umsetzung des neuen Traditionserlasses* (Berlin: Miles, 2018).

45 'Die Traditionen der Bundeswehr. Richtlinien zum Traditionsverständnis und zur Traditionspflege', 5, https://www.bmvg.de/resource/blob/23234/6a93123be919584d48e16c-45a5d52c10/20180328-die-tradition-der-bundeswehr-data.pdf (accessed 12 February 2021).

46 See, for instance, 'Die Bundeswehr hat ein Haltungsproblem', *Die Zeit*, 30 April 2017, https://www.zeit.de/gesellschaft/zeitgeschehen/2017-04/ursula-von-der-leyen-bundeswehr-kritik-haltungsproblem-soldat-terrorverdacht (accessed 9 February 2021).

47 As Sönke Neitzel has stated, a slogan and play of words using the Generalinspekteur's name could be heard within the military: 'Weak, Wieker'; Neitzel, *Deutsche Krieger*, 573.

48 See on this, Neitzel, *Deutsche Krieger*, 573–582.

49 Ibid., 571–577.

CHAPTER 4

Winning in the End: China's War Experience and the Role It Has Played in Winning Today

Kerry Brown

The foundation of the People's Republic of China (PRC) was due to World War II. The impact of that war has framed the mindset of Chinese political and military leaders ever since. While it cast a long shadow across much of the rest of the world, the depth of devastation, and the social and material ruin that the event left in China, means that today it is a live issue in ways which are not so true of Europe or North America. In the ways in which Chinese strategic thinking is shaped by defensive attitudes, and by a particular historical narrative of which the war was the culmination, the epic fight by China against the Japanese had an existential importance. To this day, the Communist Party of China (CPC) locates part of its legitimacy on the basis of having been part of the United Front forces which overcame the Japanese, and served as allies of the US and UK in the global fight against fascism. It is referred to continuously in government propaganda, in education and in the speeches of leaders to the current day. The heroic struggle against the forces of Japanese imperialism from 1937 is part of a legitimising 'myth' – the reality of the harsh battle ranged against the ways in which it has been reimagined and revivified ever since.

It is important to make clear that in the case of the PRC, the political significance of the war takes precedence over is military dimensions. This will be explained in the first section. The ways in which the war figured as part of a particular narrative sponsored by the Communist Party in its years fighting for power, and then since it has been in power, have shaped the meaning of the war and its historic interpretation in ways which continue to cause contention and argument among historians inside and outside the country to this day. The manner in which the war reinforced a victim mentality, and created a particular view of China's needs in the region and more widely is also an important dimension of this issue – specifically in how it has created a complex relationship with key neighbours from Japan, to South Korea,

Russia and even India. Finally the reimagining of the meaning of World War II and the ways in which it figures so much in contemporary nationalist discourse in the PRC will be attended to.

The battle of narratives

For the PRC, World War II continues to exist in a number of discrete areas. The first is that as part of a particular narrative of historic development underpinned by a moral teleology which the communists have embraced, and still subscribe to to this day. This in particular has political potency. It shows the ways in which the space of politics was prioritised in China, and the ways in which the Communist Party (CCP) managed to effectively monopolise this almost from the moment they came to power in 1949. For them, history has a primarily political meaning. From this everything flows. It is about the distributions and working out of power structures. This was guided by the master-ideology of Marxism-Leninism.

Within this context, much of which has been reinforced by political mobilisation and education campaigns, particularly from the 1990s, but almost all of which was implicit before this time, World War II was the final of a series of calamities that afflicted the country during its long, painful and at times tragic march to modernity. From the time of the Opium Wars in 1839, to the collapse of the Qing dynasty after over 260 years in power in 1911, and then the start of the Sino-Japanese war in 1937, China had been betrayed by political elites, vested interest and the continuing embrace of a system which was feudal, hierarchical and deeply conservative. The ways in which the outside world in the form of colonial powers like Great Britain or France exploited China's vulnerability was as much down to the culpability of these treacherous domestic forces as it was due to the greed and opportunism of outsiders. Within this historical framework, the Sino-Japanese war ended up having an almost teleological inevitability about it. It was the final act in the downfall of imperial, feudal, old China, at least as far as the communist historiography showed – something akin to a punishment for a tradition of governance that had led to the country being weak, defenceless and almost pre-modern. The simple fact was that Japan, a country that had embraced modernity since the Meiji reforms of the 1860s, was throwing the might of its industrialised, developed capacity against a country that was still overwhelmingly rural, impoverished and undeveloped. This was seen as symptomatic of China's plight – and the reason why the communists could present themselves, and subsequently did present themselves, as saviours.

That Mao Zedong, the supreme leader of the new Republic from 1949, exercised a measure of ambiguity about the war in the years afterwards is striking. The most visceral campaigns of attack and condemnation of Japan and its role in the wartime calamity for China have ironically happened in recent years – particularly since the 2000s and the escalation of tensions between the two countries over the East China

Seas territories (see below). Before this, Mao's attitude towards such a formidable enemy, once peace had been restored, was almost phlegmatic. He reportedly claimed to one visiting Japanese dignitary in the early 1970s that without Japan's onslaught, the PRC would never have been established. It was only a crisis like this that would have necessitated the radical series of events that led through the Civil War (1946–1949) to the PRC's final vindication. While some dispute whether these remarks were ever made, they do have an underlying logic. The nationalist government under Chiang Kai-shek would have probably carried on without the impact of the war on the country's economy and society. The communists would have probably continued being a marginal force, largely confined to parts of the countryside as they had been through the 1920s and into the 1930s. World War II was a catastrophe that made their radical prognosis of society's ills, and a potential solution, viable.

This narrative sponsored by the communists, one that has become the dominant once after they came to power, relegates military issues beneath political ones. The story that the CPC told was a political one. The army they created in the late 1920s was the army of the party – something that remains true to this day. It fought, but it did not think – simply because its leaders up to recent times have been political military ones, and it was under their political persona that they did their thinking, not their military one. Mao was supreme commander of the armed forces of the CPC. But he was also party leader. It was as party leader that he wrote his key works on military doctrine.

These shaped the approach of the PRC from 1949 to military matters. Through the 1940s, Mao authored a number of key works on his particular brand of guerrilla warfare. This involved subterfuge, recognition of the CPC's weaknesses (its lack of arms, technical personnel and technology) but also its great strength (public support, a strong moral message backed up by powerful propaganda, and deep, densely networked penetration of the rural areas of China). The doctrine of 'people's war' arising from this was one that was embraced, and promoted throughout the Maoist era. Marshal Lin Biao, one of the great commanders of the Chinese People's Liberation Forces during the Civil War from 1946 to 1949, produced the classic statement of this in 1965, on the eve of the cultural revolution. In 'Long Live the Victory of the People's War', Lin stated:

> How was it possible for a weak country finally to defeat a strong country? How was it possible for a seemingly weak army to become the main force in the war?
> The basic reasons were that the War of Resistance Against Japan was a genuine people's war led by the Communist Party of China and Comrade Mao Tse-tung, a war in which the correct Marxist-Leninist political military lines were put into effect, and that the Eighth Route and the New Fourth Armies were genuine people's armies which applied the whole range of strategy and tactics of people's war as formulated by Comrade Mao Tse-tung.[1]

Lin's approach outlined a series of key measures. Firstly, to ensure that the military had firm political instruction from their masters in the Communist Party – and that they were properly indoctrinated. 'History shows us', he states, 'that within the united front the Communist Party must maintain its ideological, political and organizational independence, adhere to the principle of independence and initiative, and insist on its leading role.'[2] Reliance on the core constituency of peasants and rural dwellers was key, turning a potential source of weakness into a strength. This was done through inducting them into the attractions of the liberation ideology of Marxism-Leninism as espoused by the party and its military. This entailed building a new kind of army, one where the 'people' were the key fighters, mobilising the whole of society, so that divisions between soldiers and civilians were eroded. Self-reliance was also of prime importance. Lin makes a clear declaration on the absolute priority of the party, and of politics:

> The essence of Comrade Mao Tse-tung's theory of army building is that in building a people's army prominence must be given to politics, i.e., the army must first and foremost be built on a political basis. Politics is the commander, politics is the soul of everything. Political work is the lifeline of our army. True, a people's army must pay attention to the constant improvement of its weapons and equipment and its military technique, but in its fighting it does not rely purely on weapons and technique, it relies mainly on politics, on the proletarian revolutionary consciousness and courage of the commanders and fighters, on the support and backing of the masses.[3]

Nothing better encapsulates the priority of the political over the military, and how distinctive this has been in China under the communists. The legacy of World War II can be seen clearly in the way in which the communists, who remain in power to this day, saw it as a legitimising moment – something that sanctioned the prioritisation articulated by Lin. He himself however was felled after being put in the uncomfortable position of being Mao Zedong chosen successor during the Ninth Party Congress in 1969. He died in a plane crash while reportedly fleeing to the USSR in 1969.

Liberty's and historic fact

It is important to make clear that there is World War II as it has figured in the historiography of the CCP over the last seven decades since 1949, and then history as it may actually have happened. On the latter, as in the European war, huge effort by historians and others into looking at archives and establishing a narrative of events has occurred. In the 2000s, some of this involved Japanese and Chinese scholars, trying to create consensus on profoundly contentious issues like the Rape of Nanjing in 1937 and the level of fatalities there, and then parts of the war in various areas of China up to 1945.

Despite the claims by the CPC that they played such a commanding role in the victories over the Japanese in World War II, it is far more accurate to say that as part of the United Front forces led by the nationalist government they were merely actors in a much larger effort. This is not to deny their decisive role in some of the key theatres of conflict. But it would not be a mis-representation to say that it was Chiang Kai-shek's armies that did the bulk of the fighting, and that they did so as allies of the US when they entered the war after the attack on Pearl Harbour in 1941, and of the UK. It was these armies that undertook the key campaigns in South West, South East and Central China, places where the communists were largely inactive. The communists themselves had their key headquarters in Yan'an in Central North China, in an area which was not of central importance to the Japanese. After devastating initial attacks in the early stages of the war, the Japanese imperial army soon realised that annexation of the whole of China would be time consuming, and unnecessary for their core strategic aim – of creating as East Asia Co-prosperity zone. For that vision, much of the norther area of China outside Manchuria which they had run as a puppet state since the mid-1930s was of marginal importance to them. It had little infrastructure, was often sparsely populated, was largely undeveloped, and, even if the areas did have raw materials, these were not easily exploitable. Urban centres such as Hohhot in Inner Mongolia did come under Japanese control. But as Mao foresaw, pacifying and then controlling the immense rural areas proved an investment in time and resources that the Japanese had neither the time nor the inclination to make.

The exploitation of this vulnerability was one of the key aims of the communist field armies. They harried, troubled and harassed Japanese forces. But they did not, until the end of the war, undertake any major campaigns on their own. That was left to Chiang's forces. The mistake they made once the war had concluded in their favour was to then seek total victory over the communists, now that the utility of their brief marriage of convenience had ended. Exhausted by years of fighting, and with deep issues around corruption and economic incompetence, it is unsurprising that the nationalists ended up with two million of their supports fleeing to Taiwan where they continued the Republic of China to this day.

This complex history – one made complicated by the fact that two such normally incompatible forces as the nationalists and the communists, in the exceptional circumstances of the war, were forced to work together – means that there are many subtleties and anomalies in the narrative of the conflict. One is that because of the dominant role of the nationalists, and their alliance in particular with the US and the other allied powers, the communists, through the United Front were also part of this coalition. They therefore were partners in a situation in which it was not just the USSR that worked with them but also the US. As historian Rana Mitter points out in his study of this era, China was an ally of powers it subsequently ended up being ranged against in the post war era and the Cold War.[4] This fact was, and is, often forgotten when framing China's role in the modern world as a power that has always stood outside or against the democratic, US led liberal order.

We have to remember too that for all the arguments about what events happened, what their order was and what sort of significance they might have politically, the extent of devastation visited on China in terms of loss of life, homelessness and physical destruction was immense. An estimated 20 million lost their lives; 50 million were left without homes. China's rail and road infrastructure was largely annihilated. On top of this, the city of Shanghai became a physical battlefront during one of the most intensive moments of the war in 1937. Other parts of urban China were also brutally attacked. In their encirclement and annihilation campaigns, the Japanese prosecuted a war of such savagery that it has left memory stains in the landscape to this day. Its impact on the social fabric of China through destroyed and separated families was less visible, but has every bit as last an impact. It is these aspects of the Chinese experience of World War II which were so traumatic and enduring, and which continue to frame the Chinese vision of history and of their own historic mission and development to this day.

Relations with its neighbours and the world

World War II, and its outcomes in the revolution of 1949 also fundamentally changed the PRC's relations with its neighbours. Of these, the most important were Japan, South Korea, the USSR and India. The PRC drew from the experience of the war and rethought its alliances. It eschewed formal treaty-based alliances with all but the USSR, and, a little later, with the DPRK. These were the exception rather than the rule. On the whole, as a result of the searing impact of World War II, the PRC was an increasingly isolated and maverick player, one that believed in non-alignment and absolute primacy of defending its own sovereignty over all other issues.

The PRC was created in a world already experiencing deepening division between the USSR and its satellites and the US-led west. Winston Churchill in his speech at Fulton, Missouri in the US had referred to the 'iron curtain' falling across the world in 1946. Initially, China belonged very much behind that curtain. It was recognised by only a handful of states in October, when Mao Zedong formally announced the creation of the PRC. The US was not amongst them, maintaining its recognition of the Republic of China on Taiwan – something that was to be the case till 1979. Even with the USSR, China's relations were complex from the beginning, with Mao displaying deference to Stalin, but also a willingness to assert his own country's uniqueness. The Korean War from 1950 to 1953 effectively deepened the rift between the PRC and the US and its alliances, and underlined how much China was willing to be isolated and different to its neighbours. This situation prevailed for much of the next two decades.

This was exacerbated by the particular ideology the party state subscribed to. Maoism, or Mao Zedong Thought, was related to Marxism Leninism, but had plenty of its own idiosyncrasies. The Communist Party penetrated all levels of society. Its relationship with the people was described as akin to 'fish and water.' The military was the people's army. Mao Zedong thought promoted class struggle, the cleansing of society and the need to strive for Utopian outcomes. This ideology was exported sometimes to the outside world, particularly during the period of the cultural revolution from 1966, metastasising to places like Bhutan, Cambodia and Peru, sometimes with calamitous results. The war had created a distrustful, divided region, and one where China was deeply cautious and insecure. It was able to at least resolve of these issues through negotiating border agreements. These happened through the late 1950s and into the 1990s. The most significant was with the USSR/ Russia. The most contentious with India – something that remains unresolved to this day and about which there was a war in 1962. Most others were resolved. This at least created greater certainty, predictability and stability – for everyone. Even so, politically and diplomatically, China became increasingly isolated. In the cultural revolution in 1967, it had only one formal ambassador abroad – Huang Hua in Egypt. And while rapprochement with the US with Richard Nixon's visit in 1972 alleviated this, China remained in a class of its own – something that lingers to this day, when only five countries in the world have a communist party enjoying a monopoly on power, and China stands as the by way and afar the largest of these.

The security impact of World War II on China remains today in relationships with four key regional countries – Japan, South Korea, Russia and India. It is in intercourse with these that the events of over seven decades ago still remain live. For the first, Japan, they are the most insistent and the most intractable. This is hardly surprising. Japan was the aggressor in the events from 1937. This aggression did not arise from nowhere. It was situated on a history of competition and mutual influence that stretched back over two thousand years.[5] Despite so much that was shared, in terms of written characters, Confucianist social structures, the identities of the two also have more than enough to differentiate them and create the space for animosity, misunderstanding and disagreement. The understanding of the meaning of the war, and in particular issues around culpability and what role its remembrance should play in the present, remained very much alive. It also demonstrated the very different roles of recollection in the two cultures. As former Singaporean leader Lee Kuan-yew tartly stated once, 'the problem is that Japan remembers nothing, and China never forgets!'

Under Mao, as the county reconstructed, ironically those with direct experience of the bitterness of the war took a more pragmatic stance. In the 1950s and 1960s, China's animosity was largely directed at the 'paper tiger' of the US and their imperialism, and at the 'revisionists' in the USSR after Stalin's death in 1953. Japan figured hardly at all. It was the rise of exogenous factors that brought Japan back to centre stage in Chinese concerns – along with the issues over World War II. In the 1990s, patriotic education campaigns in the PRC born from the aftermath of the 4 June 1989 shock and the collapse of the USSR and the need felt by elite leaders like the then President Jiang Zemin to create a stronger sense of coherent national identity led to a stronger desire to push back against those who had 'humiliated' and undone China. A sense of the need to 'never forget' history meant that a lot of history which had slumbered came back to life. The resources were made available to memorialise the Nanjing massacre, and to commemorate events of the war in China. School children were taught more formally in schools about this history of shame and abuse.

Japan's response in many ways inflamed this. Nationalists in the country dissented from what they saw as the perpetual quest by China to extract apologies from them that never proved sufficient, and constantly place them in a position of moral inferiority. Figures like the then governor of Tokyo Shintaro Ishihara were vocal in their frustration at the ways in which China was constantly berating them. Earlier in his career he had authored *The Japan that Can Say No* (published in English in 1991). His career had been strewn with controversial statements, ranging from denials of the large number of deaths during the 1937 Rape of Nanjing, to defence of the pre-war Japanese colonisation of Korea. While hardly a mainstream politician, it was the impact of views like these in some of the official history text books issued by the Japanese Ministry of Education which seemed to downgrade Japanese actions in the war that caused most argument. The fact that the specific textbooks in question were eventually only used by a tiny proportion of schools did not detract from their high symbolic importance. From the appearance in 2001 of the texts written by the right-wing 'Japanese Society for History Textbook Reform' and their authorisation a year later by the Ministry, 'New History Textbook' has been accused of rewriting history, refusing to engage with the immense suffering Japanese military aggression caused in its region and presenting spurious revisionist history.

All of this occurs on top of a tangible source of conflict between the two powers – the Senkaku/Diaoyutai islands in the East China Sea. Increased naval capacity in the 2000s as a result of economic development and military reform in China meant that it had the capacity to reach more into the maritime areas around it and influence the region. This brought it in direct conflict with Japan. Skirmishes between proxy actors like the Naval Life Boat agencies brought Japanese and Chinese in direct conflict. From 2009 these incidents increased, drawing the US into closer involvement. The threat by Governor Ishihara to buy the privately owned islands in 2012 led to their purchase by the Japanese government, creating a diplomatic backlash in Beijing under the new, more assertive and muscular leadership of Xi Jinping. This prickly relationship lasted till the middle of the decade. Even to 2020, Xi had yet to visit one of its most important neighbours – a visit scheduled to Tokyo in April 2020 was postponed because of the impact of COVID-19.

World War II casts the deepest shadow therefore over this particular relationship, and one that is hardly likely to shift any time soon. Japanese Prime Minister Shinzo

Abe was associated with the right wing in his early career, and was a supporter of one of the most contentious parts of the relationship – prime ministerial visits to the Yasukuni Shrine in Tokyo, where Class A war criminals are interred. While he had taken a more pragmatic stance since 2016, meeting Xi a number of times, the relationship is never one to be complacent about. With his own desire to see Japan be given a stronger role in world affairs, and to revise the pacifist constitution so that it grants Japan more rights to self-defence, it is easy to see future scenarios where the two countries, with their rising nationalism, set them on a collision course.

South Korea, Russia and India

While lacking the deep weight of the Sino-Japanese relationship, and at least united by the fact that before and during World War II both countries experienced colonisation and therefore share a narrative of victimisation, South Korea offers a constant reminder to China of the strength of the US alliance system. Since liberation from Japanese colonisation after the war, resulting in division through Soviet insistence of North and South Korea, and the Korean War to 1953, South Korea has been an ally of the US, and indeed remains to 2021 host to over 35,000 US soldiers. Threats to downscale these or bring them back to the US, even under Trump, have so far not been acted on. Though not sharing a direct border with China, South Korea is the closest of the countries which do host US military facilities. For this reason, the relationship is frequently fraught with mutual antipathy.

The introduction of a Terminal High Altitude Area Defence system (THAAD) in South Korea from 2016 has proved the most recent cause of disagreement. For South Korea, the argument was that under perpetual threat from North Korea, which was developing its own aggressive ballistic capacity, it needed a system like THAAD to detect, and then shoot down, any weapons fired at it.[6] For China however, it seemed to have a more aggressive intention. In July 2017, on a visit to Russia, Xi stated that 'The U.S. deployment of an advanced anti-missile system in South Korea gravely harms the strategic security interests of China, Russia and other countries in the region.'[7] China's anger was no so much about the potential use of the system to push back against North Korea aggression, but more about what one analyst argued was 'the sophisticated radar capabilities included in the system. These radars could be used to track China's own missile systems, potentially giving the United States a major advantage in any future conflict with China.'[8] In particular, with rising fears of US effort to contain China through the 2000s and into Xi's era, along with the PRC's own growing aspirations for a stronger and more dominant regional role because of its economic size, THAAD was an untimely reminder of just how prominent the US still was in its own backyard. It made all too visible the ability of America to operate in its region, control space around it, and even attempt to reach into its own space. This is all despite the fact that THAAD system has been partly constructed in South Korea, but is currently offering only partial coverage.

While South Korea illustrates one aspect of the legacy of the war in the region – the power of the US alliance system and how it still shapes the security environment and its capacity, despite so much else changing, the relationship with the USSR/ Russia shows a different aspect. Stalin's Soviet Union were eventually part of the alliance that defeated the Axis powers. The USSR was the PRC's principle sponsor in the period immediately after its creation. They were significant contributors of technology and aid. Their economic and governance system served as a model for Mao's China. Until the late 1950s, and their major schism, they belonged to a major alliance, facing the US and its claimed hegemony. But with the process of destalinisation under Khrushchev from 1956, the relationship cooled. By the early 1960s it had become fully confrontation, and by 1969 had escalated to an almost war footing, with a short border conflict.

The communist movement in China had never been viewed that warmly in Moscow. In the years in which Mao struggled for supreme leadership of the small group of believers in the Chinese countryside, the role of the USSR had remained contentious and sometimes fractious. Occasionally it gave significant financial and technical aid. At other times, it urged on its maverick sister party in the world communist movement actions which Mao viewed as unviable or unhelpful in the specific context of China. In World War II, the CPC's alliance with the nationalists as part of the United Front was a move blessed by Stalin. After the resolution of the war, Stalin's support for the CPC in the Civil War veered from tepid to obstructive. Part of this was the larger calculation about spheres of influence, and of ceding some areas to the US, wanting to avoid being drawn into an immediate conflict with them. As strong supporters and allies of the nationalists, the US already had a vested interest in this issue. With the surprise victory of the communists (they were viewed as the underdogs for much of the early part of the struggle) the Soviet Union was obliged to offer more support. But this never alleviated the latent mistrust between the two.

With the collapse of the USSR in 1991, after a late, brief rapprochement in the 1980s when Gorbachev was in power, China's relations with Russia from 1991 were largely shaped by pragmatism. Ideology played no major role any longer. The sizeable border issues outstanding were resolved, with significant concessions to Russia, in the Yeltsin and early Putin era. By the time of Xi Jinping, the two nations were on almost cordial terms. Russia's tensions and outright antagonisms with Europe and the US meant that it viewed China as a much less problematic partner. Even so, the reversal of power and influence between the two, with the PRC now the far stronger and more important partner, means that tensions still exist under the surface. Chinese long-term intentions to the energy rich Serbian area are one issue. So too is the growth of Chinese influence in central Asia, a place historically of great importance to Russia, and tied to it as part of the USSR before and during the war. That the Belt and Road Initiative with its mixture of aid, investment and trade is giving China a stronger role here, countering that of Russia, is a further potential source of affront to Russia's once dominant, almost hegemonic position in this area. Over one issue in particular, Russia did leave a lasting imprint in modern China – the ways in which it figured as an influence on the Xinjiang region, briefly and partially an independent entity during the war years, and then, partly through the USSR's tacit acceptance, allowed to be resumed as a part of the Republic of China, and then, after 1949, an autonomous region under the PRC. Xinjiang's restive state continues to this day.

The final major case is possibly the most problematic in the long term. India was colonised by the British, as China partially was, and gained its liberation in 1947 partly as World War II settlement, where the US insisted Britain give up most of its imperial possessions and pretensions. This meant that it was part of the broad camp of nations which claimed non-aligned status, and grouped together to oppose the domination of the major, economically developed powers in Europe and the US. China borrowed many of the ideas around its foreign policy from Nehru's India – things that appeared in its Five Peaceful Principles of Co-Existence – non-interference in domestic affairs, or instance, and defence and respect of sovereignty. Within a decade, however, India and the PRC were at odds with each other, experiencing a brief border war in 1962 which resulted in a humiliation for India. Their relationship was complicated by the hosting of the exiled Tibetan government once the Dalai Lama had fled the PRC in 1959, and further issues of strategic competition. In the Xi era, their nationalism and aspirations grate with each other. Both claim strong positions in their shared region; both have enlarging economies, strong cultural pride, and the desire for status. It is likely that while the relations China has with the three other case studies outlined above will continue to present challenges, the one with India will be the most increasingly difficult. Will Asia Pacific, and indeed the world, be large enough to accommodate two countries that constitute almost half of humanity in their populations, and yet are so different politically, and culturally?

Nationalism in modern times

The legacy of World War II in modern China exists as a framework, and as one of the most important forces that has shaped the narratives of history over the last seven decades, and of how it sees its relations with its neighbours, and into the future. The historic mission of the country, where the party aided by the people's Liberation Army seeks to restore China to its central place in the region and the world and redeliver status to it, is now well in progress. Centennial goals announced under Xi in 2013 marking the hundredth anniversary of the party in 2021, and of the

PRC itself in 2049, were shaped by the war, and through these, shape the future. The sense of humiliation and national trauma culminating in World War II is the father behind the modern phenomenon of nationalism, with its highly emotional tone, and the desire to rectify these wounds. Emotionally, therefore the war still resonates with Chinese people, and it is in that framework that it continues to be referred to by contemporary Chinese leaders.

This could be seen most vividly in the seventieth anniversary celebrations to mark the end of the war in Asia held in Beijing in 2015. Vast amounts of new military equipment were displayed in a large demonstration viewed by Xi in Beijing. Foreign leaders were invited. Few Europeans or North Americas went. Russia's Putin was present. The message of the whole spectacle was simple: China would never again be in a position where others could push it round. It had risen from the ashes of the war, and was now transformed. Its army had undergone professionalism, and modernisation, so that it was incomparable to the entity that existed in the 1980s, let along the 1940s.

While domestically, this was a powerful moment for national pride and valida-tion, externally it was viewed much more ambiguously. It showed a China which remained resolutely communist, and which seemed increasingly able to influence and dominate the world around it through its economic clout, but also its military capacity. Fears of the latter ran against the language or pacifism and desiring peace deployed in China. But they also had to counter the fact that, despite all of its new material, China had not actually engaged in any real combat experience since the 1979 clash with Vietnam, and no real major international conflict since the Korean War in the early 1950s. What was really guiding China's intentions? The desire to shape the world to become like it, or to seek some kind of historic resolution? Did the memories of the war still hold such a powerful grip over the imaginations and emotions of a country where the vast majority of the people had no memory at all of events so long ago?

In terms of military doctrine, and strategy, Chinese leaders and their generals and strategists knew well that the environment around them, the nature of war and of global politics, had changed radically since the 1940s. They knew this particularly because their own country had played such a major role in this transformation. In the war, China was a marginal, and largely ignored place, one that had been almost left to the last minute in terms of receiving help and assistance from the US and others in its struggle against the Japanese. But by 2020, for good or bad, it was one of the most important, if not the most important, territory on earth. Everywhere had changed since 1945. But China had changed more than perhaps anywhere else. It was purely in memory and the meanings inferred from memory that the war still exerted and influence. And there, despite the dramatic changes, as this chapter shows, that influence remained considerable. This is unlikely to change any time soon.

Notes

1   Lin Biao, *Long Live the Victory of the People's War* (Beijing: Foreign Language Press, 1965), 42.

2   Ibid.

3   Ibid.

4   For the demise of the Nationalists during and after World War II, see Lloyd E. Eastman, *Seeds of Destruction: Nationalist China in War and Revolution, 1937–1949* (Stanford: Stanford University Press, 1984). For the alliance between China and the US, and other allied powers, see Rana Mitter, *China's War with China, 1937–1945: The Struggle For Survival* (London: Allen Lane, 2013).

5   For an overview of this history, see June Teufel, *Middle Kingdom and the Land of the Rising Sun: Sino-Japanese Relations Past and Present* (Oxford: Oxford University Press, 2016) and Ezra Vogel, *China and Japan* (Cambridge, Mass: Belknap Harvard, 2019).

6   For background on the THAAD, see Institute for Security and Development Policy, 'THAAD on the Korean Peninsula', Stockholm, 2017, https://isdp.eu/publication/korea-thaad/.

7   Reuters, 'China, Russia share opposition to U.S. THAAD in South Korea: Xi', 3 July 2017, https://www.reuters.com/article/us-china-thaad-russia/china-russia-share-opposition-to-u-s-thaad-in-south-korea-xi-idUSKBN19O0N8.

8   Adam Taylor, 'Why China is so mad about THAAD, a missile defense system aimed at deterring North Korea', *Washington Post*, 7 March 2017, https://www.washingtonpost.com/news/worldviews/wp/2017/03/07/why-china-is-so-mad-about-thaad-a-missile-defense-system-aimed-at-deterring-north-korea/.

CHAPTER 5

The Legacy of Soviet Post-war Occupation: The Baltic States' Struggle to Return to the West

James S. Corum

The geographical location of the Baltic States dictated that the three countries found themselves in the middle of the conflict between Nazi Germany and the Soviet Union. In 1940 they were forcibly occupied by the Soviet Union. A year later they were overrun and occupied by Germany. The Soviets returned in 1944 and remained until the end of the Soviet Union in 1991.

The story of the Baltic States of Estonia, Latvia and Lithuania since 1945 falls into two clear periods: the first from 1945 and the renewed occupation of the Baltic countries by the Soviet Union and their incorporation into the USSR as constituent republics, and the second from 1991 to the present that began with regaining independence and re-establishing their cultural/political/economic position as western nations. The story centres on nationalism as each of the three countries has a distinct language and culture that they have fought to preserve and maintain against overwhelming odds. However, the other side of the distinct national identities in the Baltic States is a shared experience of being under the domination of Western powers from the middle ages to the 18th century, then more than a century under the Russian Empire, followed by successful independence wars and 20 years as national states and finally another 50 years as occupied states.

It is the shared experience from 1945 to 1991 that forms the dominant factor in Baltic security policy. Since re-independence in 1991, the Baltic nations have taken their own lessons from a shared history and formed a small, but remarkably cohesive, political bloc within the European community and NATO. By most measures of economic, political and military performance the Baltic States have an impressive level of success.

1945 to 1990: Preserving their national identity under Soviet occupation

From 1945 to 1990 the three Baltic nations persevered, despite tremendous obstacles, in preserving their national culture, their pre-occupation history and their faith in winning eventual freedom. By the end of the Soviet occupation 45 years of intensive Soviet indoctrination, Russification, constant surveillance and ruthlessly enforced compliance was quickly swept away in a revival of nationalism that had long been present just below the surface. The end of the Soviet system in the Baltic States became crystal clear on 23 August 1989 on the 50th anniversary of the Molotov–Ribbentrop Pact that had secretly divided Eastern Europe between Soviet and German spheres of influence and given Stalin the authority to claim and occupy Lithuania, Latvia and Estonia. On a warm August day approximately two million people, more than a quarter of the indigenous population of the three Soviet republics, joined hands in a continuous human chain running 420 miles that linked the capitols of Tallinn, Riga and Vilnius. The jubilant crowds waved thousands of homemade national flags and sang nationalist songs in the largest peaceful political demonstration in history.[1] The argument was proclaimed that the Molotov–Ribbentrop Pact was illegal and, hence, the Soviet occupation of the Baltic States was an illegal act.

For 50 years the Soviet Union had maintained that the secret protocols of the Molotov–Ribbentrop was a western fiction and had never existed, even though official German copies had been captured in 1945 and used as documentation at the Nuremberg Trials. Only five days before the Baltic mass protests came the first official recognition that the secret protocols of the pact were real, but then, in proper Soviet fashion, the Soviet commission set up to review the history of the supposedly non-existent pact claimed that it had no bearing on the occupation and incorporation of the Baltic States into the Soviet Empire.[2] Even in its last days, as the Soviet Central Committee railed against the Baltic States, characterising the protest organisers as 'hysterical' and 'extremist groups' and threatened 'catastrophic consequences' as the Politburo attempted re-establish the Soviet rule that was slipping away at an increasingly rapid pace.[3] Having carried out the largest and, arguably most effective, peaceful protest in history, the three states began forming political parties and moving to free elections. Full independence would soon follow with Lithuania being the first Baltic nation to declare independence in 1990 and followed by Estonia and Latvia in 1991.

The history of repression began in June 1940 with the Soviet invasion and annexation of the three Baltic nations. After making his deal with Hitler in August 1939, Stalin pressured the Baltic nations to grant the Soviet military extensive bases on their territory. Being isolated and distrustful of each other, the Baltic States acceded to Stalin's demand and hoped for the best. On 17 June 1940 the Soviet forces stationed in the Baltic States left their barracks and seized power in a coup d'état. The Baltic governments were dissolved, national leaders arrested and murdered, and after phony elections, the three nations became republics of the Soviet Union.[4]

In the first year of occupation from 1940 to the German invasion of 1941 the three Baltic States saw their national elites murdered or sent to the gulags. Collectivization of farms and nationalization of industries and businesses were imposed. Large sectors of the population that included priests and ministers, businessmen, many professionals, intellectuals, military officers, and landowners were identified for mass arrests and deportations.[5] The German invasion of the Soviet Union in June 1941 that quickly overran the Baltic States offered some respite from the heavy hand of Stalin. Although Baltic peoples had long resented the German ruling class that had remained under Czarist rule and had kicked the Germans out in 1919 after bloody fighting, one year under Soviet occupation taught the Baltic nations that the Germans were the lesser of two evils. Thousands of Latvians and Estonians fought alongside the Germans during World War II, providing two Latvian and one Estonian divisions to the Wehrmacht.[6] The fact that the Baltics had fought very well against the Soviets would remain a key source of Soviet hostility against the Baltic States from 1945 to today.

After the Soviets re-established power in the three Baltic States in 1944 they carried out several massive waves of repression lasting until the death of Stalin.[7] This period was characterised by imprisonment or forced exile of hundreds of thousands of Lithuanians, Latvians and Estonians either to the gulags or Siberia.[8] Large nationalist resistance movements were formed in the Baltic States. For almost a decade after the end of World War II, the Soviets fought anti-communist guerrilla forces, called the 'Forest Brothers,' in the rural areas. Not until 1953, after major deployments of KGB and military forces, were the Forest Brothers effectively suppressed.[9] The long guerrilla conflicts resulted in tens of thousands of casualties. The waves of Soviet repression in the 1940s and 1950s touched virtually every family in the Baltic States. Most Baltic families can recall a father who was jailed, an uncle who disappeared in the gulags or a grandfather sent to Siberia. The memories are still fresh.

While repression became less brutal after Stalin's death in 1953, the Soviet era was still a grey dictatorship maintained by a harsh criminal code that punished any expression of dissent and was backed up by the ever-present KGB. From 1953 to the 1980s, Soviet policy was to Russify the Baltic republics and Sovietise the national culture. On the surface the Baltics were 'good Soviet citizens', but under the surface the Baltic peoples worked to preserve their language, literature and unique national identities. Thanks to Lenin's decree of 1922 that encouraged the use of national languages, the Baltic peoples used their national languages to preserve their national traditions. All three Baltic nations had long associated music with their national identity and folk song festivals had attracted audiences as early as the 19th century. In all three Baltic countries song festivals featuring traditional songs in the national language became very popular as the Soviet Union loosened up in the 1960s. Estonians excelled in putting on grand song festivals while in Latvia traditional folk dancing festivals drew thousands of performers and audience members. Estonia, which had developed a film industry in the national language under Czarist rule, developed a film studio in Tallinn after 1945. By the 1960s the studio was producing high-quality films in the Estonian language. Although all films had to be approved and reviewed by the national film censors in Moscow, many Estonian films from the 1960s through the 1980s display no political content at all. Highly popular films included a nostalgic romance story set in the 1890s (*Kevade: 'Spring'*, 1969), and a musical comedy set in contemporary Tallinn (*Vana Toomas 'Old Thomas'*, 1970). One might watch these films in the national language and think that the Soviet Union had never existed. By the 1980s, with any non-Soviet political meetings forbidden, music, dance and film events were the only legal venues to express national sentiment and they became the vehicle for mobilising the populace to resist the Soviet state in the late 1980s. The term 'the singing revolution' was coined for the Baltic States and it was an apt description.

Many other Baltic nationals resorted to quiet, but highly illegal, acts to preserve their national culture. After the independence wars against Russia, large and small memorials were erected to commemorate the battles and the fallen throughout the Baltic countries. In the wake of the Soviet takeover in 1940 many of the smaller monuments and markers in the small towns were secretly removed and hidden by local residents, often buried under barns. Despite five decades of Soviet surveillance and sentences to the gulags for such acts, the memorials remained family secrets only to proudly reappear in 1990.

Russification of the Baltics, 1945–1990

After 1945, when the Soviets re-occupied the Baltic States they initiated a policy of mass deportations of Baltic peoples and the resettlement of ethnic Russians into Latvia and Estonia especially. It was a careful programme to change the ethnic nature of the countries by shipping Baltic peoples out and shipping Russians in. In the 1960s and 1970s large numbers of ethnic Russians moved into the Baltic States to work in the military industries. In 1940 the populations of the Baltic States were almost all indigenous, but by the end of Soviet rule, large Russian minorities had been established. For example, in 1935, Latvia had a population of 1.48 million ethnic Latvians and 206,000 Russians; in 1989 the population was 1.388 million ethnic Latvians and 909,000 Russians.[10] Estonia, which had only a handful of ethnic Russians in 1940, had a Russian ethnic population of 23% by 1991. Currently, Latvia and Estonia have significant Russian ethnic minorities.[11] Lithuania was the only Baltic nation that did not experience a large influx of Russians because the Forest Brothers caused so much trouble in rural areas that Stalin's plan to settle Russians on collectivised land were foiled.[12]

Almost all ethnic Russians remained in the Baltic States after independence of 1991, preferring life as non-citizens in the free and more prosperous Baltics to life in much poorer Russia. Although ethnic Russians in Latvia and Estonia can become full citizens by a simple naturalization process that requires only a five-year legal residency and a basic knowledge of the national language, many ethnic Russians still refuse to take up citizenship.[13]

1991 to the present: Baltics return to their tradition as western nations

Although the Baltic States might be geographically Eastern Europe, they are Western European nations in their history, culture, religion, language, economics and politics. Ever since the German merchants arrived on the Baltic coast in the 12th century, soon followed by German and Danish crusaders and settlers, the Baltic peoples have been tied more closely to the west than to their Russian neighbour. Latvian and Lithuanian are Baltic languages and Estonians speak a Finno-Ugric language. All three languages use the Latin alphabet, and none have any relation to Russian or the Slavic languages. In the Baltics the religion is western, with Estonia and Latvia being predominantly Lutheran in religion and Lithuania Catholic. In the Middle Ages the region was closely linked to the west in politics and economics through the Baltic cities, which belonged to the Hanseatic League and followed German law. Latvia and Estonia (then known as Livonia) were associated with the Holy Roman Empire. The rule by the Teutonic Knights in Livonia was followed by the rule of the Swedish Empire, which lasted until the conquest of Livonia by Peter the Great in 1725. Lithuania, tied to Poland in religion and politics, was annexed into the Russian Empire until Kurland was annexed in 1795.

As part of the Russian Empire the Baltic States had a special status and developed very differently from the rest of Russia. Livonia (Latvia and Estonia) was ruled by a council of ethnic German nobles and had its own laws with German being the language of government and business. As was Czar Peter's intention, Livonia maintained a strong trade relationship with the west, especially Germany and Scandinavia. Thanks to a religion of pietistic Lutheranism, Livonia had universal literacy by 1800, a century and a half before Russia met that standard. Tartu University, founded by the Swedes in 1632, became the top scientific university in Russia. Serfdom ended in Livonia 40 years before Russia ended the system, and Latvia and Estonia were the first areas to be industrialised in the Czarist Empire. The 19th century saw the rise of an indigenous and well-educated Latvian and Estonian middle class. As elsewhere in Europe, a national literature flourished along within the rise of nationalist local schools and institutions. As Czarist reforms allowed for local council elections, ethnic Latvians and Estonians came to control the city governments. By 1914 Riga was well-established as Russia's high-tech city, with automobiles and airplanes manufactured there. Riga, the largest city in the region, became Russia's great trading centre with northern Europe. With the collapse of the Russian Empire in 1917, Estonia and Latvia had both the economic infrastructure and an educated workforce and middle class to establish viable states.

The independence (or re-independence that the Baltics call it) of the three states in 1991 was seen not as a break in their political and cultural tradition but simply as a return to the west. Having gained independence, the new republics decided to immediately and completely turn western, establishing western constitutions, and privatising their economies and opening their countries to western investment. English, not Russian, immediately became the primary foreign language taught in the schools. The linkage to the west was helped by the return of many exiles and their descendants to their home countries. In 1944 approximately 10% of the Baltic population was evacuated to Germany ahead of the Russian advance. In the displaced persons camps of post-war Europe these refugees found new homes, mostly in the United States and Canada, and prospered. Forming exile groups abroad, they did not forget their national heritage.

With independence came new laws defining citizenship in Latvia, Lithuania and Estonia. Citizens were defined as residents of the three states, or their descendants, on 17 June 1940 – before the Soviet Union annexed the Baltic States. These laws immediately made the large number of Russian inhabitants and their children, who mostly knew only Russian, stateless persons and ineligible to vote in national elections. On the other side, exiles and their children could return as full citizens and reclaim property taken under the Soviet occupation. Some notable talent appeared from the exile community including Estonian academic and journalist Toomas Ilves, who had been born in Sweden to exile parents and grown up in America. Ilves became Estonia's ambassador to the United States, then foreign minister, and from 2006 to 2016 served as Estonia's fourth president. In 1999 Lithuania named retired US Army colonel Jonas Kronkaitis as its military defence chief with the consent of the US government. Kronkaitis had been born in Lithuania and his family had fled in 1944, ending up as refugees in America. He had returned to Lithuania after re-independence and was selected as defence chief specifically to bring the Lithuanian military up to standard to join NATO.[14]

The Baltic return to the west quickly succeeded in turning the three Baltic States from impoverished republics of the former Soviet Union to fairly prosperous countries with rapidly growing economies. The Baltic countries have been governed by centre-right coalitions since 1991. From the first moment of independence the Baltic States oriented their economies to the west and attracted foreign investment to establish and remake industries. At the beginning of independence, the three countries all announced their intention to become full members of the EU, a goal that was met in 2004. Today the Baltic States' per capita GDP compares well with

Central European nations and all three countries have far surpassed Russia. Compared to Russia's 2019 per capita GDP of USD 11,585, Estonia's figure is USD 23,695, Latvia USD 17,836 and Lithuania USD 19,455.[15] The Baltic countries' trade is overwhelmingly with Western Europe and have proven adept in developing new high-tech industries. For example, Skype was invented in Estonia.

In terms of security, the first objective of the Baltic States was to work with western allies and the new Russian Federation to negotiate the removal of Russian troops and bases from their territory. This was accomplished in 1994. Russia offered various security guarantees and encouraged the Baltic States to establish a neutral position. For the Baltic States, this was a non-starter. The great historical lesson of 1940 was that their neutrality and failure to form an alliance among themselves before 1940 made them easy prey for a Soviet takeover. The moment the last Russian troops left their countries in 1994, the three Baltic States all announced their goal of joining NATO.

Even before the Russians left, from 1991 to 1994 the new armed forces of all three states met regularly to coordinate security policy. This tradition continues with quarterly meetings of the three Baltic national defence chiefs where policy, procurement and training issues are discussed. The Baltic Defence College oversight consists of defence and military representatives of all countries that meet regularly, alternating the meeting venue among the three countries. The beginning of the Baltic military meetings posed an interesting language problem as there are three different Baltic languages. Of course, as former Soviet citizens, all the military leaders were completely fluent in Russian. However, it was deemed somehow unseemly for armed forces formed to defend against Russia should speak that language. So, from the beginning of the Baltic military cooperation talks the meetings were conducted in English, although it was that was the third or fourth language of the participants. Although awkward at first, it signified the determination to fully align with the west and to use NATO's common language in both speech and documents.

To achieve true security independence, the three countries formed their own security bloc and developed joint defence programmes such as a single higher staff and war college, the Baltic Defence College, established in 1999 and equally owned and operated by all three countries with English (the NATO command language) as the official language of administration and instruction. The Baltic nations sent their best officers to western military courses and sought advice and assistance not just from NATO, but from non-NATO allies such as Sweden and Finland.

Another part of the western alignment was to participate in western military operations. It started small with teams sent to support NATO's Balkan peacekeeping in the 1990s, but by 2003 all three Baltic nations were committing troops to the US-led intervention in Iraq. The Baltic forces commitment to NATO and EU missions were made in the understanding that the contribution of the three nations was to earn a 'place at the table' in NATO and EU decision-making. The Baltic States could not expect to be taken seriously or listened to unless a serious and highly visible contribution was put forward for the collective security of NATO and the EU.[16]

After joining NATO, the Baltic States made a much greater effort to support NATO in Afghanistan with Estonia and Latvia committing infantry units and Lithuania leading one of the provincial reconstruction teams (Ghor Province). The commitment to Afghanistan was not a popular one with the citizens at home, but it did serve to demonstrate the Baltic States' willingness to support the west. The highly professional performance of the Baltic troops in Afghanistan won the Baltic countries a lot of respect from western soldiers and the officer and NCO cadres of the Baltic nations won both combat experience and the experience of working effectively in a multi-national environment.[17]

The unity of the Baltic States in political and security matters was demonstrated when all three countries joined the European Union and NATO together in 2004. However, their particular position as a neighbour and likely target of Russia makes the Baltic relationship with Europe and NATO somewhat unique. Firstly, there is a clear divergence in NATO and the EU between 'Old Europe' of the Western European states and 'New Europe' of the eastern and former Warsaw Pact nations. 'Old Europe' downplays the idea of a real military threat to NATO and in the discussions of the new NATO Strategic Concept it was the older Western European nations that floated the idea of transforming the NATO mission into a vague international peacekeeping and general security organization and downplaying NATO's original mission as a collective defence alliance. This did not sit well with NATO's new Eastern European members, who are often fluent in Russian and follow Russian politics with a careful and discerning eye. The new NATO nations, and especially the Baltic States, lobbied hard and very effectively within NATO committees to ensure that the 2010 NATO Strategic Concept emphasised that North Atlantic Treaty Article 5 – collective defence against military attack – still remained the core NATO mission.

The Baltic perceptions of the threats to national security are not different than the positions of other former Warsaw Pact states such as Poland, Hungary and the Czech Republic, that joined NATO in the major expansion of NATO in 2004. In contrast to the 'Old Europe' nations, the newer Eastern European NATO nations still see Russia as a serious problem that could become an overt threat. Moreover, in terms of security, the Baltic military leaders see the Transatlantic alliance with the United States, and not Western Europe, as the most essential pillar of their own security.[18] All the Baltic States have offered to host US troops and when President Trump announced that he would reduce American troop levels in Germany by 9,500 troops the Latvian government, along with Poland, immediately announced that they would be happy to host US forces and pay for the basing. The offer is not far-fetched and comes from years of lobbying by the Baltic countries to have a permanent US military presence. US Air Force units already routinely operate out of Latvia's Ainazi

Air Base and in 2019 the US concluded a deal to place a US armoured brigade in Poland on a rotating basis.[19] In 2017 Lithuania signed an agreement to host a small permanent detachment of US troops at Lithuanian military bases to support the regular training deployments of US troops to the region.[20] Lithuania has for years put out a considerable defence investment to build military base infrastructure and training areas to a high standard to facilitate US units and American military units have carried out exercises in Lithuania.[21] In 2018 the three Baltic nations, and Poland, all made the NATO target of 2% of GDP for defence – a level of defence commitment that Chancellor Merkel of Germany has promised to meet, perhaps, by the early 2030s.[22]

The Baltic attitude of trusting in America rather than 'Old Europe' might seem a cold political calculation, but it is actually rooted in the history of World War II and the Cold War. When the Baltic States were annexed by the Soviet Union in 1940 the American response was immediate and clear: the United States would never recognise the overthrow of the Baltic States de jure or de facto. While all the other western states made some accommodation with the Soviets on this issue, some countries formally recognising the 1940 occupation, the United States never wavered in its policy. In June 1982, in his speech inaugurating Radio Liberty, President Ronald Reagan proclaimed Baltic Freedom Day and stated, 'I call upon the people of the United States to reaffirm their belief and hope that the citizens of Latvia, Lithuania, and Estonia and of all nations will one day achieve through peaceful means the goals of democratic freedom and self-determination.'[23] In several major speeches Reagan referred to the Baltic States and promised to work for their independence. It was the Reagan administration in the 1980s that stiffened the Western European resolve, against intensive European resistance, to build up NATO conventional and nuclear defences and to negotiate from a position of strength as a means to resolve the Cold War. The Baltic national leaders know their history and know that America was their only unwavering ally during the dark years of the Cold War.

After independence: The renewed conflict with Russia of history

A key objective of the Baltic States even before independence was to regain the true narrative of their national histories, which had been distorted beyond all recognition under four decades of communism. Beginning in 1988, all three Baltic States created historical commissions composed of top academics to document the extent of human rights abuses in the years of Soviet occupation. One helpful circumstance was the rapid abandonment of regional headquarters of the KGB in the Baltics and the large amounts of files left behind. Since the 1990s, the Baltic governments have published extensive historical studies carefully documenting Soviet-era arrests, mass deportations and mass murder in the Baltic States. All three Baltic States set up a series of museums and archives to document the events of World War II and the Soviet period. There was also an extensive movement to restore the past memorials to the national leaders during the independence period and to commemorate the soldiers and battles of the 1918–1920 independence wars. In each country there is a national museum of occupation that records the events of the German and Soviet occupations.

There was a brief period of détente between the Baltic States and Russia in the 1990s. The People's Congress of the USSR in December 1989 denounced the secret Soviet/Nazi protocols as unjustified and invalid.[24] After the attempted coup of August 1991 President Yeltsin formally recognised the Baltic States' independence. For a few years in the 1990s there was some opening of the Russian state archives providing some details of the Soviet occupation of the Baltic States. Baltic citizens who had been deported to the far corners of the Soviet Empire were freely allowed to return home. The work of amassing the historical record of the Soviet occupation had been made easy in the Baltics during the disorder of 1990 and 1991 when newly formed national militias forced the KGB to abandon their local and regional headquarters. The KGB left behind an enormous trove of files going back to the 1940s that documented the mass arrests, deportations and campaign against the Forest Brothers. Each of the Baltic States formed historical commissions to collect and publish the KGB records and develop comprehensive histories of the Soviet occupation era. In this effort the Baltic States have been very successful in publishing thoroughly researched and highly detailed accounts of the use of Soviet security arms to suppress the Baltic States from 1940 to 1990. One also finds a host of local museums throughout the Baltic States set up in former KGB headquarters where a visitor can see the tiny holding cells that were built to not allow a prisoner to either stand up or lie down. Former prisoners who passed through the cells on the way to the gulags are on hand to tour the visitors and the museums contain artifacts of local residents who passed through the gulags.[25] The reality of the Soviet period is still a fresh memory in the Baltic States.

When Putin came to power in 2000 the détente with the Baltics was quickly stopped and the new Russian president chose history to be a battlefield with the Baltics. One of Putin's main concerns is supporting a new Russian nationalist version of history, which was essentially the old Soviet line. Putin's feelings on the interpretation of history are not a new development. In 1994, long before he came to power, at a meeting in Hamburg, the Estonian President Lennart Meri referred to the Russians as 'occupiers' and Putin dramatically stood up and led the Russian diplomats out of the conference.[26] Putin's government has worked ceaselessly to try to delegitimise the Baltic States through state control, of the historical narrative, a constant media campaign against the Baltics and a not very subtle disinformation campaign. In 2005, Kremlin's European affairs chief, Sergei Yastrzhembsky, rejected the findings of the 1989 Baltic/Russian Historical Commission and the subsequent resolution of the Soviet government on the legality of the Soviet occupation of the Baltic States in 1940. The Kremlin insisted that the Soviet occupation of the three states was done with the approval of the Baltic governments.[27] The attack on the legal existence of the Baltic States as independent countries even accelerated. In 2015, the office of the Russian Attorney General issued a decision that the United Russian government that had recognised the Baltic States as independent nations was, in fact, an unconstitutional body and, therefore, the recognition of Baltic independence under President Yeltsin in 1991 was illegal and invalid.[28]

Since 2000 Russian regime history has again been relegated to the role of serving the state. The tone and substance of all Russian state history publications since 2000 – and almost all scholarship is under the control of the state and allied agencies – is one of aggressive Russian nationalism. In the interpretation of history promoted by the Russian government the new official view repudiates the Soviet government's admission of the Molotov–Ribbentrop Pact and insists that the Soviet occupation of the Baltic States was fully justified under international law. Baltic claims of Soviet crimes against humanity (which are carefully documented and detailed by national commissions in the Baltic States) are deemed exaggerations. Under Putin the Baltic peoples are all portrayed as Nazi supporters in World War II. Moreover, any critique of the Soviet Union and its role in the Baltics is deemed a 'revival of fascism'.[29] In 2009 Russian Prime Minister Medvedev set up a historical commission to combat the 'falsification of history' that shows the Soviet regime in a bad light.[30] This is in accord with the new Russian history of the Putin era that portrays Stalin in a positive light as a great national leader and commander in World War II.

Baltic attempts to publish accurate histories and to gain international recognition of the crimes committed against the Baltic peoples are challenged by Russian propaganda aiming to discredit the Baltic States internationally.[31] A constant theme of official Russian media depicts the Baltic peoples of the 1930s and 1940s as 'Nazis' and insist that the Baltic peoples remain deeply 'Nazi' today, thus legitimising overt Russian hostility in the past and present. Indeed, any western support for the Baltic States is interpreted as open support for the return of Nazism. A Russian News Service denunciation of a film about the Latvians in World War II stated, 'One wonders if the filmmakers stressed the fact that ethnic Latvians were amongst the most enthusiastic and willing collaborators with the Nazis during World War II …. The US government is supporting Nazi revisionists in Riga (and in Tallinn, Kiev, and Zagreb as well). How low have we fallen?'[32] Russian media cartoons show depictions of Latvia with Hitler and the Nazi flag. The Russian state media runs articles such as 'Estonia could become a haven for Nazis around the World'.[33] The characterization of all Eastern Europeans, and especially the Baltics, as Nazis is a regular theme stressed by Putin. The Baltics, as former Soviet republics that broke to the west, are special targets for Putin's ire. But Putin also uses the 'Nazi' theme as a common insult towards all the Eastern European nations that oppose him. During his invasion of the Ukraine in 2014 Putin stated that 'open neo-Nazism' has become 'commonplace' in that country, but also named Latvia and the Baltic States as guilty of that offense.[34] In October 2014, in reply to Putin's campaign, the Latvian Foreign Ministry commented that that Putin was waging an 'information war' against the Baltics and other European states.[35]

Russia's information campaign to mobilise the Russian minority in the Baltic States

Russia's policy to style itself as the protector of ethnic Russians outside of Russia is a major theme in the books of *Project Russia*, a series of four volumes published (2004–2018) by a group of academics close to Putin and forming the official ideological expression of the Putin regime.[36] From 1990 to the present the Russian regime has used historical interpretation as a means to whip up opposition of the Russian minorities in the Baltic States against the centre-right governments. In the two decades following re-independence the Baltic governments, representing the feelings of the vast majority of their populations, have taken down or moved communist-era memorials that represent the most horrendous events of their history. However, for ethnic Russian minorities in the three countries the memorials to the Red Army and its occupation of the Baltic States are a reminder of the glory days of Soviet history. In 2007, the Estonian government's attempt to move a memorial to the Red Army in Tallinn provoked a violent response from mobs of ethnic Russians. Both Tallinn and the heavily Russian northeast region witnessed days of violent demonstrations and violence that resulted in one death.[37] In Latvia and Estonia there were other incidents of violence connected with the Russian minorities and Soviet monuments. Lithuania, with only six per cent of its population ethnic Russian, is in a different position. But there is still considerable friction with Russia on the depiction of Soviet history.[38] Russia, as the proclaimed protector of all Russian speakers in the world, sees the Russian ethnic population in the Baltics as a justification to attack the Baltic governments. As recently as 2018 Putin claimed that ethnic Russians in the Baltics are victims of human rights abuses by the Baltic governments.[39] With Russia's claim to be protector of all Russian speakers one can readily see Putin justifying military intervention in the region as an excuse to defend ethnic Russian victims against western aggression.

However, despite a virulent anti-Baltic information campaign still emanating from the Soviet government, and Russian media attempts to whip up anti-Baltic sentiment by portraying the Russian minorities as victims of Baltic national governments, the relations between the Baltic governments and the Russian minorities have been steadily improving. Over time there has been considerable assimilation of the ethnic

Russians in the Baltic States. The Russian-financed ethnic parties and factions in the Baltic States have generally lost support over the last decade and present much less of a danger than they posed 15 or 20 years ago. Ethnic Russian residents of the Baltic States today do not show a high level of dissatisfaction with the national governments, something that can be readily understood when the income and living standard of a Russian living in the Baltics is far higher than their relations in Russia have. In addition, even the non-citizen ethnic Russians of Latvia and Estonia who never took up Baltic citizenship still have full travel and work rights within the EU, even with their stateless persons' passports (that recognises them as legal residents of those countries). In short, no sensible Russian would trade superior pay and benefits, a high standard of living and the right to work and travel internationally with anything that Russia has to offer – which isn't much.

Where language issues caused major protests 15 years ago in Latvia, the 2018 law that mandated that Latvian be the primary language of instruction in all national schools readily passed with only a few small protests.[40] What was notable is the lack of interest from young people in defending the Russian language. It seems that the younger generation of ethnic Russians in the Baltics are not especially devoted to the Putin's Soviet view of history nor are especially interested in following Putin's political line.[41] In short, Russia's attempt to use historical interpretation to delegitimise and discredit the Baltics in the eyes of the world failed badly in an attempt to whip up nationalist fervour among the ethnic Russians in the Baltics. The only success for Putin's ideology has been in convincing some western academics, but this is the same group that would endorse any historical interpretation or victimhood claim made against the west.

The shadow of 1945 still lingers in the Baltics, especially in the conflict over historical interpretation of the Soviet occupation of the region. But Russia's attempt to redefine the political and historical relationships of the last 75 years essentially failed when Russia took the step of invading the Ukraine in 2014. By proving that Russia was still a direct military threat to its neighbours Putin lost the support of ethnic Russians in the Baltic States, a group he was relying on to loyally support Russian politics in the region. Moreover, Putin pushed to Baltics to improve their defence build-up and to not only base American troops in their countries, but to pay for the infrastructure as well. The enthusiastic support for US troops to be permanently based in Poland and the Baltic republics reflects the general state of Eastern European opinion about Russia and defence. For one who lived for years in Eastern Europe and was involved in national defence in that region, I believe that one of the greatest legacies to come out of the long historical process since 1945 has been the rise of the 'New Europe' of the Central and Eastern European nations ready to follow a very different path in economics, politics and security than the 'Old Europe' to the west.

Notes

1   'The Baltic Way', Estonian, Latvian and Lithuanian National Commissions for UNESCO, 17 August 1989.

2   David Remick, 'Kremlin Acknowledges Secret Pact on Baltics: Soviets Deny Republics Annexed Illegally', *The Washington Post,* 19 August 1989.

3   Statement of the Central Committee on the situation in the Soviet Baltic Republics (Заявление ЦК КПСС о положении в республиках Советской Прибалтики) Pravda, 26 August 1989.

4   Andres Kasekamp, *A History of the Baltic States* (London: Palgrave, 2010), 99–105, 128–131. Kasekamp provides the best general history of the Baltic States in English.

5   All the Baltic States established historical commissions to document the victims of the Soviet period of occupation. All three states have published extensive detailed studies of the Baltic citizens killed, exiled, arrested or sent to prisons. In many cases the outcome is fuzzy with a known arrest date but nothing thereafter. Nevertheless, the enormous scale of Soviet repression and crimes against humanity committed against the Baltic States over 50 years has been very well documented. For details on the Soviet repression in Estonia in 1941–1945 see Estonian International Commission for the Investigation of Crimes Against Humanity, *Estonia 1940–1945* (Tallinn: Estonian Foundation for the Investigation of Crimes Against Humanity, 2005).

6   Latvia provided two divisions to the German Army, the 15th and 17th Waffen SS Divisions and the Estonians manned the 20th Waffen SS Division. The Western Allies after the war during the Nuremberg Trials determined that the Baltic military formations were not criminal organizations and had not committed war crimes.

7   Kasekamp, *A History of the Baltic States,* 141–146.

8   In one wave of deportations in three days in March 1949, 43,000 Latvians, including women and children, were rounded up and deported to Siberia, where many perished. In just this one wave of deportations 92,000 Baltic people were sent to Siberia. In all, hundreds of thousands of people from these small states were sent to the Gulags and to settlements in Siberia and Central Asia. See Paul Rothenhäusler and Hans-Ueli Sonderegger (eds), *Errinerung an den Roten Holocaus*t (Rothenhäusler Verlag: Stäfe Switzerland, 1999), 58–69.

9   For details on the suppression of the Latvians see Janis Straume, *Lettland im 2. Weltkrieg* (Riga: Nacionālais Apgāds, 2007), 41–46.

10 Valters Nollendorfs, Dzintra Burg, Gundega Michele, and Uldis Neiburgs, *The Three Occupations of Latvia 1941–1991* (Riga: Occupation Museum Association of Latvia, 2008), 37.

11 See the *CIA World Factbook* for recent statistics on the ethnic makeup of the Baltic States. In Latvia the population is 59.3% ethnic Latvian, 27.8% Russian, 3.6% Belarusian, 2.5% Ukrainian. 37.5% of Latvians are Russian speakers. In Estonia 68.7% of the population is ethnic Estonian and 25.6% are Russian or Russian speakers.

12 For a detailed analysis of the largest and most effective resistance movement in the Baltics see Vylius Leskys, 'Forest Brothers' 1945: The Culmination of the Lithuanian Partisan Movement', *Baltic Security and Defence Review*, Vol. 11, No. 1 (2009): 58–86.

13 On the citizenship issue and ethnic friction see Andris Runcis, 'The Citizenship Issue as a Creeping Crisis' in E. Stern and D. Hansen (eds), *Crisis Management in a Transitional Society: the Latvian Experience* (Stockholm: Swedish Defence College, 2001), 61–97.

14 Tribune News Service, 'Retired U.S. Colonel Appointed to Lead Nation's Military', *Chicago Tribune*, 13 June 1999.

15 Figures from the World Bank, GDP.pdf (worldbank.org), accessed 4 February 2021.

16 The importance of winning a seat at the table is a constant theme in the official statements and reports of the Baltic nations, as well as commentaries by leading political figures and academics.

For Baltic attitudes and policy perceptions on NATO and EU commitment see: Margarita Seselgyte, 'The Lithuanian Presidency of the EU Council and Common Security and Defense Policy: Opportunities and Challenges', in the *Lithuanian Annual Strategic Review 2011–2012*, Vol. 10 (Vilnius: Strategic Research Center, 2012), 87–120; Kestatis Paulauskas, 'NATO at 60: Lost in Transformation', *Lithuanian Annual Strategic Review 2009–2010* (Vilnius: Strategic Research Center, 2010), 31–54.; Egdunas Racius, 'Lithuania in the NATO Mission in Afghanistan: Between Idealism and Pragmatism', *Lithuanian Annual Strategic Review 2009–2010* (Vilnius: Strategic Research Center, 2010), 187–207; Martynas Zapolskis, 'NATO Transformation Scenarios', *Lithuanian Annual Strategic Review 2009–2010* (Vilnius: Strategic Research Center, 2010), 55–78; Zaneta Ozolina, 'Measuring the Effectiveness of NATO', in Zaneta Ozolina (ed), *Rethinking Security* (Riga: Zinatne, 2010), 118–167.

17 James Corum, *Development of the Baltic Armed Forces in Light of Multinational Deployments* (Carlise, PA: Strategic Studies Institute, US Army War College, August 2013).

18 James Corum, *The Security Concerns of the Baltic States as NATO Allies* (Carlise, PA: Strategic Studies Institute, US Army War College, August 2013).

19 Paul McCleary, 'Latvia wants US Troops, and is Ready to Pay for Them', *Breaking Defense*, 9 July 2020.

20 Liudas Dapkus, 'Lithuania signs agreement with U.S. on troops deployment', *Military Times*, 17 January 2017.

21 Jonas Dringelis, 'U.S. to build military bases in Lithuania', *The Baltic World*, 24 January 2019.

22 Dapkus, 'Lithuania signs agreement with U.S. on troops deployment'.

23 President Ronald Reagan, Proclamation 4948, Baltic Freedom Day, 14 June 1982.

24 For the whole story of the history commission that revised the Soviet history of the 1939 Pact see Heike Lindpere, *Molotov-Ribbentrop Pact: Challenging Soviet History* (Estonian Foreign Policy Institute: Tallinn, 2009). On the Soviet denunciation of the treaty's legality see 173–195.

25 My office at the Baltic Defence College in Tartu Estonia was located 100 metres from a large grey building that was the Regional Headquarters of the NKVD/KGB for southern Estonia. The holding and torture cells of the KGB on the basement are now preserved as a museum. There are many former prisoners of the Soviet gulags in Tart. The Tartu KGB Museum contains many documents, artifacts and photos of the Soviet Gulags, many items donated by still living local people.

26 Masha Gessen, *The Man without a Face: The Unlikely Rise of Vladamir Putin* (London: Granta, 2012), 133.

27 BBC News, 'Russia denies Baltic Occupation', 5 May 2005.

28 'Генпрокуратура РФ проверитзаконностьвыходаПрибалтикиизСССР', *Komsomolskaya Pravda*, 1 July 2015.

29 Kasekamp, *A History of the Baltic States,* 196.

30 Ibid., 197.

31 On the activities of the Baltic Historical Commissions see Eva-Clarita Pettai, 'The Convergence of Two Worlds: Historians and the Emerging Histories of the Baltic States', in Martyn Housden and David Smith (eds), *Forgotten Pages of Baltic History* (Amsterdam: Rodolpi, 2011), 262–280.

32 Voice of Russia World Service, 4 December 2008.

33 'Margolev: Estonia could become a haven for Nazis from all over the world' (Эстония может стать прибежищем для нацистов со всего мира), newsru.com/russia/30oct2011/margelov. html, accessed 4 February 2021.

34 Damien Sharkov, 'Putin Warns of Neo-Nazism in Ukraine and Europe Ahead of WW2 Memorial', *Newsweek*, 15 October 2014.

35 Ibid.

36 For an analysis of Putin's ideology see Lynn Corum, 'Project Russia: The Bestselling Book Series of Putin's Kremlin', *South Central Review*, Vol. 35, No. 1 (Spring 2018): 73–99.

37 Heiko Pääbo, 'War of Memories' Explaining the 'Memorials War' in Estonia', *Baltic Security and Defence Review*, Vol. 10 (2008): 5–28.

38 Ceslovas Laurinavicius, 'The Role of History in the Relationship between Lithuania and Russia', in *Lithuanian Annual Strateguc Review 2005* (Strategic Research Center: Vilnius, 2006), 109–125.

39 'Putin urges EU to pay attention to Russian speakers' rights in Baltics', *The Baltic Times*, 6 August 2018.

40 Una Bergmane, 'Fading Russian Influence in the Baltic States', *Orbis*, Vol. 64, No. 3 (2020): 479–488.

41 I taught a large graduate course (45 students) at Tartu University, Estonia, from 2010–2014. My students were international, but Estonians were the largest group. Among the Estonians there were always a fair number of ethnic Russian Estonians. That many ethnic Russians are able to meet the very high entrance standards of Tartu University shows that the Estonian education system had not failed the ethnic Russian population. The ethnic Russians are fully included in the university life. Some of my ethnic Russian students have told me of visiting their relatives in Russia, but they seem to have little interest in becoming Russians and displayed no deep attachment to the Russian state of Vladamir Putin. The ethnic Estonian relationship to Russia seems to mostly their connections with their cousins back in the old country. Some of my ethnic Russian students told me they had been brought up to speak a Moscow (more educated) form of Russian, while their relations in Russia often spoke dialects that were hard for them to understand.

CHAPTER 6

Beyond the 'Strange Defeat': French Defence Policy and the Memories of World War II

Olivier Schmitt

Introduction

In his *War Memoirs* published in 1954, Charles De Gaulle recalled his feeling when learning about the 1940 French military defeat: 'This is too stupid! The war is off to a terrible start, it thus has to continue.'[1] This firm belief in the fact that France had lost a battle but not the war was foundational for the entire Gaullist project: restoring France's grandeur. It just so happens that the political leader that led Free France during World War II also had a dramatic impact on French political life (and its defence policy) by establishing the Vth Republic in 1958 and being its first president until 1969: the first connection between the memory of World War II and France's post-1945 defence and security policy is embodied by De Gaulle and his legacy.

But the Gaullian epopee is far from being the only memory of World War II that shaped France's political life after 1945: a multiplicity of memories, from the micro-local to the macro-political, have contributed to constantly redefine how the war was perceived, remembered and described in public discourses, thus indirectly shaping public policies. A direct causal relationship between memories and specific policies is probably impossible to establish, and this chapter does not attempt to do so. However, memories and perceptions shape the broader normative and intellectual context in which policies are designed, thus defining the realm of possibilities.[2] The memories of an event influence policymaking in at least two ways.[3] First, policies need to be legitimised through specific narratives, which are only accepted by political communities if they fit with pre-established political myths, narratives and perceptions: it is an old political trick to justify the present by referencing the past, thus conditioning the successful adoption of policies to fit with collectively accepted memories.[4] Second, policymakers tend to think in terms of historical analogies and their perceptions of an historical event (in short, their memory of the event) influence decision-making.[5]

This chapter explores the multiple ways through which the memories of World War II have shaped French defence policy after 1945. While acknowledging the multiplicity of factors that shape decision-making, it argues that the memories of defeat and occupation have contributed to define some key strategic orientations. The chapter first discusses the diversity of memories about World War II, arguing that it constitutes a case of 'fragmented memory'. It then studies three French strategic orientations that are arguably shaped by the memories of World War II: the desire for strategic autonomy, the ambiguous relations with key allies and the willingness to rely on the colonial empire (and successor post-colonial states) as a source of power.

The French memories of World War II: Legacies of the 'strange defeat'

The first defining characteristic of the French memory of World War II is diversity. Unlike World War I, which provided a relatively similar experience of trench warfare for millions of individuals,[6] thus creating a mostly shared memory of the event among veterans, the French experience of World War II was extremely diverse. This diversity led to a 'disunited memory'[7] of the war, with several facets of this memory being more or less prevalent since 1945, depending on the political context.

One of the reasons for the diversity of memories about World War II lies in the multiplicity of fronts in which French forces were engaged during the conflict, which to a large degree (but not exclusively) mirrors the fluidity of French politics at the time (and notably the confrontation between the Vichy government and De Gaulle). The first obvious fighting experience shaping the memory of the conflict is the participation in the Free French Forces (FFF), the military wing of the government-in-exile led by Charles de Gaulle from London. However, the constitution of the FFF was far from being an easy and uncontroversial process. For example, the 1st Army (*Rhin et Danube*) commanded by general De Lattre de Tassigny, which participated in the 1944 Operation *Dragoon* in Provence and contributed to the liberation of France from the south, was awkwardly constituted in 1943 by amalgamating troops from the 'African Army' (which had remained loyal to Vichy until the 1942 allied campaign in North Africa) on the one hand, and forces which had rallied De Gaulle as early as 1940 on the other. A major difference between the two groups was the participation in the 1942 battle of Bir Hakeim, during which the 4,000 Free French commanded by General Koenig resisted for two weeks to the 40,000 Italo-German troops commanded by General Rommel, thus enabling the British troops to escape, regroup and eventually halt the Afrika Korps during the first battle of El Alamein.

The memory of Bir Hakeim, which was portrayed by De Gaulle as an example of France's fortitude after the 1940 defeat, initially acted as a strong differentiating factor between the two groups, as illustrated by a military parade on 20 May 1943, in which the troops coming from the 'African Army' paraded with the US troops, while the Gaullists paraded with the British troops. Such differences were vividly illustrated by the clashes of personalities between General De Lattre, an ambitious general who originally served Vichy before joining De Gaulle, and his subordinate general Leclerc who had joined De Gaulle as a captain and was fast-tracked to generalship. The multiplicity of fronts also contributed to the fragmentation of memories, since some troops served as part of the Free French Forces in North Africa and/or on the Western Front, some in Madagascar, but some even served on the Eastern Front, as part of the 'Normandie-Niemen' fighter regiment: this regiment was the only western military unit to fight together with the Soviets until the end of the war in Europe. The diversity of theatres in which French forces were engaged, and the difficult process that ultimately led to accepting De Gaulle's authority over the FFF, contributes to explaining the lack of unified WWII memory.

A second facet of the diverse experiences (and memories) of the war resides in the difference between French fighters abroad (fighting in conventional armed forces in high-intensity warfare) and the multiplicity of resistance networks that emerged in occupied France and who conducted sabotage, intelligence and propaganda operations.[8] The memories of the resistance are complex and have, of course, evolved over time. To begin with, the plurality of memories stems from the highly diverse social phenomenon that was the 'Resistance', which was far from being ideologically unified. The term itself is problematic, since it covers a multiplicity of attitudes and reactions to the Nazi occupation. Scholars distinguish between a 'Resistance as organisation, which only concerned a small minority, and a resistance as movement, a vastly larger social phenomenon. The latter covers all those who have conducted individual actions and whose solidarity was essential for the Resistance as organisation. The resistance as movement is not on the margins of the Resistance as organisation, it conditions its existence.'[9] However useful in terms of analytical categories, this distinction is lost in most public discourses (and thus memories), since this diversity of experiences is merged together within the unifying big word of 'Resistance'. Broadly speaking, memories of the Resistance went through two different phases. The first one, which followed the end of World War II, lionised resistance fighters, almost creating a myth of 'resistancialism' according to which the entire French population had been heroically fighting the Nazi occupant, save for a few collaborators.[10] This vision was popularised in novels or movies such as *Le Silence de la Mer* (published by Vercors in 1942 and turned into a movie by Jean-Pierre Melville in 1949), *L'Armée des ombres* (published by Kessel in 1943 and turned into a movie also by Jean-Pierre Melville in 1969) or *La Bataille du Rail* (directed by René Clément in 1946), but politicians also contributed to this image of the Resistance: the highlight was probably the inhumation of the resistant Jean Moulin in the Panthéon in 1964, which led the then-Minister of Culture (and celebrated author) André Malraux to give a famous speech. This memory was turned on its head following Marcel Ophuls 1969 movie *Le Chagrin et la Pitié*, which portrayed a French population mostly waiting to see the outcome of the war, preoccupied with survival and no stranger to collaboration on a large scale with the occupant. The movie was closely followed by the 1973 French translation of Robert Paxton's *Vichy France: Old Guard and New Order*, which demonstrated the extent to which the Vichy regime was eager to collaborate with Nazi Germany. As such, in the 1970s, the perception of the Resistance evolved and was almost entirely turned on its head: the notion of a resisting France was replaced in the collective memory by the notion of a shameful and primarily collaborationist French society. The dominating memory of the period is thus at odds with the historiography, which emphasises the overall antagonistic attitude (with varying degrees of engagement) of the French population towards the Nazi occupants.[11] There are thus multiple memories of the Resistance, a collective one which has evolved from heroism to collaboration, and a myriad of local (and even familial) memories which emphasise a vast diversity of actions against the Nazi forces, from small gestures to actually joining an active clandestine network.

The third facet is directly related to the second and has to do with the actual collaboration between the French state and Nazi Germany. It is well documented that, as time passed, the Vichy government gradually increased the scope and intensity of its collaborationist efforts, either by creating a paramilitary police force, the 'Milice'[12] or by encouraging young Frenchmen to join the Waffen-SS in what would become the 33. Waffen-Grenadier-Division SS 'Charlemagne'.[13] The memory of such engagements has been revered only by the far-right, for example in the 70s with authors such as Jean Mabire trying to romanticise and lionise his experience in the Charlemagne division. Former Waffen-SS members and 'Miliciens' also had an important role in structuring far-right networks in post-World War II France.[14] For example, the founders of the French far-right party 'Front National' (now 'Rassemblement National') include René Bousquet, a former Waffen-SS member, and François Brigneau, a former Milicien. While such figures were obviously on the fringe in post-World War II France, they add another layer of complexity to the memory of the war: being on the losing side and unrepentant.

Therefore, the memories of World War II in France are shaped by the multiplicity of experiences for French fighters: having served in Western Europe, Africa, Asia or the Eastern Front, supporting De Gaulle or Vichy, being part of the internal resistance or fighting alongside allies, or even collaborating with Nazi Germany. The diversity of experiences is compounded by the interpretative frame that has surrounded the 1940 military defeat.

The fall of France in 1940 is one of the most surprising events in military history: it was so unexpected that it prompted Heinz Guderian to talk about a 'miracle'.[15] Indeed, the campaign was a 'strange victory',[16] 'one that very few had foreseen in Berlin, Paris or London, or for that matter in Washington DC'.[17] France was considered a major military power in Europe, one whose foes and enemies alike would not imagine seeing defeated in a six-week long military campaign.[18] Compounding the military defeat and taking advantage of the political sideration created by the dramatic events, a group of anti-republican military officers and civil servants astutely manoeuvred to seize control of the government and abolish a Republican regime they abhorred: the Third Republic, which had survived (and allegedly been strengthened)[19] during the World War I, was quickly dismantled from the inside and replaced by the Vichy regime.[20]

Because it was so unexpected, the event called for interpretative frames, which Philippe Pétain was quick to provide since it established his regime's ideological foundations: for the French marshal turned politician, France lost because it had 'too few children, too few weapons and too few allies'. Therefore, this defeat was an opportunity to establish a 'national revolution', or a 'new order' (as Pétain called it in his 11 October 1940 speech) based on conservative principles, authoritarianism, state-sponsored antisemitism,[21] and organicism. Pétain and his followers thus explicitly interpreted the military defeat as a well-deserved judgement for an alleged moral decay of the French population and political institutions. While this interpretive frame was unsurprising from this side of the political spectrum, it was prolonged after World War II thanks to the publication of renowned historian Marc Bloch's *Strange Defeat* (published in 1946 but written in 1940).[22] Bloch, who was tortured and executed by the Gestapo in 1944, casts a wide net in his criticisms of the failures that led to the French defeat. First, he faults the military leadership for inadequate preparation and lack of professionalism in the conduct of the battles, with a special criticism for the intelligence services. Bloch is also particularly critical of the British ally, which is blamed at the strategic level for a lack of support and deference towards the Nazis in the inter-war period, but also at the operational and tactical level for cowardice (blowing up bridges to cover their retreat without concern for the remaining French troops) and an overall lack of professionalism (British soldiers being accused of being little more than bawdy plunderers when interacting with the French population). But Bloch is also extremely critical of the French society, laying the blame squarely on the political parties of the time, as well as the bourgeoisie and the workers alike: Bloch blamed an alleged generalised selfishness and mediocrity within the French society for the defeat. Coming from the opposite side of the political spectrum, Bloch thus had an interpretation of the defeat relatively similar to Pétain's: the moral shortcomings of the pre-war French society were reflected in the poor handling of the military campaign, which was a moment of reckoning.

This interpretative frame for the French defeat has been extremely popular and resilient in post-World War II France. For example, the combatants of the 1940 invasion have quickly been forgotten or caricatured in popular culture (for example in widely popular movies such as *La Vache et le Prisonnier*, *La Grande Vadrouille* or *La 7e Compagnie*). The perception of the defeat as an ordeal effectively led to a minimization of these soldiers' experience (and sometimes their heroism) in collective memory,[23] the 1940 campaign being predominantly perceived as a moral disaster. As such, the memory of the campaign had more political, rather than strategic (understood here as shaping defence planning), consequences. Although a number of historical works (especially from the 80s onwards) have directly challenged the notion of a decadent French society in the 30s (highlighting the military preparations, the diplomatic strategy and the relatively resilient economy while illustrating how contingent the German success was),[24] the idea that the 1940 defeat has to be explained more by moral than military factors has dominated (and allegedly still dominates) the memory of the event, thus shaping two mainstream attitudes in public and political discourses: on the one hand, a regular call for cohesiveness and transcendence of party divisions for France's sake (typical of Gaullism but also found in other movements to various degrees); on the other hand, a criticism of the elites likening their alleged shortcomings to those of the late Third Republic (with the grim implication of an impending disaster unless a radical change is made). In other words, France's 1940 defeat acts as a foil in post-World War II French politics, leading to the establishment of two rhetorical motives diversely mobilised by the political personal: a call for unity and a denunciation of the corrupted elites.

Therefore, the memories of World War II are diverse, and their influence on defence policy planning are obviously intertwined with contextual political and strategic factors, as well as other deep-seated perceptions. Nevertheless, one can identify three areas in which World War II had a distinguishable influence of French defence policy: the desire for strategic autonomy, the perception of allies and the empire as a source of power and strategic depth.

'Never Again!': Strategic autonomy as a security guarantee

In 1959, shortly after he returned to power, Charles De Gaulle gave an important speech at the French War College in which he declared:

> The defence of France must be French. It is a necessity that may have been forgotten in recent years. I know that. It is indispensable that it is French again. A country like France, if it is at war, it must be its war. The effort must be its effort. Should it not be the case, our country would contradict everything it ever was since its origins, its role, its self-esteem, its soul. Naturally, French defence policy could be, as appropriate, combined with those of other countries. It is in the order of things. But it is indispensable that our defence is our own; that France defends itself, for itself, in its own ways.[25]

This desire for autonomy was informed by the recent debacle of the 1956 Suez expedition, during which the United States had sided with the USSR to coerce France and the UK into leaving Egypt, but it had deeper roots in the perception of France having to fight nearly alone in 1940. This memory is evidently strong, since in 2019, a former French ambassador to the US tweeted, 'If the WWII experience had some bearing in rhe (sic.) French foreign policy, it's the loneliness of France in 1939/40 facing Germany'[26] and a popular history magazine, *Guerre et Histoire* led its June 2020 issue with a story titled 'The 1940 Defeat. Was France Betrayed?'. With this perception, since allies can be trusted only to a certain extent, France has to strive for strategic autonomy.[27] This perception has consistently informed the views of the security establishment (politicians and military alike) since the end of World War II, with disagreements erupting on the precise means and the exact perimeter of strategic autonomy, but not on the objective itself. To adopt a terminology developed by International Relations scholars: while post-World War II France has accepted various degrees of 'external balancing' (joining alliances and collective security mechanisms) to ensure its security, it has always considered that 'internal balancing' (developing sufficient military capabilities) was key to achieve strategic autonomy. This emphasis on strategic autonomy informs all aspects of France's security and defence policies,[28] but it is particularly visible in two areas: nuclear strategy and arms exports.

The French nuclear deterrent is the first, and most obvious, direct legacy of World War II and the invasion that followed. The defeat shaped the perception of a major strategic vulnerability which should not be allowed to happen again. Indeed, 'in the aftermath of World War II, "Never again!" became the slogan of those who would set France on the path towards nuclear deterrence. … France's acquisition of an independent nuclear deterrence force is therefore a direct legacy of WWII, both a reaction to one of the worst military defeats ever experienced by the country, and the manifestation of the engagement of a handful of nuclear specialists within Free France.'[29] Indeed, the sociology of the people involved in the origins of the French nuclear program is quite telling. Before World War II, France was already strongly involved in nuclear research through the work of Irène Curie, her husband Frédéric Joliot and his team at the Collège de France. After the fall of France, the French stock of heavy water was smuggled to the UK by two members of Joliot's team, with the aim of continuing research. The nuclear scientists who had joined De Gaulle created the group Atomiciens de la France Libre (Free French Nuclear Physicists), which was able to improve De Gaulle's bargaining power with Churchill and Roosevelt by demonstrating that France had a scientific, and thus strategic, role to play once the axis were defeated. In 1945, the government established the Atomic Energy Commission (CEA), which would ensure the development of a nuclear bomb from 1954 onwards. The spirit of the Resistance was quite important in shaping these developments, since Pierre Guillaumat, who headed the CEA between 1951 and 1958, capitalised on his experience acquired as a member of the Bureau Central de Renseignement et d'Action (BCRA), Free France's secret service. Crucially, Guillaumat appointed Pierre Buchalet, the first director of military applications at the CEA, specifically because he had been engaged in the Resistance.

Beyond the specific trajectories of the personalities involved in the French nuclear program, one cannot but notice the intimate relationship between nuclear weapons as a guarantor of autonomy and the specific set-up of the institutions of the French Republic, centred around the president. In a 1964 speech, then-Prime Minister Pompidou argued that De Gaulle had retained a key lesson from 1940: 'a country is in danger of disappearing if its institutions are not capable of withstanding the onslaught of arms, if they are not incarnate in a Chief of State who carries for the entire nation the burden and responsibility, unequivocally and undividedly, of the destiny of the country in the hours of decision.'[30] Of course, one can see how De Gaulle established a political regime which fitted his own conceptions of power, and the lessons he learned from World War II. From this perspective, the president is logically the uncontested master of nuclear deterrence, the cornerstone of the system. The president approves equipment projects and strike plans, and he decides on the alert levels and on eventual strikes: 'the presidential function is made sacred by the capacity to push the "red button". The entire organisation of the State is determined by this exclusive function. The Bomb imposes respect towards he who is his master. Deterrence is at the very heart of the French political regime.'[31] Indeed, France is the only nuclear democratic country in which the commander of the armed forces is also a head of state elected through a direct universal suffrage: the latter role being devoted to the queen in the UK and the US president being elected through an indirect suffrage. The relationship between the political regime, the strategic posture and the institutional settings thus establishes the president as the cornerstone of French defence policy. The development of French nuclear doctrine is thus an obvious result of the 1940 trauma, which was overcome through the co-development of a prestige weapon and of the political regime suited to wield it, centred around the key figure of De Gaulle, the unlikely French hero of World War II. Therefore, nuclear deterrence in France has become a quasi-theology (with its taboos and high priests), and has become so intertwined with the nature of the political regime that 'thinking through the strategic implications of a technological innovation has often meant supporting or questioning the very foundation of the Fifth Republic, the distribution of power within it, the creed of French independence and sovereignty, raising or laying to rest the spectres of the less glorious sides of France's past.'[32]

Arms exports are another example of the strive for strategic autonomy, particularly under the 5th Republic. As Lucie Béraud-Sudreau explains:

The rationale is as follows: for France to be able to act independently in the defence and foreign-policy domains, which means not having to depend on other states when it wishes to use force, it requires its own weapons-manufacturing capacity. However, the French defence industry cannot survive on domestic orders alone: it also needs to export. Arms exports are therefore both an expression and a vital component of France's sovereignty. As the defence minister, Florence Parly, put it in 2018, 'arms exports are the business model of our sovereignty'.[33]

In order to support this vision, France has built a strong administrative apparatus designed to support and facilitate arms exports, with few oversight mechanisms. Of course, this ambition comes with in-built contradictions, namely the fact that in the post-Cold War international arms market, which is buyer-oriented, French arms exports made in the name of strategic autonomy create political dependencies to other actors, which themselves reduce strategic autonomy …. However, arms exports policies are another illustration of the desire for strategic autonomy which can be traced back to the experience of defeat in 1940.

Relationships with key allies

The desire for strategic autonomy clearly informs relationships with key allies. Since a major lesson derived from World War II is that France can work with allies but, ultimately, has to guarantee its own security, alliances are never to be entirely trusted. This attitude defined France's relationship with its key alliance in the post-World War II era: NATO. As was often the case, the main terms of the debate were set by De Gaulle when he came back to power in 1958, although it must be noted that politicians of the Fourth Republic held grudges towards the way NATO was evolving which were quite similar to De Gaulle's, a sign of the shared underlying attitude towards the alliance among the French elites.[34] De Gaulle conducted a sort of psychological assessment of alliance relations, which he feared could become seductive, but dangerous, traps: to him 'the habit of dependence grows bit by bit: if a nation first becomes accustomed to relying on another to fulfil some of its needs, it risks being trapped and becoming incapable of freeing itself, especially since dependence on allied and friendly powers is rarely irksome enough to precipitate form resistance.'[35] This assessment is strikingly similar to Marc Bloch's diagnosis, discussed above, of a decadence of the French political body before World War II. Bloch (and Vichy) emphasised mediocrity and egoism while De Gaulle feared a dependence-induced moral anaesthesia, but the mechanism is the same: moral qualities are allegedly indispensable to the French nation's survival as a political entity. Clearly, the fear of complacency induced by alliance relations echoes the alleged moral decay which was perceived as having led to the 1940 disaster, thus shaping Paris's preference for flexible alliance relations, including within NATO.

The most obvious political outcome of the preference for flexible alliance relations is De Gaulle's 1966 withdrawal from the NATO military structure that followed his failure to establish a Franco-Americano-British triumvirate to lead the alliance. The rationale for the decision was a conceptual distinction between NATO as an organization and the alliance as a political commitment: for De Gaulle, NATO was a tool serving a broader political purpose: there was no need to be committed to a tool, which could be discarded when obsolete. This distinction between the alliance as a political concept and NATO as an organisation has since been accepted by generations of French security policymakers and analysts, although it usually baffles the allies. Already in the 60s, 'British and American officials complained that De Gaulle did not understand that the alliance and the organization had become inseparable. They viewed this distinction as entirely artificial',[36] a sentiment that many NATO allies would still share today. This explains a number of misunderstandings within NATO, since French policymakers are not particularly attached to the structure itself and instead prefer focusing on political relationships within the transatlantic alliance, while for many other countries the sound functioning of the organisation is in itself an indicator of the quality of the political alliance. They thus interpret France's lack of interest in the organisation or support for alternative security arrangements (such as the European Union) as a hostile attitude towards the alliance, while France has difficulties understanding the importance other countries attach to the structure. A 2019 interview by President Macron to *The Economist* in which he argued that NATO was 'brain dead'[37] is typical of this attitude: while the French president was actually complaining about political troubles in the Atlantic alliance, it was perceived as a direct attack against an organisation that was doing relatively well, if health indicators are defined in terms of longevity, numbers of activities or volumes of red tape.

Related to this fear of moral decline through alliance dependency is a tendency to 'equate power status with an ally's "nuisance value", and (...) regard "loyal allies" with a condescension bordering on contempt'.[38] This attitude is entirely related to French policymakers' quest for international status, defined as strategic autonomy (as discussed above) and is already visible in De Gaulle's retort to Anthony Eden, who was complaining that France was more difficult to handle than other allies: 'I don't doubt it: France is a great power'. This fear of being 'normalised', of losing a specific voice (and the perceived associated great power status) within the framework of the alliance informed France's relationship with NATO throughout the Cold War and after. In recent years, traces of such concerns can be found in former Minister of Foreign Affairs Hubert Védrine's line that France is a 'friend, ally, but not aligned'[39] within NATO, Jacques Chirac's dismissive comment towards Eastern European countries which supported the United States in the run-up to the 2003 Iraq War[40] or the obsession with which French politicians regularly emphasise that France is an 'independent' power. Of course, the French fear of losing international status because of an alliance regularly triggers concerns about the seriousness of the French commitment among the allies: in a classical dynamic of alliance politics, the French fear of entrapment could lead to fears of abandonment.[41]

Beyond the relationship with NATO, the memories of World War II also shaped Paris' attitude towards its major allies: the United States, the United Kingdom and the Federal Republic of Germany. Of course, World War II is not the only (or not even the most important) event influencing how those countries are perceived by French elites, since such perceptions must be put into the context of centuries of violent and complex interactions. Yet, some memories of the war have had an influence on French defence policy since 1945.

The relationship with the United States is always subject to complex feelings in France, where enthusiasm with the vitality of the US and support for another Republic coexist with a jealousy of the US power and role in the world, and contempt for what is sometimes perceived as an inferior culture.[42] When it comes to World War II, two specific experiences have been added to the repertoire of memories shaping France's perception of the United States: the US attempt to place France under the Allied Military Government for Occupied Territories (AMGOT) system in 1944, and the notion that US bomber planes were far less careful than the British ones in protecting civilian populations during the Normandy campaign (which led to the loss of about 60,000 French civilians).[43] The AMGOT project was bitterly fought by De Gaulle, but contributed to the post-World War II French tendency to 'see the US as successor to the Holy Roman Emperors with their unwelcome interference in French domestic affairs (…) NATO was called the "Holy Atlantic Empire", where the American "Emperor" ruled over his vassals',[44] thus contributing to making France a 'reluctant Atlanticist'.[45] The bombing contributed to the perception of the US as unreliable allies (since who would kill 60,000 civilians of a notionally allied country?), but has also been integrated in a broader criticism of the US way of war, which is criticised as over-technological, brutal and largely ineffective.[46] At the same time, Operation *Overlord* is regularly celebrated and framed as part of a France being the US's 'oldest ally', thus justifying the maintenance of the alliance. Those divergent narratives do not necessarily neatly espouse partisan lines, demonstrating the complex love–hate relationship France entertains with the US.

World War II also contributed to shaping the French perception of the United Kingdom. Here again, contradictory memories and perceptions emerged, due to the multiplicity of French fighting experiences during the conflict. An important, quasi-traumatic moment was the British destruction of the French fleet in Mers-El-Kebir in July 1940 (*before* Pétain was granted full powers by the National Assembly), which led to the death of 1,295 French sailors.[47] Winston Churchill decided to attack the French fleet since he did not trust that it would remain neutral (as was mentioned in the armistice terms between France and Germany) and could constitute a potent military force blocking the British access to the

Mediterranean Sea. He tasked Admiral Sommerville to ask the French fleet to defect and join the British forces (or sink the fleet), which would have violated the terms of the armistice with unknown consequences for the French population under Nazi rule and while the French government was in flux. After Admiral Gensoul declined to comply, the British forces attacked. The event was traumatic for many French decision-makers, because the two countries were still nominally allied at the time: the event thus easily fitted into the long-held characterization of the UK as a 'perfidious Albion', compounding the already-held beliefs that the UK had been the weak diplomatic link in the pre-war years and that it was, at best, of limited military value during the 1940 campaign. At the same time, London was home of the Free French, and the French troops that served alongside the British during World War II usually developed strong relationships, sometimes even importing British traditions into the French armed forces. For example, the French Navy commandos' beret is modelled on the Royal Marines Commandos': green and worn with the unit insigne on the left (all the other units in the French armed forces wear their beret with the insigne on the right), marking the filiation with the French units that were part of the British Special Service Brigade during World War II. Similarly, the 1st Régiment Parachutiste d'Infanterie de Marine (1e RPIMA) adopted the motto 'Qui Ose Gagne', a direct translation of the British SAS' 'Who Dares Wins', since the roots of the regiments were found in a French combat company originally created in 1940 in the UK as part of the SAS. Here again, a multiplicity of different memories (themselves interwoven in centuries of rocky Franco-British relations) shaped the post-war French defence policy and Paris's relationship with London. In a nutshell, this relationship can be summarised as fruitful operational cooperation stifled by grand strategic disagreements.

Military-to-military contacts are usually positive: the two countries consider themselves as the last remaining great powers in Europe and, beyond the obligatory banter, their militaries share an 'can-do' culture and vast operational experience leading to mutual respect. But France and the UK usually differ in their grand strategic preferences, notably when it comes to the relationship with the US and the future of the European Union. This pattern is largely observable in the post-World War II era, from the 1956 Suez operation which saw successful military cooperation but widely different strategic lessons learned from the two countries (London vowing never to antagonise the US again, Paris making sure its strategic autonomy would not be compromised again) to the 2010 Lancaster House treaties which drastically improved operational contacts but have not led to any significant political rapprochement. When frustrated by the lack of political progress with London, French policymakers are usually quick to revert back to the memories of World War II as an explicative framework, and notably Churchill's famously tumultuous relationship with De Gaulle: the conviction that, in the end, the UK could never be fully trusted and would ultimately always defect in favour of the

US but are worthy allies on the battlefield has shaped French defence policy and has direct roots in the memories of World War II.

Finally, memories of the conflict also shaped the perceptions of another key French ally: the Federal Republic of Germany. Georges-Henri Soutou argues that a key tenet of the French foreign policy after World War II was the establishment of a 'double security': security against the USSR through the establishment of a Western European community (including the FRG), and security against a potentially revanchist Germany through the continuous partition between the FRG and the GDR.[48] The fear of a potentially revanchist Germany informed major defence policy decisions in France, including a 'tethering'[49] policy of rapprochement initiated by the 1963 'Elysee Treaty' and President Mitterrand's initial reluctance towards the reunification after the fall of the Berlin wall.[50]

The Empire

Finally, the memories of World War II played an important role in defining France's colonial and post-colonial policies. French policymakers drew an important conclusion from World War II: France had owed its survival to the possession of its colonial empire. Colonies were the place where Gaullist troops challenged and eventually overcame the rule of the Vichy regime, they served as a large supplier of troops in the French First Army commanded by De Lattre de Tassigny[51] and were the reason why despite its loss against Germany, France was still considered an important power after World War II. This belief that the Empire had been the key to France's survival against the Axis powers informed the initial reaction by French policymakers to the first claims of decolonisation that emerged immediately after the end of World War II on the Western Front. Encouraged by the policy of 'mandates' developed by the League of Nations in the inter-war period,[52] the Lebanese and Syrian populations claimed a total independence from France, and May 1945 was a succession of riots, protests and even terrorist attacks in the area. Paris's initial reaction was to violently repress the manifestations, leading to the bombing of Damascus (27–30 May 1945) by the French artillery and air force. The same logic informed the massacre committed by French troops in the Algerian city of Setif in May 1945: troubles in the Empire could not be tolerated while France was only beginning the reconstruction process.[53] The beginning of the Indochina conflict followed a similar pattern. In March 1946, France recognised the Democratic Republic of Vietnam as a member-state of the French Union, but the word 'independence' was never mentioned. While the commander of the French expeditionary force, Marshal Leclerc, was favourable to an accommodation policy leading to an independence,[54] this was opposed by the French President of Council and later Minister of Foreign Affairs Georges Bidault and the French High Commissioner Thierry d'Argenlieu.[55] The war lasted from 1946 to 1954 and, despite the French attempt to create an artificial Vietnamese state led by Bao-Daï, the Viet-Minh troops successfully waged guerrilla warfare (with the support from communist China from 1949 onwards), which culminated in the battle of Dien Bien Phu in 1954, during which the French troops were besieged, and ultimately defeated. This defeat paved the way for the settlement of the conflict, as France recognised a partition of Vietnam and withdrew its troops from the region.

At the same time that France was embroiled in Vietnam, troubles started to emerge in Tunisia and Morocco. Here again, the initial French reaction was to try to violently suppress the demonstrations and the attacks that began to emerge in 1948. For five years, the French government adopted a repressive approach, in particular in Tunisia from 1952 onwards when the new French President Jean de Hautecloque willingly covered the brutalities and exactions committed by the police. However, the negotiations about Indochina created a window of opportunity for the French government, led by Pierre Mendès-France, to also try to solve the issues of Tunisia and Morocco, and both states become independent in 1956. On top of these issues, the Algerian war began in 1954 with the creation of the Front de Libération National (FLN) which demanded the independence for Algeria and the 'Toussaint Rouge:' a coordinated wave of terrorist attacks on 1 November 1954. The reaction of the French government was deeply hostile, and a cycle of violence was triggered between the French troops and the FLN, which caught the moderate Algerians between two extremist positions: full integration or full independence, while the majority of the population would have preferred a gradual transfer of sovereignty starting with equal voting rights. On top of the war between France and the FLN, an Algerian civil war took place, which deeply divided the country.[56] The battle of Algiers,[57] and the use of regular use of torture by the French forces[58] largely contributed to the brutalization of the conflict. Here again, preserving the Empire as a way to maintain France's great power status informed policymakers' views of the conflict and their inclination to use force. In short, 'by engaging into the wars of decolonization, French policymakers were trying to preserve the Empire, which had been identified as the indispensable asset that had allowed France's survival after the German invasion. Losing the Empire would have been losing its status.'[59] Even though the French colonial Empire was largely dismantled after 1962, practices of security cooperation were established with the former colonies, reflecting a deeply held belief (at least partly derived from the memory of World War II) that such relations are a source of power for France.

Conclusion

As discussed above, the memories of World War II shaped French defence policy in at least three major ways after 1945: it drove the desire to maintain strategic autonomy at all costs, created an ambiguous relationship with key allies and established the Empire (and later post-colonial states) as a source of power.

Arguably, the memories of the conflict still drive French defence policy in major ways in 2021: De Gaulle is more lionised than ever, the vocabulary of 'resistance' saturates public discourses, etc. It remains to be seen whether these memories end up creating a form of rhetorical entrapment that could make French defence policy unfit for the strategic challenges of the 21st century: for a declining power, not everything needs to be about 'grandeur' and 'resistance' is a word that should be used with care. In any case, it is safe to say that the future of French security and defence policy lies in its past, or more precisely, how its past lives on in memories.

Notes

1 Charles de Gaulle, *Mémoires de Guerre. Tome 1. L'Appel, 1940–1942* (Paris: Plon, 1954), 191.

2 Beatrice Heuser, 'Historical Lessons and Discourse on Defence in France and Germany, 1945–90', *Rethinking History*, Vol. 2, No. 2 (1998): 199–237; Mathias Delori, 'Le Poids de la Mémoire sur la Politique Étrangère', *Politique Européenne*, Vol. 34 (2011): 231–241.

3 Eric Sangar, 'L'Impact de la Fragmentation des Mémoires Collectives Nationales sur la Politique Etrangère: le Cas de la France', *Études Internationales*, Vol. 50, No. 1 (2019): 39–68.

4 Lawrence Freedman, 'The Possibilities and Limits of Strategic Narratives', in Beatrice de Graaf, George Dimitriu and Jens Ringsmose (eds), *Strategic Narratives, Public Opinion and War: Winning Domestic Support for the Afghan War* (New York: Routledge, 2015), 17–36; Olivier Schmitt, 'When are Strategic Narratives Effective? The Shaping of Political Discourse through the Interaction between Political Myths and Strategic Narratives', *Contemporary Security Policy*, Vol. 39, No. 4 (2018): 487–511.

5 Robert Jervis, *Perceptions and Misperception in International Politics* (Princeton: Princeton University Press, 1976); Yuen Foong Khong, *Analogies at War* (Princeton: Princeton University Press, 1992); Pierre Grosser, *Traiter avec le Diable?* (Paris: Odile Jacob, 2013).

6 Rémy Cazals et André Loez, *14-18. Vivre et Mourir dans les Tranchées* (Paris: Tallandier, 2012).

7 Olivier Wieviorka, *La Mémoire Désunie. Le Souvenir Politique des Années Sombres, de la Libération à nos Jours* (Paris: Seuil, 2010).

8 Olivier Wieviorka, *Histoire de la Résistance. 1940–1945* (Paris: Perrin, 2013).

9 François Marcot, 'Pour une sociologie de la Résistance: intentionnalité et fonctionnalité', in Antoine Prost (ed), *La Résistance, une Histoire Sociale* (Paris: Éditions de l'Atelier, 1997), 23.

10 Henry Rousso, *Le Syndrome de Vichy, de 1944 à nos jours* (Paris: Seuil, 1990).

11 Pierre Laborie, *Le Chagrin et le Venin. La France sous l'Occupation, Mémoire et Idées Reçues* (Paris: Bayart, 2011).

12 Michèle Cointet, *La Milice Française* (Paris: Fayard, 2013).

13 Pierre Giolitto, *Volontaires Français sous l'Uniforme Allemand* (Paris: Perrin, 1999).

14 Nicolas Lebourg, *Les Nazis ont-ils Survécu?* (Paris: Seuil, 2019).

15 Heinz Guderian, *Panzer Leader* (London: Michael Joseph, 1952).

16 Ernest R. May, *Strange Victory. Hitler's Conquest of France* (New York: Hill and Wang, 2000).

17 Martin S. Alexander, 'French Grand Strategy and Defence Preparations', in John Ferris and Evan Mawdsley (eds), *The Cambridge History of the Second World War. Volume 1: Fighting the War* (Cambridge: Cambridge University Press, 2015), 105.

18 Lloyd Clark, *Blitzkrieg. Myth, Reality and Hitler's Lightning War. France 1940* (London: Atlantic Books, 2016).

19 Jean-Michel Guieu, *Gagner la Paix, 1914–1929* (Paris: Seuil, 2016).

20 Jean-Pierre Azéma and Olivier Wieviorka, *Vichy, 1940–1944* (Paris: Perrin, 2000).

21 Laurent Joly, *L'État contre les Juifs. Vichy, les Nazis et la Persécution Antisémite* (Paris: Grasset, 2018).

22 Marc Bloch, *L'Étrange Défaite* (Paris: Franc-Tireur, 1946).

23 Rémi Dalisson, *Les Soldats de 1940. Une Génération Sacrifiée* (Paris: CNRS Éditions, 2020).

24 Robert Frank, *Le Prix du Réarmement Français (1935–1939)* (Paris: Publications de la Sorbonne, 1978); Robert A. Doughty, *The Seeds of Disaster: French Military Doctrine 1919–1939* (Hamden: Archon Books, 1985); Julian Jackson, *Defending Democracy: The Popular Front in France, 1934–38* (Cambridge: Cambridge University Press, 1988); Eugania C. Kiesling, *Arming Against Hitler: France and the Limits of Military Planning* (Lawrence: Kansas University Press, 1996); Peter Jackson, *France and the Nazi Menace: Intelligence and Policy Making 1933–1939* (Oxford: Oxford University Press, 2000); Maurice Vaïsse (ed), *Mai-Juin 1940: Défaite Française, Victoire Allemande sous l'Oeil des Historiens Étrangers* (Paris: Autrement, 2000); Karl-Heinz Frieser, *The Blitzkrieg Legend: the 1940 Campaign in the West* (Annapolis: Naval Institute Press, 2005); Philip Nord, *France 1940: Defending the Republic* (New Haven: Yale University Press, 2015); Simon Catros, *La Guerre Inéluctable. Les Chefs Militaires Français et la Politique Étrangère, 1935–1939* (Rennes: Presses Universitaires de Rennes, 2020).

25 Charles De Gaulle, 'Allocution du 3 Novembre 1959, École Militaire', quoted in Dominique David (ed), *La Politique de Défense de la France* (Paris: FEDN, 1989), 72.

26 Gérard Araud, 1 June 2019, https://twitter.com/GerardAraud/status/1134901498654134274?s=20

27 Beatrice Heuser, 'Dunkirk, Diên Biên Phu, Suez or Why France Does Not Trust Allies and Has Learnt to Love the Bomb', in Cyrille Buffet and Beatrice Heuser (eds), *Haunted by History: Myths in International Relations* (Providence and Oxford: Berghahn Books, 1998), 157–174.

28 Bastien Irondelle and Olivier Schmitt, 'France' in Heiko Biehl, Bastian Giegerich and Alexandra Jonas (eds), *Strategic Cultures in Europe* (Munich: Springer VS, 2013), 125–137; Alice Pannier and Olivier Schmitt, *French Defence Policy since the End of the Cold War* (Abingdon: Routledge, 2021).

29 Céline Jurgensen and Dominique Mongin, 'Introduction', in Céline Jurgensen and Dominique Mongin (eds), *France and Nuclear Deterrence. A Spirit of Resistance* (Paris: Fondation pour la Recherche Stratégique, 2020), 11–12.

30 Kosta Christitch, 'M. Pompidou définit les conditions d'une défense nationale valable', *Le Monde*, 29 September 1964.

31 Jean Guisnel and Bruno Tertrais, *Le Président et la Bombe* (Paris: Odile Jacob, 2016), 162.

32 Beatrice Heuser, *Nuclear Mentalities? Strategies and Beliefs in Britain, France and the FRG* (Basingstoke: Palgrave, 1998), 143.

33 Lucie Béraud-Sudreau, *French Arms Exports. The Business of Sovereignty* (London: IISS, 2020), 11.

34 Jenny Raflik-Grenouilleau, *La IVe République et l'Alliance Atlantique. Influence et Dépendance (1945–1958)* (Rennes: Presses Universitaires de Rennes, 2013).

35 Stanley Hoffmann, 'De Gaulle, Europe and the Atlantic Alliance', *International Organization*, Vol. 18, No. 1 (1964): 2.

36 Timothy Andrew Sayle, *Enduring Alliance. A History of NATO and the Postwar Global Order* (Ithaca: Cornell University Press, 2019), 74.

37 'Emmanuel Macron in His Own Words', *The Economist*, 7 November 2019.

38 Olav Riste, 'De Gaulle, Alliances, and Minor Powers', *IFS Info*, No. 4 (1991): 7.

39 Anon., 'Amie et Alliée mais pas Alignée, la France veut Émanciper l'Europe de l'Hégémonie Américaine', *L'Orient Le Jour*, 28 August 1998.

40 Jean Quatremer et Nathalie Dubois, 'Jacques Chirac Jette un Froid à l'Est', *Libération*, 19 February 2003.

41 Glenn H. Snyder, *Alliance Politics* (Ithaca: Cornell University Press, 1997).

42 Philippe Roger, *L'Ennemi Américain. Généalogie de l'Antiaméricanisme Français* (Paris: Seuil, 2002).

43 Stephen Alan Bourque, *Beyond the Beach. The Allied War Against France* (Annapolis: Naval Institute Press, 2018).

44 Heuser, *Nuclear Mentalities*, 117.

45 Olivier Schmitt, 'The Reluctant Atlanticist. France's Security and Defence Policy in a Transatlantic Context', *Journal of Strategic Studies*, Vol. 40, No. 4 (2017): 463–474.

46 Vincent Desportes, *Le Piège Américain* (Paris: Economica, 2010).

47 Hervé Couteau-Bégarie and Claude Huan, *Mers El-Kébir (1940). la Rupture Franco-Britannique* (Paris: Economica, 1994).

48 Georges-Henri Soutou, *L'Alliance Incertaine. Les Rapports Politico-Stratégiques Franco-Allemands, 1954–1996* (Paris: Fayard, 1996); Georges-Henri Soutou, *La Guerre Froide de la France, 1941–1990* (Paris: Tallandier, 2018).

49 In the literature on alliance formation and management, 'tethering alliances' designate security cooperation mechanisms between adversaries designed to alleviate and mitigate potential tensions.

50 Mary Elise Sarotte, *1989: The Struggle to Create post-Cold War Europe* (Princeton: Princeton University Press, 2015).

51 Eric Jennings, *Free French Africa in World War II* (Cambridge: Cambridge University Press, 2015).

52 Susan Pedersen, *The Guardians. The League of Nations and the Crisis of Empire* (Oxford: Oxford University Press, 2015).

53 Jean-Louis Planche, *Sétif: Chronique d'un Massacre Annoncé* (Paris: Perrin, 2010).

54 Jean-Christophe Notin, *Leclerc* (Paris: Perrin, 2005).

55 Ivan Cadeau, *La Guerre d'Indochine. De l'Indochine Française aux Adieux à Saïgon, 1940–1956* (Paris: Tallandier, 2015).

56 Benjamin Stora, *Histoire de la Guerre d'Algérie* (Paris: La Découverte, 2004).

57 Pierre Pellissier, *La Bataille d'Alger* (Paris: Perrin, 2002).

58 Raphaëlle Branche, *La Torture et l'Armée pendant la Guerre d'Algérie (1954–1962)* (Paris: Gallimard, 2001); Jean-Charles Jauffret, *Ces Officiers qui ont dit Non à la Torture: Algérie 1954–1962* (Paris: Autrement, 2005).

59 Olivier Schmitt, 'Decline in Denial: France since 1945', in Frédéric Mérand (ed), *Coping with Geopolitical Decline* (Montréal: McGill-Queen's University Press, 2020), 111.

CHAPTER 7

'Blood, Toil, Tears, and Sweat': Making Strategy in the United Kingdom in the Long Shadow of World War II

Jonathan Boff

In the spring of 2020, as Britain first battled the COVID-19 pandemic, World War II metaphors flew thicker and faster than Luftwaffe bombers. 'This is war', shouted journalists: '… it's time for the kind of Bulldog spirit personified by Winston Churchill.'[1] The death toll was compared with the Blitz.[2] Politicians told us that we were 'in the midst of a war against an invisible enemy' and that 'we were facing the biggest single challenge this country has faced since the war'.[3] The Queen, deliberately echoing Vera Lynn, told us that 'We will meet again.'[4] This was hardly the first time World War II got rolled out during a crisis. It is as central to the British public discourse as *Dad's Army* is to the BBC Television schedule. Brexit; Iraq; Kosovo; the Falklands; Suez: all invoked the spirit of the war in one way or another.[5] Rarely has Basil Fawlty's injunction not to talk about the war been more widely flouted.

Britain's search for a 'usable past' mobilises a wide range of different aspects of the memory of World War II.[6] One might summarise the popular memory of Britain's war in this way:

After a decade of failed attempts to appease a patently evil Hitler, in 1939 Britain found herself unprepared for war with Germany. The war effort remained half-hearted until Winston Churchill came to power in May 1940, but before he had a chance to do much, the army underwent a humiliating defeat in France and had to be rescued from the beaches of Dunkirk by an armada of little boats. Britain then stood alone against the Nazis in her Finest Hour. The Few brave pilots of the RAF defeated the Germans in the Battle of Britain, so the Luftwaffe retaliated with a campaign of night-time bombing against civilians. The Germans, however, had miscalculated again: instead of the population falling apart under the Blitz, it stiffened its upper lip and united in what became a People's War.

The defeats continued, however, as the army, navy and air force struggled to reverse years of neglect. Not until 1942 did the tide turn: Montgomery won a decisive victory in the desert at El Alamein. From then on, victory was a matter of when, not if. D-Day saw 'Monty' lead the way back to liberate France. Eventually, Hitler committed suicide in the ruins of Berlin and the Third Reich conceded defeat. A few months later the atomic bomb dropped on Hiroshima brought the war to a close with victory over Japan. Britain alone had fought from the first day of the war to the last, struggling through even when it had seemed all hope was lost. The war bankrupted Britain. She was forced to give up her empire and accept that her glory days of international power were over. Not all was lost, however. To celebrate victory and reward the hard-working ordinary people who had won it, Britain set up a welfare state to provide 'cradle to grave' care, including a National Health Service which remains, like her armed forces, the best in the world.

This story is, of course, a myth. Not in the sense that it is not true – although some of it is demonstrably false, much of the rest is, at best, a half-truth, and it leaves much out. (To take just three examples of its shortcomings as an account: Britain was in fact one of the strongest military powers in the world in 1939; she never stood alone; and the welfare state was at least as much the outcome of mundane and shabby political compromises as of a quest for a New Jerusalem.) But it is a myth in the sense that it is the story the British people seem to need. It captures some of what Professor Mark Connelly describes as 'the big facts' about World War II: 'that Britain won, the British people fought for the best reasons and showed great heroism, and that the war was won by a collective act of fortitude and self-sacrifice.'[7] Myths like this are the stories we tell ourselves about who we are and how we got here. It doesn't much matter how true they are.

There are two possible historical approaches to myths of this nature. One is to highlight deviations from the historical record in an attempt to correct the mistakes of the myth.[8] The other approach is to accept that popular myths of this kind are typically too deep-rooted to shift and instead to study the myth itself. That is what this essay does. Myths are, after all, rich phenomena which bridge past, present and future. They are representations of yesterday, created today, which seek to shape tomorrow. They can teach us much about how those who believe them see all three. It is striking, for instance, as Mark Connelly points out, that the myth 'is skewed towards the early years of the conflict because this suits Britain's self-perception: resolute in a crisis and at its best when alone ...'. The bombing campaign of Sir Arthur 'Bomber' Harris, especially late on in the conflict, on the other hand, is often downplayed, regarded as in some sense unsporting and un-British.[9] There are in fact three competing narratives about Britain's history during the 20th century, and World War II lies at the centre of all three. One is the story of Britain's decline from global superpower to international also-ran, attributed largely to the strength-sapping effect of two world wars. Another narrative looks at the same shift from the perspective, not of international politics, but of a national identity shifting from citizens of the world to British exceptionalism. And the third is a tale of dramatic social and economic progress at home, much of it led by state intervention and a welfare state born during wartime, which left Britons immeasurably healthier, wealthier and happier at the end of the century than their grandparents had been at the beginning.[10]

This essay focusses on one particular dimension of Britain's World War II myth: the shadow it has cast on her military and political thought, and in particular on how she conceives of, and constructs, strategy. By strategy, I mean the art or science of directing the threat (however disguised and remote) or use of force to persuade or compel someone else to do what we want.[11] It is about power, and it always involves the 'who, whom?' question that Lenin famously asked.

There can be no doubt that Britain, having leveraged the US relationship during the Cold War to outstanding effect to get what it wanted at relatively low cost, has enjoyed little success over the last couple of decades. The Chilcot Report offers just one example: it found that efforts in Iraq 'fell far short of strategic success'.[12] A rich literature has sprung up to explain why this was. The reasons proposed are many and complex, and this essay will not rehearse them all.[13] Instead, it will focus on one of the common themes running through much of this literature: the idea that underlying it all is an end, ways and means problem: some mixture of setting the wrong objectives, choosing the wrong methods, and/or allocating insufficient or inappropriate resources. In particular, this essay has been inspired by, and seeks to develop, an article by Professor Sir Hew Strachan which argued that policymakers have been unable to transcend the 'major war mindset' engendered by the two world wars and Cold War and that Britain has 'reached the point where it seems incapable of thinking about strategy for itself.'[14] This left it unable to see the conflicts of today for what they are: not existential threats to the whole world order, but nasty little regional limited wars which the United States and United Kingdom lacked the conceptual equipment to manage successfully.[15] Both Britain and America have been trying to fight the high-tech, high-tempo, modern, industrial, military-led wars they are set up to fight, rather than the low-tech, low-intensity, primarily political conflicts with which they have actually been confronted, and have been slow to adapt to the reality they have faced.

This essay suggests that the underlying problem has been less shortcomings in policy and strategy leading to a mismatch between objectives set, available resources, and how those resources were utilised, than a failure to realise that these were unwinnable wars, because they were political problems not susceptible to military solutions in the first place. British policymakers, still in the grip of the 'major war mindset', lack the mental equipment or language to identify or manage more limited conflicts.[16] The solution is not to set better ends, find smarter ways, or allocate more appropriate means: bringing British ends, ways and means into balance in the 21st century is a problem too complex – possibly, indeed, 'wicked' – to break down into separate, soluble sub-problems. We in the west need, instead, to recalibrate our ideas, and the way we talk, about war itself. We spend too much time thinking about war as a political activity and seeing strategy as a rational process. We need instead to realise that in fact the defining characteristic of war, for most people most of the time, is what economists call 'radical uncertainty', where rational calculation counts for less than human intuition and creativity. Strategy is less science than art. Recognising that fact challenges us to reconsider the way we think about strategy, and to improve the strategy-making apparatus, with better integration of civil and military decision-making, broader and deeper education of those charged with carrying it out, and a better-informed and more involved electorate.

On 13 May 1940, shortly after becoming prime minister, Winston Churchill addressed the House of Commons and encapsulated, in what later became known as his 'blood, toil, tears and sweat' speech, the 'major war mindset':

> You ask, what is our policy? I say it is to wage war by land, sea, and air. War with all our might and with all the strength God has given us, and to wage war against a monstrous tyranny never surpassed in the dark and lamentable catalogue of human crime. That is our policy.
>
> You ask, what is our aim? I can answer in one word. It is victory. Victory at all costs – Victory in spite of all terrors – Victory, however long and hard the road may be, for without victory there is no survival.

Here Churchill provided a clear statement of intent and an aim behind which the whole nation could unite. Over the next five years, politicians, military advisers, civil servants and allies together developed a machinery for formulating strategy far superior to anything the Axis ever managed. The job they faced was never easy, but it was relatively straightforward. There was a strong consensus among both elite and popular opinion that the war had to be fought. It was not a 'war of choice', for Britain and the Allies at least. The ends for which it was fought soon became unlimited and absolute: literally a war to the death. It made unlimited demands of means. Resources were mobilised on an unprecedented scale to fight it: few corners of the economy and society remained untouched. Those means were employed in unlimited ways, with a violence and ruthlessness rarely before seen. Importantly, it seemed a morally simple, black and white war, with good and evil clearly defined. Further, the fact that it was the second time in a generation that a war of this kind had been fought, and that many of the measures taken to fight in 1939–45 had first been rolled out in 1914–18, suggested that this was part of a pattern, rather than a one-off. It could not be dismissed as an outlier in the historical record. So, the scale and immediacy of the threat Britain faced made the national interest clear, aligned right with might, and simplified decision-making such that it was able to maintain sufficient consensus behind the war effort to play its part in victory. Inevitably, mistakes and setbacks occurred. Public support fluctuated at times. On the whole, however, the rhetoric of major war matched the danger and suited the public mood.

The same did not apply to the efforts of Tony Blair or David Cameron to speak in similar terms in the new century. Their attempts to mobilise support for military adventures against Saddam Hussein or Islamic terrorism failed to chime with citizens. The threats they warned of failed to resonate on the streets of Britain, which the security services mostly succeeded in keeping safe. When the voters' natural scepticism about the threat from Iraqi weapons of mass destruction proved justified, the politicians reacted by shrinking from further debate and scrutiny. They made sure to finance the wars in Iraq and Afghanistan by borrowing, rather than taxation.[17] The perception spread that the British public doubted the utility of force, full stop.[18] The possibility that it was not the use of force in general that the electorate was disagreeing with, but the particular uses to which the government was trying to put it, was not an idea which politicians seemed prepared to confront.

During World War II, in other words, the national interest appeared clear and uncontested, as it tends to in major wars, but rarely does today. This contributed to a perception that somewhere out there lies an objective national interest, waiting to be discovered. As soon as we find it and see it for what it is, we will all be able to unite around it. Those who disagree with us about it are poor benighted fools who do not understand what we initiates do, but once we show them the true light, all will be well. This is, of course, elitist claptrap, often peddled by strategy professionals keen to stake out a claim to unique expertise in a realm where common sense has real value, but its roots lie in the experience of existential conflict in the 20th century. The national interest is in fact always subjective and contested. It always was, too, even in Britain during World War II, but the popular memory forgets the disputes that occurred because they get flattened out with the passing of time. The national interest emerges only from political debate, and since that debate never ceases, circumstances are always changing, and our ways and means are fluctuating, our ends are never finally fixed. Strategy formulation is, therefore, an unending process. Consequently, we need an extremely robust process for thinking about and debating such matters.

Judging by results over the last couple of decades, however, we seem to be going about it the wrong way. The approach we have tended to take is the traditional method for dealing with large, 'wicked', problems: breaking them down into smaller, simpler, sub-problems which we hope can be resolved, delegating them to specialists, and betting that the parts will fit back together at the end. In this case that often means leaving policy to the politicians, strategy to the generals, planning to their staffs and execution to the soldiers, sailors and airmen in the front line. There are five problems with such an approach. First, formulating strategy is not, like Adam Smith's pin-making, improved by the division of labour. No one is actively trying to stop the pin-manufacturer so he is free to improve absolute efficiency as he chooses, while strategy is relative and cannot be maximised through efficiency savings alone.[19] Secondly, strategy requires an integrated view, so breaking the task up into its component processes and delegating specific tasks to specialists in each only gets in the way. Thirdly, it makes accountability difficult. In the event of failure, each group can and will blame the others. Fourthly, the institutions entrusted with the task of coordinating these sub-groups must be robust, and they must be used. The example of the National Security Council (NSC), set up in 2010 after criticisms of 'sofa government' under Tony Blair to formalise and improve the top-level coordination of security strategy, is discouraging. The very name echoes the body set up in the US in 1947 to fight the Cold War. The British version is under-resourced and ever vulnerable to prime ministerial neglect.[20] So, in early 2020, the NSC, which David Cameron and Theresa May tended to convene weekly, did not meet for four months. The role of National Security Adviser has become, not a standalone job, but just another of the Cabinet Secretary's hats.[21]

A fifth, deeper, conceptual weakness is evident, too. On Tuesday 17 March 2020, the House of Commons Defence Committee met to hear oral evidence from Lord (Peter) Ricketts, UK National Security Adviser (2010–12), and Lord ('Jock') Stirrup, Chief of the Defence Staff (2006–10) as part of its inquiry into the Integrated Security, Defence and Foreign Policy Review. The Chairman, Tobias Ellwood, MP, expressed surprise at the disjointed approach being taken by the government to the review:

> On our visit to Andover last week, we discovered that submissions are already being demanded of the top team in the Army – the land forces – by this coming Friday. You talked about the foreign policy baseline, Britain's place in the world, but they have not even been told what that is, what our approach should be to the Gulf – any themes at all – yet they are making submissions. At the same time, we pick up that the Foreign Office are presenting five separate essays on their view of the world, yet the Armed Forces have not seen this work ....[22]

There are two underlying assumptions in this, both of which were shared by Ricketts in his response. First, that strategy can be broken down in this way, into a step-by-step process where only once foreign policy objectives have been set can the armed forces start to lay out what means might be necessary and the ways in which they might use them. Secondly, that the military are subordinate technicians who should be called in only once their bosses, the politicians, have set the ends of policy. The generals, admirals and air marshals are only there to advise on ways and means. There is currently a view that 'a serious defence review must begin with an attempt to define the country's desired strategic end-state. The task of each of the three services would then be to decide upon the equipment and force structure needed to achieve the grand strategic goal, after which the task of the Treasury would be to foot the bill.'[23] We have already discussed some of the problems with that approach, but there is a more fundamental issue at work, too. These two assumptions conform to Samuel Huntington's model of 'objective military control'. This contrasts with the 'subjective military control' tradition which sees political intent and military capacity fused in the citizen-soldier, as, for example, in revolutionary France.[24] At least two of the assumptions embedded in Huntington's model, however well they may have applied in fact to 1950s America, are demonstrably false in 21st-century Britain. First, the idea that the national interest is clear and the ends of policy are uncontroversial is an example of 'major war mindset' and does not fit well with the complex multipolar international environment, shorn of the simplifying dynamics of World War II and Cold War, that we inhabit. Secondly, the assumption that ends are separate from ways and means, if it were ever true, is so no longer. The severity of the existential threats posed by Nazi Germany and the USSR justified mobilisations of resources, and methods of employing them, which the lower stakes of today do not. It is impossible in our less dangerous world to define ends without understanding what ways and means make possible, just as the ends one hopes to achieve must affect the means that are made available, and the methods employed. Ends, ways and means are intricately bound up with each other in complex reciprocal relationships and feedback loops, some of them hard to predict, and all of them open to challenge and debate.

Consequently, the common complaint about the UK's periodic defence reviews, that they have a tendency to be 'led by resources rather than requirements' instead of the other way around, rather misses the point.[25] There is no correct order for the consideration of ends, ways and means. The three cannot be disentangled but must all be considered together. The idea that politicians alone make policy, informed by objective specialist advice from the military and civil service, is unrealistic. Likewise, there is no possibility of carving out apolitical operational or tactical spaces within which the soldiers can get on with their business free from political interference, as Strachan has pointed out.[26]

Yet Ellwood and Ricketts are clearly thinking in terms of strategy as the rational application of ways and means to previously defined policy. The underlying problem is that they (and we, generally) have tended to focus on a particular and narrow understanding of war and so have formed too rational and mechanistic an approach to strategy. The mistake is to listen too hard to Clausewitz's famous insistence that war is 'an instrument of policy, which makes it subject to reason alone'.[27] This fitted the 20th century neatly, but applies less well to the past 30 years, to the present, or to the likely future.

I do not mean to suggest that the nature of war has changed, nor that Clausewitz got it wrong. War is and always will be 'an act of force to compel our enemy to do our will.'[28] War as 'an instrument of policy', however, is just a single facet of Clausewitz's multi-dimensional presentation of war, the 'paradoxical [*wunderlich*] trinity'. There are another two legs to the Clausewitzian stool: 'primordial violence, hatred and enmity, which are to be regarded as a blind natural force'; and 'the play of chance and probability within which the creative spirit is free to roam.'[29] The mix between these continually shifts, and it is the combination of all three which defines the character of any given war.[30] It is the 'play of chance' to which I suggest we need to pay more attention in the future.

The idea that war is 'the continuation of policy by other means', with its emphasis on rational action, has an obvious attraction to the politicians or civil servants involved in strategic decision-making, and, indeed, to political historians, but it is a very top-down, mandarin and rather bloodless perspective on the phenomenon.[31] That is not how most humans through history have experienced war. For the ordinary human, cowering in a cellar under enemy bombardment, for instance, the politics of war feel very distant. Distinctions between limited and major wars seem nothing more than semantics. What felt like a limited war on the TV news in Virginia, probably did not to a peasant in Vietnam, and no mother was ever consoled to learn that her child died in a 'war of choice'. Individuals caught up in a war exist in a state of what economists sometimes call 'radical uncertainty'. They have no idea, and no way of knowing, what the future holds. In this state 'there is', as Maynard Keynes put it, 'no scientific basis on which to form any calculable probability whatever. We simply do not know.'[32] This may arise because we don't know enough about the world we live in to form a judgement of probabilities; or because we cannot predict the effects of our actions. Either way, a state of radical uncertainty is very different from the world of 'risk', or 'resolvable uncertainty', where it is possible to assign probabilities to outcomes, plot the paths of a range of possible futures and draw up plans for each.[33] The 2010 and 2015 UK strategic reviews were explicitly risk-based, and at least one Chief of the Defence Staff has described the armed forces as 'the country's risk managers of last resort.'[34] Risk management, however, presupposes an ability to quantify both the probability of loss and the likely extent of any loss incurred. Neither is genuinely possible, in fact, when it comes to defence. The rhetoric of risk management is, therefore, misleading, and introduces a spurious and impossible level of certainty. It may provide fleeting reassurance, but clarity and honesty might form better foundations for policy.

Seeing war primarily as the domain of radical uncertainty, rather than of political calculation, would have three significant advantages. First, it would help us remember the effect on ordinary humans of the decisions we take, and so would reinforce the ethical foundations of our strategy. In major wars, overwhelming existential threats sometimes force even the highest-minded nation to act in ways they would not be proud of to achieve a greater good. Limited wars, on the other hand, give us the freedom not only to do the right thing, but also to do it in the right way. This is important in itself. The moral authority this generates is also vital, secondly, to maintaining support both with the domestic public and in the international community. As people all over the world become ever better connected and informed, the importance of gaining and maintaining that support only grows. There are, inevitably, occasions when strategy cannot be made in the full glare of democratic debate, but that only makes it more important that those making decisions understand and try to act in the best interests of the electors who will eventually hold them accountable for the actions they take. Thirdly, it would better reflect the complex reality that surrounds us. The idea that we are autonomous decision-makers of unbounded rationality has come under increasing challenge, not only from the evidence of cognitive psychology, but also from greater understanding of the social constraints we are all subject to. The merging of values and interests, possible now that there is no overwhelming existential threat, makes a calculus which must incorporate both inherently more complicated. Also, in place of a world divided in two by active fighting, as in 1939–45, or by the nuclear stand-off which followed, we live in a multipolar world with many more actors and a more intricate web of relationships. The recent escape from the bottle of the populist genie only increases the instability of the world order, by apparently putting the value even of long-standing alliances such as NATO up for renegotiation, and undermining many of our international organisations. In this shifting world, it is ever harder to predict the effects of our actions. In other words, not only have the problems themselves become harder, but it has also got more difficult to work out how to answer them. Imagining what we want our ideal world to look like has grown more challenging at precisely the moment that it has become much harder to work out how in practice to build it.

Changing the emphasis of how we view war, from an extension of the political calculus to a world epitomised by radical uncertainty, may sound at first like nothing more than a theoretical shift. If strategy is anything, however, it is a pragmatic art, concerned with resolving real-world problems, and the practical implications of recalibrating our understanding of war to escape the 'major war mindset' and the long shadow of World War II and equip ourselves better to create 21st-century strategy are fourfold. We will need a different approach to strategy; we will need to re-engineer the machinery which produces it; we will need to ensure that those involved in that machinery are adequately prepared to play their part; and we will need engaged citizens who are fully educated about the constraints on strategy, and the opportunities and threats it brings. Let us take these in turn.

First, we need to take a broader, more holistic approach to strategy, explicitly seeking to integrate values and interests, ends, ways and means; accepting that every choice is political; and embracing uncertainty. Strategy should be less like a road map and more like an operating manual, perhaps along the lines proposed by Professor Sir Lawrence Freedman's more fluid and adaptable model, where we are not necessarily aiming at reaching some particular set of objectives, but instead constructing a flexible framework for action capable of allowing for a wide range of contingencies.[35] Of course, we will need some idea of 'a desired end-state', but it may be unrealistic to plot a course from here to our final destination today. Strategy must be driven, not by how we want the world to be, but by a clear-sighted and cold-eyed appreciation of how it is, and of what is possible in the foreseeable future.[36] Maybe all that can be achieved for now is to keep the car on the road. That does not mean, of course, that we should just make it up as we go along, as the German General Staff of World War I sometimes seemed to believe, with ultimately disastrous results.[37]

Making strategy of this kind in a world of radical uncertainty, of course, where we possess only imperfect knowledge of the present as well as the future, is difficult. We need to accept that the application of reason has limits, particularly when the third leg of the trinity, 'primordial violence, hatred and enmity' starts to exert its influence. We have to transcend pure intellect and embrace intuition, flair, and the subconscious.[38] We need the *coup d'oeil* to grasp the essentials of a given situation quickly, and the moral courage to make and stick to decisions in the face of uncertainty.[39] That is what Churchill was putting on display in his 13 May 1940 speech, which was, for all its vehemence, pretty vague: the policy was to fight, the aim victory, and the desired end-state for now nothing more ambitious than survival. There was no talk here of making the world safe for democracy and freedom, much less of how the map of Europe might be re-drawn. In May 1940 it was far from clear to Churchill or anybody else that he or Britain would survive long enough to catch a hare, much less cook one.[40]

Ideally, according to Winston Churchill, the strategist must have 'that all-embracing view which presents the beginning and the end, the whole and each part, as one instantaneous impression retentively and untiringly held in the mind.' Churchill was talking about painting a picture as much as about fighting a battle, but the point holds.[41] When Clausewitz or Churchill thought of military genius, they had men like Napoleon in mind: warrior leaders who possessed supreme authority over policy, strategy, and execution and so were able to exercise their strategic genius in ways that might seem difficult today, especially in the democracies we are lucky enough to inhabit. We can be sure that Churchill, for one, thought individual strategic genius still possible in the 20th century, however, not least because he believed himself blessed with it. In his World War II memoirs, he presents himself as the master strategist. Where he mentions his Chief of the Imperial General Staff (1941–6), General Sir Alan Brooke, at all, it is purely as his professional adviser.

This is another World War II myth. In fact, Brooke and Churchill, perhaps because their minds worked so differently, formed a very effective partnership. The soldier, sometimes aided by other members of the Chiefs of Staff, did a good job of 'nannying' the occasionally puerile politician and reconnecting some of Churchill's loftier visions with mundane realities.[42] Perhaps it is too much these days to expect any single person to be able to carry the whole strategic picture in their mind, as Churchill suggested; but teamwork may fill the void. It is clear, however, that the double act Churchill and Brooke established during World War II set a standard for integrated command which their successors have rarely succeeded in emulating recently. The relationship was not always one of consensus and concord, as the myth would have it: rather their success was built on frequent, hard-nosed, but ultimately fruitful, debates. The same cannot be said for operations in both Iraq and Afghanistan.[43]

Especially since we cannot rely on individual genius to do it all, we need to re-engineer the machinery of strategy, better to integrate expert opinion and mastery of detail with political aspiration. This is the second implication of revising our view of war and escaping the 'major war mindset', and it concerns both the institutions we use and how we use them. Let us take these in turn. Just because we do not know what is going to happen does not mean that thinking about possible futures is without value. As Eisenhower said, 'plans are worthless, but planning is everything'. The process of regular UK defence reviews is useful, even if their outputs tend quickly to be overtaken by events or budgetary pressures. There was a time when such paperwork was superfluous. The days when tight coteries of like-minded oligarchs, such as the Pitts, Castlereagh and Palmerston, directed strategy over the port and nuts are long gone, however, at least in theory; and a more complex government machine of course demands a more institutional, less personal, approach. No doubt the current process could be improved. The debates which surround our periodic defence reviews often generate more warmth than enlightenment, but robust discussion is necessary over choices which, given the long lead times and service lives of military equipment, will constrain capabilities for decades.[44] Perhaps, if anything, we need to moderate our expectations of the likelihood of the review getting everything right.

More generally, in the councils of strategy, both the decision-makers and their advisers need to take responsibility for proper debate and shared decisions. The military men need, not only to answer the questions they are asked, but to answer the questions that should have been asked; and to ensure that they make their views clear. Equally, 'politicians should not be passive recipients of whatever expertise comes their way, but should rather engage with the experts to explore alternative options and their empirical foundations.' They need to be asking the right questions. The politicians must not hide behind the science.[45] Strategy must be 'the product of the dialogue between politicians and soldiers … its essence is the harmonisation of the two elements, not the subordination of one to the other.'[46] The late Professor Sir Michael Howard summed up the role of the strategist in what he called 'wars of intervention', by which he meant wars fought to 'preserve or overthrow foreign regimes':

> First, to determine whether military force should be used at all, and the burden of proof lies with those who advocate it. If it is judged to be absolutely necessary, it should be regarded as one 'instrument of policy' among many – including financial subvention, humanitarian aid, economic development, international diplomacy – and by no means the most important. As in 'total war', the direction of such strategy is too complex to be left to the military. However, whereas in the total war of the twentieth century all other instruments were ultimately subordinated to the military, in wars of intervention military force should serve the purposes of political, social and economic requirements.

It is necessary, therefore, for strategists to be able to pull together political, social, economic and military considerations. Such a war will be fought as much in the hearts and minds of the local population as on any battlefield, and maintaining the support of one's own domestic population will be no less crucial than progress in theatre.[47] Consequently, generals and other expert advisors need to think more like politicians, and vice versa. Both groups need to share moral responsibility for the decisions they reach together, even if it is and should always be the case that it is the politicians who are directly accountable to the public.

Clearly, the ability to think broadly yet clearly about fiendishly complicated problems requires skills of the highest level. It demands leaders with a superior tolerance for ambiguity and complexity, with high levels of empathy.[48] This introduces the third implication of changing the way we think about war: the need for those who aspire to make strategy to educate themselves properly in preparation. In Britain we elect our politicians, rather than select them, so there are limits to what we can expect of their strategic education. We shall just have to hope that they construed their Homer properly at school. We are lucky, however, to have a long tradition of able and dedicated public servants. Institutions such as the Royal College of Defence Studies have historically done a good job of preparing those destined for high command in the civil service and armed forces in a formal manner. Exercises, wargames, and other simulations have a role to play. As important are organisations which promote informal education through debate and discussion, such as RUSI or CHACR. Suggestions for reading, similar to the professional reading programme put forward by the US Chief of Naval Operations, or the RAF Chief of the Air Staff, may help.[49] In all cases, however, it is important to make sure that we are making the best use of these channels and are giving people the time and space to read and reflect independently. This is tough: high-fliers are inevitably busy people anyway, and the pressure of events and finances will always get in the way. The temptation to slip back into training drills, rather than teaching skills, will always be present.

The final implication of the new approach to war and strategy proposed in this essay concerns the population as a whole. The gap in understanding and expectations that exists between government and electorate about strategy needs to be closed. As citizens we all share responsibility for the choices made in our name. This is never more important than when lives are at risk. Strategic decisions cannot be taken by plebiscite, or even, always, by parliamentary debate, but that only makes it more important that the principles which underpin choices are better understood in the country at large. As things stand, security policy rarely forms part of the national conversation. There are a number of reasons for this: foreign policy by definition takes place overseas and out of sight; spending on defence forms a relatively small part of annual government expenditure; and press interest tends to centre on a narrow, predictable and unrepresentative range of defence stories, sometimes even once the shooting starts. To raise the profile of national security as an issue would involve considerable investment in public education and debate. Social media offers fascinating opportunities for democratising such a debate, although it brings with it, of course, unique risks, too.[50] Devising robust structures and forums, virtual and real, for considered discussion might prove difficult but open up remarkable opportunities. Alternatively, we can carry on endlessly trotting out the same old tired World War II clichés which obstruct, rather than stimulate, intelligent debate and public understanding.

This book is concerned with the long-term impacts of World War II on political and military thinking. This essay has concentrated on the British experience of one particular but important aspect of that: the formulation of strategy. It has argued that the travails of British strategy over the last couple of decades can be traced, in part, to a failure to jettison the 'major war mindset' engendered by the memory of World War II. This has left the UK less able to manage the more complicated uncertainties of the present century. Approaches, based in a misunderstood past, which seek to break the 'wicked' problems of strategy down into simpler, soluble sub-problems, cannot succeed. We need instead to re-think the entire problem and in particular to reconceptualise war itself. Perhaps if we think of war less as a domain of politics and policy susceptible to pure reason, and more as a realm of radical uncertainty which can only be navigated and unlocked by creative spirit, we will get closer to moving away from the legacy major war mindset from the last century and begin to acquire the skills we will need for success tomorrow.

Notes

All websites cited in this chapter were accessed between 19 and 29 May 2020.

1   Piers Morgan, 'Coronavirus has declared war on the world', *Daily Mail*, 11 March 2020.
2   Ryan Merrifield, 'Coronavirus death toll in London now worse than at the height of the Blitz in World War Two', *Daily Mirror*, 29 April 2020.
3   Health and Social Care Secretary Matt Hancock's statement, 2 April 2020, https://www.gov.uk/government/speeches/health-and-social-care-secretarys-statement-on-coronavirus-covid-19-2-april-2020; Prime Minister Boris Johnson statement, 27 April 2020, https://www.gov.uk/government/speeches/pm-statement-in-downing-street-27-april-2020.
4   The Queen's broadcast to the UK and Commonwealth, 5 April 2020, https://www.royal.uk/queens-broadcast-uk-and-commonwealth.
5   Amy Walker, 'Do mention the war', *The Guardian*, 4 February 2019; https://www.thetimes.co.uk/article/blair-attacks-appeasement-in-our-time-60nckrf7czb; Prime Minister Tony Blair, speech to Labour Party Conference, 28 September 1999, https://www.theguardian.com/politics/1999/sep/28/labourconference.labour14; Mark Connelly, *We Can Take It! Britain and the Memory of the Second World War* (Abingdon: Routledge, 2014 [2004]), 11–12; Prime Minister Anthony Eden, debate, House of Commons, HC 12 September 1956, Hansard Vol 558, cc 15, https://api.parliament.uk/historic-hansard/commons/1956/sep/12/suez-canal.
6   Britain, Great Britain, and the United Kingdom are used here interchangeably. None of them is, of course, strictly correct but the fact that they all apply to the United Kingdom of Great Britain and Northern Ireland is, I hope, clear. Robert G. Moeller, *War Stories: The Search for a usable Past in the Federal Republic of Germany* (Berkeley: University of California Press, 2001). I am grateful to Professor Daniel Todman for bringing this book to my attention.
7   Connelly, *We Can Take It!*, chapter 1, 6–7; see also Angus Calder, *The Myth of the Blitz* (London: Pimlico, 1992 [1991]), chapter 1; Dan Todman, *The Great War: Myth and Memory* (London: Hambledon Continuum, 2005), xi–xiii.
8   See, for example, Brian Bond, *Britain's Two World Wars against Germany: Myth, Memory and the Distortions of Hindsight* (Cambridge: Cambridge University Press, 2014).
9   Connelly, *We Can Take It!*, 14.

10 Peter Clarke, *Hope and Glory: Britain 1900–1990* (London: Allen Lane, 1996); David Edgerton, *The Rise and Fall of the British Nation: A Twentieth Century History* (London: Allen Lane, 2018).

11 For useful definitions of 'strategy' and 'policy', see Hew Strachan, *The Direction of War: Contemporary Strategy in Historical Perspective* (Cambridge: Cambridge University Press, 2013), 11–13, 26–45; Colin S. Gray, *Modern Strategy* (Oxford: Oxford University Press, 2010), 17–18; Colin S. Gray, *The Strategy Bridge: Theory for Practice* (Oxford: Oxford University Press, 2010), 18; Lawrence Freedman, *Strategy: A History* (Oxford: Oxford University Press, 2013), especially xi–xii and 609–15; and David Morgan-Owen, 'History and the Perils of Grand Strategy', *Journal of Modern History*, Vol. 92, No. 2 (June 2020): 351–85.

12 'Report of the Iraq Inquiry: Executive Summary', HC 264, 6 July 2016, paragraphs 788–98, pp. 109–10, https://assets.publishing.service.gov.uk/government/uploads/system/uploads/attachment_data/file/535407/The_Report_of_the_Iraq_Inquiry_-_Executive_Summary.pdf

13 There is useful analysis in: Jonathan Bailey, Richard Iron, Hew Strachan (eds), *British Generals in Blair's War* (Farnham: Ashgate, 2013), especially Strachan's conclusion: 327–46; Adrian L. Johnson (ed), *Wars in Peace: British Military Operations since 1991* (London: RUSI, 2014); Christopher L. Elliott, *High Command: British Military Leadership in the Iraq and Afghanistan Wars* (Oxford: Oxford University Press, 2015); Theo Farrell, *Unwinnable: Britain's War in Afghanistan, 2001–2014* (London: Bodley Head, 2017); Patrick Porter, *Blunder: Britain's War in Iraq* (Oxford: Oxford University Press, 2018). See also, for an oblique view, John Kiszely, *Anatomy of a Campaign: The British Fiasco in Norway, 1940* (Cambridge: Cambridge University Press, 2017). There are plenty of more journalistic accounts, of course, and some books so mad and bad that one can only hope that the authors at least found them cathartic to write.

14 Hew Strachan, 'Strategy and the Limitation of War' in *Direction of War*, 98–118: 108. The theme runs through many of the other essays in that collection. Others voices singing a similar tune include Peter Ricketts, 'How British Foreign Policy lost the Art of Grand Strategy', *New Statesman*, 26 February 2020, while Lawrence Freedman identified similarities in British strategy-making over Iraq and COVID-19: 'Strategy for a Pandemic: the UK and COVID-19', *Survival,* Vol. 62, No. 3 (2020): 25–76. The theme extends back at least to the House of Commons Public Administration Select Committee reports of 2010 and 2011 on 'Who does UK National Strategy?', HC 435, https://www.parliament.uk/business/committees/committees-a-z/commons-select/public-administration-select-committee/inquiries/uk-grand-strategy/, and perhaps to Paul Cornish and Andrew Dorman, 'Blair's wars and Brown's Budgets: From Strategic Defence Review to Strategic Decay in less than a Decade', *International Affairs,* Vol. 85, No. 2 (2009): 247–61.

15 Strachan, 'Strategy and the Limitation of War'. The last point was developed in Strachan, 'Strategy in Theory, Strategy in Practice', *Journal of Strategic Studies*, Vol. 42, No. 2 (2019): 171–190. See also Strachan, 'Strategy and Democracy', *Survival: Global Politics and Strategy*, Vol. 62, No. 2 (2020): 51–82; Hew Strachan with Ruth Harris, *The Use of Military Force and Public Understanding in Today's Britain,* Research Report, RAND Corporation, 2020, https://www.rand.org/pubs/research_reports/RRA213-1.html; and Hew Strachan, 'Clouds of War and Strategic Delusions', *Standpoint* (March 2020): 18–19.

16 I am grateful to the members of Phillips O'Brien's World War Lockdown virtual seminar who discussed a version of this paper on 25 June 2020 for their comments and questions, and in particular for the point about language.

17 Strachan, 'Strategy and Democracy', 53–4, 68; for context, see Rosella Capella Zielinski, *How States Pay for Wars* (Ithaca: Cornell University Press, 2016).

18 Strachan with Harris, *The Use of Military Force*, 3; Tom Coghlan, 'General fears "mawkish" view of military', *The Times*, 13 November 2010.

19   Adam Smith, 'Of the Division of Labour', Book I, chapter 1 in *An Inquiry into the Nature and Causes of the Wealth of Nations* (London: Penguin, 1999).

20   Joe Devanny and John Harris, 'The National Security Council: National Security at the Centre of Government' (London: Institute for Government, 2014), https://www.instituteforgovernment.org.uk/publications/national-security-council.

21   National Security Council, gov.uk, https://www.gov.uk/government/groups/national-security-council.

22   House of Commons Defence Committee Public Hearing, Oral evidence: The Integrated Security, Defence and Foreign Policy Review, HC 165, Tuesday 17 March 2020, Q61, https://committees.parliament.uk/download/file/?url=%2Foralevidence%2F204%2Fdocuments%2F1527&slug=oral-evidence-session-transcript-integrated-review-session-two-170320pdf.

23   Cited, but not shared, by Paul Cornish and Andrew M. Dorman, 'Complex security and strategic latency: the UK Strategic Defence and Security Review 2015', *International Affairs,* Vol. 91, No. 2 (2015): 351–70, 363–4.

24   Samuel P. Huntington, *The Soldier and the State: The Theory and Politics of Civil–Military Relations* (Cambridge, MA: Belknap Press, 1957), 3, 163–4; Strachan, 'Strategy and Democracy', 69–72.

25   Douglas Barrie, 'UK Defence Review: Repent at Leisure', *Military Balance* blog, 31 January 2020, https://www.iiss.org/blogs/military-balance/2020/01/uk-defence-review.

26   Strachan, 'Strategy and the Operational Level of War'.

27   Carl von Clausewitz, *On War* (Michael Howard and Peter Paret, eds and trans.) (Princeton: Princeton University Press, 1976), 89. The German word *Politik*, translated by Howard and Paret as 'policy', could equally well be rendered as 'politics': luckily the difference does not affect my argument here.

28   Ibid., 75.

29   Ibid., 89.

30   Hew Strachan, *Carl von Clausewitz's On War: A Biography* (London: Atlantic Books, 2007), chapter 4: Kindle edition: loc. 2097–2108; see also Christopher Bassford, 'The Primacy of Policy and the 'Trinity' in Clausewitz's Mature Thought' in Hew Strachan and Andreas Herberg-Rothe, *Clausewitz in the Twenty-First Century* (Oxford: Oxford University Press, 2007), 75–91.

31   Clausewitz, *On War*, 87.

32   John Maynard Keynes, 'The General Theory of Employment', *Quarterly Journal of Economics* (February 1937), reprinted in Donald Moggridge (ed), *The Collected Writings of John Maynard Keynes,* Vol. XIV, *The General Theory and After,* Part II, *Defence and Development* (Cambridge: Cambridge University Press, 2013 [1973]), 113–4.

33   John Kay and Mervyn King, *Radical Uncertainty: Decision-Making beyond the Numbers* (New York: W.W. Norton and Company, 2020), 12–16.

34   Andrew M. Dorman, Matthew R. H. Uttley and Benedict Wilkinson, 'The Curious Incident of Mr Cameron and the United Kingdom Defence Budget: A New Legacy?', *Political Quarterly,* Vol. 87, No. 1 (2016): 47–53; General Sir Nicholas Houghton, Annual RUSI Lecture, December 2014, https://www.public-sector.co.uk/article/0e348ac1834fb21ddac90001ceb1d1e9.

35   Freedman, *Strategy*, xi–xii.

36   Ibid., 609–11.

37   Jonathan Boff, *Haig's Enemy: Crown Prince Rupprecht and Germany's War on the Western Front* (Oxford: Oxford University Press, 2018), 207–8, 278–9.

38   Freedman, *Strategy*, 612–15.

39   Clausewitz, *On War*, 100–12.

40   David Reynolds, *In Command of History: Churchill Fighting and Writing the Second World War* (London: Allen Lane, 2004), 170–3.

41 Winston S. Churchill, *Painting as a Pastime* (London: Bloomsbury, 2014 [1932]), DOI: 10.5040/9781472580016.0006, 23, cited in Freedman, *Strategy*, 141.

42 Reynolds, *In Command of History*, 404–6, 514–9; Alex Danchev and Daniel Todman (eds), *Field Marshal Lord Alanbrooke, War Diaries: 1939–1945* (London: Phoenix Press, 2002 [2001]), xi–xxx.

43 Anthony King, 'Military Command in the last Decade', *International Affairs*, Vol. 87, No.2 (2011): 377–96.

44 A concept known as 'strategic latency': Paul Cornish and Andrew M. Dorman, 'Complex security and strategic latency: the UK Strategic Defence and Security Review 2015', *International Affairs*, Vol. 91, No. 2 (2015): 351–70.

45 Freedman, 'Strategy for a pandemic', 63.

46 Hew Strachan, 'Making Strategy Work: Civil-Military Relations in Britain and the United States' in Strachan, *The Direction of War: Contemporary Strategy in Historical Perspective* (Cambridge: Cambridge University Press, 2013), 64–97, 78.

47 Michael Howard, 'The Transformation of Strategy', *RUSI Journal*, Vol. 156, No. 4 (2011), 12–16.

48 Peter Gray, *The Leadership, Direction and Legitimacy of the RAF Bomber Offensive from Inception to 1945* (London: Continuum, 2012).

49 'The Chief of Air Staff's Reading List 2019–20', Air Media Centre, 2019, https://www.raf.mod.uk/what-we-do/centre-for-air-and-space-power-studies/documents1/cas-reading-list-2019-20/.

50 My thanks to Professor Anthony King for raising this point.

CHAPTER 8

Total War, Total Victory: World War II in American Memory and Strategy

Michael S. Neiberg[1]

'We have seen their kind before. They're the heirs of all the murderous ideologies of the 20th century. By sacrificing human life to serve their radical visions, by abandoning every value except the will to power, they follow in the path of fascism, Nazism, and totalitarianism. And they will follow that path all the way to where it ends in history's unmarked grave of discarded lies' – President George W. Bush, address to Congress, 20 September 2001[2]

'All the murderous ideologies'

It was a stirring speech, delivered just days after the stunning attacks of 9/11 from a president who had entered office under a cloud of controversy and only after a narrow ruling in his favour from the US Supreme Court. President Bush and his speechwriters went naturally enough to the anchor point that they knew the American people would most easily recognise and embrace. Just as the military forces of the United States, which included Bush's own father, had vanquished the Nazis and the Japanese, so too would they defeat this newest in the line of American foes. Moreover, the American ideals of democracy and individual liberty would surely vanquish al Qaeda's 'lies' just as American values had destroyed the lies of Hitler and Tojo. By anchoring his listeners to the familiar and available historical example of World War II, Bush could simultaneously promise success and reassure the American people that they sat on the right side of history.

The actual historical linkages between the members of al Qaeda and the Nazis, of course, were incredibly weak. Osama bin Laden's influences ran much deeper than 1930s Germany; he anchored his own thinking in the time of the Prophet, the Islamic defence against the Crusaders, and, more recently, the struggle against those he defined as post-Ottoman European colonisers like the United States and Israel. His long, detailed response to President Bush opened with two quotations from the Koran. It made no reference to World War II at all.[3]

The lack of any direct connection between bin Laden's fundamentalist vision of Islam and the 'murderous ideologies' Bush attacked in his speech did not stop neoconservatives from trying to popularise a conflated concept called 'Islamofascism'. Historically nonsensical, the idea of Islamofascism had the advantage of rhetorically linking bin Laden to Hitler and Mussolini to make it appear as though bin Laden's own ideology derived from fascism.[4] In hindsight, it should strike us as remarkable that the evils that al Qaeda had committed were insufficient on their own; Americans still felt the need to continue to link their enemies to those of World War II. Rather than rally the American people exclusively around the images of the World Trade Center and the Pentagon, Bush and his team chose to base his speech in images from six decades earlier.

A brief examination of the concept of cognitive biases helps us understand why they did so. Scholars like Daniel Kahneman, Amos Tversky and Dan Ariely argue that human behaviour is not always based in rationality. It is instead conditioned by cognitive biases and mental shortcuts called heuristics that help the brain process the vast amount of new information it receives every day.[5] In short, when we see something new and unfamiliar (especially if that something is terrifying, like a terrorist attack) we quickly scan our brains to find some experience or knowledge we already possess that looks similar to the problem at hand. By finding mental analogies the new information looks less unfamiliar to our imaginations and thus gives us a structure to both comprehend the event and begin to organise our response to it. Those responses, the scholars argue, are natural and occur instinctively.

Behavioural economists have identified numerous such cognitive biases, but two in particular are relevant to our discussion here. First, our brains tend to look for examples most widespread in the surrounding culture because they already exist in our brains. Rather than head to a library or archive for obscure case studies that might be more relevant to the data at hand, we naturally think of the analogy that comes to us most easily. In effect, our brain scans its hard drive not for the most appropriate analogies backed by data but the ones with which we are already most familiar. Scholars call this the availability bias. In an ideal world, one should over time add more data to one's analogy and correct for its limitations, but not all people do so, in part because of the second bias.

That bias is called the confirmation bias, and scholars argue that it is even more powerful than the availability bias in driving human responses. The confirmation bias explains the tendency of all humans to look for evidence and analogies that best support what they already want to believe whether it is the right mental shortcut or not. Rather than reject ill-fitting evidence that might challenge what we have already 'learned,' we tend to adapt evidence to fit our pre-existing beliefs. Cognitive bias shapes what we remember, what information we seek out, and how we interpret the information we receive.[6] Because of these biases, the World War II analogy has proven irresistible and adaptable for Americans since 1945.

As Tom Englehardt has argued, the war 'was especially effective as a builder of national consciousness because it seemed so natural, so innocent, so nearly childlike and was so little contradicted by the realities of invasion or defeat.'[7] In other words, it confirmed the bias inherent in America's own self-image. It was also distinctly available as an historical reference point. All American presidents from the 1952 election of Dwight Eisenhower to the 1992 election of Bill Clinton were World War II veterans, with the veteran experience being especially important to the political careers of John F. Kennedy and George H. W. Bush.[8] The first 12 chairmen of the Joint Chiefs of Staff were World War II veterans, the last one not retiring from his post until 1989. The office of chief of staff of the US Army was held by a World War II veteran until 1979. The last chief of naval operations with World War II service retired in 1982.

As this essay will show, World War II experience has been so fundamental to American identity at the individual and national levels that it has become the nation's most available historical analogy when it faces a new crisis of almost any kind. Americans have 'learned' facile lessons about the war that weave a narrative perfectly suited to the confirmation bias. In the American telling, the war began when innocent Americans were viciously struck by a sneak attack on what President Roosevelt famously called a 'date that will live in infamy.' The country then united and rallied to fight a war on several continents against an enemy driven by unspeakable evil. The final result was the well-photographed deck carrier moment when the enemy surrendered in full, paving the way for the implementation of a lasting peace. Moreover, this war ended an age of economic depression and ushered in a period of sustained growth perhaps unprecedented in human history, lifting millions of Americans out of poverty and into the middle class. Of course, the reality was not so clean or neat, but the point is that this version of events became the dominant, and most available, one for Americans of virtually all backgrounds. In his September 2001 speech, Bush was in effect promising a new generation that they would have their own war of good versus evil and their own opportunity to contribute to the inevitable human march toward freedom.

World War II thus became the natural analogy for the frightening world America faced after September 2001, whether it was the most appropriate one or not. In preparing his speech, George W. Bush and his speechwriters might well have drawn on other examples. They might, for example, have thought about long, drawn-out wars against non-governmental groups far away from American shores like the American war in the Philippines from 1898 to 1902. But to do so would not have confirmed what they most wanted to believe themselves and what they most wanted their audience to believe, namely that a nation powerful enough to defeat Nazi Germany and Imperial Japan in four years could surely defeat the global challenge of al Qaeda, or perhaps even terrorism itself, in even less time. They could also have used another historical example easily available to Americans, the long and frustrating failure in Vietnam, to indicate that Americans should not expect an easy road or complete success. Doing so, however, would obviously have sent exactly the wrong signal to their audience by suggesting the possibility of a long, inconclusive war, or even a defeat.

Bush and those trying to push the convoluted idea of Islamofascism used World War II analogy to put a comforting definition on the uncertain new world Americans faced after 9/11. Instead of signalling that the nation now faced a war of indeterminate length and cost against an ambiguous adversary motivated enough to fly hijacked airplanes into the Pentagon and World Trade Center, the president told his audience that America would naturally prevail, all while producing a new generation of heroes, like those on Flight 93.[9] Those heroes would join the long line of fighters in the war for the universal triumph of liberty against the lies of the likes of Hitler and bin Laden. Without having to do so expressly, the speechwriters used Bush's speech in those emotional days to leverage the cognitive biases that already existed in the minds of their audience.

It hardly matters that this version of the history of World War II hides a lot of ugly truths under layers of myths. The reality of the war was hardly as positive as Americans like to believe. To cite just a few examples, the United States fought a war for freedom with a segregated army, showed scant concern for the fate of Europe's Jews even after evidence of genocide had become irrefutable, and interned Japanese-Americans into squalid camps on unfounded charges of treason. Nor was the world in the years immediately after 1945 as uniformly stable as Americans like to remember. The feeling of triumph and the dancing in the streets would soon enough be replaced by the anxieties of the Cold War and the sense of vulnerability of the Atomic Age.

Moreover, in the years of the Cold War, the contribution of the Soviet Union to Allied victory became largely forgotten despite the enormous scale and scope of the German-Soviet War.[10] The American relationship with the Soviets from 1941 to 1945 simply added too much grey to the war of black and white that Americans preferred to remember. Thus came a vision of World War II as one that the United States won with minimal allied help, especially after Operation *Overlord* gave the United States the dominant western voice in the Grand Alliance. In his recent book on Operation *Market Garden*, historian Antony Beevor cites British failures in the operation (which stood in stark contrast to the success of the American 82nd and 101st Airborne Divisions) as the moment when the United States lost faith in its British allies. Beevor lends credence to the episode from the film *A Bridge Too Far* that American commanders were furious at their British comrades for committing the unpardonable sin of pausing their advance to brew tea. Max Hastings, another notable British historian, concurs, writing that '[Generals Matthew] Ridgway, [James] Gavin, and [Maxwell] Taylor, all of whom became important figures in the post-war US Army, never recovered the respect for the British Army that they lost while witnessing its abysmal show in Market Garden.'[11]

In the Pacific theatre, American memory of the war is even more focused on America's success without significant allied help. In American minds the United States won the war through the heroic island-hopping campaign and then the atomic bombing of Hiroshima and Nagasaki. The image of American Marines raising the stars and stripes on Iwo Jima has become the iconic image of the Pacific War, memorialised in a statue in Arlington, Virginia near the Pentagon. As a result, while the United States did rely on help from allies after 9/11, Bush felt comfortable going forward unilaterally or with a largely ambivalent 'coalition of the willing' as his global war on terror shifted in 2003 from Afghanistan to Iraq. The lesson that the United States achieves its greatest successes in wars when it fights as a part of a global coalition did not fit the cognitive biases and was thus largely forgotten.

World War II also stands out in American history in being fought with almost complete domestic support and major contributions from all sectors of the society. The exceptional service of the African American pilots in the Tuskegee Airmen, the Japanese-Americans of the 442nd Regimental Combat Team (featuring future US Senator Daniel Inouye) and the Navajo Code Talkers seemingly proved that even populations ill-treated by the United States government made their own critical contributions to victory. The war has become an enormously important event for a divided country that has almost no other modern events that serve as universal rallying points. Americans thus remember World War II as 'the good war,' fought for the right reasons against the right enemies and producing the right outcome, in this case turning the former enemies of Germany, Japan, and Italy into longstanding allies and trade partners.

The war became the founding myth of a modern America dedicated to quickly solving large international problems with the mass application of resources. Certainly, this version of the memory of the war has some basis in fact. American military force did destroy the evils of Nazism and Japanese militarism, even if it did so as part of a wider international coalition. The more Americans learned about the depths of that evil, of course, the more worthwhile the sacrifices became. American analysts even during the war noted that soldiers had a harder time understanding what they were fighting for in Europe than they did in Asia, where a sense of revenge against Pearl Harbor and Japanese treatment of American POWs motivated men to fight. After the discovery of the Nazi death camps late in the war, however, Americans understood better the larger purpose of their struggle in Europe. After seeing the Ohrduf camp, Dwight Eisenhower famously remarked, 'We are told the American soldier does not know what he is fighting for. Now, at least, we know what he is fighting against.'[12] Such a war could only inspire pride in the American people. Little wonder then that even an imperfect memory of it fits the availability and confirmation biases so well.

No substitute for victory

Nevertheless, the decision for the United States to commit to Europe and become proactive in overseas defence matters after 1945 was far from automatic. Before the cognitive biases set in, there were important American leaders, including for a time President Truman himself, who argued for limiting American commitments overseas in order to focus on domestic issues and cutting the federal budget. At the Potsdam Conference of July and August 1945, Truman repeatedly stated that the United States was willing to help Europe, but that Europeans could not expect the American people to finance their recovery as they had after World War I. Nor could they expect a permanent presence of American military forces to maintain their security. Truman hoped instead for a long-term agreement with the Soviet Union and a short-term occupation of Germany to make such a commitment unnecessary.

It seemed for a time that such a non-military model might work in the post-war years. In NSC (National Security Council) Memorandum 20/4 of November 1948, legendary American strategist George Kennan argued that Soviet territorial goals under Joseph Stalin's leadership would differ little from those of Lenin or even the Tsars. The United States, moreover, had a nuclear monopoly and budding alliances with Great Britain, France, (West) Germany and Japan that could balance Soviet desires to force any radical changes to the status quo in Eurasia. There was, therefore, little reason for the United States to spend heavily on a military challenge that the Soviets were unlikely to present while they recovered from the inhuman suffering they had experienced during the war. Kennan wanted the United States to be ready to combat the Soviets in the global war for ideas and execute a strategy of containment, using mainly non-military means like the Marshall Plan to keep Soviet expansion to a minimum.[13] Following the logic of the memorandum, the United States ended conscription, reduced or eliminated most military hardware production, and continued a demobilization from 12,000,000 men and women in uniform in 1945 to 1,400,000 in 1948.

But such an approach ran against the popular association of World War II's triumph via military means, especially as tensions with the Soviets continued to rise. Within a few months of NSC 20/4, the growing threat of the Soviet Union convinced Americans that the militarised model of World War II was the right one to follow in order to meet the Soviet challenge. As the world grew more dangerous, the United States decided that it could not risk the mainly non-military approach called for by Kennan. The Berlin blockade crisis, which began as Kennan was writing NSC 20/4, forced even Kennan to call for getting tougher with the Soviets and returning to a strategy based heavily on military instruments of national power. The rapid reconstruction of Soviet military power, the success of the communists in the Chinese Civil War, and the Truman Doctrine's pledge that America would help fight communism worldwide made the views in NSC 20/4 look antediluvian by the beginning of 1950. They also clearly signalled that the United States would not respond to the world of the 1950s the way that it had the world of the 1920s. The founding of NATO in 1949 marked a major departure for the United States, introducing collective security as a cornerstone of American defence policy and making the United States responsible for the security of its European allies.

By that point, moreover, World War II had already bequeathed at least three major 'lessons' that underpinned the new American transition in its thinking on national defence. The first one might call the Pearl Harbor lesson, the fear of a sneak attack. In this case the fear cantered on an attack by the Soviets on West Germany, Turkey, or somewhere else with their massive ground forces. American estimates concluded that such an attack could slice through Germany and France before the west could mount an effective response. The stunning Soviet detonation of an atomic bomb in 1949 and the victory of communist forces in the Chinese Civil War massively increased these fears. Collective security and nuclear deterrence served as two insurance policies against a surprise Soviet attack. Although neither offered any sure guarantee, they seemed a better approach than trying to deal with the Soviets primarily through economic or diplomatic means.

Second, American planners recalled how woefully underfunded and unprepared the American military had been in 1940, when the fall of France exposed its weaknesses. At that time, the United States had not launched any capital ships since World War I and had not increased its army's size since the early 1920s. In April 1950, the United States tried to address that problem by passing NSC 68, which argued that a future lack of spending on modernising American military forces since 1945 would provide the Soviet Union an opportunity to attack in the near future. It called for massive spending to build an army, navy, and air force so large that the Soviets would not dare to challenge the west. It did not even try to estimate how much such a program might cost, asserting that national defence had become so important that tax increases and cuts to spending elsewhere would be needed. The purpose, as historian Odd Arne Westad wrote, was 'to put the United States on war footing in a conflict that could last for a very long time.'[14]

Never again would the United States find itself in a position of being too weak militarily to defend itself or deter potential enemies. The age of parsimony on the military had ended, as had the pre-1940 belief that the United States could count on the British and the French to underwrite American security. Thereafter, the strategic calculation would have to be reversed. The United States began to build a massive standing army and navy of a kind quite unusual in its history. Its new air force would have what its architects called a 'global reach' that would give the United States a massive power projection capability. The consolidation of the armed service branches into a Department of Defense increased the shift in the American government's approach away from the soft power of diplomacy and toward the hard power of a nuclear-capable military.

The third, and perhaps most important, intellectual legacy of World War II was the association of any kind of conciliation with the discredited appeasement spirit of Munich. The rise of McCarthyism in the United States and the 'fall' of China (which the opposition Republicans blamed on Democratic foreign policy blunders) underscored the domestic political price that any politician or political party might have to pay for appearing weak. The Munich analogy informed Truman's thinking in deciding to resist the North Korean invasion of the South in June 1950, just weeks after NSC 68 provided the blueprint for building a much more powerful American military. Korea, Truman insisted, was not an isolated war, but a battleground on the global stage to resist Soviet expansion. As a result, the United States sent more soldiers to Europe than to Asia from 1950 to 1953, then built a military force through conscription so large that it even drafted Elvis Presley to fill the ranks by the end of the decade.

The start of the war in Korea seemingly confirmed all three of these World War II lessons. North Korean forces, presumably part of a global communist monolith and backed by the Soviet Union and communist China, had struck without warning against beleaguered American forces too weak to defend themselves. Just five years after the great triumph over Germany and Japan, America had too few military resources to meet this new challenge. The only rapid response capability the United States possessed was a half-strength formation of just 400 soldiers known to history as Task Force Smith. Only one in six soldiers had combat experience. The task force had limited ammunition, poor communications equipment, and just two days' worth of food. It suffered 40% casualties and quickly became a symbol of the ills that NSC 68 was written to cure.

The war in Korea was a conventional limited war that was both familiar to American strategists and frustratingly new. The three American commanders in Korea, Douglas MacArthur, Matthew Ridgway, and Mark Clark, were all heroes of World War II. As in World War II the two opposing forces were symmetrical, and the war had the familiar metric of ground gained as a proxy to measure success. General Douglas MacArthur's brilliant amphibious landing at Inchon in September 1950 came straight from the playbook of World War II amphibious operations that he had used so effectively to defeat Japanese armies in the Central Pacific.

Unlike World War II, however, the war in Korea represented something new on the strategic level. As American President Harry Truman understood it, the United States-led coalition was not only fighting the North Koreans but sending a signal to the Soviets and the Chinese that the free world would resist any Munich-style aggressions. Upon ordering American forces to Korea, Truman said, 'The attack on Korea makes it plain beyond all doubt that Communism has passed beyond the use of subversion to conquer independent nations and will now use armed invasion and war.' The lesson Truman and others learned from Nazi aggression in the 1930s taught them that any response to such aggression had to be strong and swift. As no less a World War II figure than Dwight Eisenhower said in his support of Truman, 'We'll have a dozen Koreas soon if we don't take a firm stand.'[15] The real foe, in this formulation, was not the North Koreans, but the Soviet and Chinese masterminds trying to undermine America's worldwide position via their proxies. These ideas formed the basis of the 'domino theory' that soon emerged to argue for an American intervention in Vietnam in order to contain communist expansion throughout Southeast Asia.

But a firm stand in Korea, Berlin and (later) Vietnam did not mean total war on the 1941–1945 model. Truman well understood that the war in Korea had to be prosecuted within strict limits. However important Korea was in the grand strategic picture, the United States could not return to a full wartime mobilization and it could not risk nuclear war, although at various points the administration did discuss the possibility of using atomic weapons. The new intellectual ground of limited war proved difficult to navigate, especially for World War II veterans who wanted to take the war not just to North Korea but directly to China as well. The total war mindset of 1941–1945 proved difficult to set aside.

The inability of Douglas MacArthur to recognise the tensions inherent in this new kind of war contributed to Truman's decision to fire him. After his removal, MacArthur famously told the United States Congress that 'there is no substitute for victory.' Although he noted that Korea 'created a new war and an entirely new situation, a situation not contemplated when our forces were committed against the North Korean invaders; a situation which called for new decisions in the diplomatic sphere to permit the realistic adjustment of military strategy,' he called for fewer limits, not more. His speech remained rooted in the concepts of strategy from World War II. He spoke of fighting simultaneously on multiple fronts, the danger of the enemy conducting lightning attacks, and, above all, the need to fight any war as a total war.[16] His desire to lead American soldiers across the Yalu River and into Chinese territory showed how uncomfortable he was with the new paradigm of limited war.

Cathal Nolan has recently argued that World War II was the last to end with the belief that winning battles equated to winning wars. In reality, Nolan argues, modern war from Napoleon to Nagasaki was almost always attritional; winning big battles and having brilliant generals mattered far less than a society's ability to stay in the fight and a government's ability (in both its civilian and military leadership) to devise a political and economic strategy to best apply its resources toward victory. In effect, he argues, the quest for battles of annihilation ended up annihilating even the idea of strategy itself, leaving armies with little in their intellectual toolkit but a predilection to fight large, costly and ultimately indecisive battles.[17] So it was in Korea, where even lopsided victories on the battlefield proved unable to produce the political outcome the United States sought.

MacArthur may have been an extreme case of the inability to make the adjustment from total war to limited war, although he was obviously an important one. Still, he was far from alone in being deeply influenced by the total war mentality of the 1940s and the availability and confirmation biases that World War II all too easily provided. One clear consequence of this failure was the concomitant unwillingness of the American military to return to its roots in irregular war. John Grenier, in his appropriately titled book on the subject, *The First Way of War*, argued that the United States Army's true intellectual heritage came not from fighting large battles in Europe and Asia, but from its war making on the frontier. From fighting Native American nations in New England in the colonial period through the American counterinsurgency effort in the Philippines from 1898 to 1902, the American Army spent most of its history fighting light, irregular conflicts that looked more like guerrilla warfare than the large-unit combat of the two world wars.[18]

Brian Linn agrees, noting the success of American forces in the unconventional war in the Philippines under the command of Douglas MacArthur's father, General Arthur MacArthur. Linn argues that the United States Army learned how to fight a war that combined limited violence with diplomacy to subdue a rebellion against the American presence in the Philippines.[19] Unconventional war was always dirty, but in the 19th century it could also be heroic and was, both Grenier and Linn argue, central to the fulfilment of Manifest Destiny and the creation of an American overseas empire.

But the small war mindset of Arthur MacArthur did not fit the cognitive biases Americans like his son had in their minds in the 1950s. In relying on the memory of World War II, Americans found a new and far more appealing model for war, one that leveraged the industrial overmatch and phenomenal logistical capabilities of the new American superpower. Moreover, having given the Philippines its independence in 1946 without violence, the United States, unlike France and Britain, had little incentive to think deeply about small wars in the 1950s. Instead, the military model of World War II-dominated thinking both in NATO and Korea. In large-battle war, the Americans had found an ideal type better suited to the kinds of wars they could prepare to fight than the actual wars the nation would soon find itself fighting. In Nolan's formulation, World War II and its focus on big battles produced for American audiences 'an uncritical hero literature … in a long morality play of good versus evil.'[20]

This disconnect between the wars the nation fought and the war the nation chose to idolise would have deadly consequences from Vietnam to Iraq. World War II model might have satisfied cultural, economic and political beliefs about war, but it was ill-suited to the radically different environment of America's next major war after Korea, the war in Vietnam. If Grenier and Linn are correct, then the United States would have been better served to look even further back in its history, far beyond World War II to the irregular warfare models of early centuries.[21] As Gregory Daddis and others have shown, the American generals of the Vietnam era certainly recognised that they were fighting a new kind of war in Vietnam.

Their ways of thinking, however, remained stubbornly industrial and based on the massive application of firepower. Strategic bombardment, airborne operations (this time from helicopters) and an attritional mindset as expressed in the now notorious 'body count' remained at the centre of American strategy despite the obvious fact that they were not working. Even Daddis, who has written a sympathetic assessment of World War II veteran William Westmoreland's war in Vietnam, argues that the Westmoreland generation was smart and professional enough to recognise that they were fighting a very different war in Vietnam than the one of their youth. Still, Daddis concludes that change was 'unnatural' for them, most of whom held a strong 'cultural affinity toward conventional war.'[22]

Yuen Foong Khong, in his marvellous book *Analogies at War*, found that the Munich warning played a central role in American strategic thinking. Senators in 1965 opposed to intervening in Vietnam like Wayne Morse received umbrellas (a symbol of British Prime Minister Neville Chamberlain) in the mail. American policymakers who argued for intervention frequently cited Munich as a way to argue that the United States could not yield in Vietnam or else it would face further aggression in the future. In one meeting of the NSC that year, US Ambassador to Vietnam Henry Cabot Lodge, Jr. snapped at an opponent of sending American troops to Vietnam 'Can't we see the similarity to our own indolence at Munich?'[23]

The price of freedom

The desire to move past the negative model of Vietnam and back to a more familiar one proved strong. The American AirLand Battle concept, introduced in 1976, looked to the Yom Kippur War of 1973 as its model instead of Vietnam. Betting that Vietnam was an aberration, AirLand looked to a future conventional war fought with tanks, close air support, and heavy infantry on large battlefields that resembled a modern version of World War II. One internal study on the new doctrine written in 1988 used George Patton's Third Army campaign in France and Germany in 1944 and 1945 to establish a baseline for estimating the kind of war that the AirLand doctrine envisioned fighting. It expressly warned that the United States had to relearn the lessons of operational warfare in the European theatre that it had forgotten as a result of its wasteful focus on the anomalous unconventional environment in Vietnam.[24] The AirLand doctrine played an important role in helping to develop the concepts that the American-led coalition used to evict Iraqi forces from Kuwait in 1991, although it did little to prepare the Army and Marine Corps for the counterinsurgency challenges that emerged soon afterward.

The success of American-led forces in the First Persian Gulf War led the United States to return to World War II heuristics. On the battlefield, tanks and heavy infantry dominated Iraqi forces, once again creating a war that could be measured by ground gained. Journalists covered the war as part of a tightly controlled system of embedding reporters with military units, and the short duration of the war prevented any significant anti-war movement from developing. President (and World War II veteran) George H. W. Bush proudly exclaimed 'By God, we've kicked the Vietnam syndrome once and for all.'[25] With the Persian Gulf War having supposedly cured the United States of its malignant syndrome, the way was clear to return to the more familiar and comfortable analogy of World War II, updated with new technologies for the modern age.

Not coincidentally, the importance of World War II in American culture grew exponentially in the decade between the First Persian Gulf War and the attacks of 9/11. Included in this cultural renaissance were countless examples of World War II as a moment of heroic American achievement in the face of unspeakable barbarity and evil. In 1993, the United States Holocaust Memorial opened on the National Mall and Steven Spielberg's *Schindler's List* won seven Oscar awards. It is now the sixth most highly rated movie on the popular internet site IMDB. Together the museum and the movie emphasised the American role in World War II in assuring the deliverance of Europe from the horrors of genocide.

Just five years later, Spielberg released the movie that sits on the IMDB list at #27, *Saving Private Ryan*. The two movies brought World War II to a new generation of Americans, with the first clearly identifying the barbarism of the enemy and the second showing the heroism of average Americans like Captain Miller, a former teacher whose martyrdom makes possible the subsequent life of the title character. In the same year (1998), famed journalist Tom Brokaw published *The Greatest Generation*, a book that, like *Saving Private Ryan*, underscored the heroism of the average American in such desperate times.[26] Together, the movie and the book transferred much of the celebrity of victory from leaders like Dwight Eisenhower and George Patton to the aging Americans in every community who had served in uniform or supported the war effort from the home front. Brokaw's book became a national bestseller and its title has become shorthand for the men and women of that era.

In 2000 (notably on 6 June), the National World War II Museum opened in New Orleans. Originally conceived as the D-Day Museum, it was the brainchild of New Orleans businessman Nick Mueller and Stephen Ambrose, author of a number of best-selling books that chronicled the experiences of American soldiers during the war. The museum has become a runaway success and one of the most visited American museums outside of Washington and New York City. In 2019 it welcomed almost 800,000 visitors and now occupies a multi-building campus thanks in part to the generosity of American corporate sponsors.

In the symbolic month of September 2001, the United States broke ground on the World War II Memorial on the National Mall. The sprawling, massive memorial sits just across the Reflecting Pool from the Lincoln Memorial and is visible from parts of the White House grounds themselves. It features 56 pillars, an enormous central fountain and a 'freedom wall', marked with the words 'Here We Mark the Price of Freedom'. The memorial seemed so over the top that newspaper editorials criticised it as fascist in both spirit and design.[27] (The first time I went there, a visitor said loud enough for me to overhear that it looked like what Albert Speer would have built if the Nazis had won). In the same week, the first episode of the successful mini-series *Band of Brothers*, based on Ambrose's books, aired.

The triumphal tone of the memorial was part of the point. It was always intended to stand in sharp relief to Maya Lin's now iconic subterranean black granite wall listing the American dead of the Vietnam War (1982) and the haunting Korean War Memorial with its wraith-like soldiers and their thousand-yard stare (1995). There is still no national memorial in Washington to World War I, although there are plans to refurbish the run-down Pershing Park on the opposite side of the White House from the National Mall. The redesign will include a memorial to the war if enough money can be raised.[28]

The omnipresence of World War II in American popular culture strongly suggests that it remains a critical reference point for reasons of both availability bias and confirmation bias. The former means that World War II references are everywhere, in cinemas, in bookshops, on television and as stops on summer vacations. The latter means that by relying on World War II as a model, Americans can convince themselves that they can once again win a total victory against a terrible enemy without major reliance on allies all while maintaining near total support for the war on the home front. Whether or not this vision of the war is consistent with historical reality hardly matters: these are, after all, cognitive biases.

The answer came very quickly

The influence of World War II remains in American culture, as do the cognitive biases. Analogies between World War II and the COVID-19 crisis abound despite their obvious limitations. In his remarks on the 75th anniversary of VE Day in May 2020, President Trump compared COVID-19 to the unanticipated Japanese attack on Pearl Harbor as a way of explaining his administration's slow response to this new 'invisible enemy'. He used the analogy both in an attempt to rally the American people to his side and to pass the blame for this 'surprise' outside America's own borders; in this case he blamed China for mishandling the crisis and forcing the United States to assume a war-like mobilization.[29] This way of thinking has manifest flaws, and unlike George W. Bush's use of World War II analogy in 2001, this one seems not to have gained much purchase with the American people. Yet the rhetoric proves that it remains World War II model, with its emotive pull, that becomes the first analogy for Americans facing new and troubling situations.[30]

In 2019, the United States Army introduced a new uniform that looked quite familiar, even if most Americans would have only recognised it from museums and movies. It featured dark gabardine wool coats worn over khaki trousers. As the *New York Times* observed, 'Probably not by coincidence, that's what the Army was wearing the last time the nation celebrated total victory in a major war.' As the sergeant major of the Army himself said, 'We went back and asked, when is the most prominent time when the Army's service to our nation was universally recognised, and the answer came very quickly …. That victory, that impact on the nation, is still felt today by the sons and daughters and grandsons and granddaughters of the "Greatest Generation."'[31] As George W. Bush did in September 2001, the designers of the new uniform went back to the most useful and available historical model they had, World War II.

Notes

1   The views presented in this article are those of the author and do not represent the views of the Department of Defense or any of its components. The author thanks Jonathan Boff for his helpful comments on an earlier draft.

2   'Text: President Bush Addresses the Nation', *Washington Post*, 20 September 2001, https://www.washingtonpost.com/wp-srv/nation/specials/attacked/transcripts/bushaddress_092001.html.

3   'Full Text: Bin Laden's Letter to America', *The Guardian*, 24 November 2002, https://www.theguardian.com/world/2002/nov/24/theobserver.

4   See Christopher Hitchens, 'Defending Islamo-fascism: It's a Valid Term. Here's Why', *Slate*, 22 October 2007, https://slate.com/news-and-politics/2007/10/defending-the-term-islamofascism.html.

5   A decent short summary is Ben Yagoda, 'The Cognitive Biases Tricking Your Brain', *The Atlantic*, September 2018, https://www.theatlantic.com/magazine/archive/2018/09/cognitive-bias/565775/

6   Daniel Kahneman, *Thinking Fast and Slow* (New York: Farrar, Strauss, and Giroux, 2011) and Drew Weston, *The Political Brain: The Role of Emotion in Deciding the Fate of the Nation* (New York: PublicAffairs, 2007).

7   Tom Englehardt, *The End of Victory Culture: Cold War America and the Disillusioning of a Generation* (New York: Basic Books, 1995), 5.

8   Jimmy Carter is a partial exception here. He was a midshipman at the US Naval Academy during the war.

9   Four al Qaeda hijackers took control of United Airlines Flight 93 with the intent of crashing it into the US Capitol building. Passengers took action themselves to subdue the hijackers, but the plane crashed in Pennsylvania. Today a large memorial marks the spot, and the phrase 'Let's Roll', spoken by one of the passengers to inspire others, has become shorthand for the heroism of that day.

10 One recent survey found more than half of Americans believe that the United States made the single greatest contribution to victory in Europe; the next closest country was the Soviet Union with just 15%. See Lucy Fisher, 'We Led the War Effort, Say British – Others Disagree', *The Times*, 8 May 2020, https://www.thetimes.co.uk/edition/news/who-won-the-war-nations-divided-over-which-allied-power-played-the-biggest-role-8wpcr0wwr.

11 See Max Hastings, 'Botch on the Rhine', *New York Review of Books*, 28 May 2020, 38; Antony Beevor, *The Battle of Arnhem: The Deadliest Airborne Operation of World War II* (New York: Viking, 2020).

12 Connie Gentry, 'What We Fought Against: Ohrdruf', National World War II Museum blog, 4 April 2020, https://www.nationalww2museum.org/war/articles/ohrdruf-concentration-camp.

13 John Lewis Gaddis, *George Kennan: An American Life* (New York: Penguin, 2011), 326–327.

14 Odd Arne Westad, *The Cold War: A World History* (New York: Basic Books, 2017), 104.

15 David McCullough, *Truman* (New York: Simon and Schuster, 1992), 780–781.

16 James M. Lindsay, 'TWE Remembers: General Douglas MacArthur's Speech to Congress', *Council on Foreign Relations*, 19 April 2012, https://www.cfr.org/blog/twe-remembers-general-douglas-macarthurs-speech-congress.

17 Cathal J. Nolan, *The Allure of Battle: A History of How Wars Have Been Won and Lost* (New York: Oxford University Press, 2019).

18 John Grenier, *The First Way of War* (New York: Cambridge University Press, 2005).

19 Brian M. Linn, *The U.S. Army and Counterinsurgency in the Philippine War, 1899–1902* (Chapel Hill: University of North Carolina Press, 1989).

20 Nolan, *The Allure of Battle*, 5.

21 President Kennedy did create the Green Berets, but that small change did not fundamentally change the mindset of the American military, simultaneously worried as it was about the Cold War threat the Soviets posed.

22 Gregory A. Daddis, *Westmoreland's War: Reassessing American Strategy in Vietnam* (New York: Oxford University Press, 2014), 9.

23 Yuen Foong Khong, *Analogies at War: Korea, Munich, Dien Bien Phu and the Vietnam Decisions of 1965* (Princeton: Princeton University Press, 1992), 3, 174. The remark is fascinating when one considers that 'we' (i.e., the United States) had no representative at Munich.

24 Douglas Skinner, 'AirLand Battle Doctrine' (1988), https://apps.dtic.mil/dtic/tr/fulltext/u2/a202888.pdf.

25 William Schneider, 'The Vietnam Syndrome Mutates', *The Atlantic*, April 2006, https://www.theatlantic.com/magazine/archive/2006/04/the-vietnam-syndrome-mutates/304891/. For a critical view that argues that the United States has exaggerated the Munich analogy to justify wars of choice, see Christopher Layne, 'Why the Gulf War Was Not in the National Interest', *The Atlantic*, Vol. 268 (July 1991): 54–81.

26 Tom Brokaw, *The Greatest Generation* (New York: Random House, 1998).

27 Inga Saffron, 'Monument to Democracy, The National World War II Memorial Deserves Its Prominent Location in Washington, as a Tribute to Heroes and a Great Cause', *The Philadelphia Inquirer*, 28 May 2004, E01.

28 Most of the money for the World War II Memorial came from private donations, so this model is not unusual.

29 'Trump Says Coronavirus Worse Attack than Pearl Harbor', BBC, 7 May 2020, https://www.bbc.com/news/world-us-canada-52568405.

30 Ishaan Tharoor, 'The Shadow of World War II Hangs Over the Pandemic', *Washington Post*, 11 May 2020, https://www.washingtonpost.com/world/2020/05/11/shadow-world-war-ii-hangs-over-coronavirus-age/.

31 Dave Phillips, 'To Stand Out, the Army Picks a New Uniform With a World War II Look', *New York Times*, 5 May 2019, https://www.nytimes.com/2019/05/05/us/new-army-greens-uniform.html. The popular military-themed satire site, Duffle Blog, welcomed the new uniforms with a headline that read 'Army to bring back WWII-era uniforms in lieu of WWII-era victory', https://www.duffelblog.com/2017/10/army-pinks-and-greens.

CHAPTER 9

The Beginning of the End: The Legacy of World War II in Africa

Richard Reid

Introduction

In 1943, a young Kenyan, Waruhiu Itote, found himself in Burma fighting the Japanese. He was a soldier in the King's African Rifles, the British East African regiment, which had been deployed to the Southeast Asian theatre of operations. One day, Itote had a conversation with a British soldier who wondered what he, a Kenyan, was actually fighting for. It was clear to the Englishman why *he* was fighting: 'for England, to preserve my country, my culture …'. But the young African? Why would *he* fight for Britain, or the Empire? The conversation struck Itote forcefully. A few months later, he had another encounter, this time with an African-American GI, who wondered why Africans had accepted so uncritically the notion of white superiority and who introduced, in Itote's mind, the idea of the great racial struggle to come. These were life-changing interactions, and Waruhiu Itote would later return to Kenya to become one of the leaders of the Mau Mau uprising against the British in the early 1950s.[1]

Of course, not every African serviceman would have these kinds of experiences. Thousands would return home to be demobilised, and to transition more or less seamlessly back into civilian life with little or no interest in politics – or at least none that seemed to flow directly from wartime service.[2] But more generally World War II had a profound impact on Africa, and in a multitude of ways. The legacy of the war on the continent is complex, and there is no single narrative, whether from the perspective of imperial metropoles or from the standpoint of African societies themselves. But in broad terms the experience of the war heightened political consciousness among millions of Africans, not least because it increased awareness of the fallibility of European empires; and it shaped imperial thinking in hugely important ways, particularly in terms of political and military strategy.[3]

In operational terms, Africa was a zone of combat – or at least key regions were. If China's war started earlier than Europe's, with the Japanese invasion in

1937, Africa's war began even earlier – in 1935, with fascist Italy's invasion of Ethiopia. Mussolini's long-planned conquest of Africa's lodestar of independent sovereignty was part of a larger project to build a new Roman Empire. But for our purposes it illustrates two key themes. Firstly, swathes of Ethiopia remained outside Italian control, even after the 'formal' victory by May 1936 when Italian forces entered Addis Ababa and Haile Selassie fled into exile. While it is true that Italian success had owed much to alliances with local leaders hostile to Haile Selassie, Ethiopian resistance – the 'Black Lions' – continued throughout the period of Italian occupation, and *Il Duce* could never truly claim to be in control of the entire territory.[4] It demonstrated the limitations of European imperialism when access to firearms and robust identity were available. Indeed, even the claims of the fascists to be embarking on a civilising mission made British and French diplomats uncomfortable, so anachronistic did they seem. Secondly, Britain and France had decided early on in the 'Abyssinian crisis' – whatever their misgivings about Mussolini's vulgar language and disingenuity – that appeasement was best. Italy could have Ethiopia. This was in part because of the enduring suspicion that Haile Selassie's state was itself an unfortunate anachronism, a semi-civilised state which had somehow survived the European partition 40 years earlier.[5] But more importantly, it represented the essential anxiety behind appeasement – that another major war would be disastrous. In London, appeasement of both Germany and Italy was driven by the conviction held by imperial strategists after 1918 that war would spell the end of the British Empire, and the emergence of a new world order in which British decline was inevitable.[6] In that sense the conquest of an African state in 1935–6 tells us quite a lot about what lay ahead: the dilemmas and decisions of metropolitan imperial governments, and the nationalist movements in Africa as a result of the war itself.

The physical manifestation of the war in Africa was limited but significant. The Horn of Africa was the scene of major combat in 1940–41, when British and Allied forces – including troops from West, East and South Africa, and French and Belgian units from central and equatorial Africa – launched offensives into Italian colonial territory, including Somalia, Eritrea and Ethiopia. Fighting was particularly ferocious in Eritrea, where the battle for the town of Keren represented some of the stiffest resistance offered by Italian forces.[7] Addis Ababa was captured in April 1941 – Emperor Haile Selassie was returned to the throne, although he continued to have a somewhat tense relationship with the British occupying administration – and thereafter only pockets of resistance remained. The other major zone of combat was the narrow coastal strip in Egypt and Libya, where Axis forces – the dominant component of which was Erwin Rommel's Afrika Korps, although Libya was an Italian territory – engaged in a back-and-forth with British and Commonwealth forces between 1940 and 1942. Britain's overwhelming concern was the defence of Cairo and the Suez Canal, the vital artery to India, and only with the defeat of German forces at the battle of El Alamein in October 1942 did that immediate threat subside. Thereafter British and Australian forces pushed steadily westward, joined at the other end of the Mediterranean by US forces which landed in Morocco and Algeria during Operation *Torch* in November 1942. The arrival of the Americans – their first major combat operation in the European-North African theatre – ended the uneasy political ambiguity in French North Africa which was the outcome of the Vichy regime.[8] Together, Allied forces closed in on the remaining Axis forces in an enormous pincer movement, meeting in Tunisia in May 1943 when the last German and Italian troops withdrew. Finally, it should be noted that the Allied war effort in the Mediterranean was aided, firstly, by the support of the Sanusiyya sect in Libya who were broadly anti-Italian and, pragmatically, pro-British;[9] and by far-flung supply routes stretching across much of Sahelian and Equatorial Africa, where a number of French colonial administrators had offered their allegiance to de Gaulle's Free French movement rather than Vichy.[10] The expulsion of Axis forces spelt the end of combat operations on African soil, but not of the African contribution to the war effort. African regiments served in Europe and Asia as well as in Africa itself under British, French and Belgian colours. By 1945, some 370,000 Africans were serving in the British armed forces – many of them in Southeast Asia, as we noted at the beginning of the essay – and it was an experience which was formative for many of them.[11] It is certainly true that many veterans returned to lead peaceable lives in their home communities, remaining proud of their service for the rest of their days. But many others – including Waruhiu Itote, with whom we began the essay – had become politically and socially conscious as a result. They had served alongside Europeans, and seen them scared and killed; the myth of white supremacy, intrinsic to the entire imperial project, was exploded for many of them.

Experiencing the war: Political and socio-economic impacts

Beyond combat operations, the impact of the war on African politics and society – and indeed economies – was profound. Britain in particular sought to mobilise the human and material resources of its African territories: the empire was not merely something to be 'defended', but actively relied upon by the Mother Country in the existential struggle against Germany and Japan. In many respects, the vigorous economic interventionism of the war years dated to the pre-war period, when the Great Depression of the 1930s had necessitated more systematic management of production than allowed for by the more laissez-faire approach of early colonial regimes.[12] The British, the Free French, and the Belgian government-in-exile relied heavily on the natural resources and productive capacity of their respective African territories: rubber, copper, palm oil, cotton, cocoa and numerous other commodities which were overwhelmingly the product of African labour but which were now channelled into the war effort. In Belgian Congo, for example, copper, rubber, gold and tin were requisitioned on a grand scale, and perhaps most importantly – during the war and afterwards – Congolese uranium had been critical in the development of the atomic bombs which were eventually dropped on Hiroshima and Nagasaki.[13]

As a result, the war intruded on Africans' lives in dramatic ways. Across the continent, inflation and declining prices for exports hit African workers and producers hard, while trade itself was obviously significantly disrupted. In many ways this exacerbated some of the problems experienced in the years immediately preceding the war itself. Unlike during World War I, when coercion and conscription had been the order of the day, from 1939–40 the British sought to persuade their African subjects through propaganda of the righteousness of the great struggle at hand. Films, radio broadcasts, newspapers and pamphlets exhorted Africans to cooperate and contribute, with the war framed in Manichean terms as a struggle between good and evil.[14] To some extent it marked a major shift in colonial thinking, reflecting a recognition that loyalty could not be taken for granted, and even an acceptance that empire itself was not quite as secure as might once have been believed. When war broke out, there were certainly anxieties across both French and British Africa about the potential for disorder and large-scale protest; in an age of unprecedented threat and insecurity, confidence in the imperial order was not what it had been, despite Churchillian exhortations about finest hours and fighting on beaches.

The miners of Northern Rhodesia certainly understood that the British seemed to value copper: when they went on strike in 1940 (for the second time, following a major strike in 1935), Britain was engaged in existential combat against the Luftwaffe over the skies of southern England, and local administrators had little choice but to offer better pay and conditions.[15] Thus did African workers begin to realise their own economic muscle. But there were political anxieties for the British, too. Under the terms of a 1936 treaty, Britain was able to use Egypt as a base for their operations in the eastern Mediterranean and the Middle East. While the young and inexperienced King Faruq remained loyal and controllable, the prime ministers who served under him were either determinedly neutral or in some way sympathetic to the Axis powers, in large part reflecting their hostility to the British. Egyptian nationalists were not quite as clear in their minds about the difference between European imperialism and European fascism as the British were; at the very least, they were certainly more pragmatic. Nationalist sentiment – expressed, for example, through the Muslim Brotherhood – was on the increase as Rommel pushed ever closer toward the Suez Canal. The credibility and popularity of the Wafd, the dominant nationalist party in the inter-war years, declined rapidly during the war, owing to its association with a weak monarchy and the British imperial presence. The British themselves thought it prudent to station tanks around government buildings in Cairo to discourage any outbreak of open dissent within government. This in itself merely enflamed anti-British feeling, as did wartime hardships, notably inflation and food shortages.[16] In the Gold Coast, Britain implemented new constitutions in 1942 and 1946 which increased African representation on a legislative council and facilitated the emergence of political organisations; in Nigeria, 1944 saw the foundation of the National Council of Nigeria and the Cameroons, one of the earliest nationalist movements in the territory.[17] Elsewhere, the British sought to co-opt elites through rank and uniform in order to legitimise the war effort at the local level. In the Uganda Protectorate, for example, the ruler of the most important kingdom, Buganda, *Kabaka* Edward Mutesa II, was commissioned as an officer in the Grenadier Guards at the express wishes of King George VI. It was a logical step, given that he had joined the Officer Training Corps while at Cambridge University – although it is important to note that at the time and for a number of years subsequently, the *Kabaka* was an unpopular figure locally, precisely because he was seen as being under too much British influence and patronage.[18]

More broadly, African readership and listenership expanded dramatically during the war, and Africans became ever more aware of global issues, through local newspapers in particular. News of the Atlantic Charter of August 1941 reached a wide audience, and its explicit reference to the rights of all peoples to self-determination and protection against aggression and persecution caused considerable excitement. Churchill – arch imperialist that he was – might hastily clarify that the peoples under benign British imperial government were to be discounted, but in a sense the damage was done: the moral weakness of imperial rule was increasingly exposed, and even the co-author of the charter, lifelong critic of European empire US President Franklin Roosevelt, was less than persuaded by the British position – more on which later.[19]

On the French side, relations with North African rulers were delicate. In Morocco, Sultan Sidi Mohammad remained broadly loyal to the Allied cause throughout the war, having been given assurances – including by Roosevelt himself – that full independence would follow an Allied victory. Likewise in Tunisia, the nationalist leader Habib ibn Ali Bourguiba was pro-Free French, no doubt believing that his efforts would be rewarded after the war. The US military presence in Algeria served to spur the nationalist cause, and in 1943 a group of activists, including Ferhat Abbas, produced their *Manifesto of the Algerian People* which demanded economic and political reform. De Gaulle promised full French citizenship for a local elite, prompting Abbas to increase the pressure by founding the Amis du Manifesté et de la Liberté, which had as its core aim the creation of an Algerian republic to be federated with France. Abbas was condemned by white settlers as an extremist, and by the more radical Parti du Peuple Algérien under Ahmed Messali as too moderate. When violent protests erupted in 1945, the French suppressed it brutally, and detained both Abbas and Messali.[20]

More broadly, however, de Gaulle recognised the importance of the French African colonies to the war effort, especially after these territories – nominally under Vichy administration – gradually disavowed Vichy and declared for de Gaulle. In January 1944, at a conference in Brazzaville in French Equatorial Africa, a suite of reforms was announced, including greater economic and political freedoms. These reforms in no way promised – nor did they even anticipate – eventual independence for the French colonies, but they did represent the first step toward autonomy and a recognition that the very basis of colonial governance needed to be fundamentally reconfigured.[21] Locally, people were beginning to organise. Later in 1944, cocoa and coffee farmers in Côte d'Ivoire established the Syndicat Agricole Africain with the primary aim of having the hated policy of periodic forced labour abolished; the following year elections led to the dispatch to Paris of the Syndicat's leader, Felix Houphouet-Boigny, as a regional representative, and he secured the abolition of forced labour.[22] Still, the French could be brutal when challenged. Later that year, in November and December, a mutiny over pay and conditions on the part of Tirailleurs Senegalais units of the French army led to a massacre of dozens of African soldiers at Thiaroye in Senegal.[23] Concerned about morale and order, de Gaulle nonetheless swiftly ensured that one of the key causes of the mutiny – the issue of backpay – was resolved in the recruits' favour, although the massacre itself was airbrushed from mainstream French histories.

By the end of the war, momentum was building among a new cohort of African political activists – young, educated and radicalised – who had often travelled abroad before and during the war itself. They had seen colonialism in the context of the global conflagration, and were ever more ferocious in their critiques. They were emboldened by the advances made by Indian nationalists, for example, which seemed to signify a much weakened British Empire – and even, briefly, by the sight of a rampant Japan which had so convincingly overwhelmed European empires in Southeast Asia. It is true that Japan's influence was less overt in Africa than in Asia itself, but nonetheless Japan had offered up a model of non-western modernity, even if Japan's own behaviour in the territories it occupied tarnished its own reputation.[24]

In October 1945, just weeks after the Japanese surrender, the Fifth Pan-African Congress was held in Manchester, England – the first such meeting since the Congress of 1927 in New York. Much had changed in the intervening 18 years. The delegates now demanded full independence for Africa, and issued a statement condemning imperialism, racism, and capitalism.[25] The experience of the war itself accounts for much of the new momentum behind the demand for the unconditional dismantling of the old European colonial order, although detailed plans of action for how this would be achieved were as yet absent. At the same time, however, the remaining colonial powers – chief among them Britain, France, Belgium and Portugal, neutral during the war itself – were ever more convinced of the need to retain their colonial possessions in pursuit of post-war recovery. The war had unleashed desires and sentiments which were seemingly diametrically opposed, and the forces of metropolitan imperialism and nationalism were destined to clash in the wake of the Axis defeat.

Aftermaths and consequences

In the immediate post-war period, the colonial powers sought to consolidate their respective empires. Just as African territories had been critical in the war effort, so they were seen as vital in the new post-war world. The Western European imperial powers may have ultimately been on the winning side in the war itself, but they were now economically exhausted and desperate to use the raw materials of their empires to recover in both economic and political terms. The late 1940s have even been described, for the British as witnessing a 'second colonial occupation' during which colonial administrations sought to mobilise local resources more systematically than previously.[26] The economic potential of eastern and central Africa, for example, was identified as remaining largely untapped, and as offering a way out of heavy dependence on and indebtedness to the US. After 1945, governments became more directly involved in crop production, notably, and this vigorous interventionism was manifest in the re-energising of marketing boards, some of which pre-dated the war itself. The British aimed at economic stability and the maximisation of production through the West African Produce Marketing Board, while the British government made funds available for colonial development. The French had also established marketing boards by the end of the 1940s to take advantage of the agricultural boom, although the recovery in the colonies took rather longer than elsewhere, as the war had witnessed a collapse in investment and foreign trade. But British and French ambitions went further still. There emerged new visions of economic transformation in Africa, and capital-intensive projects were implemented which witnessed the attempt to bring to parts of the continent North American-style mechanised agriculture on a large scale. Britain launched the groundnut scheme in Tanganyika, which was supposed to herald new forms of partnerships between the state and private capital. But the scheme was a disaster – in much of Tanganyika the soil was too dry and thin for mechanised agriculture – and it collapsed amidst something of a public outcry in the early 1950s.[27] In a scheme which in fact dated to the 1930s but which was now dusted down and relaunched, the French committed large funds to the construction of dams on the Niger, the aim being to create an extensive area of irrigated land for the production of cotton. But again, the results were disappointing. Cotton production never reached projected levels, and African farmers quietly moved in and used the land to produce sugar and rice for the domestic market.[28]

Within a few years, the global post-war recovery involved a rise in prices for a number of export crops which meant something of an economic boom, for some at least. But if increasing state involvement in the management of African production had been an important legacy of World War II, so too was the marginalisation of African producers within economic systems. Marketing boards, again, had been first introduced in the 1930s to mitigate the vagaries of the global market during the depression: they set a fixed price which would be paid to farmers for their produce regardless of the state of the global economy. The theory was that in good years, when the global price was higher than that being paid to farmers, boards would build up a surplus which would then be used to pay farmers during periods of economic downturn. This was prudent, in principle. In reality, however, Africans were only ever paid a small proportion of the actual value of their produce, and while boards did indeed build up surpluses, these were not used to support farmers but were instead siphoned off into schemes for capital development. There was a longer-term political consequence, too. Marketing boards were part of state-controlled commercial structures which allowed governments to earn foreign currency on the back of African farmers' labour which was systematically undervalued. Once they became independent, many African governments retained these structures and frequently used the profits for political purposes.[29]

The failings of certain capital-intensive schemes notwithstanding, Britain and France recovered relatively quickly after the war and in time – as we see below – were able to contemplate decolonisation (or a form of it), even if decolonisation came rather sooner than either Paris or London would have envisaged in 1945. For economically weaker powers, however, that was not an option. For Portugal – along with Spain one of only two surviving fascist regimes in Europe after the war, in large part the dividend of their neutrality – its African colonies were seen as absolutely critical to its standing in the world and its economic position, as well as providing outlets for 'surplus' population. The Portuguese (with US support, ironically) came down hard on emerging nationalist protest in the 1950s.[30] Similarly, in the Belgian Congo, the post-war boom in minerals – including uranium, increasingly and dangerously significant in the Cold War context – was deemed critical to Belgium's economic recovery, as well as supporting the emergence of an African middle class in the territory, and so for much of the late 1940s and 1950s Brussels would not countenance any meaningful transfer of power to increasingly vocal political activists.[31] Dramatic shifts in the balance of power both globally and within Europe itself in the aftermath of the war meant that African colonies were seen in various ways as core components of metropolitan economic planning.

The war had brought about important shifts in political thinking, too. Again, the roots of some of these shifts can be traced to the immediate pre-war period: the destabilising effects of the depression had led to a critical questioning of the nature and purpose of colonial rule. But the war forced the pace of change. The post-war reassessment of political priorities and strategies reflected the fact that the African colonies had made a major contribution to the war effort, and followed on from promises made during the war itself – as in the case of de Gaulle at Brazzaville. France now began to consider a limited transfer of power to Africans, but one which would be to the benefit of both former colony and metropole: the latter would be closely linked to the latter in a form of conditional autonomy, a federated community, with Paris maintaining both economic influence and control over key aspects of local politics, including defence and foreign policy.[32] In Britain, against the backdrop of the withdrawal from India in 1947 – long the centrepiece in Britain's modern empire and, ostensibly at least, the justification for Britain controlling a huge swath of northeast and east Africa in the first place – the Attlee government signalled a shift toward the incorporation of an emerging educated elite in Africa and away from the system of indirect rule through 'traditional' chiefs, in place since the end of the 19th century. A very gradual transfer of power was still envisaged – for the economic reasons noted above – even in the late 1940s and early 1950s. In both London and Paris, cautious, constitutional reform would facilitate the incorporation of educated moderates, who would implement policies favourable to, and represent the putative values of, the outgoing colonial powers. This was as true in British territories from the Gold Coast to Uganda to Northern Rhodesia as it was across French West Africa.[33] (A somewhat different plan was envisaged for colonies of white settlement, including Algeria, Kenya and Southern Rhodesia, where settler regimes were regarded as key to those territories' future. South Africa, loyal to Britain during the war under the terms of the Statute of Westminster of 1931, would also soon go down a very different path, following the apartheid election of 1948.)

The central idea – that pliable and ideologically compatible systems of authority would be created to safeguard metropolitan interests – was also applied to territories which had not originally been under British or French rule. Italy, as a defeated former Axis power, was now a spent force in colonial terms – a ten-year trusteeship over Somalia notwithstanding. In former Italian Libya, the UN oversaw the granting of independence to the territory under Britain's wartime ally, the Sanusi leader Sayyid Mohammed Idris, who now headed a monarchy which was by no means accepted as legitimate by all Libyans and which was heavily dependent on US and British support as a result.[34] These monarchical and authoritarian regimes – replicated across North Africa and the Middle East in the aftermath of World War II – would face crises of legitimacy in the years to come, with devastating consequences for millions of people.

At the same time, of course – and arguably the single most significant legacy of World War II in terms of global politics – the Cold War, and the ideological bipolarity of the new world order, intruded on these events and processes in often dramatic ways. US–Soviet rivalry had a profound impact on Africa, even if Africa itself was not immediately regarded as a priority battleground; that dubious honour fell to

Southeast Asia, among other places. But Cold War exigencies shaped decolonisation and African politics in important ways.[35] One of the earliest manifestations of a war legacy in this context was in the Horn of Africa. Here, the US swiftly identified Ethiopia under Haile Selassie as a key regional ally against global communism – Haile Selassie portrayed himself as precisely that – and ultimately supported the emperor's claims over the former Italian colony of Eritrea, despite the fact that by the late 1940s a sizeable proportion of the Eritrean population aspired to independence. To Washington, keeping Ethiopia on side in the Cold War was more important than any local aspirations to national self-determination, and by the early 1950s Eritrea had been federated with Ethiopia and the US had a defence agreement with Haile Selassie – including an enormous military base in Asmara, the Eritrean capital. In time, these attempts to control an already-volatile region would result in violent conflagration, not least a 30-year war for Eritrean independence, the consequences of which are still being felt today.[36]

In broad terms, the western Allies – including the US, despite its avowed historical hostility to European imperialism – regarded empire as a bulwark against the spread of communism after 1945, and so at first Cold War dynamics militated against decolonisation, or at least justified brutal responses to particular forms of nationalism. Washington, notably, was prepared to temper its anti-imperial agenda – as already noted in the context of the Horn – in order to defend the so-called 'Third World' against the predations of communism, and this was as true in Africa as it was in Southeast Asia or Central America. In the meantime, colonial administrations themselves sought the suppression of movements with left-leaning inclinations, and to carefully manage the transfer of self-government to those movements deemed ideologically aligned with their own interests.[37] At the same time, however, the Soviet Union and – in time – China represented alternative models of both resistance to western imperialism and distinctive paths of national development. The important caveat to this is that neither the Soviet Union nor China showed much interest in Africa for the first few years after the war. Only once Stalin was dead and Khrushchev securely in post did Moscow begin to offer material support to particular African states and movements deemed worthy of such backing, and often to counter American influence, especially after the implementation of Kennedy's counterinsurgency policy in the early 1960s. China entered the field even later, notably by providing military and ideological training to rebel groups and – in the case of the Tanzania–Zambia railway – investing in local infrastructure projects.

While many African nationalist movements would position themselves in the non-aligned camp, others made dextrous use of post-1945 global rivalries to shore up their own positions and attracted both military and economic support. Over the longer term, the Cold War along with the enduring drive for influence on the part of former imperial powers led to 'neo-colonialism': the attempt to maintain a degree of control over nominally-independent states in both economic and political terms.[38]

Meanwhile, however, the nationalist challenge to colonial regimes across the continent became ever more aggressive. Across North Africa, where nationalist politics were initially more robust and better organised than south of the Sahara, political movements came to the fore which were more strident and radical than anything before the war. In Egypt, strikes and open protest were increasingly common in the late 1940s, while the Muslim Brotherhood and the Young Egypt Party, among others, became ever more vociferous in their critique of both the British presence and the ineffectual government of King Faruq. In Algeria, Abbas and Messali, following their release from prison, founded rival nationalist parties, and while the French created a new constitution widening political representation, politics in Algeria became increasingly contested by the late 1940s, with nationalists frustrated by French dissemblance and persistent defence of the sizeable settler community there. In Tunisia, King Moncef Bey began to lobby for political reform and was deposed and exiled by France for his trouble; Bourguiba, formerly a supporter of the Free French movement and now leader of the nationalist Neo-Destour party, began to organise abroad for the struggle for independence. And in Morocco, Sidi Mohammad – formerly loyal to the Allied cause – became a key figure in the nationalist movement, embittered by what he saw as a betrayal of promises by the Allies.[39] Across the continent, African leaders perceived a casual casting aside of pledges made by the Allied powers, lack of reward for the African contribution to the war effort, and sensed both moral and political weakness in the imperial order, making them increasingly confident in the challenge they posed to that order.

This played out in different ways in different colonial contexts. Across much of British and French Africa, elections were permitted which themselves encouraged political mobilisation and the creation of more coherent political platforms. In territories such as the British Gold Coast – which became independent as Ghana in 1957 – a combination of colonial pragmatism and the dexterity of the nationalist movement under Kwame Nkrumah could lead to a relatively peaceful decolonisation process.[40] The same was true of French West Africa, where an initial acceptance of French metropolitan hegemony – with the exception of Guinea – on the part of regional leaders was followed by full independence in 1960.[41] Post-war metropoles could claim to have remained in charge of the process, with varying degrees of accuracy; nationalists could claim to have firmly but with respect to due process steered colonial officials toward the exit. Elsewhere, however, there was violence. In Kenya, from the early 1950s, the British – now occupied in wars of various levels of intensity across the globe – were confronted with the Mau Mau uprising.[42] Even more ferociously, from 1954 France was waging war in Algeria against the Front Liberation Nationale (FLN).[43] The Portuguese were by the early 1960s were dealing with major uprisings in Guinea-Bissau, Angola and Mozambique.[44] In each case, these were armed insurgencies who knew only too well of the capacity of imperial nations – the victors of the war against Axis aggression – to counterattack; but they also sensed empires which were weakened – certainly politically, and economically, and morally, and for all their armed might, militarily too – for in the aftermath of the war, the colonial powers discovered that, in a much changed world, their military capacity was ultimately of little consequence when it was not underpinned by moral righteousness, political will, or economic strength.

The British crushed the Mau Mau revolt, in military terms; the French won the battle of Algiers. But nonetheless, Kenya became independent in 1963, and Algeria in 1962. Events which were directly or indirectly the legacy of World War II had overtaken them. In particular, there was Egypt in 1956, when Britain and France – acting in a way which they felt their status as imperial powers, victors of World War II, and permanent members of the UN Security Council permitted – sent forces into the Suez Canal zone following the decision by Gamal Abdel Nasser (who had recently overthrown wartime British ally King Faruk) to nationalise the Suez Canal Company. Britain and France were roundly condemned, including by the US, where the Eisenhower administration – for all its ties to two of its closest western allies – denounced an action which seemed to belong to the age of high imperialism half a century earlier. Humiliated, Britain and France – and Israel, which had also been involved – withdrew, and it seemed to herald a different kind of post-war order than that which London and Paris had envisaged.[45] Soon after, in Britain, a scandal unfolded around events at Hola Camp, a detention centre for Mau Mau suspects in Kenya. At Hola, detainees had been tortured, some beaten to death, and subjected to forced labour and brainwashing, reflecting the idea that the revolt had been symptomatic of a psychological illness on the part of the Kikuyu people rather than an expression of legitimate grievance.[46] A government enquiry followed, although it would be many decades before some semblance of truth emerged; but more importantly, as with Suez, the revelation delivered a body-blow to Britain's image of itself as an essentially benign, civilising force. Harold Macmillan, at the head of a conservative government, now regarded empire as an electoral liability and as morally unjustifiable, and thus felt able to deliver his famous speech in Cape Town, South Africa, in 1960, in which he declared that a wind of change was blowing across the continent.

It was perhaps fitting that the Suez debacle happened just months after the final departure from the political frontline of Winston Churchill, Britain's great war leader but who held, to modern eyes and indeed to some at the time, a profoundly racialised view of the world and who was in many ways the product of the late 19th century. It fell to the unfortunate Anthony Eden, who had waited for so long as the heir apparent to the great man, to preside over the beginning of the end of Britain's African empire; and then to Macmillan, long-serving minister and former adviser in the Mediterranean theatre in particular, to largely oversee it. It was a slow-burning legacy of the war itself. Britain still had the capacity to crush a rebel network such as the Mau Mau in Kenya; but in the wake of World War II it had neither the political will nor the economic facility to win the larger war, namely the struggle against a tide of nationalist movements which, conversely, had been invigorated by the experience of the war, albeit in a myriad of ways. The same was true of the French in Algeria: de Gaulle, the complex war hero who had witnessed German tanks drive through the Ardennes in May 1940 and who had both symbolised and galvanised the French spirit of resistance to Nazism, had no answer to the FLN in Algeria – no more than Churchill could comprehend, or at least control, the forces which now challenged a much-weakened Britain.

Conclusion

When the war began in September 1939, the idea was still prevalent that European empires in Africa would last for many decades to come. Six years later, much had changed. The war by no means meant that decolonisation was either imminent or inevitable, but the strains and pressures and traumas of the period between the late 1930s and the mid-1940s had unleashed forces which both shaped metropolitan imperial strategies and empowered continental nationalisms, and left enduring legacies for both. Fundamentally, empires were weakened, in both material and moral terms, and led to new strands of political thought around the future of empire – and indeed of 'imperialism', however defined – although of course there was diversity across the various empires themselves. Those strands of thought evolved from conceiving former colonies as part of an extended Francophone community of new nations led by the metropole, in the case of the French, to rethinking the nature of the Commonwealth in Britain as a network of influence and cultural connection which was a useful counterbalance to American hegemony.

One of the key drivers behind appeasement among British imperial thinkers in the 1930s had been the belief that another major world war would spell the rise of the US to global hegemony and, in essence, the end of the British Empire. That certainly proved correct, in Africa and elsewhere. World War II exposed the vulnerabilities of British imperial control, and specifically the overstretch which had long engendered anxiety among imperial planners. Britain, France and Belgium emerged from the war on the side of righteous triumph but, exhausted and depleted, they each, in their different ways, soon had to grapple with the fact that the very experience of the war had unleashed forces for change which they could not control – or at least not in the ways they believed they might. The focus soon turned to the creation of moderate regimes through the decolonisation process which would guarantee continued influence in the Cold War world, and on targeted military interventions to ensure that outcome. In a sense this represented the evolution of counterinsurgency thought rooted in the late 19th century. But more specifically, World War II represented a last charge for large-scale military operations on the part of Africa's imperial powers, and in its wake came a recognition of severe limitations on military and political capacity.

On the African side, the legacy of the war was manifold. In fairly specific terms, the interventionist state model which was honed during and after the war, was further utilised by later independent governments, in both economic and political spheres, and in many ways came to be seen as a model for governance and 'development' – with variable results. More broadly, on many levels of society there was a growing understanding of, and a critical engagement with, global forces for change, which Africans could harness to their own ends and which also intersected with ongoing social and political change within the continent as a result of colonial rule. In particular, there was an intensifying and ever more articulate critique of the very ideological and moral basis of European imperialism. Yet at the same time there was also an understanding that Africans – whether as territorial nationalists or as Pan-Africanists (and political activists were frequently both) – had to engage with and play a part in the international system which was the direct outcome of the war itself. The consequences of such engagement were diverse, and not always to the benefit of the majority, but across the board – whether as producers, soldiers, or simply colonial subjects – Africans understood with ever greater clarity the nature of the global order and the ways in which they might participate in, and indeed influence, that order.

Notes

1   Waruhiu Itote (General China), *'Mau Mau' General* (Nairobi: East African Publishing House, 1967), 9–12.
2   This is one of the arguments in David Killingray's *Fighting for Britain: African soldiers in the Second World War* (Woodbridge: James Currey, 2010).
3   A sample survey of relevant scholarship would include: 'World War II and Africa', special issue of the *Journal of African History*, Vol. 26, No. 4 (1985); R. Rathbone and D. Killingray (eds), *Africa and the Second World War* (Basingstoke: Macmillan, 1986); K. Jeffrey, 'The Second World War', in J. Brown and W. R. Louis (eds), *The Oxford History of the British Empire, Vol 4: The Twentieth Century* (Oxford: Oxford University Press, 1999); Judith A. Byfield, Carolyn A. Brown, Timothy Parsons, and Ahmad Alawad Sikainga (eds), *Africa and World War II* (Cambridge: Cambridge University Press, 2015).
4   Anthony Mockler, *Haile Selassie's War: the Italian-Ethiopian Campaign, 1935–1941* (Oxford: Oxford University Press, 1984). See also a range of fascinating, and very different, contemporary sources: Evelyn Waugh, *Waugh in Abyssinia* (London: Longmans, Green & Co, 1936); Edward Ullendorff (tr and ed), *The Autobiography of Emperor Haile Selassie I: 'My Life and Ethiopia's Progress', 1892–1937* (London: Oxford University Press, 1976), chaps. 34–50; Andrew Hilton, *The Ethiopian Patriots: forgotten voices of the Italo-Abyssinian War, 1935–41* (Stroud: The History Press, 2007).
5   Esmonde M. Robertson, *Mussolini as Empire-Builder: Europe and Africa, 1932–36* (London: Macmillan, 1977).
6   David Reynolds, *Britannia Overruled: British policy and world power in the 20th century* (Harlow: Longman, 2000).

7   A. J. Barker, *Eritrea 1941* (London: Faber, 1966).

8   The tense interstitial ambiguity of French Morocco is of course beautifully, and famously, captured in the classic wartime movie *Casablanca* (dir. Michael Kurtiz, 1942).

9   The reach and power of the Sanusiyya across a chunk of central-northern Sahara had long prevented meaningful Italian control beyond a coastal strip of Libya. Notably, during World War I, the Sanusiyya had initially been funded and armed by Germany and the Ottoman Empire, but following the emergence of pro-British elements the brotherhood had reached a truce with the British and the Italians: see the classic anthropological study, E. E. Evans-Pritchard, *The Sanusi of Cyrenaica* (Oxford: Clarendon Press, 1949).

10   Ruth Ginio, *French Colonialism Unmasked: the Vichy Years in French West Africa* (Lincoln, NE: University of Nebraska Press, 2006).

11   Killingray, *Fighting for Britain*; Anthony Clayton & David Killingray, *Khaki and Blue: Military and Police in British Colonial Africa* (Athens, OH: Ohio University Center for International Studies, 1989).

12   For example, see John Iliffe, *A Modern History of Tanganyika* (Cambridge: Cambridge University Press, 1979), 342–80; David Meredith, 'The Colonial Office, British business interests, and the reform of cocoa marketing in West Africa, 1937–1945', *Journal of African History*, Vol. 29, No. 2 (1988).

13   Phyllis M. Martin, 'Le Congo Belge durant la Seconde Guerre Mondiale: Recueil d'Etudes', *Journal of African History*, Vol. 26, No. 4 (1985); Susan Williams, *Spies in the Congo: The Race for the Ore that Built the Atomic Bomb* (London: Hurst, 2018).

14   Wendell P. Holbrook, 'British propaganda and the mobilisation of the Gold Coast war effort, 1939–1945', *Journal of African History*, Vol. 26, No. 4 (1985).

15   Andrew Roberts, *A History of Zambia* (New York: Africana Publishing, 1976), 186, 193, 203; I. Henderson, 'Early African leadership: the Copperbelt disturbances of 1935 and 1940', *Journal of Southern African History*, Vol. 2 (1975).

16   Artemis Cooper, *Cairo in the War, 1939–1945* (London: John Murray, 1989); Afaf Lutfi Al-Sayyid Marsot, *A Short History of Modern Egypt* (Cambridge: Cambridge University Press, 1985), chap. 5.

17   D. Austin, *Politics in Ghana, 1946–1960* (London: Oxford University Press, 1970); J. S. Coleman, *Nigeria: Background to Nationalism* (Berkeley, CA: University of California Press, 1971).

18   Richard J. Reid, *Warfare in African History* (New York: Cambridge University Press, 2012), 150; and see also his own account in The Kabaka of Buganda, *Desecration of my Kingdom* (London: Constable, 1967).

19   R. D. Pearce, *The Turning Point in Africa: British Colonial Policy, 1938–1948* (London: Cass, 1982).

20   Adria K. Lawrence, *Imperial Rule and the Politics of Nationalism: anti-colonial protest in the French Empire* (Cambridge: Cambridge University Press, 2013), chaps. 4 and 5.

21   For example see Joseph R. De Benoist, 'The Brazzaville Conference, or Involuntary Decolonization', *Africana Journal*, Vol. 15 (1990).

22   Tony Chafer, 'Education and Political Socialisation of a National-Colonial Political Elite in French West Africa, 1936–1947', *Journal of Imperial and Commonwealth History*, Vol. 35, No. 3 (2007); James E. Genova, *Colonial Ambivalence, Cultural Authenticity, and the Limitations of Mimicry in French-Ruled West Africa 1914–1956* (New York: Peter Lang, 2004); Frederick Cooper, *Citizenship between Empire and Nation: remaking France and French Africa, 1945–1960* (Princeton: Princeton University Press, 2014).

23   The official narrative was that some thirty-five mutineers died, but *Tirailleurs* veterans claimed the number was actually over three hundred. See Martin Mourre, *Thiaroye 1944: histoire et mémoire d'un massacre coloniale* (Rennes: Presses universitaires de Rennes, 2017).

24 For example Li Narangoa and Robert Cribb (eds), *Imperial Japan and National Identities in Asia, 1895–1945* (London: Routledge Curzon, 2003).

25 Hakim Adi and Marika Sherwood, *The 1945 Manchester Pan-African Congress Revisited* (London: New Beacon Books, 1995).

26 D. A. Low and J. M. Lonsdale, 'Introduction: towards the new order, 1945–1963', in D. A. Low and Alison Smith (eds), *History of East Africa, Vol. III* (Oxford: Oxford University Press, 1976), 12–16.

27 Alan Wood, *The Groundnut Affair* (London: The Bodley Head, 1950).

28 Patrick Manning, *Francophone Sub-Saharan Africa, 1880–1995* (Cambridge: Cambridge University Press, 1998), 114–15.

29 For a comprehensive survey, see D. K. Fieldhouse, *The West and the Third World: trade, colonialism, dependence and development* (Malden, MA: Blackwell, 1999).

30 Patrick Chabal et al, *A History of Postcolonial Lusophone Africa* (Bloomington, IN: Indiana University Press, 2002).

31 R. F. Holland, *European Decolonisation 1918–1981: an introductory survey* (Basingstoke: Macmillan, 1985), 175–90; Manning, *Francophone Sub-Saharan Africa*, 114–15.

32 Cooper, *Citizenship between Empire and Nation*.

33 Ronald Hyam, *Britain's Declining Empire: the road to decolonisation, 1918–1968* (Cambridge: Cambridge University Press, 2006), chap. 2. These developments are also documented in Lord Hailey's monumental quasi-official work, *An African Survey* (London: Oxford University Press, 1957), which is a rich resource for historians of the immediate post-war period.

34 John Wright, *A History of Libya* (London: Hurst, 2012), chap. 16.

35 Arthur Gavshon, *Crisis in Africa: battleground of East and West* (London: Penguin, 1981); Elizabeth Schmidt, *Foreign Intervention in Africa: from the Cold War to the War on Terror* (Cambridge: Cambridge University Press, 2013); and see also Odd Arne Westad, *The Global Cold War: Third World Interventions and the Making of Our Times* (Cambridge: Cambridge University Press, 2007).

36 Harold Marcus, *The Politics of Empire: Ethiopia, Great Britain, and the United States, 1941–1974* (Berkeley: University of California Press, 1985); Okbazghi Yohannes, *Eritrea: a pawn in world politics* (Gainesville, FL: University Press of Florida, 1991), esp. chap. 7; Richard J. Reid, *Frontiers of Violence in Northeast Africa: genealogies of conflict since c.1800* (Oxford: Oxford University Press, 2011), esp. chap. 6.

37 Holland, *European Decolonisation*, remains a useful survey.

38 Kwame Nkrumah, *Neo-Colonialism: the last stage of imperialism* (London: Nelson, 1965); Colin Leys, *Underdevelopment in Kenya: the political economy of neo-colonialism, 1964–1971* (London: Heinemann, 1975).

39 Lawrence, *Imperial Rule*, chaps. 4 and 5.

40 Basil Davidson, *Black Star: a view of the life and times of Kwame Nkrumah* (London: Allen Lane, 1973); Austin, *Politics in Ghana*; and Nkrumah's own account, *Ghana: the autobiography of Kwame Nkrumah* (New York: Nelson, 1957).

41 Manning, *Francophone Sub-Saharan Africa*, 139–40; Cooper, *Citizenship Between Empire and Nation*, passim; Elizabeth Schmidt, *Mobilising the Masses: gender, ethnicity and class in the nationalist movement in Guinea, 1939–1958* (Portsmouth, NH: Heinemann, 2005); Mairi MacDonald, 'A vocation for independence: Guinean nationalism in the 1950s', in Tony Chafer & Alexander Keese (eds), *Francophone Africa at Fifty* (Manchester: Manchester University Press, 2013).

42 Huw Bennett, *Fighting the Mau Mau: the British Army and counterinsurgency in the Kenya Emergency* (Cambridge: Cambridge University Press, 2012); Dan Branch, *Defeating Mau Mau, Creating Kenya: counterinsurgency, civil war, and decolonisation* (Cambridge: Cambridge University Press, 2009).

43 Alistair Horne, *A Savage War of Peace: Algeria 1954–1962* (London: Macmillan, 1977).

44 Allen Isaacman, *Mozambique: from colonialism to revolution, 1900–1982* (Boulder, CO: Westview, 1983); David Birmingham, *Frontline Nationalism in Angola and Mozambique* (London: James Currey, 1992).

45 Barry Turner, *Suez 1956: the inside story of the first oil war* (London: Hodder & Stoughton, 2006); Wm Roger Louis, *Ends of British Imperialism: the Scramble for Empire, Suez, and Decolonisation* (London: I.B. Tauris, 2006).

46 David Anderson, *Histories of the Hanged: Britain's dirty war in Kenya and the end of empire* (London: Weidenfeld & Nicholson, 2005); Caroline Elkins, *Britain's Gulag: the brutal end of empire in Kenya* (London: Pimlico, 2005).

CHAPTER 10

Adhere to 'Complete' Armed Forces: The Security and Defence Policy of the Netherlands since World War II

Jan Hoffenaar

Introduction

For a good understanding of the security and defence policy of the Netherlands since World War II, it is necessary to first go further back in history. After all, as is the case for every state, the Dutch policy is and was determined by its geographical and political position, the general development of warfare, and its ambitions and traditions with regard to foreign politics.

The Netherlands, located by the sea and at the mouth of several major western European rivers, has always been surrounded by larger powers. Initially, the United Kingdom, France and Germany, then after World War II the United States and the Soviet Union too. In terms of the size of its territory and population, the Netherlands is a relatively small country. It has also always been relatively prosperous, focused on trade and the protection of its economic interests in all corners of the world. Together with its high population density, this has made the Dutch economy highly dependent on foreign countries. To protect its trade and economy it has always had a large fleet, and, for the protection of its territory against obtrusive larger powers, an army.

During the course of the 19th century, warfare increasingly developed to the disadvantage of small states, including the Netherlands. Up until then, money had been the most important factor with regard to establishing and sustaining strong armed forces. What a state did not have, such as military personnel for example, it could buy elsewhere. As a result, the Netherlands could still be considered a major power until the first half of the 18th century. Since the French Revolutionary Wars and the Napoleonic Wars, and especially after the military success of Prussia and subsequently the American Civil War, wars and war preparations became increasingly more 'total' and national. The course of World War I and II showed that a modern, industrial war demanded the efforts of all civilians, and the country's full potential. The country's military capability had become dependent on the number of young citizens that it could mobilise and the maximum potential power of its economy. Small states, including prosperous ones, were up against major powers. If they were attacked, they would only be able to stay standing with the help of allies. In reality this meant ever less sovereignty.

In addition to war taking on a more and more total character, since the mid-19th century there had been another development that reduced the military options for a relatively small country like the Netherlands: the increasing complexity and multifaceted nature of modern warfare. It became increasingly difficult, especially from World War I onwards – during which an unprecedented number of technological innovations were launched – for smaller countries in Europe to keep up with all military-relevant developments.

Against this geopolitical and military backdrop, since the mid-19th century, Dutch governments have always been strongly inclined to place the law above power in international relations, and to take a politically neutral position and exercise military restraint. After all, the Netherlands had too little military power to make a real show of strength in order to force results, while its economic interests were best served by peace and clear international rules. This ethical policy was sometimes paired with a feeling of moral superiority. In addition, the possession of a large colonial empire in East Asia – present-day Indonesia – resulted in an overestimation of the global dominance of the Netherlands.

When building up and sustaining its army – its renowned fleet from the 17th and 18th centuries had since been reduced to a small sea power, mainly with tasks in the waters of the Dutch East Indies – political neutrality and military restraint did not prevent the small, proud Netherlands from continuing to compare itself with the larger powers, increasingly difficult though that was as a result of the aforementioned developments in warfare. Defence was focused on both deterring the enemy, and on being an attractive potential ally. In the 19th century, up until World War II, the policy was based on the implicit assumption that in the case of an enemy attack, the United Kingdom would come to the aid of the Netherlands. The Netherlands performed this balancing act – which brought the well-known security dilemma to the fore in a singular way – by organising and arming itself as a major power on a small scale. Almost all types of operational, support and logistics elements of the armed forces of the larger powers could also be found in the wartime organisations of the Dutch armed forces, including a large field army. At times Germany served as the prime example, at other times the United Kingdom (and after World War II, the United States.) Alternative defence options, such as a form of mass mobilisation, types of defence more specifically tailored to national circumstances (water!), and more symbolic defence preparations, were definitely discussed from the 19th century onwards, but their advocates never managed to gain enough support for these plans.

A possible explanation for this is that the defence organisation had practically always been the province of regular and retired regular military personnel who wanted to 'play with the big boys' and looked to the leading nations for their policies.

This principled choice meant that the Netherlands has always tried to field a fully fledged, modern military with the most up-to date equipment, whose deployability and qualities could be a match to the major players in the world. This also meant that just like the great powers, the country prepared its armed forces and society for total war. The consequence of this choice was that the Netherlands faced a perpetual struggle to establish and sustain both a modern army and a modern navy. Without foreign support this hardly ever succeeded. At the same time, the question is whether there were realistic political and military–strategic alternatives for independent assertive national defence. Given the geopolitical position of the Netherlands, entering into alliances in peacetime would almost certainly have led the country to war. By remaining neutral, the Netherlands had good hope of staying out of armed conflict for a long time.

In the eyes of the political and military establishment, the course of World War I (1914–1918) demonstrated that the chosen defence course had been the right one. The mobilisation of almost 200,000 military personnel had been swift and efficient and was believed to have had a deterrent effect on potential invaders. After all, none of the major powers had dared to violate the neutrality of the Netherlands on a large scale. The fact that the Netherlands had been lucky and that the United Kingdom and Germany had other important reasons outside the sphere of influence of the Netherlands for leaving the Dutch armed forces be, was a viewpoint that only a few people openly communicated.[1] Nonetheless, drastic cuts were made to defence in the years after the war. A majority of politicians advocated the cuts, and the military leadership realised it had little choice but to accept them. Recovering the economy and social stability was the highest priority. They were confusing times. The German threat may no longer have been present, but the balance of power in Europe, which had allowed the Netherlands' policy of neutrality, had been completely turned on its head. France was now the dominant power on the continent, without any meaningful rival. The newly established League of Nations, which intended to provide a system of collective security, could not offer a credible alternative. The Netherlands fell back on a historic reflex and behind the scenes it followed the British foreign policy with regard to Europe.[2] It should be noted that the military establishment was still committed to a large army comparable to that of the major powers with regard to structure.[3]

It was not until the second half of the 1930s, when Germany, under Adolf Hitler, started rebuilding strong armed forces, that defence expenditure rose sharply. A rapid attack on and occupation of the Netherlands was suddenly a very real possibility again. It was only then that real effort was put into expanding the air force, for which the first steps had been taken in 1913 with the acquisition of several aircraft.

THE LONG SHADOW OF WORLD WAR II

In 1940, the aviation section of the army had over 125 aircraft ready for combat.[4] The threat of violations of neutrality by air had already led to the establishment of anti-aircraft artillery in 1917.[5] In the 1930s, this new capability was significantly expanded. Anti-tank artillery was also acquired on a large scale. Tanks, which had manifested themselves as the weapon of the future during World War I, were not given a place in the army. They were considered unsuitable for the partially marshy terrain in the Netherlands.

Furthermore, tanks were not necessary for the execution of the static-defence operational concept, which had been opted for out of necessity in the 1930s. The field army was weakened and untrained and therefore incapable of mobile operations. Almost all units were bound to lines. There was no longer any preventive effect (in the event of an attack on the Netherlands, an aggressor would gain an additional strong opponent, who could possibly be the decisive factor in the outcome of the conflict). The Dutch could only hope and pray that their armed forces could hold up the defence long enough for their allies to come to their aid.[6]

The cutbacks had less far-reaching consequences for the navy, except for the fact that there was insufficient support for the expansion of the fleet and its tasks in parliament. Its main deployment area continued to be the Dutch East Indies. On Java, the Royal Netherlands East Indies Army, a separate colonial army, had the leading role in the enforcement of neutrality. The navy came second there. For the islands other than Java, those in the outlying regions, the navy was leading. During the interbellum, the navy was assigned submarines (as the core of the fleet, a fairly remarkable situation worldwide), new cruisers, destroyers, gunboats and aircraft for these tasks, and the Royal Netherlands East Indies Army was modernised. At the end of the 1930s, an air fleet of medium bombers, the largest in South-East Asia, was established at a rapid pace, with the purpose of guarding the colony's external borders alongside the navy. As a result of the German invasion on 10 May 1940, parliament did not act on a plan that government had previously approved for the construction of battle cruisers with which the navy could damage the Japanese by attacking their supply lines, which were considered vulnerable.[7]

This invasion by a major power was disastrous for the small state of the Netherlands. More or less in line with their expectations, the German troops achieved victory on the flank – after all, the German attack to the west focused on France – in five days. The Dutch Army's lack of training, the fact that the lines and positions were not ready, the lack of confidence within large units and the shortage of arms and equipment were not solely responsible for this tragic course of events. The excellent German planning, command and control, and armament, as well as the German air superiority were decisive. The allies could not provide the expected aid. The security policy of the Netherlands had failed.[8] After capitulation, the army demobilised. In 1942, most of the regular officers were taken prisoner, followed in 1943 by some of the regular NCOs and lower-ranking military personnel, as well as some of the reserve officers and NCOs.[9] The navy, on the other hand, continued to exist. Many ships, aircraft and personnel were able to escape the Dutch waters to the United Kingdom. They came under British command shortly after their arrival.[10]

Most of the fleet was still in the Dutch East Indies. In Asia the war started with the Japanese attack on the American naval base Pearl Harbor on 7 December 1941. The Netherlands entered into an alliance with the United States, the United Kingdom and Australia, but that offered little solace. Op 27 February 1942, a large part of the fleet went under in the battle between the allied Combined Striking Force under the command of the Karel Doorman and the Japanese fleet in the Java Sea. The Royal Netherlands East Indies Army capitulated on 9 March of the same year.[11] The Dutch East Indies were occupied by Japan. Many Royal Netherlands East Indies military personnel were taken prisoner. Dutch people and people of the Dutch East Indies disappeared into internment camps. The structural weakness of Dutch defence – dependence on allied support – also took its toll on the other side of the world.

Fully fledged armed forces of a small power

The disastrous and, for many, traumatic outcome of the battle in May 1940 and of the battle for the Dutch East Indies in 1941–1942 formed a watershed in Dutch security policy. It was the definitive unmasking of the neutrality policy of the Netherlands. Immediately after these defeats, it was clear to most politicians and military personnel that the Netherlands could now only guarantee its security by entering into alliances with major powers during peace time. In view of the course of World War II,[12] the United States, in addition to the United Kingdom, would also have to be involved. During the first years after the war, little came of this. In Europe, the allies from the war primarily concentrated on Germany's future position. They were also occupied with licking their wounds and primarily with sorting out matters at home, in their own spheres of influence and in their own colonies.

This also applied to the Netherlands. On 17 August 1945, two days after the capitulation of Japan, nationalists declared the independence of the Republic of Indonesia. A conflict followed that was fought both at the conference table and with military means, during which the Netherlands became almost completely isolated internationally. The United Kingdom, under whose operational command the Dutch East Indies fell at the time of the Japanese capitulation, could not and did not want to pave the way for the restoration of the Dutch colonial authority by military means. The Dutch government was forced to send huge numbers of military personnel. War volunteers (over 25,000) and a marines brigade at first, soon followed by conscripts (around 95,000 in total), joined the 60,000 military personnel of the Royal Netherlands East Indies Army to fight an increasingly better organised opponent dedicated to guerrilla warfare. The deployment of the conscripts was accompanied by a great deal of political and social upheaval and emergency legal measures, as up until then it had not been possible to send conscripts to the colonies without their consent. The role of the Dutch air forces and navy in the decolonization war was small.

Initially, the United States tacitly stood behind the Netherlands, but from the summer of 1948 it shifted to openly supporting the Republic of Indonesia. At the time, it had a very open and fiercely ideological, economic and military conflict of power with the Soviet Union. In connection with the Cold War, it attached great value to stability in the region. The United States believed that sustaining and recognising the new, apparently well-governed, non-communist state was a better guarantee for this than the progress of the hopeless attempt of the Netherlands to restore its authority. The Netherlands could not achieve its goal on its own. Two large-scale military operations, called police actions, could not bring about a change in that either. What the Netherlands had achieved with great difficulty and brute force in the 19th century and the early 20th century it could not repeat in the space of a few years. The determination of the people of the Dutch East Indies was too great, and political stubbornness on the part of the Netherlands, caused by it being out of touch with global politics following its aloofness on the active political world stage for more than a century, did the rest in combination with the wrong military–strategic policy. On 27 December 1949, sovereignty over Indonesia was handed over. The retention of Netherlands New Guinea only served as a plaster on the wound.[13]

Meanwhile, the Cold War demanded everyone's attention. In 1948, the Netherlands joined the Western Union and subsequently, on 4 April 1949, the North Atlantic Treaty Organization (NATO). This laid the foundation for a new security policy.[14] For the time being, however, security was by no means guaranteed. Joint build-up plans still existed mainly on paper. This changed following the invasion of South Korea by North Korean troops in June 1950. Under the compelling leadership of the United States, which suspected the hand of Soviet leader Stalin behind the invasion, the NATO member states drastically increased their defence efforts. Under US command, the first peace enforcement operation of the UN was launched in Korea. A Dutch voluntary detachment, as well as several navy ships, also participated.[15] In Europe, the rearmament of the Federal Republic of Germany ('West Germany') was discussed openly. It was considered necessary for the construction of a credible allied defence. The stationing of more American and British troops in Europe and the launch of a large-scale American military aid program had an immediate impact on the strengthening of the joint defence.[16]

However great the American and to a lesser extent the British influence was, NATO remained dependent on what the individual sovereign member states themselves were prepared to make available for allied defence. The realisation of the Dutch military contribution in the form of three 'complete' services was a clear example of this. There was soon international agreement regarding land and air forces. They were much needed for the direct defence on the continent. That did not apply to the maritime contribution of the Netherlands. The United States and the United Kingdom wanted to limit the Dutch role to the coastal waters, i.e. to pre-war proportions. They themselves would ensure the security of the Atlantic supply routes. This was not what the Royal Netherlands Navy had had in mind. It had learned from the experience of the war that the Netherlands had to have as harmonious a fleet as possible in order to have its voice heard loud and clear internationally and to look after its interests worldwide. It had to ensure that it did not allow itself to be banished from the ocean, because otherwise it would become a 'vassal state' of the United States. During the war, the navy had made great plans for the fleet, and after the war it defended a watered-down version with verve. In doing so, it repeatedly pointed out the interests of shipbuilding. However, it had the most success with its appeal to the Netherlands' glorious past at sea, particularly in the 17th century. The Netherlands was a maritime trading nation. A majority in parliament responded well to this, thus continuing a long historical line of public sympathy for the fleet. As a result, the government, which initially focused on the high costs of the plans for the fleet, changed its mind. Its decision was partly informed by the serene calm that the navy emanated, compared to the great unrest of the army. Thus, the long-cherished wish of the navy to become a fully fledged blue water navy was finally fulfilled. This course of events also meant that the navy did not deeply mourn the loss of its regional task in the Dutch East Indies. This task may have been its main raison d'être for a very long time, but at the same time it had kept it from its 'true' calling on the high seas.

The NATO allies had little choice but to accept the Dutch maritime offer. Moreover, their reluctance soon dissipated, because the maritime contribution was of high quality. The Royal Netherlands Navy had an aircraft carrier (the Karel Doorman), two cruisers, a number of bombers, frigates and submarines, a large number of mine sweepers and dozens of fighter aircraft. It contributed in this way to the security of shipping in the Atlantic Ocean, in the English Channel and in the North Sea, and helped to keep the latter two areas mine-free. Den Helder Naval Base grew to become the operational centre. The navy had arranged its affairs well. Proud and united, it cherished its independence.[17]

This was in stark contrast to the situation in the Royal Netherlands Army. The troop deployment to Indonesia had been a difficult organisational feat that it had pulled off. However, it had difficulty making the shift to establishing fully deployable units in the NATO context. This was, incidentally, unsurprising. The process started when tens of thousands of military personnel were still in the Dutch East Indies. At the same time, the entire Royal Netherlands Army, which had initially been entirely in line with the British Army, had to fully convert to the American organisational model. This was a condition for obtaining equipment under the US military aid program. In addition, there were quite a few delays in these weapon deliveries. On top of all this, Dutch officers had little experience of operating in international alliances. They also had little or no combat experience in Europe. The problems were so acute – according to NATO estimates there was already a significant chance of a Soviet attack at the end of 1952 – that NATO helped to manage the establishment of the Royal Dutch Army in the first few years. Officers and NCOs went on training with allied units in the Federal Republic of Germany. Future commanders of the army corps and divisions had to first complete an internship there before starting their job. The Supreme Headquarters Allied Powers Europe (SHAPE) even sent a mission to assist the Royal Netherlands Army in training its units. But the period of adjustment was short. In a few years, an army corps had been realised with one combat-ready division and almost four mobilisable divisions. NATO commanders were satisfied with their performance, although they did continue to criticise the small number of regular soldiers, the high percentage of mobilisable units and the large number of territorial troops.[18]

The air force had very few problems operating under allied command. Three Dutch squadrons had already operated in the British Royal Air Force in World War II. This trend was continued after the war. It included setting up allied air defence in the 'front garden' of the United Kingdom. The international cooperation was followed up within NATO. The great importance of air power had been undisputed since the war. The establishment of allied air forces was given a high priority. It was therefore logical that the air force became an independent service in 1953. The Royal Netherlands Air Force grew rapidly with day and night bomber squadrons for air defence, tactical bomber squadrons, a reconnaissance and transport squadron and light aircraft squadrons for artillery observation. The air force was for the most part focussed on the technique of flying and on its own service.[19]

Thus, in the 1950s, the Netherlands had three fully fledged services in its armed forces, each organising and operating in their own separate directions.[20] This situation would not change for the next 50 years. After World War II, the Royal Netherlands Marechaussee was in danger of being assigned only military-police tasks, but in the end it was again given a number of civilian tasks, such as guarding members of the Royal Family, border control with limited police powers, police assistance, and security tasks for De Nederlandsche Bank.[21]

Fully fledged armed forces with nuclear tasks

The armed forces of the Netherlands were an instrument for the implementation of the political and military strategy agreed jointly by the sovereign NATO member states. In the 1950s and 1960s, this strategy underwent quite some changes. Initially, the member states tried to establish with great urgency a force that could stop any Soviet attack at the Rhine and the IJssel, after which a counter-attack could be deployed. At the insistence of the Netherlands, the IJssel Line was included in the allied plans. Large parts of land on either side of the river could be submerged by an ingenious feat of 'water management', creating a great obstacle for an opponent. Above the major rivers, it was up to the Dutch corps to carry out defensive operations behind this line.[22] Nonetheless, the first allied plans were unsatisfactory in the view of the Dutch, because the north and east of the Netherlands would be relinquished.[23] However, NATO had the intention from the outset to advance the defence as far as possible. The first step was only taken in 1958, four years later than originally intended. The main defence line of the allies then shifted to the River Weser and the River Fulda. The Dutch corps was then given its own 'sector' west of Bremen. The defence was only truly advanced as far as possible from 1963, when the line moved to the Elbe, by the Inner German Border. The Royal Netherlands Army was then faced with the major problem of whether the divisions of the army corps could reach their sector in time. The stationing of a brigade and some smaller units near the deployment area, in Seedorf and Hohne, in the course of the 1960s was in the opinion of many insufficient to remedy this problem of maldeployment.[24]

The forward defence was possible as a result of the accession of the Federal Republic of Germany to the alliance and the 'nuclearisation' of the NATO strategy. Germany became a member in 1955, after a difficult attempt a year earlier to contain the former enemy in a close-knit Europe Defence Community with own European armed forces had failed.[25] In response to the accession, the Soviet Union and its satellite states, including the German Democratic Republic ('East Germany'), proceeded to establish the Warsaw Pact as an equivalent to NATO. With American aid, the Federal Republic of Germany was soon able to bring a large number of new units into the field.

The 'nuclearisation' of the alliance strategy was the second factor that enabled the defence behind the Elbe. NATO made a shift from a defence strategy to the ultimate deterrent strategy. This strategy of massive retaliation meant that all forms of aggression, including those of only conventional means, would immediately be responded to by massive deployment of nuclear resources (also known as the 'sword'). At the same time, the combat-ready units in the front line (the 'shield') were given a large arsenal of tactical nuclear weapons, which were to compensate for the allegedly outdated conventional arms. It was expected that this 'nuclearisation' could reduce the number of conventional armed forces needed and thus reduce defence costs. However, this quickly proved to be an inaccurate assessment. Nuclear warfare and forward defence actually required more combat-ready and mobile troops, and they were more expensive than the largely mobilisable troops for the static defence behind the IJssel Line. Moreover, the modernization of the armament had become an almost continuous process, which put permanent pressure on the defence budgets. In addition, the strategy of massive retaliation soon became less credible. It became clear more quickly than expected that the Soviet Union could deploy nuclear weapons on a large scale and over long distances. In the event of an all-out war, mutual destruction would be guaranteed. This called into dispute the 'link' between the American and European security interests. The European member states feared that, in the event of an attack by the Warsaw Pact on Western Europe, the United States would no longer automatically use nuclear means to come to their aid because that would also mean their own destruction. Now that its nuclear superiority was out of date, the United States was checkmated as a result of the all-or-nothing strategy. That strategy was no longer credible.

The solution was found in the strategy of flexible response, which officially entered into force in 1967. In the future, NATO would respond to all forms of aggression, except a large-scale nuclear attack, with direct defence. In doing so, it would use the same amount and type of assets as the opponent. The significance of combat-ready and very rapidly deployable conventional armed forces became relevant again. If direct defence were not successful, NATO would proceed to deliberate escalation of the conflict, for example through the deployment of tactical nuclear weapons. NATO would only turn to the large-scale deployment of nuclear weapons in the case of a large-scale nuclear attack. The United States strongly stressed the need for direct defence, so that a conflict would be contained in Europe; while the European member states, in view of the 'link', strongly stressed the possibility of deliberate escalation. This dispute led France to withdraw from the integrated NATO command structure. This increased the political and military significance of the Netherlands, because American, Canadian and British military reinforcements now had to reach the Central Sector via Dutch ports and roads.

The described developments from the end of the 1950s led, on balance, to a permanent conventional and nuclear arms race. The Netherlands, small as it was, participated in full. It wanted to be a loyal ally, especially in the field of defence (in foreign policy matters it sometimes expressed its own alternative view with some persistence). NATO in general and the security guarantee of powerful America in particular were the cornerstones of its security policy. All three services of the armed forces benefitted from this. They almost entirely focused on their NATO tasks and each one was given one or more (tactical) nuclear tasks.[26] The Royal Netherlands Navy, which of the three services of the armed forces had initially been the most reticent towards NATO – it claimed that the Netherlands had interests to defend worldwide, including outside the regional NATO – started to specialise in the fight against submarines and mines from the 1960s onwards, after the transfer of sovereignty of New Guinea in 1962.[27] It formed escort groups, composed of bombers and frigates with on-board helicopters and supported by submarines and land-based maritime patrol aircraft. As a result, the Naval Air Arm was assigned nuclear depth bombs. The Karel Doorman was withdrawn from service and sold to Argentina in 1968. Ultimately, the Marines Corps was also given clear NATO tasks. It was reorganised and from 1973 started participating in what later became the United Kingdom/Netherlands (UK/NL) Landing Force, a directly deployable unit for the vulnerable north flank of the treaty area.

The Royal Netherlands Army made a second division combat-ready, converted to a division structure with independently operating brigades and increased the mobility of its troops through the introduction of armoured and mobile weapons systems. It was assigned three nuclear tasks: the Honest John missiles, the 8-inch artillery and atomic demolition munitions ('atomic mines').[28] The Commander Corps, like the Marine Corps, was entirely geared to NATO tasks. In 1964, the 104 Observation and Reconnaissance Company were formed, to gather as much data as possible by means of long-distance patrols in enemy territory. In these years, the Royal Netherlands Air Force was given the highest priority in NATO. The lack of allied air defence was a particular concern. In the 1960s, it became an integrated system under the command of Supreme Allied Commander Europe (SACEUR). An important part of this was the belt of surface-to-air guided weapons, which ran straight across the Federal Republic. For this 'belt', the Netherlands supplied units with Nike weapons (radar-guided, surface-to-air missile weapon systems) for high-flying targets, and units with Hawk weapons (guided missiles) for low-flying targets. The Nike missiles could be fitted with a nuclear charge.[29] In the 1960s, the armed forces were, for the first time, to contribute to crisis management in the context of NATO. For example, the navy participated in the NATO Standing Naval Force Atlantic that is continuously available at sea, and the air force made available one squadron of bombers to the AMF, the Allied Command Europe Mobile Force, also known as the 'NATO fire brigade'.

Sustaining 'complete' armed forces was a very costly matter. In the early 1950s, critics had already pointed out that the Netherlands could not continue to deliver on its commitments – and with regard to the navy, we can even speak of 'ambitions' – in the longer term. Their criticism was ignored at that time, because the need was very high and the expectation was that international tensions would decrease over a foreseeable number of years. When that did not happen, the Netherlands was one of the first member states to put on the agenda the problems of sustaining the defence efforts within the alliance. In the late 1960s/early 1970s, the Dutch military contribution to NATO ran into serious problems. The flexible-response strategy called for an increase in conventional defence efforts and at the same time significant replacement investments had to be made. Moreover, the United States, which had come into financial difficulties partly as a result of its involvement in the Vietnam War, demanded more from newly reconstructed Europe. However, several European member states, partly in view of the relative reduction in tension between the east and west during that period, were inclined to reduce their efforts. In the Netherlands, ministers and state secretaries, political parties and committees offered various solutions to this complex problem. They ranged from an increase in the budget to greater task specialisation, task rejection, international division of tasks, integration of armed forces into national and international alliances, and more standardisation and cooperation.[30]

In the mid-1970s, the centre-left Den Uyl government cut the Gordian defence knot. Minister of Defence Henk Vredeling again stated that the small state of the Netherlands could not possibly afford three fully fledged services in the 1980s. Together with the Secretary of State Bram Stemerdink he made far-reaching proposals under the motto 'quality over quantity'.[31] In the context of the allocation of tasks, they did not shirk from calling into question the maritime long-distance aircraft, submarines and Nike missiles of the Royal Netherlands Air Force either. The Netherlands seemed to be out of step with NATO. In practice, however, that was not really the case. Following NATO consultations, the ministers and state secretaries went back on their proposals or made them dependent on positive outcomes of discussions between NATO and the Warsaw Pact about reductions in arms. The government did not take unilateral decisions on the allocation of tasks either. International consultation on the matter was unsuccessful. In the early 1950s, it became clear that the Netherlands had once again condemned itself to sustaining three fully fledged services and that it could no longer decently escape from this 'obligation' to the alliance.[32]

NATO, on balance, would not have been dissatisfied with the decisions that the government did take. They gave all the armed forces a clear perspective for the future. The navy received funds for a comprehensive modernisation and replacement program. The future of the air force was secured by the planned replacement of the 'Starfighters' (by the F-16s).[33] Greater emphasis was placed on tactical air support than had been the case in the past. Following a reorganisation, the army would have a corps with three, almost identical, rapidly deployable mechanised divisions, two of which would be combat-ready and mobilisable. However, implementation of the developments was not without problems. The question of financing in particular remained a major concern. Several factors played a role in this: the great optimism behind the plans of Vredeling and Stemerdink, financial changes, the high costs of new technologies, and additional costs resulting from defence orders placed with Dutch companies. However, there were no insurmountable problems. It is striking that from the mid-1970s, the heated public debates on the introduction of 'neutron bombs' and the deployment of Pershing II missiles and Tomahawk cruise missiles did not have any impact on the modernisation of the armed forces. Hundreds of thousands of Dutch citizens participated in protest demonstrations. For the first time since their relatively noiseless introduction in the 1950s and 1960s, nuclear weapons played an important autonomous role in the security debate.[34] On the sidelines of the public debate, the armed forces were given the space and means to develop the services into some of the most modern in Europe.[35]

Fully fledged armed forces and new tasks

The 'complete' armed forces of the Netherlands were thus still standing proud when in the second half of the 1980s the security situation in Europe changed dramatically. Under the leadership of Mikhail Gorbachev, the Soviet Union introduced a new policy aimed at openness and relaxation. The subsequent developments progressed extremely quickly. On 9 November 1989, the Berlin Wall fell. On 3 October 1990, 'West Germany' and 'East Germany' were united. On 19 November of that year, the NATO member states and the Warsaw Pact signed the Treaty on Conventional Armed Forces in Europe. On 1 July 1991, the Warsaw Pact was dissolved. At the end of that year, the Soviet Union even fell apart into independent republics. Before everyone had time to properly realise it, the Cold War was over.

Everything that had been self-evident a few years earlier was that no longer. No one had a clear picture of the threats and security situation anymore, nor therefore of the future tasks of the armed forces, let alone the structure and means needed. At the same time, almost everyone in the Netherlands – as was the case in most countries – believed that the armed forces could make do with less money. It was time for the 'peace dividend' to be collected. Various 'efficiency operations' were started to achieve that goal. However, most of the money was found by restructuring and, above all, by reducing the armed forces. In this way, successive governments took a path shrouded in darkness, which they had to feel and search their way along because of a lack of light to lead the way (vision). Some general remarks follow about continuity and discontinuity regarding developments in the past.

The most notable change in the defence policy was that it was no longer exclusively 'threat-driven'. For more than two centuries, the Dutch defence efforts, based on the implicit or explicit support of one or more major powers, were primarily focused on general defence of the territory. That was the main task. Now the defence efforts were also shaped by the level of political ambition. The government and parliament would determine, with ever decreasing budgets, what the capabilities of the armed forces should be, so the Netherlands could make a realistic contribution to the enforcement and promotion of the international rule of law. That became its second main task. More than before, the armed forces became an active instrument of foreign policy. Defence operations shifted from deterrence and defence to out-of-area operations and interventions all over the world. Task and territory were separated. Issues that had previously caused a major headache, such as the limited depth of the Dutch and Western European territory and the maldeployment of the Dutch Army corps, became irrelevant. The implicit or explicit support of a major (Anglo-Saxon) ally, an almost 300-year-old pillar of Dutch security policy, initially seemed less important, now that the direct threat from the east had disappeared. 'Seemed' because the new threats ('risks') that were soon identified, such as terrorism, the deployment of weapons of mass destruction by 'rogue states', and cyber-attacks, cannot be combated independently by any state and therefore force a global, jointly agreed approach, in which the United States often takes the lead and small states follow. The new threat assessment has also ensured that support from national civil authorities in law enforcement and disaster relief has been given a high priority. That is now the third, national, main task of the Netherlands armed forces. The distinction between the three main tasks is becoming increasingly blurred. After all, the reason for taking part in international missions is that it is better to go to the problems before they reach us.

In recent decades, an old question that the dependent Netherlands has had to constantly ask itself since the second half of the 18th century has once again came to the fore: how much defence effort on the part of the Netherlands is enough? Until World War II, the question was how much was enough to sustain the battle until the allies came to help. During the Cold War, the question – explicitly formulated like this at the beginning – was how much Dutch defence spending would be sufficient as 'insurance premium' for the American security guarantee. Since the 1990s, it has been a question of how great the Dutch contribution to military missions needs to be to continue to count internationally. How high should the level of political ambition be? And following the terrorist attacks in New York and Washington on 11 September 2001, the question arose as to how much defence is enough to deal with the new threats mentioned above.

The most visible continuity in the Dutch defence policy is adhering, for as long as possible, to the old 'complete' armed forces structure, with the capability to participate at all levels of force.[36] As there were no clear agreements in the EU and NATO regarding the allocation of tasks and with a view to the international reputation of the Netherlands, it wanted to have as many military capabilities at its disposal as possible, so that it could in principle always respond to a request to participate in a mission. The level of ambition and the structure of the armed forces associated with it were based on the existing structure and capabilities of the armed forces at the end of the Cold War. In this sense, the defence policy was also 'capability-driven'. Even before the Defence White Paper ('Defence Priorities Review') of 1993 discussed the 'level of ambition' for the first time, several notable extensions took place. In view of the new concept of the 'mobile contra-concentration' developed by SACEUR, the army was assigned an airmobile brigade, while the strategic transport capacity of the navy and the air force was significantly increased. The decisions leading up to this were made known in the Defence White Paper of 1991. The Warsaw Pact and the Soviet Union were still in existence at the time, and the 'red menace' had not yet been lifted completely. At the same time, crisis management and peace-keeping tasks increased in importance. More flexible and mobile armed forces emerged, which remained suitable for the more limited overall defence task but which could also be deployed in crises outside the treaty area and could contribute to peace operations.

These 'complete' armed forces formed the basis for a long-term process of restructuring and reduction. The politically sensitive nuclear tasks quickly disappeared from the package. The army was initially hit the hardest during the successive reorganizations. The number of 'heavy' units with tanks and artillery was drastically reduced, and other elements did not come off unscathed either. The army corps was reduced and eventually merged with German units into the German/ Netherlands Army Corps. The organisation of the National Sector was simplified and reduced. The same applied, for example, to the training programs. Moreover, the army was the service most severely affected by the actual transition from an army comprised of regulars, volunteers, and conscripts to a professional army in 1996.[37] Suddenly it had to find thousands more recruits per year. The navy and the air force also suffered losses, but – until the first few years of the 21st century – on a more modest scale and more across the board: in each austerity round, one or more frigates, mine sweepers and/or squadrons were cut. The structure of these services of the armed forces remained untouched for a long time. The Marechaussee is one of the few elements of the armed forces that have increased in size since the end of the Cold War. Its civil tasks in particular have increased considerably. These include reinforcing border control, introducing mobile surveillance of foreigners at the southern and eastern borders, assisting in the fight against cross-border crime and taking over police and security tasks at Schiphol and other airports. In 1998, the Royal Netherlands Marechaussee was granted the status of an independent service of the armed forces. This brought an end to a long emancipation process that had started as early as the late 1960s.[38]

The expansion of the Marechaussee is one of the logical organisational adjustments to the tasks that the armed forces started to perform in practice after the Cold War. The most striking aspect is its continued commitment to various types of international operations, which are carried out for the most part under the flag or with a mandate from the United Nations.[39] The main areas of deployment in recent decades have been former Yugoslavia, Iraq, Afghanistan and, since 2014, Mali, and at sea in the Adriatic Sea, around the Arabian Peninsula and near the Horn of Africa.[40] UN missions are, incidentally, nothing new. Between 1979 and 1985, for example, a Dutch battalion and then a company were part of the United Nations Interim Force in Lebanon and Dutch officers have been part of an observation mission in the Middle East since 1956.[41] The frequency and diversity of the deployments is new, however.

The structure of the armed forces has been largely adapted to this in recent years. A shift was made to modest modular expeditionary armed forces that operated jointly and were tailored to the new tasks. It still has almost all the functionalities of the Cold War, only in much smaller numbers. Until now, it has lost only a few major weapons systems. With a smaller fleet, the Royal Netherlands Navy increasingly focuses on operations in coastal waters and in support of land operations. Its 'eyes above water', the Orion patrol aircraft, disappeared from the organization in 2005.[42] In the Royal Dutch Army, the army corps and division structures have been phased out and all units are grouped in three brigades.[43] Major cutbacks due to the credit crisis led to the painful decision to dissolve all tank units in 2011.[44] The continued existence of the Royal Netherlands Air Force has been secured by the planned purchase of an operationally minimum number of Joint Strike Fighters.

The cuts over the past decades were driven by budgetary motives. Although the world certainly had not become safer in this period following the terrorist attacks in America on 9/1,1 in practice defence was a closing entry in the budget. This has led the Netherlands to lower its level of ambition from four operations of battalion size in the first half of the 1990s to one today, with limited capability for sustainment.[45] The modest European operational cooperation at a lower level could not compensate for this loss of capacity. The obstacles had proved insurmountable.

Since 2014, the defence situation has become even more acute because Russia openly embarked on a revanchist approach with the annexation of Crimea and the support of separatists in Eastern Ukraine. Defence of NATO territory in Europe again requires a great deal of attention and resources. Despite cautious increases in the defence budget, many good intentions and several new cooperation initiatives, the capabilities of the Dutch armed forces are far too small to be able to carry out all their tasks in a military and internationally acceptable manner. That is, incidentally, not only the case for the Netherlands. It is a symptom of the incapability of Europe to manifest itself as a power factor in our multipolar world.

Constants and variables

At the end of this chapter on Dutch security and defence policy since World War II, when we focus more on the most important constants and variables regarding this policy, a number of things stand out. The Netherlands has always defended two interests in its international relations: its territorial integrity and its trade and service activities. At the end of the 1970s, foreign policy expert and later Minister of Defence Joris Voorhoeve characterised the basic principles of Dutch foreign policy over the past two centuries – and thus also of security and defence policy – in three key terms: 'peace, profits and principles'. In doing so he referred to respectively the neutralist-abstentionist, the maritime-commercial and the idealistic-internationalist tradition of the Netherlands. Although there is a lot to be said about this characterization – certainly when the idealistic argumentation is compared to day-to-day policy practice – it is broadly correct for the period up to World War II. As a small country with a worldwide trading network, the Netherlands benefited greatly from peace and legal order in international relations. The Dutch authorities often substantiated it with idealistic arguments, which they, especially with regard to colonial 'civilization policy', often firmly believed themselves.

A legacy of World War II was the departure from the neutralist-abstentionist tradition. The Netherlands realised that it could only defend its own security within an alliance. It therefore took an active stand in the Western Union and NATO from the start. The other two traditions remained intact. As a trading nation, the Netherlands sought above all far-reaching economic and financial cooperation in a European context; in the political field, on the other hand, it made great efforts to prevent that the three large Western European countries were given too many powers, including over the policies of smaller countries such as the Netherlands. One of the strategies to counter this threat was to link the security of Europe with that of the United States as much as possible through NATO. The Netherlands also saw its trade and financial interests served through a pro-active membership of globally operating organizations such as the General Agreement on Tariffs and Trade, the International Monetary Fund and the World Bank. Traces of the idealistic-internationalist tradition of the Netherlands can be found in its active policy with regard to international law and the social and cultural organizations of the United Nations, and above all in its activist policy in the field of development cooperation and human rights from the early 1970s. The latter was given space and time thanks to the existence of the protective military and economic bell jar of the Cold War.

After the fall of the Berlin Wall, foreign political certainties crumbled. No major military threat was perceived anymore. In addition to Europe, the United States increasingly turned its focus to East Asia, particularly China, which left Europe more on its own. At the same time, due to developments such as globalization, international terrorism, refugee flows and the Internet, the concept of 'security' changed from a primarily military concept to the much broader concept of 'human security'. In line with its idealistic-internationalist tradition, the Netherlands initially followed the worldwide optimism with regard to a much greater role for the United Nations in promoting peace and prosperity in the world. However, the trauma of the Dutch UN battalion in Srebrenica in July 1995 made the country realise that the world was still ruled by power politics. Nevertheless, it continued to advertise itself as the country of international law.

The United States and NATO have remained the most important security policy landmarks, while the Netherlands has taken cautious steps towards more European cooperation. This is not easy in a domestic political climate with a strong nationalist-populist headwind. European cooperation has become more necessary in recent years since Russia tinkers with Europe's borders. It is already visible in defence cooperation by a (bilateral) bottom-up approach, such as the German–Dutch Army Corps and the Admiralty Benelux. However, the main motive for the formation of these units was the drastic defence cuts since the end of the Cold War, the collection of the 'peace dividend'. While the Netherlands continued to hold on to a 'complete' armed forces for as long as possible – a long-standing constant in defence policy – it increasingly lost its strength and with it its international influence. The increasing threat to both European security and human security therefore means that the position of the Netherlands as a small but still economically prominent country is less and less comfortable.

Notes

1   Wim Klinkert, *Defending neutrality. The Netherlands prepares for war, 1900–1925* (Leiden/Boston: Brill, 2013).

2   R. van Diepen, *Voor Volkenbond en vrede: Nederland en het streven naar een nieuwe wereldorde 1919–1946* (Amsterdam: Bakker, 1999).

3   R. P. F. Bijkerk, 'Nederlands defensiebeleid in de jaren '20. Het bestaande beeld nader bezien', *Militaire Spectator*, Vol. CLXIV (1995): 90–96; Herman Amersfoort, *Een harmonisch leger voor Nederland. Oorlogsbeeld, strategie en operationele planning in het Interbellum* (Breda: Nederlandse Defensie Academie, 2007).

4   Dirk Starink, *De jonge jaren van de luchtmacht. Het luchtwapen in het Nederlandse leger 1913–1939* (Amsterdam: Boom, 2013).

5   Erwin van Loo a.o., *Verenigd op de grond, daadkrachtig in de lucht. Een eeuw grondgebonden luchtverdediging 1917–2017* (Amsterdam: Boom, 2017).

6   G. Teitler (ed), *Tussen crisis en oorlog. Maatschappij en krijgsmacht in de jaren'30* (Dieren: De Bataafsche Leeuw, 1984).

7   G. Teitler, *De strijd om de slagkruisers 1938–1940* (Dieren: De Bataafsche Leeuw, 1984).

8   H. Amersfoort and P. H. Kamphuis, *May 1940. The Battle for the Netherlands* (Leiden/Boston: Brill, 2010); Tobias van Gent, *Het falen van de Nederlandse gewapende neutraliteit, september 1939 – mei 1940* (Amsterdam: De Bataafsche Leeuw, 2009).

9   J. W. M. Schulten, *De geschiedenis van de Ordedienst: mythe en werkelijkheid van een verzetsorganisatie* (Den Haag: Sdu Uitgevers, 1998).

10 Ph. M. Bosscher, *De Koninklijke Marine in de Tweede Wereldoorlog* (Franeker: Uitgeverij Wever/ Uitgeverij Van Wijnen, 1984–1990). For the Dutch contribution to the battle in the air see: Erwin van Loo, *'Eenige wakkere jongens'. Nederlandse oorlogsvliegers in de Britse luchtstrijdkrachten 1940–1945* (Amsterdam: Boom, 2013).

11 Petra Groen and Elly Touwen-Bouwsma (eds), *Nederlands-Indië 1942. Illusie en ontgoocheling* (Den Haag: Sdu Uitgeverij, 1992); J. J. Nortier, P. Kuijt and P. M. H. Groen, *De Japanse aanval op Java. Maart 1942* (Amsterdam: De Bataafsche Leeuw, 1994); P. C. Boer, *De Luchtstrijd om Indië. Operaties van de Militaire Luchtvaart KNIL van december 1941 tot maart 1942* (Houten: Van Holkema & Warendorf, 1990).

12 Christ Klep and Ben Schoenmaker (eds), *De bevrijding van Nederland 1944–1945. Oorlog op de flank* (Den Haag: Sdu Uitgeverij, 1995).

13 P. M. H. Groen, *Marsroutes en dwaalsporen. Het Nederlands militair-strategisch beleid in Indonesië* (Den Haag: Sdu Uitgeverij, 1991); J. J. P. de Jong, *Diplomatie of strijd. Het Nederlands beleid tegenover de Indonesische revolutie 1945–1947* (Meppel/Amsterdam: Boom, 1988); J. J. P. de Jong, *Avondschot. Hoe Nederland zich terugtrok uit zijn Aziatische imperium* (Amsterdam: Boom, 2011); Elly Touwen-Bouwsma and Petra Groen (eds), *Tussen banzai en bersiap. De afwikkeling van de Tweede Wereldoorlog in Nederlands-Indië,* (Den Haag: Sdu Uitgevers, 1996); G. Teitler and P. M. H. Groen (eds), *De Politionele Acties* (Amsterdam: De Bataafsche Leeuw, 1987); J. Hoffenaar and G. Teitler (eds), *De Politionele Acties. Afwikkeling en verwerking* (Amsterdam: De Bataafsche Leeuw, 1990); J. A. de Moor, *Westerling's oorlog. Indonesië 1945–1950: de geschiedenis van de commando's en parachutisten in Nederlands-Indië 1945–1950* (Amsterdam: Balans, 1999);

J. A. de Moor, *Generaal Spoor: Triomf en tragiek van een legercommandant* (Amsterdam: Boom, 2011); Gert Oostindie, *Soldaat in Indonesië, 1945–1950. Getuigenissen van een oorlog aan de verkeerde kant van de geschiedenis* (Amsterdam: Prometheus Bert Bakker, 2015); Rémy Limpach, *De brandende kampongs van generaal Spoor* (Amsterdam: Boom, 2016). The Netherlands also retained Suriname and the Netherlands Antilles, both of which had to be defended. See: Ellen Klinkers, *De troepenmacht in Suriname De Nederlandse defensie in een veranderende koloniale wereld 1940–1975* (Amsterdam: Boom, 2015); Anita van Dissel and Petra Groen, *In de West. De Nederlandse krijgsmacht in het Caribisch gebied* (Franeker: Van Wijnen, 2010).

14 D. A. Hellema, *Dutch Foreign Policy. The Role of the Netherlands in World Politics* (Dordrecht: Republiek der Letteren, 2009); P. B. R. de Geus, *Staatsbelang en Krijgsmacht. De Nederlandse defensie tijdens de Koude Oorlog* (Den Haag: Sdu Uitgevers, 1998).

15 M. D. Schaafsma, *Het Nederlands Detachement Verenigde Naties in Korea 1950–1954* (Den Haag: Staatsdrukkerij en Uitgeverijbedrijf, 1960); Bernadette Kester, Herman Roozenbeek and Okke Groot, *Focus op Korea. De rol van de Nederlandse pers in de beeldvorming over de Korea-oorlog 1950–1953* (Den Haag: Sdu Uitgevers, 2000); Martin Elands (ed), *Vechten, verbeelden en verwerken. Nederland en zijn Korea-veteranen* (Amsterdam: Boom, 2001); Anselm J. van der Peet, *Out-of-area. de Koninklijke Marine en multinationale vlootoperaties 1945–2001* (Franeker: Van Wijnen, 2017).

16 Ine Megens, *American aid to NATO allies in the 1950s: the Dutch case* (s.l.: Thesis Publishers, 1994).

17 D. C. L. Schoonoord, *Pugno Pro Patria. De Koninklijke Marine tijdens de Koude Oorlog* (Franeker: Van Wijnen, 2012).

18 J. Hoffenaar and B. Schoenmaker, *Met de blik naar het Oosten. De Koninklijke Landmacht 1945–1990* (Den Haag: Sdu Uitgeverij, 1994), 67–138.

19 Quirijn van der Vegt, *Take-off. De opbouw van de Nederlandse luchtstrijdkrachten 1945–1973* (Amsterdam: Boom, 2013). For an overview of the history of the Royal Netherlands Air Force see: Rolf de Winter, *Een eeuw militaire luchtvaart in Nederland. Bakermat Soesterberg* (Amsterdam: Boom, 2013).

20 J. Hoffenaar and G. Teitler (eds), *De Koude Oorlog. Maatschappij en Krijgsmacht in de jaren '50* (Den Haag: Sdu Uitgeverij, 1992).

21 Herman Roozenbeek a.o., *Een krachtig instrument. De Koninklijke Marechaussee 1814–2014* (Amsterdam: Boom, 2014).

22 J. R. Beekmans and C. Schilt (eds), *Drijvende stuwen voor de landsverdediging: een geschiedenis van de IJssellinie* (Utrecht: Stichting Menno van Coehoorn, 1996).

23 Jan Hoffenaar, "Hannibal ante portas': The Russian Military Threat and the Build-up of the Dutch Armed Forces, 1948–1958', *The Journal of Military History*, Vol. 66 (2002): 163–191.

24 Hoffenaar and Schoenmaker, *Met de blik*, 143–212; B. Schoenmaker and J. A. M. M. Janssen (eds), *In de schaduw van de Muur. Maatschappij en krijgsmacht rond 1960* (Den Haag: Sdu Uitgevers, 1997); Jan Hoffenaar and Dieter Krüger (eds), *Blueprints for Battle. Planning for War in Central Europe, 1948–1968* (Kentucky: University Press of Kentucky, 2012).

25 Jan van der Harst, *European Union and Atlantic Partnership: Political, Military and Economic Aspects of Dutch Defence, 1948–1954; and the Impact of the European Defence Community* (Florence: European University Institute, 1987).

26 J. Hoffenaar, 'Kans of verplichting. Nederlands complete krijgsmacht in de Koude Oorlog' in G. J. Folmer e.a., *50 jaar NAVO en Nederland* (Den Haag: Atlantische Commissie, 1999); R. M. Verbeek, 'Fighting apart together. Het optreden van de Nederlandse krijgsmacht in NAVO-verband', *Militaire Spectator*, Vol. 169 (2000): 70–82; J. van der Harst, "Kernwapens? Geen bezwaar.' De IRBM-discussie en de opslag van tactische kernkoppen in Nederland, 1955–1970', *Transaktie*, Vol. 4 (1997): 495–518.

27 R. E. van Holst Pellikaan a.o., *Patrouilleren voor de Papoea's. De Koninklijke Marine in Nederlands Nieuw-Guinea* (Amsterdam: De Bataafsche Leeuw, 1989–1990); Martin Elands (ed), *Afscheid van Nieuw-Guinea. Het Nederlands-Indonesisch conflict 1950–1962* (Bussum: Uitgeverij Thoth, 2003).

28 D. Starink, 'De nuclearisering van de krijgsmacht' in Schoenmaker and Janssen, *In de schaduw van de Muur*, 82–99.

29 Rinus Nederlof, *Blazing Skies, De Groepen Geleide Wapens van de Koninklijke Luchtmacht in Duitsland, 1960–1995* (Den Haag: Sdu Uitgevers, 2002).

30 Jan Hoffenaar and Robin Bleichroth, 'Defensiehervormingen in de Jaren '70. Rondom de generaalsruzie', *Tijdschrift voor Geschiedenis*, Vol. 128 (2015): 407–431.

31 *Handelingen Tweede Kamer*, 1973–1974, nr. 12994 (Defence White Paper 1974).

32 Jan Willem Honig, *Defense Policy in the North Atlantic Alliance. The Case of the Netherlands* (Westport: Praeger, 1993); Hoffenaar and Schoenmaker, *Met de blik*, 287–298.

33 D. Starink, *Gevechtsvliegtuigen voor de KLu. De geschiedenis van de keuzebepaling en de aanschaf* (Den Haag: Sectie Luchtmachthistorie, 1991); Bert Kreemers, *Hete hangijzers: de aanschaf van Nederlandse gevechtsvliegtuigen* (Amsterdam: Uitgeverij Balans, 2009).

34 Coreline Boot, *Het leger onder vuur. De Koninklijke Landmacht en haar critici 1945–1989* (Amsterdam: Boom, 2015).

35 J. Hoffenaar a.o. (eds), *Confrontatie en ontspanning. Maatschappij en krijgsmacht in de Koude Oorlog 1966–1989* (Den Haag: Sdu Uitgevers, 2004).

36 For a more comprehensive overview of the development of defence policy since the end of the Cold War see: J. Hoffenaar, 'Een politieke aangelegenheid. De ontwikkeling van de hoofdtaken en het ambitieniveau van de Nederlandse krijgsmacht na de Koude Oorlog', attachment to *Verkenningen – Houvast voor de krijgsmacht in de toekomst* (Den Haag: Ministerie van Defensie, 2010).

37 Officially, administratively, conscription still exists, but call-up has been suspended. As of 1 January 2020, conscription in the Netherlands also applies to women.

38 Roozenbeek, *Een krachtig instrument.*

39 Christ Klep and Richard van Gils, *Van Korea tot Kabul. De Nederlandse militaire deelname aan vredesoperaties sinds 1945* (Den Haag: Sdu Uitgevers, 2005); https://www.defensie.nl/onderwerpen/historische-missies.

40 Thijs Brocades Zaalberg and Arthur ten Cate, 'A gentle occupation. Unravelling the Dutch Approach in Iraq, 2003–2005', *Small Wars & Insurgencies*, Vol. 23, No. 1 (2012): 117–143; Christ Klep, *Uruzgan. Nederlandse militairen op missie, 2005–2010* (Amsterdam: Boom, 2011; Arthur ten Cate and Martijn van der Vorm, *Callsign Nassau. Dutch Army Special Forces in action in the 'New World Disorder'* (Leiden/Chicago: Leiden University Press, 2016); Van der Peet, *Out-of-area.*

41 Ben Schoenmaker and Herman Roozenbeek (eds), *Vredesmacht in Libanon. De Nederlandse deelname aan UNIFIL 1979–1985* (Amsterdam: Boom, 2004); Arthur ten Cate, *Waarnemers op heilige grond. Nederlandse officieren bij UNTSO, 1956–2003* (Amsterdam: Boom, 2003).

42 *Handelingen Tweede Kamer*, 2003–2004, 29.200-X, No. 4 ('*Op weg naar een nieuw evenwicht. De krijgsmacht in de komende jaren*').

43 These are 11 Airmobile Brigade and 13 and 43 Mechanised Brigade. At the time of writing – in accordance with the letter from the Minister of Defence to the President of the House of Representatives, BS2013031445, 25 October 2013 – 13 Mechanised Brigade has been converted into a motorised brigade (with wheeled rather than tracked vehicles).

44 *Handelingen Tweede Kamer*, 2010–2011, 32.733, No. 1 ('*Defensie na de kredietcrisis*'). In 2016, a German/Netherlands tank unit was established.

45 *Handelingen Tweede Kamer*, 2013–2014, 33.763, No. 1 (White Paper '*In het belang van Nederland*').

CHAPTER II

The Ambivalent Results of 1945:
The Case of Austria and her Central
European Neighbours

Lothar Höbelt

Introduction: Geography versus history

When Europe was commemorating World War I as the seminal catastrophe of the 20th century a few years ago, the prime minister of Croatia is supposed to have said: 'I know: That is one of those old wars where we still don't know whether we won or lost.'[1] Of course, few politicians would run the gauntlet of political correctness by allowing themselves to be quoted in similar terms about the results of World War II.[2] Yet the ambivalence of Zoran Milanovic's answer would appear to sum up very well the results of 1945 over large parts of Central Europe. Few lamented the downfall of Hitler, or his acolytes. Even 'unreconstructed rebels' would have to admit that no regime had ever come to quite such a disastrous end. It was easy to agree that the end of the most destructive war the world had ever experienced was 'a good thing'. It was far from clear whether what came next was a good thing, too.

1945 – and the two or three years after – were a great watershed in Central European history, far more so than in the history of Western Europe (where 1945 simply corrected the fluke of 1940). For most of Western Europe, the number of casualties during World War II was much lower than in the 'Great War' of 1914–18. For most of East and Central Europe – except for the Czechs – it was the other way round. 1945 ended the turmoil of the Thirty Years War of the 20th century, to borrow General de Gaulle's phrase, and paved the way for a period of extraordinary stability that lasted until 1989. For Austria, that period turned a 'state that no one had wanted' during the inter-war years into an 'island of the blessed'.[3] For Hungary, it was an almost unmitigated disaster – few analysts think that the country ever stood a chance of escaping the clutches of Soviet rule. For Czechoslovakia, 1945 initially seemed to open 'a window of opportunity' to revive the good old days of the post-1918 First Republic – a window that slammed shut in 1948. In Yugoslavia the charismatic dictatorship of Marshal Tito was often given the benefit of the doubt in retrospect because it had at least managed to keep the country together.

Geography, not history, dictated the post-war fate of Central Europe. That's why the crossroads of 1945 lead to slightly paradoxical results. To all intents and purposes Austria had lost the war as part of the 'Third Reich', but it still managed to disassociate itself from Germany and win western support. Hungary had been the last ally of Germany (except for Japan). In 1944, it unsuccessfully tried to copy the Italian model and switch sides. These efforts failed and were not appreciated. In contrast to the Austrian experience, the Cold War cut off Hungary from all hopes of western support. The Czech lands had been occupied by Nazi Germany before the war had even started, and they were only occupied by the Soviets after the war had all but ended. Before World War II, Hungary and Czechoslovakia had followed quite different and often antagonistic paths in more ways than one. Hungary had been a monarchy without a king, run by a semi-authoritarian conservative regime, Czechoslovakia a multi-ethnic democracy, governed by centrist coalitions. Czechoslovakia was the most heavily industrialised part of the old Austro-Hungarian monarchy, Hungary was still dominated by aristocratic great landowners. Nevertheless, both countries were subjected to a very similar dose of orthodox communism after 1947/48.

Slovakia had for the first time in her history enjoyed a limited form of independence as a German satellite. In 1945, the country was reintegrated into Czechoslovakia. Yugoslavia had disintegrated after the Axis attack in the spring of 1941 and experienced years of bloody civil wars among a multitude of warlords, selectively supported by the great powers. Tito's communist-dominated resistance movement (Antifascist Council for the Liberation of Yugoslavia, with AVNOJ as its acronym) emerged victorious from the chaos. However, in 1948, when 'western-style', half-way democratic Czechoslovakia vanished behind the Iron Curtain, Tito made the most of his geographical position and managed to cut his ties with the Eastern Bloc.

Austria: Liberated, defeated – or neutral

Of course, Austrians paid lip-service to the notion that they had been liberated from the German yoke by the Allies. For many of the politicians who formed its provisional government in April 1945, there was a certain element of authenticity to that assertion. Most of them, at one time or another, had been arrested by the Nazis or even spent a few years in a concentration camp (like Leopold Figl, Chancellor of Austria from late 1945 to 1953).[4] His predecessor Karl Renner was closer to the mainstream, when he told the civil servants who returned to duty in late April 1945, that the 'Anschluß' (union with Germany) had been a dream that had ended badly. Now at least they knew that it was over for good.[5]

At the same time, the claim to be a sort of clandestine victor of World War II rang hollow. More than a million Austrians had fought with the German 'Wehrmacht', only a few thousand émigrés had joined one of the allied armies.[6] The behaviour of the Red Army did little to improve the image of the liberators: the monument erected in their honour in down-town Vienna was often referred to as the 'monument of the unknown rapist'. Peter Kenez's summary about Hungarian attitudes would seem to apply to Austria as well: 'It is highly unlikely that more than a small minority of the population at the time greeted the arrival of the Red Army with unalloyed enthusiasm and felt themselves liberated.'[7] That general rule allowed for certain exceptions as far as the western powers were concerned: the British who entered Carinthia on VE Day were certainly cheered as saviours – because they had arrived just in time to prevent a take-over by Tito's feared partisans from the south.[8]

Bruno Kreisky, Austrian chancellor after 1970 and himself an émigré, always stressed that he regarded Austria as a defeated country.[9] However, there were some obvious benefits in sticking to the legal fiction that Austria had not been annexed in 1938, but only occupied by German troops. Thus, whatever individual Austrians might have done, the reborn state could not be blamed for their actions. The western powers were far from being firm believers in the Rip van Winkle-like character of the Austrian Republic that claimed to have been dormant through six years of warfare. But as a thoughtful US official once minuted: 'Since, as a matter of national policy, we encourage a separate Austrian nationalism, we cannot be surprised, and should in fact find comfort in the fact that most Austrians deny ever having had anything to do with Germany.'[10]

In 1945, just like the remainder of Germany, Austria had been divided into four different zones of occupation. Having got rid of the Germans, Austria was looking forward to getting rid of its 'liberators' at roughly the same time that the peace treaties with Hungary, Romania and Italy were signed in 1947. Once these expectations turned out to be wrong, they put their hopes on the 'roll-back' promised by Truman. After all, the communist take-over in Prague seemed to have galvanised the west into action. Austrian Foreign Secretary Karl Gruber fondly talked about ten thousand bombers ready to be unleashed against the Soviets.[11] But the roll-back did not come to pass. The Korean War did – and raised the spectre of a Soviet advance to the Atlantic. After that sobering experience, faced with the threat of a partitioning of the country along the lines of Germany, Chancellor Julius Raab after 1953 opted for an 'appeasement' of Stalin's heirs.

Once again, it was geography that provided a helping hand. A neutralization of Austria – following the example of Switzerland – cut NATO in two but did not materially affect the strategic position of the emerging Warsaw Pact. That is why the Soviet Union told its clients within the fairly small Austrian Communist Party in no uncertain terms that they were not interested in creating an Austrian GDR in miniature.[12] The US was predictably sceptical about the prospects of a neutral Austria with a capital only 30 miles away from the Iron Curtain. In 1955, they only agreed to give the State Treaty the benefit of the doubt once the Austrians promised to provide some sort of deterrent against a hostile take-over by creating an army of their own. At the back of their minds, once Eisenhower's 'New Look' had dispensed with the idea of maintaining huge and costly conventional forces in Europe, the US could rely on tactical nuclear missiles as a weapon of last resort to close the gap in the western defences opened by their withdrawal from Austria.[13]

The 'Second Republic': Anti-communism, de-Nazification – and machine politics

Austria had been well-known for its divisive politics during the inter-war years, culminating in two brief civil wars in 1934. Social democrats had positioned themselves to the left of their comrades in most of Europe, antagonising the middle classes but incidentally preventing the growth of a sizeable native communist party. Catholic conservatives had opted for an authoritarian government with pseudo-fascist trappings in 1933. National socialism – as a hybrid nationalist white-collar party – had originated in Austria but returned to power via Munich and Berlin during the 1930s. The Nazis gobbled up all the minor middle-class parties during the Great Depression, besides attracting support from both farmers and workers as the first modern 'catch-all party'.

After 1945, socialists and Christian democrats outlawed the Nazis and joined forces against the communists who only received 5% of the vote – despite or because of their association with the Soviets. From a general humanitarian point of view, there was little to choose between the totalitarian systems of Hitler and Stalin who had both sent many millions of innocent victims to their death. The difference was that Hitler had lost the war, Stalin had won – which is what made him far more dangerous. A leading Austrian socialist summed up the priorities: 'Within the next twenty years, a Hitler-style concentration camp is impossible, a Stalin-style one is not.'[14]

The Marshall Plan aid was intended to keep Austria firmly within the western orbit, but at the same time gave a big boost to nationalised industries. Big business, the commanding heights of the economy, remained state-owned and was administered by managers selected on a strictly bi-partisan model labelled 'Proporz'. The remnants of war-time controls were delegated to the 'social partnership', a high-level combination of chambers of commerce and trade unions. Competition was stifled, but strikes averted.[15] Austria remained staunchly anti-communist but established a neo-corporatist economy. In 1951, an up-and-coming Austrian statesman already coined the phrase, usually associated with Harold Macmillan half a dozen years later: 'You've never had it so good.'[16]

The ten years during which Austria was occupied by the Allies also gave rise to a peculiarity of the Austrian post-war political system. Austrians aimed at presenting a united front against the occupation forces in general, Soviets and native communists in particular. That is why the preservation of the Great Coalition of Christian Democrats (ÖVP) and Socialists counted as a patriotic necessity. The US had usually encouraged the formation of centre-right governments like Alcide de Gasperi's in Italy and Konrad Adenauer's in West Germany. But in Austria they insisted on keeping the socialists in government as their working-class supporters were the ones who were supposed to act as the main bulwark against communist subversion. Once the occupation forces left, the Great Coalition seemed to have taken on a life of its own. Austria was dominated by machine politics to an unusual extent. Benefits from civil service jobs to subsidised council flats were parcelled out according to political clientelism. No less than a third of all adults were card-carrying members of one of the two big parties.

De-Nazification has become a scholarly growth subject in recent years. It seems there are a number of misperceptions about the sort of anti-fascist fervour prevalent in 1945. The Allies organised detention camps for a motley collection of suspects to guard against any inkling of werewolf activities. This kind of arrest was 'a preventive, not a punitive' measure. Maybe its arbitrariness was balanced by the fact that during the immediate post-war years the inmates of the US camps often received bigger rations than the average Austrian. Chancellor Renner was quite prepared to hang a few Nazis '*pour encourager les autres*', but then call an end to the vicious circle of successive waves of persecution that had overtaken Austria for the last dozen years. Few thought that it was a good idea to enact sweeping laws indiscriminately penalising the rank-and-file members of the Nazi party (10% of the population, up to 20% of male adults).

However, exactly such a law was passed in February 1947 because the Soviets insisted on it – and the Austrians hoped they would be rewarded by the speedy conclusion of the State Treaty. At that point in time, a few weeks before the official start of the Cold War, the US was still unwilling to oppose the Soviets openly. They thought the law was inoperable but encouraged the Austrians to go through the motions and simply find a way to mitigate its effects afterwards. Foreign Secretary Gruber went so far as to tell his colleagues that the law was the result of 'a Communist manoeuvre supported by the Russians and the French.' (After all, the communists still formed part of the French government at that time.) The Austrians heeded the advice of the Americans: the law was duly passed and followed by an amnesty the year after.[17]

It was not quite so easy to define what exactly Nazis were supposed to want in the post-war world. The Nazi programme had been a hodgepodge mixture of sometimes contradictory ideas stolen from both left and right, enforced by totalitarian methods, an 'extremism of the centre' (Martin Seymour Lipset). One could as easily persuade oneself to carry on its essence in prolonging the anti-communist crusade on the side of conservatives and the western powers, or espouse the socialist element of Nazism that militated in favour of an interventionist state, deficit spending and the 'antiplutocratic' left. After 1945, Austrian parties each had their own pet criteria as a litmus test for reformed characters: Christian Democrats stressed Austrian patriotism and a heartfelt farewell to Anschluß, socialists directed their ire at dictatorship in general (with a swipe at the conservative pre-1938 regime). Communists targeted NATO by identifying revanchism and remilitarisation as the prime danger. When communists staged demonstrations against Wehrmacht nostalgia in 1952, their immediate target happened to be a Hollywood film with a script by a British general, Desmond Young's *Rommel – the Desert Fox*.

The Bundesheer: The Cinderella of Austria

In terms of national identity, tradition and ethnicity, the post-1918 Republic of Austria as the German rump of the monarchy had hovered uneasily between the pull of pan-German ideas and Habsburg traditions. After 1945, both options were no longer available. Nostalgia for the Habsburgs might give a boost to the film industry, but links to the Central European neighbours had been severed by the Iron Curtain. The idea of union with Germany had been fatally contaminated by Hitler's policies. But contrary to their post-1918 reaction, Austrians gradually learnt to no longer even think of themselves as Germans. Pan-Germanism was frowned upon, but economic integration with West Germany boomed, as there were few viable alternatives. Austrian identity clearly refuted the dictum that the flag follows the trade, or in Marxian terms: that being determines consciousness.

Austrian diplomats were certainly told to forget about their service in the German army (even if one of them, First Lieutenant Kurt Waldheim, was later on chastised for following orders, on these and earlier occasions). However, 'civil society' did not have to toe the official line: veterans continued to wear their war-time decorations (and proudly showed them off when Queen Elizabeth and Prince Philip visited the country in 1969). During the 1960s, Chancellor Alfons Gorbach – who had lost a leg in WWI and spent years in a Nazi concentration camp during WWII – epitomised the compromise consensus when he publicly praised the veterans of both world wars for their sense of duty.[18] His successor Josef Klaus (1964–70) was the only Austrian chancellor who had himself served in the Wehrmacht; his cabinet included two ministers who had lost a limb during the fighting in World War II.[19]

When an Austrian 'Federal Army' (Bundesheer) was re-founded in 1955, one of the clauses of the State Treaty read that no officer who had held the rank of colonel or above in the German Wehrmacht was allowed to serve in the Bundesheer of the Second Republic. But then he could either claim that his promotion papers had no longer reached him during the chaotic last days of the war – or if all else failed, he was simply hired as a civilian consultant.[20] It will not come as a big surprise that the first three inspector generals of the Austrian Army all happened to be lieutenant colonels of the Wehrmacht, to be followed by two men with less predictable career patterns, Hubert Wingelbauer (1978–80) – who had been expelled from the German army because of his Jewish ancestry – and Heinz Scharff (1981–85), a Knight's Cross holder who had spent no less than eight years as a POW in Russia. Baron Karl Lütgendorf, Minister of Defence during the 1970s, had been a German intelligence officer sent to the US for de-briefing in 1945.[21]

At the same time, the Bundesheer indulged in a certain kind of schizophrenia. Even if the leading cadres owed their military experiences to World War II, service in the German Army was not supposed to form part of its tradition. Thus, the Military Academy in Wiener Neustadt was not allowed to cherish the memory of Erwin Rommel who had briefly commanded the Academy in 1939. The image of Rommel whom Churchill had called 'a great general' and who had been forced to commit suicide by the Nazis, might appear as a fortunate combination of professional renown and opposition to Hitler. But then he had never served in any Austrian army. Socialists were equally weary of the legacy of the old Habsburg Empire. Kreisky once summed up his scepticism: many Austrian officers had already sworn four different oaths (which was no longer quite so plausible during the 1970s). A long feud erupted over the adoption of either peaked caps (like the Wehrmacht) or kepis (like old Austria or the French, but also the Stormtroopers). The Swiss continued to use German-style neck-protection helmets and Austrians adopted the American model (partly because it was for free).

Ideologues might debate the merits of the Wehrmacht as a suitable role model for an Austrian army because of the political misgivings attached to the Nazi regime it had served, even if the professional quality of German officers was generally appreciated by specialists, not excluding western ones. The real question was whether the lessons of blitzkrieg and its aftermath were any longer relevant to a small country likely to be quickly overrun in any confrontation of the great powers. If any experiences were valid, perhaps Rommel springs to mind again – not the desert fox, but the commander in Normandy who always warned that given allied air superiority the defenders would be unable to move by daylight – or indeed at any other time. Austrians had their allotment of tanks (because they were expected to buy all the home-produced ones that could not be exported) but they were inadequately equipped in terms of air defence. They were not allowed to own 'rockets'. (And even legal experts weren't quite sure whether the term in the State Treaty refer to latter day V 2s only or to bazookas, too.) The jets they bought from Sweden in the 1960s were actually built to a Messerschmidt design but they were trainers only.

Austrians had promised to defend their neutrality. But per capita they spent only about a sixth as much on defence as the Swedes. A British observer once christened the Bundesheer the Cinderella of Austria.[22] Perennial budget constraints – and the reduction of service time to a mere six months in 1971 – paved the way for a militia army. In the 1970s the Army Commander, Count Emil Spannocchi, tried to make the best of it by advocating a concept of local defence rather than reliance on a rapid deployment force. Incidentally, the Soviets had a way of taking their guests to the sites where they had been once before – during World War II. When Spannocchi was shown the spot not very far from Moscow where he had fought in 1941, he turned round and promised his hosts: 'In the name of the Bundesheer, I promise we'll never again advance that far.' Coming from an Austrian, his comments caused general merriment. Perhaps, a similar joke by a West German general would not have elicited such an amused reaction.

Hungary

Hitler had annexed Austria in 1938, but he was willing to support the conservative regimes in Hungary and Romania rather than putting his money on the wild cards of those countries pro-Nazi Arrow-Cross and Iron Guard movements. Thus, until October 1944, Hungary continued to be run by Admiral Miklos Horthy, the last commander of the Austro-Hungarian navy. Just like the system of the post-war months (when right-wing parties were not allowed to compete) his regime can best be characterised as a system of impaired pluralism (with socialists not allowed to proselytise in the countryside). It was only when Hungary tried to follow the Italian example by jumping ship in 1944 that German troops occupied Hungary in March and appointed the Arrow Cross leader, Ferenc Szalasi, as their henchman in October.

After World War I and the interlude of a Soviet Republic in 1919, Hungary had remained a kingdom as a symbol of national unity and continuity, albeit without a king. It had lost more than half of its territory under the terms of the peace treaty of Trianon in 1920 but had gone a long way towards reclaiming territories lost between 1938 and 1941. All these windfall profits – Transylvania, Carpatho-Ukraine, the Bacska and the southern rim of Slovakia – were lost again in 1945 (though Hungarians – even the Hungarian communists – argued that after all Slovaks and Romanians had been German allies, too). At least, Hungarian minorities in those areas were not generally expelled. Deportations soon stopped.

Like the Austrian Christian Democrats, the peasant-based Smallholders Party succeeded in winning an overall majority in 1945. Communists won only 17%, compared to 38 % in Czechoslovakia. Nevertheless, Hungary actually succumbed to communism much earlier than Czechoslovakia. Matyas Rakosi and his communist-led Bloc relied on 'salami tactics' by slicing the Smallholders Party apart in the course of 1946 and 1947, frightening some of their leaders into exile, winning over others and coercing the rest. After the elections of 1947, the communist-led Bloc still fell short of an overall majority but took a leaf out of Hitler's book who in 1933 had simply outlawed the communists to emasculate the opposition. Communists – with a docile Smallholder still formally running the government – outlawed enough right-wing MPs to make sure they could no longer be defeated in parliament. [23]

The Smallholders' plight served as a warning to parties further west, exposed to the rough wooing of Soviet suitors. Yet, too much blame should not be laid at the door of the smallholders appeasement tactics. There was no window of opportunity. Even before the war ended, the Soviets had occupied all of Hungary. No matter what the (in)famous percentage agreements were supposed to have said, in the Allied Control Commission set up to run Hungary the western powers were only given an observer's role (just as the Soviets had not been invited to participate in the Italian one). The Smallholders' leaders hoped to play for time and last long enough for the Soviets to leave once the peace treaty had been ratified. The treaty was actually signed in February 1947, but Stalin argued that his troops needed to stay put to safeguard their lines of communications with the Soviet troops in Austria. Thus, the onset of the Cold War already found Hungary on the wrong side of the Iron Curtain. The US had long since lost hope of keeping Hungary out of the Russian orbit. Predictably, in his speech commemorating a hundred years of Trianon in 2020, Hungarian Prime Minister Viktor Orban highlighted this betrayal of Hungary by the west.

Czechoslovakia

Austrians had fought on the German side in WWII and said goodbye to world politics after 1955. In the case of its northern neighbour, the Czech heartland of Czechoslovakia, there could hardly be any doubt that it had been occupied by Germany against its will in March 1939. Hitler's march into Prague had none of the trappings of his earlier flower campaigns. Once the war started, ex-President Edvard Benes successfully tried to win recognition for his government-in-exile. Benes originally resided in London (Grosvenor Place 8) but returned to Czechoslovakia in the wake of Soviet troops. On 5 May, there was a Czech uprising in Prague, started by pro-western police units. The Soviets were none too eager to give a helping hand. The Germans crushed the uprising in the last few hours before the armistice. A Czech contingent under Ludvik Svoboda had fought with the Soviet army. Maybe more memorable was the contribution of close to a hundred Czech pilots during the Battle of Britain. But few of those RAF volunteers were welcome in post-1948 Czechoslovakia.

In Czechoslovakia, the communists won no less than 38% of the vote in 1945. Czechoslovakia had always had a strong Communist Party. Once before, in 1925, it had emerged as the country's largest party. Moreover, in 1945, all the parties of the centre-right, Agrarians and national democrats, as well as the Slovak Catholics, to say nothing of Germans and Hungarians, had been outlawed. The communists got the lion's share of jobs in the all-party government established in 1945. When their coalition partners showed signs of growing restive and were tempted to join the Marshal Plan, the communists browbeat the social democrats into cooperating and grabbed power in the 'Victorious February' of 1948. Benes had earlier told his confidants: 'My task was to defeat Hitler. The job before your generation will be to defeat the other dictator. You know whom I am talking about.' But he did not play a heroic part during the final crisis. As one participant said: It was 'either collaboration or resignation – tertium non datur.' In a repeat performance of the classic 'defenestrations' for which Prague had become famous, Foreign Secretary Jan Masaryk, son of the founder of the First Republic, was found dead below his windows two weeks later. [24]

Three million Sudeten Germans were expelled from Czechoslovakia in 1945–46. Plans of large-scale ethnic cleansing had been mooted by both Czechs and Germans since 1938. Originally, Benes had envisaged a partial solution: he was willing to cede a little bit of territory to Germany but in return either expel or forcibly assimilate the rest of the German population. In 1945 the first part of the deal had become superfluous. Towards the end of the war, Germans from East Prussia, Pomerania and Silesia had most of them fled before the Red Army. When Poland was handed Wroclaw and Szczecin as compensation for Vilnius and Lvov, there were few Germans left in those provinces. But the Czech lands had been held by the Wehrmacht far longer than almost any other part of the Third Reich. Expulsions thus had to be conducted in peacetime by what claimed to be a democratic government. The western powers agreed to the population transfer with some misgivings mostly because they hoped that a more homogenous Czechoslovakia would be better able to stand up to bullying by either the Germans or the Russians. [25]

Ethnic cleansing left a bitter taste. It also had unforeseen consequences. Bohemia had been spared most of the ravages of the war. [26] In 1945 it seemed a far more promising country than all the surrounding German lands. With hindsight, however, Sudeten Germans were (most of them) expelled into the West German 'economic miracle' while Czechs were condemned to languish behind the Iron Curtain. Czechs had two sorts of grievances against the Germans. First of all, obviously, the destruction of the First Republic, Munich and its aftermath. But the backlash against Hitler's expansionism was not welcome either. The war Hitler had unleashed helped to propel Czechoslovakia into the Eastern Bloc. What had been imposed on Hungary as a penalty, was awarded to Czechoslovakia as a prize. As one Czech journalist put it: 'You Germans marched all the way to Stalingrad, and as a result the Russians decided to stay put in Bohemia.' [27]

Thus, the legacy of 1945 was a liberation by the wrong sort of liberators – and a reunification of Czechoslovakia that had been dismembered in 1938–39. Slovaks had for the first time enjoyed statehood in 1939 under the leadership of Jozef Tiso, a Catholic priest. Tiso's regime was a dictatorship, allied to the Axis powers, that sent a few regiments to fight the Soviets. It met with fervent opposition from Protestants who started an uprising in mid-1944. After the war, Czechoslovakia was re-established – except for its easternmost Ukrainian province that was annexed by the Soviets. In 1993, the Czech Republic and Slovakia negotiated a peaceful parting of the ways, helped by the fact that there were few minority disputes on either side of the border – and that both have little difficulty understanding each other's language. Since 2017, the Prime Minister of the Czech Republic, Andrej Babis, actually has been a Slovak.

Yugoslavia

If Austrians lost the war, Czechs lost the peace and Hungarians both, Yugoslavia's Marshal Tito (nee Josip Broz) undoubtedly won his war, or rather: he won any number of disjointed civil wars, or at least watched his rivals go down in defeat. Yugoslavia had disintegrated after the military coup d'etat in March 1941 and the subsequent attack of the Axis powers. Germany, Hungary, Bulgaria and Italy – both on her own account and on behalf of Albania – had all laid claims to part of the booty. Croatia (including all of Bosnia) and the rump of Serbia were established as client states of the Axis powers.

The communist party had proven adept at exploiting ethnic grievances rather than class warfare even during peacetime. After the dismemberment of Yugoslavia, its partisan drive found any number of takers, starting with Montenegrin clans who staged a successful uprising against the Italians already in the summer of 1941, but especially among the diaspora of Orthodox Serbs subjected to the terror regime of Ante Pavelic, the Croatian dictator whose genocidal tactics upset even his far from soft-hearted German allies. In Serbia proper Draza Mihailovic's 'Cetniks' grew out of the remnants of the royal army. The intricacies of local antagonisms made for strange bedfellows at times. Whereas Mihailovic established links with the Italians, Tito in early 1943 tried to entice the Germans into an armistice, by appealing to their common interest in preventing a western landing in the Adriatic.

Yugoslavia suffered huge losses in low-tech warfare and massacres of up to two million, almost 10% of the population, i.e. on the scale of the Russian losses. As in the Russian case, that civil war actually dragged on far beyond VE Day. Tito was a survivor who narrowly escaped capture on several occasions. After 1943, he profited from the collapse of Italy and from the British decision to back him rather than Mihailovic.[28] Tito's trump card was that he represented not just a makeshift government-in-exile that the Allies had deigned to recognise but he was the one who was actually in possession once the Germans under their Austrian commander Alexander Löhr beat a retreat. (In the end, Löhr voluntarily returned to captivity in Yugoslavia where he was sentenced to death.)[29] Tito claimed to lead the fourth-largest allied army in Europe (even if that claim might conceivably have been disputed by de Gaulle). This is what gave him a unique position among the resistance movements of Europe.[30] Stalin and Churchill might engage in a tug-of-war over who was going to run Poland or Hungary, but Randolph Churchill already told his father, Winston, in mid-1944: 'Whether we help Tito or not, after the war, he will be the master of Yugoslavia.'[31]

Like Mao on the other side of Eurasia, for Tito the Soviets were allies, not liberators. Yet both Mao and Tito started out by being more Popish than the Pope. In 1945, Stalin did not want to provoke the US, but persuade them to go back to normalcy and no longer bother about Europe. Tito on the other hand seemed eager to pick a fight with the west, in particular the British almost everywhere, from Carinthia and Trieste to the Greek border in Macedonia and Albania. Maybe by doing so he was actually playing the British game because his truculence succeeded in alerting the US to the dangers of communist expansionism. He was certainly not playing Stalin's game by his misplaced zeal. His old partisan fighters pretended to be unimpressed when Molotov warned them about the west: 'Don't you realise they have the atomic bomb?'[32] Tito added insult to injury when after having wrecked Stalin's approach, he went on to make the most of his geographical position by risking a break with the Kremlin in early 1948.[33]

US observers compared Tito's rupture with Stalin to either Martin Luther's or Henry VIII's with the Pope. Was that conflict going to lead to a schism or to a thoroughgoing reformation? In many ways, not just in terms of lifestyle, Tito – who cost the state far more than King Alexander – preferred the Tudor example. Like Henry VIII, he persecuted adherence to the old faith as treason, not heresy. After Stalin's death, his relations with Moscow were subject to a number of ups and downs. He certainly relied on assistance from the west – both in terms of armaments and grain supplies, but still supported the Soviet suppression of the 'counter-revolution' in Hungary in 1956. Yugoslavia looked to an international role as a leader of the non-aligned countries, with special emphasis on relations with India. In Tito's favourite holiday resort of Brioni – the Austro-Hungarian U-boat station in World War I – one can still visit the elephant that Indira Gandhi gave him as a present.[34]

Tito's image as a more benevolent kind of communist would not have been shared by the relatives of the victims of the 'foibe', the caves in the Karst mountains where tens of thousands of Croatian soldiers, Slovene militia or Italians vanished in 1945. But Tito's rebuilding of Yugoslavia followed a federalist pattern. Pre-war Yugoslavia had been run by a Serb dynasty, the Karadjeordjevic. All its prime ministers had been Serbs. Tito was a Croat (with a Slovene mother) who had even briefly fought against the Serbs during World War I as a NCO under Habsburg colours.[35] Most of his support during the years from 1941 to 1944 came from the ex-Habsburg lands in the Western half of Yugoslavia. Tito's version of 'Socialism in One Country' was a socialism in six republics (and two autonomous regions, one of them the Kosovo). In 1974, the republics were even accorded the right to secession – in a way, almost reminiscent of Austria-Hungary, only the army and foreign policy were any longer supposed to be run by Belgrade.

'Titoism' toyed with the concept of 'self-management', with power devolved to factory collectives rather than a central planning agency. It is not always clear what that system meant in terms of investment and prices.[36] Behind the scenes, there was a tug-of-war between the Slovene Edvard Kardelj as a proponent of reforms and relations with western social democrats, and Serb secret police boss Aleksandar Rankovic who preferred 'democratic centralism' of a more orthodox kind and mending fences with the Russians. Differences in per capita income between the republics were huge. But the emphasis on local autonomy probably did help to reduce ethnic tensions. Like Habsburg Prime Minister Count Edward Taaffe, Tito succeeded in keeping most of his subject – or constituent – nations in a state of 'well-tempered discontent'.

The legacies of 1945 and the 'politics of memory'

The legacies of 1945 were diverse: Austria was finally reconciled to its independence and sooner or later even started to take pride in having become a nation of its own; Hungary remained a classical nation state, if no longer a kingdom, with a lot of grievances against her neighbours; Czechoslovakia and Yugoslavia were reconstituted as multi-ethnic units before falling apart during the 1990s, peacefully in one case, much less so in the case of the warring tribes of Serbo-Croat speakers, rent apart by religion and history in a way almost resembling the case of Ireland.

For the Austro-German losers 1945 was the unequivocal beginning of a success story that propelled them into an 'economic miracle' on a par with West Germany. The 1951 book *The Mouse that Roared* – later turned into a film by Peter Sellers – seems to sum it up in a nut-shell: the perfect way to prosperity is to lose a war against the Americans. But their Central European neighbours were painfully aware that the western powers had not fought the war on their own. Thus, for Hungarians 1945 marked the continuation of a tragedy, from the SS to the NKVD, and from Szalasi to Rakosi. For Czechs the interval between the German and the Russian tyrannies has assumed greater significance than in the Hungarian case, as a kind of unfulfilled hope, even if those years also saw the expulsion of minorities and the first steps on the way to communist domination. For Yugoslavs Tito's Frank Sinatra-style communism ('I'll do it my way'), framed as it was by two eras of civil wars, comes closest to an ambivalent legacy. For all its faults, Tito's dictatorship was pragmatic and increasingly willing to open the country to western tourism (and western employers eager to hire migrant labour).

The two totalitarian movements claimed a lot of victims. It is a truism that all these movements obviously also had a great number of followers in Central Europe, of both the enthusiastic and the opportunistic variety. The electoral statistics from both the pre- and the post-war years point to the conclusion that fascism – under different labels – was more popular with Austrians and Hungarians, communism in its different varieties with Czechs and Yugoslavs. That finding in itself begs the question whether these sympathies had that much to do with ideological convictions or were not more influenced by traditional notions about 'auld alliances', i.e. the popularity of a German versus a Russian 'great brother'. Since 1989, the geopolitical context has changed dramatically, but the ideological debates of yesteryear have to some extent been given a new lease of life under the heading 'politics of memory'.

The celebration of 'national holidays' is one way to chart the 'politics of memory' at its most official level. In Austria, the day to remember in connection with 1945 had usually been 27 April when Karl Renner announced the re-founding of the Republic. When Austrians debated the adoption of a national holiday during the 1960s, the two options both by-passed 1945: 15 May (when the State Treaty was signed in 1955) or 12 November (when the Republic had been proclaimed in 1918). Only recently have Austrians caught on to the coattails of VE Day, 8 May, that is routinely celebrated by a concert in front of the Hofburg (where Hitler held his victory speech in 1938).[37] So do Czechs who had usually celebrated the war's end one day later, on 9 May – the day when the Red Army reached Prague. In the Bohemian town of Klattovy, the memorial to the Russian liberators is still in place. But a plaque with a footnote has been added: Patton was already here a few days earlier. The Czech opposition to the totalitarian regimes of the 20th century is epitomised by 17 November – as it happens, the commemoration of the day when the SS rounded up scores of university students in 1939, turned into the beginnings of the Velvet Revolution 50 years later.[38] Yugoslavia used to celebrate 29 November, the anniversary of the founding Congress of AVNOJ in 1943, not the doings of the great powers. For a few years Tito's (fake) birthday on 25 May was also celebrated in public, but replaced by a 'Youth Day' when the 'cult of personality' had ceased to be fashionable. Hungary held fast to the 15 March, the start of the revolution of 1848, under most regimes. The communists added 4 April as the day when the Red Army had conquered all of Hungary in 1945. After 1989 it was replaced by 23 October, to commemorate the beginning of the (abortive) revolution of 1956.[39]

It will not come as a surprise that the incentive behind the 'politics of memory' usually has less to do with scholarly findings than with 'scoring points' against your present-day political rivals.[40] One way of conducting such campaigns is by way of iconoclastic pin-pricks about street names. Examples can easily be spotted everywhere in Central Europe (and not only in Central Europe). As a particularly lurid example, in Vienna a local district council recently fielded a motion to re-christen the square named after the Battle of Blenheim (Höchstädtplatz) in honour of Johann Koplenig, the communist party leader who had his office there after 1945.[41] In Austria, with few native communists to fight, the Iron Curtain surrounding half the country had kept anti-communism alive. The collapse of the wall – and the emergence of a vibrant right-wing opposition – sparked a revival of anti-fascist 'muck raking' from the late 1980s onwards.

Kreisky had scoffed at the often-repeated slogan of 'coping with the past' (*Vergangenheitsbewältigung*) but a new generation of left-wingers threw themselves into the battles of the past with abandon. The controversies surrounding Kurt Waldheim's election as president in 1986 are often cited as a watershed. A few months before, there had already been a debate about a plaque honouring Löhr for his part in building up an Austrian air force during the 1930s. One commander of the Defence Academy, a conservative nobleman, supported the idea, but his socialist successor had it removed.[42] The significant feature of both these debates was indeed the timing: They happened a few years before the 'Fall of the Wall' but at exactly the time when the war generation – except for heads of state – was leaving office and entering retirement.[43] Western appreciation of the Wehrmacht's fighting qualities had receded into the background – and Austria had ceased to be 'the darling of the Cold War'.[44]

In Hungary and Czechoslovakia, it was the other way round: anti-fascism had been the stale diet of an unloved regime. 1989 provided a chance to catch up on anti-communism that had for so long been a taboo. Czechs in particular find it easy to condemn both of the totalitarian movements that engulfed them in the same breath. They are very much alive to the danger that focusing exclusively on the misdeeds of one variety of totalitarianism has traditionally been a recipe of their opposite (but equally deadly) numbers. They also find it easy to identify with the pre-World War II First Republic. The traumatic turning points of the 20th century are not associated with 1945, but with the number 8 years – 1938 (the Munich Conference), 1948 (the communist take-over) and 1968 (the invasion by the Warsaw Pact).

In Hungary, the quarter of a century of the Horthy regime (1919–1944) is more controversial than the Czechoslovak First Republic but does provide an element of continuity for a country that does not regard itself as a creation of Saint Germain (or even worse, Trianon) a hundred years ago but as an '*antemurale christianitatis*' (bastion of Christianity) for the last thousand years. The Crown of St Stephen returned to Hungary from Fort Knox already in 1978, Horthy's remains followed suit in 1993. The one date in recent history that is interpreted in different ways but commands universal respect is the 1956 split of the Communist Party and the subsequent fight against the Soviet intervention. In (ex-)Yugoslavia, more recent conflicts have usually overshadowed debates about 1945. However, it is probably fair to say that like most of Europe they resent the subliminal suggestion that because Germans have difficulties with their history and identity, everybody else should renounce theirs, too.

At the same time, it would probably be rash to assume that official propaganda is taken all that seriously by the public, especially in a Central European context which during the 20th century provided such a perfect example of the difficulty of predicting the past. Maybe the cynicism towards official pronouncements has abated with a new generation that has no longer experienced any of these 1984-like

U-turns in political correctness. But then they are probably no longer listening to the Sunday speeches of their political leaders, anyway (unless the messages arrive via twitter). The restricted, but authentic tunnel vision of the participants, has been replaced by the carefully crafted but somewhat fairy-tale like messages of the media and Hollywood variety. These days, we are able to add colour to old black-and-white movies. But the lingering taste for a Manichean view of the world in black and white survives despite all the evidence about different shades of grey presenting a more realistic view of the past.

Notes

1   Tvrtko Jakovina, 'Ein großer Krieg, über den niemand spricht', in Bernhard Bachinger and Wolfram Dornik (eds), *Jenseits des Schützengrabens. Der Erste Weltkrieg im Osten* (Innsbruck: StudienVerlag, 2013), 105–120, here: 106.
2   In 1994, the Italian right-wing leader Gianfranco Fini was one of the last to return an ambivalent verdict about the consequences of D-Day 50 years after. But even he – or he in particular – changed colours soon after.
3   Those were the titles of two popular books on Austrian 20th-century history by Hellmuth Andics.
4   On Figl's career in 1945 by far the best book is Helmut Wohnout, *Leopold Figl und das Jahr 1945. Von der Todeszelle auf den Ballhausplatz* (St. Pölten: Niederösterreichisches Pressehaus, 2015).
5   Eva-Marie Csaky (ed), *Josef Schöner. Wiener Tagebuch: 1944–1945* (Vienna: Böhlau, 1992).
6   Thomas Grischany, *The Austrians in the German Wehrmacht, 1938–1945* (Chicago: University of Chicago Press, 2007); Thomas Grischany, 'The Integrative Impact of Wehrmacht Service on the Austrian Soldiers during World War II', *Austrian History Yearbook*, Vol. 38 (2007): 160–178.
7   Peter Kenez, *Hungary from the Nazis to the Soviets: The Establishment of the Communist Regime in Hungary, 1944–1948* (Cambridge: Cambridge University Press, 2006), 38.
8   Gabriela Stieber (ed), *Consolidated Intelligence Reports. Psychological Warfare Branch Military Government Kärnten Mai 1945 bis April 1946* (Klagenfurt: Kärntner Landesarchiv, 2005); Manfried Rauchensteiner, *Under Observation. Austria since 1918* (Vienna: Böhlau, 2018), 246–9.
9   Bruno Kreisky, *Im Strom der Politik. Der Memoiren zweiter Teil* (Vienna: Kremayr & Scheriau, 1988), 45.
10 Reinhold Wagnleitner (ed), *Understanding Austria. The Political Reports and Analyses of Martin F. Herz, Political Officer of the US Legation in Vienna, 1945–1948* (Salzburg: Neugebauer, 1984), 214 (16 June 1947), 132 (18 March 1947).
11 Lothar Höbelt, *Die Zweite Republik und ihre Besonderheiten* (Vienna: Böhlau 2020), 21 (quote from the Cabinet Meeting on 19 October 1948).
12 Peter Ruggenthaler, 'Warum Österreich nicht sowjetisiert wurde. Sowjetische Österreichpolitik 1945–1953/54', in Stefan Karner & Barbara Stelzl-Marx (eds), *Die Rote Armee in Österreich. Sowjetische Besatzung 1945–1955. Beiträge* (Graz: Leykam, 2005), 649–726; here: 671; on the foreign policy context Gerald Stourzh & Wolfgang Mueller, *A Cold War over Austria and the Struggle for the State Treaty, Neutrality, and the End of the East-West Occupation, 1945–1955* (Cambridge, Mass: Lexington Books, 2018); Michael Gehler, *From Saint Germain to Lisbon. Austria's Long Road from Disintegrated to United Europe* (Vienna: Österreichische Akademie der Wissenschaften, 2020).
13 Andrew P. N. Erdmann, 'War No Longer Has Any Logic Whatever': Dwight D. Eisenhower and the Thermonuclear Revolution', in John L. Gaddis (ed), *Cold War Statesmen confront the Bomb. Nuclear Diplomacy since 1945* (Oxford: Oxford University Press, 1999), 87–119; Bruno

Thoß, 'Österreich in der Entstehungs- und Konsolidierungsphase des westlichen Bündnissystems (1947–1967)', in Manfried Rauchensteiner (ed), *Zwischen den Blöcken. NATO, Warschauer Pakt und Österreich* (Vienna: Böhlau, 2010), 19–87.

14   Höbelt, *Zweite Republik,* 22 (Party Congress 1949, 75).

15   Randall W. Kindley, 'The Evolution of Austria's Neo-Corporatist Institutions', *Contemporary Austrian Studies,* Vol. 3 (1995): 53–93; Jill Lewis, *Workers and Politics in Occupied Austria 1945–55* (Manchester: Manchester University Press, 2007).

16   Höbelt, *Zweite Republik,* 148 (ÖVP-Club, 16 May 1951).

17   The standard account is Dieter Stiefel, *Entnazifizierung in Österreich* (Vienna: Europaverlag, 1981); Höbelt, *Zweite Republik,* 60.

18   The speech was printed by his party's regional mouthpiece, *Südost-Tagespost,* 19 September 1963.

19   Minister of Defence Georg Prader had lost a leg in Normandy and Minister of Finance Stefan Koren his right hand when his recce plane was shot down in 1941.

20   Peter Barthou, *Der 'Obersten-Paragraph'. Der Umgang mit Obersten und Generalen der Wehrmacht im Österreichischen Bundesheer* (Vienna: BM für Landesverteidigung, 2008); Bastian M. Scianna, Rebuilding an Austrian Army: The Bundesheer's Founding Generation and the Wehrmacht Past, 1955–1970', *War in History,* Vol. 26 (2019): 105–123.

21   For short biographies see Stefan Bader, *An höchster Stelle. Die Generale des Bundesheeres der Zweiten Republik* (Vienna: BM für Landesverteidigung, 2004).

22   Martin Kofler, *Kennedy und Österreich. Neutralität im Kalten Krieg* (Innsbruck: Studienverlag, 2003), p. 120.

23   Kenez, *Hungary from the Nazis to the Soviets,* 134, 205 seq., 218; Laszlo Borhi, *Hungary in the Cold War, 1945–1956* (Budapest: CEU Press, 2004).

24   Igor Lukes, *On the Edge of the Cold War: American Diplomats and Spies in Postwar Prague* (Oxford: Oxford University Press, 2012), 193, 199; Jiri Slama and Karel Kaplan, *Die Parlamentswahlen in der Tschechoslowakei 1935–1946–1948* (Munich: Oldenbourg, 1986).

25   One of the best in-depth studies is by a Slovak author: Emilia Hrabovec, *Vertreibung und Abschub der Deutschen in Mähren 1945–47* (Francfort: Peter Lang, 1995); Alfred J. Rieber (ed), *Forced Migration in Central and Eastern Europe, 1939–1950* (London: Frank Cass, 2000).

26   Bombing raids on the so-called Protectorate of Bohemia and Moravia were restricted to a very few chemical factories, like Aussig or Pardubice. The fighting in Prague destroyed half the old town hall but did not seriously damage one of the most beautiful early modern cities of Europe.

27   The quote was part of a debate at the Czech Embassy in Vienna in 2017.

28   Walter B. Roberts, *Tito, Mihailovic and the Allies, 1941–1945* (Rutgers: Rutgers University Press, 1973); Peter Batty, *Hoodwinking Churchill: Tito's Great Confidence Trick* (London: Shepheard-Walwyn, 2011).

29   Erwin Pitsch has written a three-volume biography of Alexander Löhr (Salzburg: Österreichischer Milizverlag, 2004–9).

30   Klaus Schmider, *Der Partisanenkrieg in Jugoslawien 1941–1944* (Berlin: Mittler, 2002); Jozo Tomasevic wrote two volumes on *War and Revolution in Yugoslavia, 1941–1945* (1975, 2001) but unfortunately could not finish the third one that was going to be dealing with Tito's partisans.

31   Joze Pirjevec, *Tito and His Comrades* (Madison: University of Wisconsin Press, 2018), 128.

32   Ibid., 167.

33   There are many accounts of the ideological battles between Stalin and Tito. Lorraine M. Lees, *Keeping Tito Afloat: The US, Yugoslavia and the Cold War, 1945–1960* (Penn State: Penn State University Press, 2010) provides the logistic details.

34   Pirjevec, *Tito,* 147, 204, 275.

35 His three wives were a Russian, a German and a Serb partisan captain from the diaspora, the Lika region not far from the Adriatic, Jovanka, who was violently anti-Croat during the crises of the 1970s.

36 Pirjevec, *Tito*, 227 seq., 296, 324, 394 seq.; Gorana Ognjenovic & Jazna Jozelic (eds), *Revolutionary Totalitarianism, Pragmatic Socialism, Transition* (London: Palgrave Macmillan, 2016).

37 For obvious reasons, though, the New Year's Concert, first broadcast in 1941, has not been affected by the desire to cancel all traditions tainted by their birth certificates between 1938 and 1945.

38 In a tacit admission of the writing on the wall, Communist boss Jakes had tried to buy popularity a year earlier by declaring 28 October, the birthday of the First Republic, as a national holiday, too.

39 Laszlo Peter & Martin Rady (eds), *Resistance, Rebellion and Revolution in Hungary and Central Europe: Commemorating 1956* (London: University College, 2008).

40 Kenez, *Hungary from the Nazis to the Soviets*, 290.

41 Apparently, the motion was supposed to celebrate the 100th birthday of the Austrian Communist party. In February 2020, the proposal was turned down by the City Council.

42 I am grateful to Friedhelm Frischenschlager, Minister of Defence from 1983 to 1986, for looking at his notes for me. In 1992 Werner Fasslabend as Minister of Defence still prevented Löhr's name from being removed from another memorial plaque in the Hofburg chapel. In the 2010s one of his successors no longer did so.

43 The return of Walther Reder, an invalid Lieutenant-Colonel in the Waffen-SS and the last POW in Italy, created even more of a stir in early 1985 but in that case the debates were clearly overshadowed by a complex web of political intrigues and infighting within all parties; see Höbelt, *Zweite Republik*, 262–4.

44 Bruno Kreisky, *Der Mensch im Mittelpunkt. Der Memoiren dritter Teil* (Vienna: Kremayr & Scheriau, 1996), 238; Oliver Rathkolb, *Die paradoxe Republik* (Berlin: Hanser 3rd Ed., 2015), 408.

CHAPTER 12

'A distant past draws near'[1]: World War II's Impact on Danish Security and Defence Politics

Niels Bo Poulsen

In December 2019, the Danish parliament debated the findings of a recently published inquiry report *Hvorfor gik Danmark i krig? (Why did Denmark go to war?)*.[2] The 2,000-page-long report had been ordered by the parliament some two years earlier in an attempt to learn from Denmark's participation in military interventions, from the 1999 Kosovo war to Afghanistan and Iraq.[3] After an MP from the far-left party Enhedslisten criticised that the parliament had sent Danish troops to war based on a simple majority vote, a member of the populist right-wing party Dansk Folkeparti replied that he found such criticism 'shameful'. In his view, it came from a party that had never done anything to ensure 'that the Danish population since World War II has been able to live in a free nation'. During the same debate, another MP (from the libertarian party Liberal Alliance) delivered a brief overview of international security politics since World War I, as he saw it. This parliamentarian also invoked World War II. Its reverberations, he declared, had been felt until around 1990. As can be seen, in the said speeches World War II was used as a means of periodization and as a standard for how to define Denmark as a free and sovereign nation. The abovementioned interventions were, however, the sole examples of references to the war during a 2½-hour-long debate, in which about a dozen MPs and the foreign minister spoke. In fact, no other speakers ventured further back in history than the Yugoslav civil war and the genocide in Rwanda, i.e. the 1990s.[4]

Studying other debates in the Danish parliament during the last five years concerning Denmark's security and defence politics, one does find additional examples of how World War II is occasionally used as a point of reference and as a measuring stick, for example in the following statements: 'This is the worst crisis, we have seen since the Second World War' (referring to the 2015 Syria refugee crisis) and 'not since the end of the Second World War' has the world experienced a disrespect for national borders similar to Russia's annexation of the Crimea.[5] In addition to such illustrative and evaluative uses of the war, in one case a politician explicitly drew a lesson from the war, stating that, in his opinion, respect for human rights and democracy is the best way to avoid war.[6]

As the above examples indicate, World War II still plays a certain role when Danish parliamentarians debate security and defence politics. What is not clear, however, is whether we should understand such references as purely rhetorical, as a vicarious approach to contemporary challenges, or as a central point of reference when addressing present and future affairs? In other words, how has Danish strategic culture been shaped by the war experience? And how about the military culture of the Danish defence force? How has it related to the legacy of the war? In this chapter, these questions represent central pillars in the analysis of the legacy of World War II. The chapter will, however, move beyond these questions and offer a broader and more inclusive perspective by combining a study of the mental impact of the war with a study of the physical legacy of the war. Consequently, the text falls in four parts. First, a brief outline of the theoretical basis for my inquiry. Second, a brief overview of Denmark and World War II and an outline of the physical legacy of the war. Third, a discussion of how the war has influenced the impacted Danish strategic culture Finally, the war's direct and indirect influence on the Danish armed forces and their military culture. The crux of the matter is – as the headline of this chapter suggests –whether World War II, as Prime Minister Mette Frederiksen stated in her liberation day speech on 4 May 2020, still represents 'a distant past [which] draws near', or has ceased to matter in earnest in Danish security and defence politics?

Denmark and World War II – a brief overview and the material legacy of the war

The format of this text does not allow a long exposé on Denmark during World War II – arguably the most studied period in Danish history.[7] The history of Denmark's experience during World War II has been greatly contested, and any attempt to summarise the events between the German occupation of Denmark on 9 April 1940, and the liberation on 5 May 1945, is doomed to simplify what were highly complex and multi-layered developments. In addition, the very focus on the state of Denmark in itself represents a considerable simplification, as World War II obviously was a transnational event. From a historiographic perspective, three generations of Danish historians have offered quite different interpretations of this period. During the first decades after the war, a consensus narrative emerged, telling the story of a united nation uniformly opposing the Germans and, to early scholars, exploring the history of the resistance movement was paramount. Beginning in the 1970s, a new generation of historians focused on internal divisions and conflicts in Denmark, for example based on affiliation with different classes and social groups, and they painted a more nuanced picture of how resistance and collaboration manifested itself. This included a study of how the political establishment was highly suspicious of the resistance movement due to its extra-parliamentarian character and its many activists from the far left and right. Later – beginning in the 1990s – the perspective broadened even further. A new generation of historians increasingly challenged the narrow focus on Denmark, and they also scrutinised how Denmark and the Danes had played other roles than those of victims and resisters, for example by studying the role of Danes in Hitler's *Vernichtungskrieg* on the Eastern Front.[8] Also, the Holocaust has become an important focal point in recent historiography. Breaking down the time separation between the occupation period, the inter-war period and the post-war period, historians also began studying the Danish refugee policy after Hitler's ascension to power and the treatment of German refuges after the war.[9]

This increasingly nuanced and complex understanding of Denmark in World War II among historians has nevertheless only had limited implications for the general memory culture. As demonstrated by Bryld and Warring in their study of Danish memory culture and the German occupation, a widespread and generally accepted narrative gradually emerged after the war. Its main claim was that 'resistance had been the characteristic Danish stance during the occupation', and that the majority of the population and the political establishment had engaged in active or passive resistance, save a limited group of clearly defined traitors.[10] A recent study of how the youth in Denmark, Finland, and Germany view World War II indicates that not much has changed since Bryld and Warring conducted their study in the late 1990s.[11]

In the context of studying the legacy of World War II in Danish security and defence politics, a number of events are especially relevant. First, in 1940, when invaded by Germany, Denmark had a limited defence force, and the liberal-social democratic government had no faith in the utility of fighting the Third Reich if it attacked. Rather, it hoped to repeat what had happened during World War I: by subtle diplomacy, avoid being involved in the war.[12] Thus, when – in the early morning hours of 9 April 1940 – offered the opportunity to accept the German occupation of Denmark in exchange for assurances that the government would enjoy inner autonomy, leading politicians from all major parties accepted the German fait accompli. After the sporadic fighting between Danish and German troops had ceased, the Danish armed forces went back to their garrisons. Until August 1943, Denmark had its own defence force as well as a democratic government, albeit frequently pressed to make additional concessions to the Germans. However, increasing resistance activities resulted in a German demand that the government should introduce the death penalty as punishment for sabotage. In response, the government resigned on 29 August 1943. With the blessing of the politicians, a civil servants' administration continued to govern. Yet, the conditions had changed significantly. The very day when the government resigned, the German Wehrmacht executed *Unternehmen Safari* (Operation *Safari*): the disarmament and dissolution of the Danish armed forces. In several barracks and naval installations, the Germans met armed resistance, and the navy managed to scuttle a significant part of its ships while a number of smaller ships escaped to Sweden.[13] The Germans now introduced the death penalty for sabotage and, as the war dragged on, the suppression of the growing resistance movement became more and more draconian. Nevertheless, for various reasons – the most important being the desire not to disrupt the export of Danish agricultural products to the Third Reich – the German authorities were hesitant to escalate the repression beyond a certain point. Thus, compared to other occupied countries, the Danish population was spared the worst excesses and enjoyed a relatively high living standard.

Despite the creation of a unified non-partisan Resistance Council, the Danish resistance movement never played a military role as such. Neither did the 5,000-strong Danish Brigade (including a miniscule air force and flotilla) organised by Danish refugees in Sweden. In contrast, approximately 1,000 Danes saw action as volunteers in the Allied armed forces, but an even more decisive contribution to the Allied cause was rendered by around 6,000 Danish sailors on Danish ships in Allied service. Also, around 6,000 other men served under the ranks of the Waffen-SS and other German formations. They fought on the Eastern Front, suffered considerable casualties and committed a number of crimes abroad as well as in Denmark.

Although impressive fortifications and a considerable military infrastructure had been established by the German Wehrmacht, Denmark was liberated without any fighting as part of the German surrender of north western Germany to Field Marshal Montgomery on Lüneburg Heath on 4 May 1945. There were notable exceptions to this rule, however. Two parts of the Danish realm, Greenland and the Faroe Islands, had since 1940 been occupied by American and British forces, and at the other end of the kingdom, the small island of Bornholm was only liberated by Soviet forces on 9 May 1945. Despite overtures from the political establishment to the British and American governments, Denmark was not accepted as an allied nation until the war ended. It was nevertheless invited to join the United Nations, and a Danish delegation participated in the establishment of the UN at the San Francisco Conference in autumn 1945.

Based on the above, the material legacy of World War II in Denmark may be summed up as follows: by the end of 1945, Denmark found itself in the precarious situation that it had no armed forces of its own, and virtually all military stocks had been taken over by the Germans. On the other hand, there were substantial amounts of German armaments and military installations in Denmark. In addition to the regular officers' corps – which remained relatively intact as the men had been released from German custody on 29 August 1940 after a brief internment following – there were also potential new sources of military expertise to tap, namely the men who had done military service during the war in Allied uniform and, more controversially, the abovementioned pool of former Waffen-SS officers and soldiers.

It should be added that in contrast to most other European countries, the political and social fabric of society was little affected by the war. During the early post-war years, the voting behaviour demonstrated that the population not only endorsed the policy pursued during the occupation, it also favoured the construction of a welfare state with more focus on social security and economic prosperity than on military spending and hard security. As a small agrarian-based economy, Denmark was dependent on import of most raw materials and energy, and only high prices for its agricultural exports could ensure a balanced economy. Albeit Denmark had come out of the war with almost no physical destruction or large numbers of civilian casualties, the state of its financials was not good, and this had an impact on the reconstruction of the armed forces, as Denmark, save its shipbuilding industry, had to import most military equipment.

World War II and Danish strategic culture

The impact of World War II on Danish strategic culture is deeply intertwined with other historical experiences. Among these are long periods of Danish neutrality, namely 1720–1807, 1814–1848, 1850–1864, and 1864–1940, typically accompanied by good earnings from the merchant marine.[14] On the other hand, the disastrous war with Austria and Prussia in 1864 led to the loss of the Duchies of Schleswig and Holstein – almost eradicating Denmark as an independent country. The defeat in 1864 together with the occupation in 1940, are by most scholars of Danish foreign policy seen as the fundamental – and highly traumatic – experiences of the 19th and 20th centuries.[15] Historically significant is also the establishment of a politically stable, increasingly wealthy and ethnically homogeneous nation state after 1864. According to Rasmussen, this sum of historical experiences has created two principal stands in Danish strategic thinking, cosmopolitans versus defencists. The first position – often represented by the influential centrist party Radikale Venstre – finds the use of armed force in international politics unnecessary and counterproductive. Furthermore, it is believed that 'the rest of the world would enjoy peace and prosperity Scandinavian-style if only Scandinavian values were adopted.'[16] Thus, this position has a certain optimistic and moralistic tone. In contrast, the defencist position is more pessimistic with respect to a norm-based world order and believes 'that Denmark ought to be integrated within the European [alliance] system with an active foreign policy and the military capacity to back it up.'[17] Although the cosmopolitans were much more sceptical towards maintaining a substantial defence force and towards NATO membership than the defencists, Denmark's security and defence politics since entering NATO in 1949 have generally been subject to broad political compromises that have managed to span both positions.

The transformation from neutralism to membership of NATO was, however, never unconditional and, in the words of Villaume, Denmark became a 'reluctant ally'.[18] Investment in hard security was deliberately kept low in order to maintain one of the most generous welfare states in the world. As Ringsmose and Brøndum put it in their study of Denmark's defence budget during the Cold War, the unspoken motto was 'how low can you go.'[19]

Although NATO membership implied an acknowledgement that Denmark's main adversary was now found to the east and not to the south, the former foe, Germany, still loomed large in Danish security politics. From the end of the 1940s and well into the 1960s the question of how to relate to Germany represented one of the most significant and persevering dilemmas in Danish defence and security politics.[20] The combined lessons from the period 1864–1945 made it almost a dogma in Danish foreign policy that Germany was destined to be the eternal great power at Denmark's doorstep. Considerable restraint was shown after the war to make sure that Denmark was not perceived as a predator aiming at devouring the corpse of the collapsed Third Reich. Consequently, Danish politicians had to navigate between public sentiments, including demands for revising the border with Germany, fear of a possible German restoration as a great power, and realization that without a strong German defence Denmark would be vulnerable to an attack from the east.[21] While the circles demanding a border revision had effectively been marginalised by the late 1940s, a sound modus vivendi with the new German Federal Republic was not established until 1955 with the Copenhagen-Bonn declarations – two unilateral, but coordinated declarations in which it was stated that the two states would respect the joint border and protect the German and the Danish minorities, respectively. Two years before, the last German war criminals had been released from Danish prisons.[22] Thus, the road was paved for Denmark to accept Germany's rearmament and consent to admitting it into NATO.[23] This process did not happen without internal opposition. As mentioned, the image of Germany was rather negative, and shifting governments had to take public opinion into account.[24] The communist party especially attempted to mobilise the population against the remilitarization of Germany by invoking images of Nazi officers and officials once again taking control over Denmark, this time by means of a formal military alliance.[25] The litmus test of the public mood came in the early 1960s when a unified Danish–German command over the Baltic Sea, Denmark, and Schleswig-Holstein (BALTAP) was established under the auspices of NATO. Joint BALTAP manoeuvres in Denmark in 1962 saw German troops and naval vessels in Denmark for the first time since the occupation. In several locations, the troops were met with sit-downs, blockades and pickets.[26] Nevertheless, the uproar was manageable as leftist fringe groups were behind most protests. Gradually losing its grip on the population, the use of the occupation as a means of discrediting

German–Danish military and political cooperation did, however, continue until the collapse of the Berlin Wall. While not necessarily very efficient or for that matter sophisticated, this sort of political propaganda nevertheless tapped in to a popular trope as demonstrated by the fact that also major newspapers occasionally would publish cartoons depicting German politicians and citizens in Wehrmacht and Nazi-like postures and outfits.[27]

The war experience not only affected how Germany was perceived, it also served as a prism though which to understand the new security threat from the Soviet Union.[28] The most significant lessons derived from the war in this respect were to parallel the Soviet system with the Nazi system and to ascribe to it similar schemes for conquest and domination. The proponents of this interpretation argued that rather than the failed appeasement and disarmament policy before the war, a policy of deterrence and military balancing should be pursued.[29] This lesson was summarised under the catch phrase 'never again April 9'. As noted by Bryld and Warring, the dates of Denmark's occupation and liberation came together in one joint narrative:

> 9 April and 5 May became important dates in the historical basic founding myth about NATO membership and the affiliation with the Western world. Peace and freedom were [...] associated with a strong defence, representing a negation of 9 April 1940, and an alliance which confirmed 5 May 1945 and the armed resistance by the resistance movement, aimed at causing a political break with the Germans and the subsequent liberation.[30]

During the first decades after the liberation, World War II legacy was often referred to in debates about security and defence politics. Consistently, social-democratic and right-wing parties pointed out that the war experience demonstrated the need for a credible defence and strong allies, whereas the most leftist parties (especially the communists) claimed that the threat to Denmark came from neo-fascism and American imperialism – often portrayed as one and the same.[31]

The legacy of World War II entered a new stage with the end of the Cold War and German reunification. Despite a statement in November 1989 by the Danish Prime Minister Poul Schlüter that German reunification was not in the interest of Denmark, the public in general accepted the unification of the two German states.[32] It seemed at the time that Denmark, like other European countries, had finally moved out of the shadows of 'the long Second World War'.[33] The demise of the war's influence was also noted by Bryld and Warring. Comparing the parliamentary debates about the occupation in 1955 with that of 1995, when the parliament addressed the 50-year anniversary of the liberation, they found that by 1995, 'one may in earnest talk about a de-historization of the occupation period among the political elite in Danish society.'[34]

With the dismemberment of the Soviet Union and the dissolution of the Warsaw Pact, the risk of large-scale conventional warfare involving Denmark was eliminated.

In the next decades, Denmark radically reduced and reformed its armed forces, gearing them towards peacekeeping and expeditionary warfare in a coalition framework, not towards territorial defence.[35] This included participating in UN and NATO led interventions in Yugoslavia, Kosovo, Afghanistan, and Libya, but also joining the United States in invading Iraq in spring 2003. On 29 August 2003, six months after the invasion of Iraq, a commemorative event illustrated that although Denmark's security landscape had changed, the war experience had not lost its foothold as a point of reference. Having involved Denmark in the invasion of Iraq against considerable political opposition, Prime Minister (and later NATO Secretary General) Anders Fogh Rasmussen used the occasion of the 60-year anniversary of 29 August 1943 to present his reading of Denmark's role in World War II. The prime minister declared that although there were logical reasons why Danish politicians had initially opted for cooperation with the German invaders, it was the events on 29 August 1943 that saved the honour of Denmark. The government's attempt to accommodate the Nazis had, in the words of the prime minister, been 'reprehensible'. He added that it would always be immoral to stay neutral in 'a mortal struggle between being free and unfree, between democracy and dictatorship'.[36] The speech caused considerable debate as it was widely seen as the prime minister's not too subtle defence of his government's controversial foreign policy and because his own party during the war had been among the staunchest supporters of the policy of accommodating Germany.[37] While controversial at the time, Prime Minister Rasmussen's point was essentially repeated by his successor Helle Thorning-Schmidt when she presided over the 70-year commemoration of 29 August ten years later. In her speech she paraphrased his message by stating that 'back then, like today, we realise that when all other paths have been tried in vain, the world's free countries have an obligation to do what we can to stop the forces of war and tyranny. Denmark is a country you can count on.'[38]

In contrast to her predecessor, the speech by Prime Minister Thorning-Schmidt did, however, not generate controversy. By 2013, most parties had come to support the deployment of Danish troops abroad on combat missions, including a substantial contribution to the air campaign against the Gaddafi regime in Libya in 2011. At the same time, Denmark's continuous participation in expeditionary warfare had begun to generate a new group in society – war veterans – and along with them the number of war casualties was also growing. Having not fought a major war since 1864, Denmark lacked a veterans' policy and a corresponding commemorative culture.[39] The occupation period stood apart as an exception, but could not really serve as a model, because almost all victims of the occupation were civilians – either bystanders or people belonging to the resistance movement. 1,300 monuments and other memorial parks devoted to World War II and another 370 celebrating the liberation make World War II the military event with most monuments dedicated to it.[40] The most significant memorial park is the former German execution site for Danish resistance fighters, Ryvangen, on the outskirts of Copenhagen, where around 200 men were executed and buried during the war. Since its inauguration in 1950, Ryvangen has been the place where foreign dignitaries lay flowers and wreaths and where the main commemorative acts take place on the anniversaries of the occupation, the liberation and the resignation of the government.[41] However, the politicians evidently believed that Danish military losses in the post-war period represented a new beginning rather than a continuation of the resistance. That was made very clear when a new national monument for all post-war Danish military casualties abroad was established in 2011 at the Citadel of Copenhagen. To the public, this was a place devoid of symbolic reference to World War II.[42] The same is true for the new memorial day for war veterans, *Flagdagen*, namely 5 September, a date lacking reference to Danish wars, including World War II. So far, the new memory culture associated with Denmark's international missions has in no manner overshadowed the memory culture related to World War II. As in Norway, the veterans' day seems primarily to be an event attended by officials, staff of the armed forces and their relatives.[43] Nor have the dates associated with World War II faded from memory. In 2020, the 80-year anniversary of the occupation was marked with official ceremonies as was the 75-year anniversary of the liberation that same year. 2020 also became the year when the Museum of Danish Resistance was reopened after its premises had been destroyed by a fire in 2013. The new museum represents a more user-friendly, more digitalised and less text heavy approach to the history of Denmark and the resistance movement – causing a number of leading Danish historians to criticise the curators for popularising and trivialising history.[44]

The legacy of the war is important – not just as part of the collective memory, but also because of its consequences. Below, there are a number of examples from the armed forces. However, a strategic challenge inherited from the war – Greenland – deserves to be mentioned first. Originally admitted into Greenland in 1940 by the Danish ambassador to Washington, Henrik Kaufmann, against the will of the government in Copenhagen, the American bases in Greenland were made permanent in 1951 by an open-ended agreement between Denmark and the United States and without any formal consultation of the Inuit population of the island. The American presence in Greenland is a sensitive matter, mainly because Danish governments are believed to have used Greenland as a pawn during the Cold War, but also because of environmental issues (including pollution from fuel dumps from World War II). In 2019, based on a growing US strategic interest in the Arctic region, President Trumps offered to buy the island – a proposal which was flatly rejected both by the Danish government and by the self-rule government of Greenland.[45]

The armed forces and the legacy of World War II

Albeit not studied in detail, it may be argued that there is a heterogeneous memory culture concerning World War II in the Danish armed forces.[46] One service branch – the air force – only became an independent branch after the war. This branch of the armed forces has always been the most technology driven, and its memory culture seems only superficially to relate to the war. This is illustrated by the fact that of the three branches, the air force devotes the least number of lessons to military history – including the war – in the syllabus of its officer education.[47] The army on its side is still tapping substantially into the war experience in its officer education, and some regiments even commemorate their soldiers' military actions on 9 April and 29 August (the Royal Lifeguard, the Royal Hussars and the Schleswig Regiment of Foot). The navy is in a similar situation. Calling itself the oldest service branch (being established in 1510), it devotes considerable energy to its own history, and 29 August 1943, is observed in the navy as one of its most important commemorative dates.[48]

In 1945, the Danish armed forces had to be rebuilt virtually from scratch. In contrast to the low priority assigned to the military during the 1930s, most parties in parliament agreed that a more robust defence force was now called for. The initial vision was to build a defence force capable of fighting under the auspices of the UN – the foreseeable threat being German resurrection. The first steps were taken in cooperation with the UK which delivered equipment and an advisory military mission in exchange for the pledge of a Danish army division to assist in manning the British occupation zone in Germany.[49] The process of setting up a post-war defence force was, however, long and complicated. In 1946, the parliament appointed a commission, the goal of which was to propose how to organise the future armed forces, but due to the rapid political changes in Europe during the initial post-war years, the committee chased a moving target. When Denmark joined NATO in 1949, its work had not been completed, and only in 1950 did the parliament adopt a new comprehensive defence bill.[50] The reconstruction of the Danish defence force right after the war essentially became a combination of drawing on the 1937 defence bill, ad hoc measures, and seeking guidance from whatever lessons the war offered.

In an editorial in the navy's periodical *Tidsskrift for Søvæsen,* published shortly after the liberation, its editor, Commander Paul Ipsen, not too subtly hinted that the politicians were solely to blame for the surrender on 9 April 1940, as they had neglected the armed forces' warnings about Denmark's military unpreparedness. Quoting the navy's actions on 29 August 1943, and the alleged involvement of most naval officers in resistance work after that date, Ibsen declared that the navy was blameless during the war. He also stated that he hoped that the population had learned its lesson from the war and would no longer neglect the

Danish defence force. However, to reconstruct the navy was a daunting task, he stated, because of the rapid military and technological changes during the war. 'In virtually all regards', Ibsen declared, 'the war has created new naval challenges and radically changed [...] the tactical, technical, and organizational opportunities and threats.'[51] On the positive side, the reconstructed navy would benefit greatly from 'no longer being impeded by long outdated war material'.[52] Shortly after, a new editor-in-chief, E. J. Saabye, in another editorial encouraged 'the many naval officers who served foreign [i.e. Allied] powers [...] to introduce' the readers to their war-time experiences.[53]

Despite this call for contributions, the articles from *Tidsskrift for Søvæsen* as well as the content of the other leading military periodical, *Militært Tidsskrift*, demonstrate that a main challenge associated with reconstructing the Danish defence force after the war was the lack of war experience.[54] Not only did the members of the Danish armed forces in general lack combat experience from the war, it could even be argued that the pool of 'Danish military experience has been virtually non-existent since 1864'.[55] When considering which types of weapon systems to acquire and when appreciating the doctrinal lessons of World War II, the defence force thus had to look abroad. In fact, many of the early articles in *Militært Tidsskrift* about the war were not written by Danish authors, but were translations of articles published in the military periodicals of other countries (most notably Sweden). There were, however, exemptions. The first volumes of *Tidsskrift for Søvæsen* after 1945, for example, saw articles about modern motor torpedo boats and submarines based on the authors' own experiences abroad.[56] Also, an article about 'Nationalt Værn' in *Militært Tidsskrift* in 1945 drew on the authors own war experience and simultaneously addressed one of the most contested topics of the summer and fall 1945 – what was to happen to the resistance movement after the liberation? The article was both a presentation of a resistance group which conservative officers and likeminded had organised during the war, *Nationalt Værn*, and a proposal for a future home guard of volunteers.[57] The idea of creating a home guard had been born in autumn 1943 when the Danish army clandestinely began planning for a post-war reconstruction and found inspiration in the British and Swedish armed forces. After the liberation, the resistance movement also embraced the idea. To some resistance fighters, most notably the communists, this was a way of preserving an extra-parliamentarian role for the resistance movement. On their side, the major political parties saw the home guard as a vehicle preventing the existence of militias outside of the state's control. Hardly surprising – as the author was closely associated with the defence command – the article opposed the idea that former resistance groups should become autonomous home guard units. Instead, the author advocated the establishment of a home guard under political control and with the army being responsible for its operational role. Until 1948, an uneasy compromise existed between the two approaches: former resistance fighters could establish their own home guard formations and keep their individual weapons if submitted to inspection by the army. Eventually, in 1948, a unified home guard was established. As a new service branch, the home guard was headed by a politically appointed civilian, social-democrat politician (and resistance fighter) Frode Jacobsen, and all prospective members were screened for their loyalty to the state. Thus, most communists were soon purged from the ranks of the home guard, making it a potential first line of defence in case of a sudden Soviet attack similar to the 1940 German invasion, but also making it a force to be used against a possible communist takeover.[58]

Although – as demonstrated above – the military press contained several articles written by persons who had hands-on experience from duty abroad, the careers of these individuals paradoxically did not sky-rocket after the war. Often, the opposite was the case, as with Kaj Birksted. During the war, Birksted had been in the Royal Air Force, and he was generally regarded as both a very capable pilot and a good staff officer. Nevertheless, Birksted was completely marginalised within the Danish armed forces after the war and eventually left service for a civilian career in NATO.[59]

One of the areas where the Danish experience in World War II had a long-term influence on the armed forces was the suddenness of the German attack in the morning of 9 April 1940. The unpreparedness for the German onslaught has consistently been brought forward as an important lesson, not just in terms of civil-military relations (the political will to fight), but also from the perspective of maintaining a high level of readiness in order to secure the country against an unwarned attack, or for that matter a situation where it was unclear to the troops what their orders were. In 1952, a royal contingency order was issued in order to address this type of situation. The order which was valid for all Danish military units, stated that in case of an enemy attack, the forces should immediately fight back without waiting for superior orders. Simultaneously, mobilization should start automatically, and all reservists should without further notice meet in at their barracks.[60] The lessons of 9 April were also used in intra-service rivalries. In 1959, when facing severe budget cuts, in a memorandum to the minister of defence, with explicit reference to 9 April, the army high command stated that it would make no sense to finance the two other service branches at the expense of the land forces because they would be of limited use if an enemy already had established himself in Denmark.[61] On its side, the navy did its very best to make sure that it was not caught off guard, as shown by a large number of articles in *Søfart for Søvæsen* about Pearl Harbor.[62] Even the maritime doctrine, according to which the navy planned to fight a possible Eastern Bloc amphibious attack, was – until around 1985 – based on a combination of Denmark's experience on 9 April, the configuration of the navy, and the expected Soviet behaviour in case of war.[63]

Another problem arising from the war was the nuclear bomb, and from the early post-years it was debated how this new weapon would affect the Danish armed forces.[64] However, as the nuclear weapons grew more powerful and as the general technology advanced, the number of articles related to the war in the military periodicals studied for this article diminished significantly, indicating that the war was deemed less relevant for the military profession. Figures 1 and 2 illustrate the trend: while about 75 articles explicitly addressed World War II in the two above-mentioned military periodicals during the period 1945–1950, the next decade saw just over 50 articles published and after that, the figure dropped even further. The nadir came during the 1970s with only around ten articles. While the figures picked up slightly during the ensuing decades, the writings underwent an important transformation: they became more descriptive and were less geared towards offering lessons to the current Danish defence force.[65]

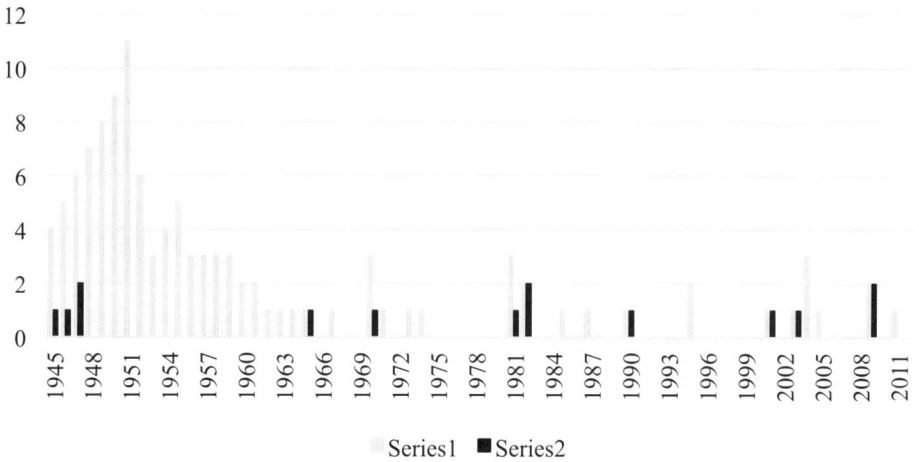

Figure 1: Articles about World War II in *Militært Tidsskrift* 1945–2012

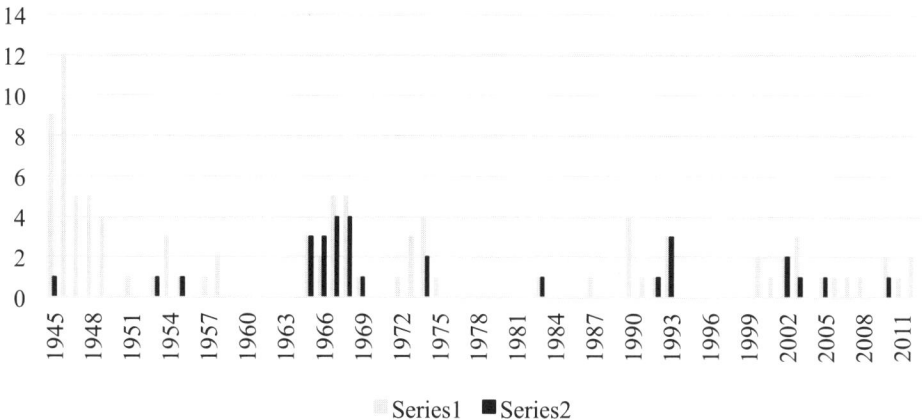

Figure 2: Articles about World War II in *Tidsskrift for Søvæsen* 1945–2012

When the Cold War manifested itself and Denmark opted for NATO, it became clear that the German coastal defences erected in Denmark during World War II by and large pointed in the wrong direction. Nevertheless, a number of individual German bunkers from the coastal defence system were put to use by the Danish armed forces – as ammunition depots, signal stations, command posts etc. In one case, namely with the Bangsbo fortification in Northern Jutland, an entire German fort was converted into a defence position which should help to prevent Eastern Bloc vessels from entering the North Sea in case of war.[66] Two other Danish coastal forts – both located along the Danish straits and erected in the early phase of the Cold War – had German World War II naval guns as their main guns. While the army and home guard were able to use some of the military infrastructure constructed by the Germans, it was the air force – established as an independent service branch in 1950 – that benefitted the most. As the airspace over Denmark had represented an important avenue to northern and eastern Germany for Allied strategic bombers, the Germans had established an elaborate air defence in Denmark, including major airfields. The Danish air force inherited these facilities. From the time of the Cold War and until today, all airbases have been located in places where the Germans established their bases.[67]

In 1947, *Militært Tidskrift* published an article in which the author informed the readers how the engineer unit of the Danish brigade had operated during the war and how, since then, it had been engaged in supervising German prisoners of war who did mine sweeping along the Danish beaches where about 1.4 million mines had been left.[68] Like in many other countries, German 'volunteers', PoWs whose main motivation was better food and treatment, did the clearing itself. The article was not silent about the terrifying casualties during the work, but the author claimed that in comparison with other countries, the treatment of the Germans had been good and their relative casualties low.[69] When the German PoWs returned to Germany in 1947, the task was almost completed. Nevertheless, one of the long-term consequences of the war was the continuous engagement of both the army's engineers and the navy in handling mines and other explosive devices left from the war. The last land mines from World War II – a minefield with some 11,000 remaining mines at Skallingen in western Jutland – were cleared between 2006 and 2012 as a result of Denmark joining the Ottawa Treaty.[70] While the clearing itself was commissioned to a private contractor, the process was planned and supervised by a subunit of the Danish engineer regiment, Danish Demining Centre. This unit destroyed mines and other explosive devices from the war when found on land, while the Navy had a similar assignment in Danish and international waters. By 2006, it was estimated that there were still 6,000 sea mines in the Danish waters and still today, a Danish navy mine clearing unit occasionally handles WWII explosive devices.[71]

A few weapon systems designed during the war still survive in the Danish armed forces. The model 2001 12.7 mm heavy machine gun was originally introduced to the armed forces as an anti-aircraft weapon in 1950. Although modified, the weapon is essentially the American-built inter-war Browning M2 gun. Physically, the main frame of some of the weapons still used today was produced during the war. Likewise, it has been less than a decade since the army's light machine gun – the LMG M/62, modeled over the German MG42 – was replaced by the M60 E6.[72] While modifications and updates contributed to an increase in the performance of these weapons over time, the soldiers were keenly aware of their origin in the war, not least what concerns the MG42. As an example, this author some years ago received a photo taken by a Danish soldier in Afghanistan, depicting a book about World War II next to an LMG M/62 in a camp watchtower. This example also illustrates a challenge that is not unique to the Danish armed forces, namely a fascination among smaller groups of servicemen with the German armed forces during World War II.[73] The most notorious case is from 1954 when a newspaper disclosed that a former Waffen-SS captain had unofficially been tutoring a number of cadets at the army officers' school. The involved cadets were dismissed from the school, the general inspector of the army – who knew about the arrangement – was sent into retirement, and the head of the school was transferred to another duty.[74] The swift reaction by the authorities demonstrated that semi-official contacts to former Danish SS volunteers were off-limits to members of the armed forces.

Conclusion

As all historical events, World War II has been subject to diverse interpretations over time, and different memory communities and individual actors have derived varying lessons from it. While earlier generations of politicians and defence specialists especially tapped into the memory of World War II in order to find military lessons or to prove their point about Denmark's security politics, the speech on the 75-year anniversary of the liberation on 4 May 2020, by present Prime Minister, Mette Frederiksen, is a good illustration of the plasticity of history politics. In contrast to previous jubilees where military security threats have been the reference point, Prime Minister Frederiksen pointed towards a different threat: 'Today we are not at war. We do not fight evilness. We fight a disease [COVID-19].'[75] As Philip Zelikow reminds us, it usually takes a new collective trauma to deprive past traumas of their ability to serve as 'master scripts that can mold public policies across whole eras.'[76] Evidently, while the shadow cast by World War II have underwent different interpretations over time, the war has still not ceased to play the role of a master narrative in Denmark's security and defence politics, and hopefully, the new trauma, which may replace the war experience will fail to materialise in the near future.

Notes

1   'Statsminister Mette Frederiksens tale ved fejring af 75-året for Danmarks befrielse den 4. maj 2020', address by Prime Minister Mette Frederiksen on the 75th anniversary of Denmark's liberation, 4 May 2020. Available at https://www.stm.dk/_p_14945.html.

2   Literally translated: *Why did Denmark go to war?* The authors, however, have used the English translation *Denmark at war.*

3   The report is summarised by its two authors in R. Mariager and A. Wivel, 'Denmark at War: Great Power Politics and Domestic Action Space in the Cases of Kosovo, Afghanistan and Iraq' in Kristian Fischer and Hans Mouritzen (eds), *Danish Foreign Policy Review* (Copenhagen: DIIS, 2019), 48–73. The full report is by Rasmus Mølgaard Mariager and Anders Wivel, *Hvorfor gik Danmark i krig? Uvildig udredning af baggrunden for Danmarks militære engagement i Kosovo, Afghanistan og Irak,* Vols 1–4 (Copenhagen: Københavns Universitet, 2019). Available at https://krigsudredning.ku.dk/.

4   Folketinget 19.12.2019, *Folketingstidende,* 2019, Appendix F, 12–36.

5   Martin Lidegaard (RV), Folketinget 14.12.2016, *Folketingstidende,* 2016, Appendix F, 51. Michael Aastrup Jensen (V), Folketinget 12.4.2016, *Folketingstidende,* 2016, Appendix F, 36.

6   Christian Juhl (EL), Folketinget 7.4.2015. *Folketingstidende,* 2015, Appendix F, 31.

7   Erland Kolding Nielsen, 'Serieredaktørens forord', in John T. Lauridsen, *Samarbejde og modstand, Danmark under den tyske besættelse 1940-45. En bibliografi* (Copenhagen: Museum Tusculanums Forlag, 2002), 5.

8   Bo Lidegaard, *Kampen om Danmark* (Copenhagen: Gyldendal, 2005), 588. For a historiographic overview in English with almost similar periodization, see Carsten Holbraad, *Danish Reactions to German Occupation. History and Historiography* (Chicago: Chicago University Press, 2017), chapter 3. For a discussion of whether it makes sense to organise historiography concerning the occupation, see Palle Roslyng-Jensen, 'Besættelseslitteraturen 2001–2006. Postmodernistisk variation og fortsat hausse', *Historisk Tidsskrift,* Vol. 106, No.1 (2013): 198–242.

9   Ibid.

10   Claus Bryld and Anette Warring, *Besættelsestiden som kollektiv erindring* (Roskilde: Roskilde Universitetsforlag, 1998), 554–560.

11   Kevin Wolnik, Britta Busse, Jochen Tholen, Carsten Yndigegn, Klaus Levinsen, Kari Saari & Vesa Puuronen, 'The long shadows of the difficult past? How young people in Denmark, Finland and Germany remember WWII', *Journal of Youth Studies,* Vol. 20, No. 2 (2017), 162–179.

12   The most recent study about the Danish government and the German invasion of Denmark is by Steen Andersen, *'Der er intet foruroligende for Danmark' – Danmark mellem stormagterne frem mod 9. april 1940,* (Odense: Syddansk Universitetsforlag, 2020).

13   Søren Nørby, *Sænk skibene! Flådens sænkning 29. august 1943* (Aarhus: Turbine, 2018).

14   Carsten Holbraad, *Danish Neutrality. A Study of the Foreign Policy of a Small State* (Oxford: Clarendon, 1991).

15   Mikkel Runge Olesen, 'Dansk udenrigspolitik i skyggen af katastrofen', in Lars Bangert Struwe and Mikkel Vedby Rasmussen, *Læren af 1864. Krig, politik og stat i Danmark i 150 år* (Odense: Syddansk Universitetsforlag, 2014). Hans Branner, *9. april 1940 – et politisk lærestykke?* (Copenhagen: Jurist og Økonomforbundets Forlag, 1987), 230.

16   Rasmussen, *Læren af 1864. Krig, politik og stat i Danmark i 150 år,* 73.

17   Ibid., 73.

18   Poul Villaume, *Allieret med forbehold. Danmark, NATO og den kolde krig* (Copenhagen: Eirene, 1995).

19   Jens Ringsmose and Christian Brøndum, *Frihedens pris – så lav som mulig. NATO, Danmark og forsvarsbudgetterne* (Odense: Syddansk Universitetsforlag, 2018).

20 Poul Villaume, 'Den lange dansk-(vest)tyske afspændingsproces. Fra fjendtlig stormagtsnabo til tæt alliancepartner, 1945–1990', in Rasmus Mariager and Niklas Olsen, *Venskab og fjendskab i Danmark og Tyskland i det 19. og 20. århundrede* (Copenhagen: Den danske Historiske Forening, 2018), 291.

21 Karl Christian Lammers, *Hvad skal vi gøre ved tyskerne bagefter? Det dansk-tyske forhold efter 1945* (Copenhagen, Schønberg, 2005), 120f, 137ff.

22 Lammers, *Hvad skal vi gøre ved tyskerne bagefter? Det dansk-tyske forhold efter 1945,* 55–57.

23 Ibid., 89ff.

24 Villaume, 'Den lange dansk-(vest)tyske afspændingsproces. Fra fjendtlig stormagtsnabo til tæt alliancepartner, 1945–1990', 291f; Thomas Wegener Friis, '1945–2008', in Ole L. Frantzen og Knud J. V. Jespersen (ed), *Danmarks krigshistorie*, Vol. 2 (Copenhagen: Gads Forlag, 2008), 298f.

25 Bent Jensen, *Ulve, får og vogtere. Den kolde krig i Danmark 1945–1991*, Vol 1 (Copenhagen: Gyldendal, 2014), 227, 352, 361; John T. Lauridsen (ed), *Den kolde krig og Danmark* (Copenhagen: Gad, 2011), 718.

26 Lammers, *Hvad skal vi gøre ved tyskerne bagefter? Det dansk-tyske forhold efter 1945,* 157–160.

27 Ibid., 139. See also Villaume, *Allieret med forbehold,* 283, note 16 and picture No. 149.

28 Villaume, *Allieret med forbehold,* 20.

29 Ibid., 812.

30 Bryld and Warring, *Besættelsestiden som kollektiv erindring,* 250.

31 See for example debate about the findings of the parliamentary commission of 12 February 1955, in *Folketingstidende* 1954, 2189, 3584, 3596, 3616; debate about Danish foreign policy 23 January 1958 in *Folketingstidende* 1958, 2040; debate about a defence bill on 12 March 1959, in *Folketingstidende* 1958, 3666, 3696; and sporadic use in other debates on 2 June 1954, *Folketingstidende* 1954, 6016; 23 January 1958, *Folketingstidende* 1958, 2040; 13 January 1966, *Folketingstidende* 1966, 2608; 28 November 1967, *Folketingstidende* 1967, 1708.

32 Lammers, *Hvad skal vi gøre ved tyskerne bagefter? Det dansk-tyske forhold efter 1945,* 258ff.

33 R. J. B. Bosworth, *Explaining Auschwitz and Hiroshima: history writing and the Second World War 1945–1990* (London: Routledge, 1993), 4.

34 Bryld and Warring, *Besættelsestiden som kollektiv erindring,* 250.

35 Mariager and Wivel, *Hvorfor gik Danmark i krig?,* 117–145.

36 'Statsminister Anders Fogh Rasmussens tale in anledning af 60 året for 29. August 1943', address by Prime Minister Anders Fogh Rasmussen on the 60-year anniversary of 29 August 1943. Available at: https://www.stm.dk/statsministeren/taler/60-aaret-for-29-august-1943/.

37 For the Prime Minister's speech and the ensuing debate, see Holbraad, *Danish Reactions to German Occupation. History and Historiography,* 209ff.

38 'Statsministerens tale ved mindehøjtidelighed i Mindelunden den 29. august 2013 – 70 året for den 29. august 1943', address by the Prime Minister at the memorial ceremony at Mindelunden 29 August 2013 – the 70 year anniversary for 29 August 1943. Available at: https://www.stm.dk/statsministeren/taler/statsministerens-tale-ved-mindehoejtidelighed-i-mindelunden-den-29-august-2013-70-aaret-for-den-29-august-1943/.

39 Niels Bo Poulsen and Jakob Brink Rasmussen, 'The Long Road Towards an Official Danish Veterans' Policy, 1848–2010', *Contemporary Military Challenges*, Vol. 19, No. 2 (2017): 89–106.

40 Inge Adriansen, *Erindringssteder i Danmark. Monumenter, mindesmærker og mødesteder* (Copenhagen: Museum Tusculanums Forlag, 2010), 130ff, 181ff.

41 Adriansen, *Erindringssteder i Danmark. Monumenter, mindesmærker og mødesteder,* 125f.

42 Ibid., 136. It should be added that the Citadel was taken by the Germans early in the morning of 9 April 1940, and that the Museum of Danish Resistance is located just outside it.

43 T. L. Haaland and E. Gustavsen, 'From commemoration to celebration: The making of the Norwegian Liberation and Veterans Day', *Memory Studies* (2019): 1–16.

44 Steen Andersen, 'Hvor er fagligheden?', *Weekendavisen*, 10 July 2020; Hans Bonde, 'Det nye frihedsmuseum er en overfladisk udstilling med politisk slagside', *Berlingske Tidende*, 8 August 2020.

45 Niels Bo Poulsen, 'Impact of War on Colonial Areas – the Case of Greenland', Paper for the 43rd ICHM Congress World Wars and Colonies in history, 7 September 2017.

46 On the military culture of the three major services of the Danish armed forces see, Michael Clemmesen *Værnskulturerne og forsvarspolitikken* (Copenhagen: Politica, 1986).

47 The author of this article is heading the institute charged with teaching military history at all the defence force institutions of education.

48 See for example E. J. Saabye, 'Tradition', *Tidsskrift for Søvæsen* (1949): 421–434; A. H. Vedel, '10 år efter', *Tidsskrift for Søvæsen* (1955): 193–198.

49 Friis, '1945–2008', 264ff.

50 Hans Chr. Bjerg, 'Forsvarskommissioner gennem 125 år', in Henning Sørensen (ed), *Forsvar i forandring*, (Copenhagen: Samfundslitteratur, 1991), 12ff.

51 Paul Ibsen, 'Danmark er frit', *Tidsskrift for Søvæsen* (1945): 169–171, here: 171.

52 Ibid., 170f.

53 E. J. Saabye, 'Ved redaktørskiftet', *Tidsskrift for Søvæsen* (1945): 233.

54 In preparation for the article, the present author has done a complete survey of *Militært Tidsskrift* and *Tidsskrift for Søvæsen* between 1945 and 2012 in order to determine when, what, and how much was written about the lessons of the war.

55 Bertel Heurlin, 'Militær forskning i Danmark', *Militært Tidsskrift*, Vol. 140, No. 1 (2011): 21–35, here: 21.

56 K. Bang, 'Motortorpedobaade i Fremtidens danske Søværn', *Tidsskrift for Søvæsen* (1945): 250–258, here: 258. J. Petersen, 'U-Baade i Fremtidens danske Søværn', *Tidsskrift for Søvæsen* (1945), 348–355.

57 Skjoldager, 'Hvad er 'Nationalt Værn'', *Militært Tidsskrift* (1945): 271–273.

58 Friis, '1945–2008', 272. Mads Kr. Petersen, 'Hjemmeværnet', in John T. Lauridsen, Rasmus Mariager, Thorsten Borring Olesen and Poul Villaume (eds), *Den Kolde Krig og Danmark* (Copenhagen: Gad, 2011), 346–348. Michael Clemmesen, 'Udviklingen i Danmarks forsvarsdoktrin fra 1945 til 1969', *Militærhistorisk Tidsskrift* (1987), 7–82, here: 13.

59 Peter Hoved, *Kaj Birksted: dansk jagerpilot i allieret tjeneste: et mindeskrift* (Copenhagen: Frihedsmussets venner, 2010).

60 'Anordning om forholdsordre for det militære forsvar ved angreb på landet og under krig', contingency order regarding the military defence of the country during invasion and war, 6 March 1952. Available at https://www.retsinformation.dk/eli/lta/1952/63.

61 Clemmesen, *Værnskulturerne og forsvarspolitikken*, 61.

62 There were no less than four articles about Pearl Harbor between 1945 and 1950.

63 K. Winther, '9. april 1940 – læren og arven', *Tidsskrift for Søvæsen*, No. 1 (2000): 1–5.

64 Preben Holm, 'Nogle Tanker over et dansk Forsvars Muligheder på Basis af Krigserfaringerne', *Tidsskrift for Søvæsen* (1946): 60–65.

65 The above is based on an ongoing study of Danish military writing in *Militært Tidsskrift* and *Tidsskrift for Søvæsen*.

66 Henrik Gjøde Nielsen, 'Bangsbo Fort – fronten mod øst', in Jens Andersen (ed), *Atlantvolden i Nordjylland*, Vol. 2 (Aalborg: Museum Thy, 2018), 126–161.

67 Thomas Tram Petersen, 'Flødeskumsfronten klædt i beton – tyske anlæg i Danmark 1940–1945', 'Med frygt skal man forsvar bygge – den Kolde Krigs forsvar og bygninger 1945–1989', both

chapters in Mette Bom (ed), *I krigens fodspor – forsvarsbyggerier i Danmark* (Copenhagen: Kulturarvsstyrelsen, 2010), 65–74, 75–87.

68 D. A. Wieth-Knudsen, 'Den danske brigades pionerkompagni i Sverige', *Militært Tidsskrift* (1947): 241–264.

69 John V. Jensen, *Livsfare – **Miner!** Minerydningen på den jyske vestkyst 1945* (Varde: Vardemuseerne, 2019).

70 Peter Borberg and Thorsten Asbjørn Lauritsen, *Minerydning Skallingen. Historien om Danmarks sidste minefelt* (Århus: Turbine, 2012).

71 Jens Ejsing, 'Søværnet jager stadig miner fra krigens tid', *Jydske Vestkysten*, 1 November 2012. Available at https://jv.dk/artikel/s%C3%B8v%C3%A6rnet-jager-fortsat-miner-fra-krigens-tid-2012-11-1(3); Søværnet, 'Danske minerydder hjælper til med at rydde op i Østersøen', 31 May 2018. Available at https://www.facebook.com/sovaernet/posts/1692234400858815/.

72 'Hæren får nyt let maskingevær', *Dronningens Livregiments Soldaterforenings blad,* 2014. Available at http://drlrsf.dk/Blad4-15/H%C3%A6ren%20f%C3%A5r%20et%20nyt%20let%20maskin-gev%C3%A6r.pdf.

73 For fascination with WWII German armed forces in general, see Ronald M. Smelser and Edward J. Davies, *The Myth of the Eastern Front: The Nazi-Soviet War in American Popular Culture* (Cambridge: Cambridge University Press, 2008).

74 Sten Krarup, 'Lærum-sagen 1954', *Krigshistorisk Tidsskrift* (April 2006): 3–26.

75 'Statsminister Mette Frederiksens tale ved fejring af 75-året for Danmarks befrielse den 4. maj 2020', address by Prime Minister Mette Frederiksen on the 75th anniversary of Denmark's liberation, 4 May 2020. Available at https://www.stm.dk/_p_14945.html.

76 Zelikow, Philip, 'The Nature of History's Lessons', in Hal Brands and Jeremi Suri (eds), *The Power of the Past. History and Statecraft* (Washington, DC: Brookings Institution Press, 2016), 281–309, here: 286.

CHAPTER 13

Destiny Interrupted: The Legacy of World War II and Iran's Path to the 1979 Revolution

Ali Parchami

World War II seldom receives the attention it merits in the history of the post-war Middle East. Its long shadow can oddly be inconspicuous because of the way post-war events are described and presented: too often it is acknowledged only tangentially, either in the context of the founding of the state of Israel, or as an afterthought in reference to British decline. Nevertheless, World War II left the Middle East with a profound legacy. Its immediate impact was in the rapid disintegration of British hegemony and the acceleration of the process of de-colonisation. These events, in turn, precipitated numerous state-building projects, the forging of new national identities and a restructuring of the post-war regional order. Its intermediate legacy was epitomised by the Cold War and the conflict's spill-over into the region. Beginning in the 1950s, and spanning into the early 1970s, the United States found itself stepping into the vacuum left by the British as it sought to contain Soviet influence and prevent Moscow from establishing a foothold in the Middle East. In an already volatile strategic arena, the east–west ideological struggle succeeded only in exacerbating inter-state hostilities and intensifying the enmity of rival ethnic and political groups. Concurrently, Middle Eastern states took advantage of the opportunities presented by bipolarity to manipulate the superpowers and, under the veneer of the Cold War, to pursue their own narrow aims and interests.

Iran fits into this tapestry almost seamlessly, but it also provides a unique insight into how the legacy of World War II converged with post-war developments to give birth to the modern Middle East. First and foremost, Iran has the distinction of being the only ostensibly independent Middle Eastern country to be forcefully dragged into World War II. Despite proclaiming its neutrality, it was invaded in 1941 and jointly occupied by the Anglo-Soviet allies. Second, Stalin's prevarication in withdrawing from Iranian territory contributed significantly to the souring of US–Soviet relations.

The 1946 'Iran Crisis' – as the standoff came to be known – is now widely regarded as one of the nascent battlegrounds of the Cold War. Third, Iran was at the fulcrum of events that led to the weakening of Britain's grip over the region. Its wartime humiliation and occupation – and the financial and economic devastation that accompanied this experience – heightened amongst its population a nationalistic fervour that was saturated with strong anti-British and Russian undertones. This fervour reached its peak in the early 1950s when the Iranian government set out to nationalise the oil industry and claw back its lucrative profits from the British. Although thwarted and forced into yet another humiliating climb-down, Iran's defiance reverberated throughout the Middle East and was to be echoed by Nasser during the 1956 Suez Crisis.

Fourth, post-war Iran became one of the few non-western countries to experiment with democracy. The elected government's drive to nationalise the oil industry turned out be its undoing, however, as it was to be insidiously overthrown in an Anglo-American engineered coup. The episode not only convinced many Iranians that the claim to champion democracy was a hollow western slogan, but it also sowed the seeds of the popular resentment that was violently manifested in 1979. Last, but not least, the forced abdication of Reza Shah[1] in 1941, and his subsequent exile by the British, left a bitter and lasting impression on his young son and successor. Muhammad Reza Shah's determination to tilt post-war Iran towards the United States was borne, partly out of his wartime experience, and partly out of his conviction that the Americans were the panacea to the century-old influence that Britain and Russia had exerted over his country. The Shah's flirtation with the United States was to have far-reaching consequences for Iran, and after the 1979 revolution, for the wider Middle East and beyond.

Reza Shah and World War II

For the first four decades of the 20th century, the defining feature of Persian history was the competition for dominance between Britain and Russia, punctuated by periods of nationalist resistance. Persia – as Iran was known internationally – entered the century as a country ravaged by political corruption, administrative ineptitude, financial insolvency, social malcontent, and tribal and ethnic dissent. Permitted only the semblance of independence, the country had been divided by the 'Great Game' into spheres of influence. Under the weight of foreign intervention, its Qajar[2] government had become progressively impotent, spurring the two imperial powers to make of it ever greater demands.[3] Tightening their grip over the economy, the British and Russians had secured vast concessions, wavers on import-export duties, and tax exemptions. Even as the British siphoned off Persia's oil for a token fee, the traditional engines of the Persian economy – notably its textile industry – had been pushed to the brink of extinction. With its income rapidly shrinking, the Qajar government had been directed by the two powers to accept a series of costly loans, forcing it to sell off more and more of its assets to pay off the interest rates.[4]

Beset by turmoil, in February 1921, a nationalist army officer seized power by marching on Tehran. A colonel in the Cossack Brigade, Reza Khan was initially content with the title of Commander-in-Chief and Minister of War. But in December 1925 he ended the debacle of the Qajar monarchy by proclaiming himself Shah and inaugurating the Pahlavi era.[5] Modelling himself on Turkey's Atatürk, he set about transforming the country. Power was centralised, the bureaucracy reformed, and tribal agitations quelled. The Shah oversaw the construction of new roads, a Trans-Persian railway network, and the re-organisation of the armed forces – now equipped and trained by European instructors. The economy was modernised with the institutionalisation of banking and the establishment of industrial factories; and the Shah broke the power of the Shia Ulama (senior clerics) by confining them to religious seminaries. Persian society was further transformed with the forced unveiling of women and the introduction of a western-style university, schools and department stores.[6]

Alongside his policy of modernisation, Reza Shah was also determined to end the century-old machinations of the British and Russians by pursuing and cultivating relations with Germany. Economic cooperation was precipitously expanded as hundreds of German engineers, technicians and their dependents were invited to Persia to overhaul its infrastructure.[7] The growing German influence caused dismay in London and Moscow, but these concerns were heightened after 1933 when Berlin began courting oil-rich Persia as part of its wider strategy of undermining British influence in the Near East. Nazi propagandists fuelled British suspicions by offering Persia equivocal protection against 'predatory powers' and by brandishing the vague notion of a common 'Aryan ancestry'.[8]

The Persian court found considerable appeal in the prospect of the German Reich acting as a bulwark against its Anglo-Russian tormentors. It may have played a part in the Shah's 1935 decision to formally ask the diplomatic community to stop referring to his country as Persia. Instead, Tehran sought international recognition for the name that had been used by the country's indigenous population since antiquity: Iran – the 'land of the Aryans'.[9] A year later, the German Reichstag declared Iranians to be immune from the Nuremberg Laws by recognising their ancestors as 'Aryans'.[10] Between 1939–1941, as Europe was ravaged by war, Nazi Germany became Iran's leading trading partner – with half of the country's commercial activity concentrated in German hands.[11] However, by stringently maintaining Iran's neutrality, the Shah demonstrated that his anti-British and anti-Russian sentiments outweighed his pro-German sympathies.

Once Operation *Barbarossa* was underway, Britain became alarmed at the possibility of Iranian oil fields falling into German hands. The Iranian government was issued with an ultimatum demanding the expulsion of all German nationals from

Iranian soil. Even as Iran insisted on its sovereignty and neutrality, on 25 August 1941 Britain and the Soviet Union jointly launched a surprise invasion with aerial power, mechanised units and some 140,000 troops.[12] Under the codename Operation *Countenance*, the Soviets moved swiftly into northern Iran, as the British dispatched troops from neighbouring Iraq and advanced north from the Persian Gulf. Sporadic pockets of resistance notwithstanding, the Iranian military was quickly overwhelmed and brushed aside. Six days into hostilities, Iran formally surrendered.[13] Forced to abdicate in favour of his son, Reza Shah was exiled by the British first to Mauritius and then South Africa. His 22-year-old son and successor, Muhammad Reza, was compelled in January 1942 to sign the Tripartite Treaty of Alliance. The convention stipulated that Iran's sovereignty and territorial integrity would be restored six months after the end of hostilities with Germany.

The 'Persian Corridor' allowed the western Allies to dispatch over 5 million tons of war materials to the Soviet Union.[14] Hailed as a strategic 'bridge to victory', the impact of Iran's occupation for its people was catastrophic. With transportation networks and distribution facilities diverted in aid of the war effort, and with tens of thousands of foreign troops on Iranian soil competing for basic amenities, scarcity and food shortages led to widespread famine, disease and inflation. One author estimates that over 4,000,000 Iranians – a quarter of the population – lost their lives during the occupation.[15] As unscrupulous profiteers took advantage of the economic downturn, hyper-inflation reached as high as 450% on some basic goods. The Allies neither bothered to ease the pressure on the Iranian people nor showed much regard for their well-being.[16] In fact, the exiled Shah's bureaucracy was allowed by the British to crumble, creating a ripple effect that intensified the rise in local abuse and crime.

Amidst social and economic uncertainties, reports of the maltreatment of Iranians by Allied troops provoked popular anger and led to sporadic urban rioting and tribal uprisings.[17] These developments encouraged pro-German sympathies among some members of the Iranian intelligentsia and, in particular, the humiliated army officer corps. Under the leadership of General Fazollah Zahedi, a small resistant movement reached out to German agents, engaged in acts of sabotage, and encouraged ethno-tribal rebellions. Although its impact was negligible, and it was quickly rooted out, its activities led to Allied pressure on the Iranian government to declare war on the German Reich on 9 September 1943.[18] Iran's status as a secure and subjugated country was all but confirmed by December 1943 when it hosted Churchill, Roosevelt and Stalin at the Tehran Conference.

Marxists, the 1946 Crisis and the Soviets

World War II cast an immediate shadow over the internal dynamics of Iran and its relationship with the outside world. The experience left a deep scar on the national psyche. Despite enduring years of exorbitant taxes and heeding Reza Shah's demands for self-sacrifice, the promise of a modern and powerful Iran had come to naught. Any relief the populace may have felt at the cession of hostilities soon turned into indignation once they learned about the shambolic demise of their military and the swift collapse of the Shah's seemingly unassailable autocracy. Iranians of all classes were particularly shocked by the nature of the country's capitulation: never before, in its long and illustrious history, had Iran succumbed to a foreign adversary so pitifully without a fight. There was palpable resentment towards the exiled Shah – a man who had treated his people with brutality but had withered away within six days of the invasion. An American Presbyterian minister, who was living in Tehran during the mid-1940s, noted that many Iranians viewed the Allied occupation not only as an expression of national disgrace, but also as a loss of personal honour.[19]

Iranian anger should be understood in the context of a culture which, contrary to reality, continued to view itself as an imperial power. Even though Iran had been subjected to foreign influence since the early 19th century, it had retained the illusion of independence – with the majority of the population oblivious of the extent to which Britain and Russia had exerted control over Iranian affairs. This changed with the Allied occupation when every segment of Iranian society came to experience, first-hand, the bitterness of being treated as underlings in their own towns and villages. This overarching sense of humiliation fuelled an upsurge in nationalism, leftist radicalism, and religion. All three had been significant movements in the first two decades of the 20th century – at least until Reza Shah had suppressed the last two and re-branded nationalism around the Pahlavi dynasty. But as the authority of the central government evaporated after 1941, all three movements found new outlets. Tapping into the prevailing mood of discontent, each recruited a younger generation of supporters and, by channelling their anger, succeeded in building national organisations with local chapters.

The radical left was the first to make a play for power. Freed from imprisonment during the wartime occupation, leftist leaders had formed the Marxist Tudeh (Party of the Masses) in October 1941 with Soviet assistance. War had left Iranian society both vulnerable and receptive to leftist ideologues. By 1946, Iran had become one of the poorest countries in the world.[20] Alongside wartime profiteers, the major beneficiaries of the occupation had been the large landowners. Taking advantage of adverse circumstances, they had either forcefully snatched the plots of small farmers or had bought the land on the cheap when the latter fell into debt. Abandoning their rural habitats in their thousands, peasants swarmed into the cities to become an angry underclass. They were to be joined by small merchants and urban labourers, whose wartime plight had been made worse when parliamentary deputies passed tax laws that favoured their own kind – fellow members of the nobility and the upper-middle-classes.[21]

With Soviet logistical and financial support, Tudeh Marxists grew rapidly by reaching out to the underrepresented masses and by expanding their network of open and clandestine cells.[22] Intent upon seizing control of the government, their first goal was to force parliamentary elections to increase the number of Marxist deputies in the Majlis (parliamentary assembly).[23] The party's strategy was to outflank its nationalist rivals – who dominated the assembly – and to undercut the Shia Ulama with their large and devoted religious followers. During the war, Tudeh activities were supported by the Soviets in the northern provinces they occupied. Outside the Soviet zone, they were aided by the apathy the British had shown for the indigenous population and, after 1945, by acts of sedition designed to foment urban unrest and ethno-tribal agitation.[24] The Tudeh were thus willing collaborationists when the Soviets triggered the 1946 'Iran Crisis' – an event with far-reaching international consequences.

An opening salvo in the Cold War, the crisis encapsulated how the events of World War II were shaping developments in Iran, and how these developments, in turn, were determining the distribution of power in a polarised international system. The crisis was occasioned by Moscow's decision to renege on the 1942 Tripartite Agreement which required the Allies to withdraw from Iranian territory within six months of Germany's defeat. Stalin initially prevaricated by insisting that Soviet forces would be withdrawn six months after Japan's surrender. The west suspected foul play, with the British fearing the fate of the vast Anglo-Persian oil refineries in Abadan; and the Americans expressing concern for the future of Iran altogether.[25] The western powers recognised that Iran's oil deposits, and access to the warm sea ports of the Persian Gulf, had been coveted by the Russians since the 19th century. What they were not sure of was whether the Soviets intended to turn Iran into a buffer state – consistent with Stalin's policy in Eastern Europe – or to incite turmoil so they could carve off the country one slice at a time.

The west's worst suspicions were confirmed in November 1945 when the Tudeh Party, at Soviet behest, proclaimed a People's Republic in the north-western Iranian province of Azerbaijan. Under the leadership of Jafar Pishevari, a prominent Marxist with a record of secessionist activity, the newly formed Azerbaijani Democratic Party assumed power in the province. The Soviets immediately granted the Pishevari government diplomatic recognition, and propped it up with money and the deployment of Soviet troops. To give the Azerbaijan People's Republic a veneer of legitimacy, in December 1945 Moscow encouraged a group of Iranian Kurds to form their own independent Republic of Mahabad in the eastern half of the province. While ostensibly an ethnic Kurdish homeland, with no Communist affiliation, the Kurdish entity depended entirely on Soviet military and financial support. Neither the west, nor the Iranian authorities, were oblivious of the fact that – during the occupation years – it was the Soviets and their Tudeh agents who had fanned the flames of hostility among Azerbaijan's Turkic and Kurdish peoples. In particular,

Kurdish ethnic identity had been encouraged in direct opposition to the 'Persian' central government in Tehran.[26]

Matters came to a head when the Iranian government formally submitted a motion of complaint to the newly established United Nations. The 'Iran Crisis' instigated a bad-tempered confrontation in the Security Council (UNSC) between the Soviet ambassador, Andrei Gromyko, and his Western counterparts. But when nine UNSC members voted in Iran's favour by demanding an immediate Soviet withdrawal, the Soviets responded with a veto – occasioning its first ever use. The standoff ended under considerable American pressure, and after the Iranian government signed the 1946 Qavam-Sadikov Agreement. Under its terms, the Soviets abandoned their puppet regimes in Azerbaijan and Mahabad and removed their troops from northern Iran. In return, the Iranian government conceded to Moscow a 51% share of the petroleum in its northern provinces and the Shah allowed members of the Tudeh Party to be appointed to Prime Minister Ahmad Qavam's cabinet. In December 1946 Iranian troops re-occupied Azerbaijan.[27]

The 1946 'Iran Crisis' had three repercussions. First, the incident hardened US attitudes towards the Soviet Union. As one contemporary American diplomat put it, the Cold War started on 4 March 1946 when 15 Soviet armoured brigades poured into Iran's Azerbaijan province.[28] The episode was certainly one of a series of events that culminated in the 1947 Truman Doctrine and the formalisation of the Cold War.[29] Second, and as we shall see later, the episode was important in how the Shah came to view the Americans and was a contributing factor to his erstwhile dependency on the United States. Third, the events of 1946 helped shape Iranian policy towards the Kurds – not just under the Shah but, arguably, also under his Islamist successors. After the establishment of the Mahabad Republic, Iranian leaders came to view Kurdish aspirations for autonomy – much less statehood – as seditious and sought to stamp out Kurdish identity and culture. At the same time, even as the Shah – and later the Ayatollahs – pursued a brutal policy of Kurdish suppression within Iran, they intermittently armed the Kurds in neighbouring Iraq and Turkey to use them as leverage.[30]

Nationalists, oil and the British

As we have seen, Iran's wartime defeat stirred among its population strong nationalist feelings which, during the occupation, morphed into anti-foreign sentiment. Whereas Soviet Russia had a natural constituency in Iran in the form of the Marxist Tudeh, pro-British sympathisers lacked a party-political organisation. If anything, Britain's role in the 1941 invasion had served to alienate many admirers. For all its claims to the moral high-ground, there could be no denying that Britain had committed an act of aggression against a neutral and sovereign country on the justification that it harboured German nationals and their dependents.[31] The Iranian intelligentsia, who already viewed Britain's rationalisation of the invasion as flimsy, soon came to realise that their country had been occupied so that its transportation network could provide relief to the Red Army.[32] Attacked by the left and the right, Britain would never again be accepted by Iranians as a paragon of democracy and an observer of international law.

If the 1946 Iran Crisis epitomised how wartime occupation had energised the Iranian left in collusion with the Soviets, the late 1940s was characterised by the struggle of Iranian nationalists against the British. With anti-British sentiments running high, the government's announcement of further oil concessions to Britain caused political outrage in 1949. Galvanised by their wartime experience and post-war Soviet mischief, nationalist deputies in the Majlis began organising themselves into a powerful bloc: the National Front. Its leadership made its express objective to end the 'malign' influence of the British once and for all. When the Shah clumsily tried to rig the parliamentary elections in favour of loyalists, National Front deputies passed laws that set-in motion plans to turn Iran into a democratic state under a constitutional monarchy and to divest the Shah of the autocratic powers his father had exercised. In April 1951 the deputies forced the Shah, by a vote of 79–12, to appoint a National Front leader as prime minister.

The 69-year-old Muhammad Mossadegh was a princely scion of the Qajar dynasty. A patriot with impeccable nationalist credentials, he was an intellectual, a moderniser, reformer and a Francophile. He was also mercurial with a propensity for showmanship and demagogic outbursts. His government implemented a raft of reforms to address the social-economic malaise of the war years. Focusing on the plight of peasants and the working classes, Mossadegh introduced unemployment and sickness benefits, protection for workers, and tackled illegal activities of feudal landlords in the countryside. These and other measures made his government immensely popular with the masses and strengthened the political hand of the National Front against the Shah and his loyalists.[33] Banking on his popularity, in May 1951 Mossadegh moved against the British by nationalising the Anglo-Iranian Oil Company (AIOC).[34] Oil was to be the battleground, as well as the prize, of the National Front's struggle to rid Iran of British imperialism. Oil concessions were cancelled and AIOC's assets were seized, including the oil refineries in Abadan – the biggest in the world.[35]

For the British this was unfathomable. Imperial pride aside, the financial burden of World War II had made it even more pressing for Britain to tighten its grip on Iranian oil. Ernest Bevin, the British Foreign Secretary, noted that without Iranian oil there would be no hope of achieving the standard of living Britain was aiming for.[36] In conjunction with financial considerations, there was genuine concern in London that weakness against Iran would fatally harm Britain's prestige at a time when it was desperately fighting to hold on to its standing as a 'great power' and to the remnants of its Empire.[37] Unwilling to compromise, Britain referred the case to the International Court of Justice and the UN Security Council. When an equally intransigent Mossadegh refused to back down, Britain used its considerable leverage to organise an international embargo against Iranian oil, and to institute wide-ranging sanctions against Iran's financial transactions. It also enforced a naval blockade of Iranian shipping in the Persian Gulf.

These measures caused severe disruption to the Iranian economy by reducing the sale of oil to nearly zero and put an even greater strain on the government's meagre income.[38] Despite the setbacks, Mossadegh's anti-British stance boosted his popularity with the masses, retained the support of the rank-and-file of the Nationalist Front, and met with the approval of the powerful Shia Ulama. With momentum on his side, Mossadegh held snap elections and, with a much-improved popular mandate, now doubled-down on his previous policies. The Shah, feeling threatened, and under pressure from the British, engineered Mossadegh's resignation and re-appointed in his place Ahmad Qavam – the man who had negotiated the treaty with the Soviets that had ended the 1946 Crisis. But Mossadegh, riding high on anti-British nationalism, was swept back into office after his supporters organised mass demonstrations. Emboldened, the prime minister began confronting the Shah openly and attacked his base of power by purging the army's officer corps of pro-Shah supporters. The Shah and his family fled into exile, first to Baghdad and then to Rome.

Mossadegh's victory was short-lived. The British, with the aid of pro-Shah sympathisers, convinced the Americans that a cohort of leftist radicals – led by the Marxist Tudeh – had been instrumental in Mossedgh's success. Mossadegh was no communist sympathiser, but the British claimed that he was either too feeble to control the Tudeh or was being manipulated by them. Either way, the British insisted, the political fallout from Mossadegh's policies could only have one outcome: communists' empowerment in Iran.[39] The US Secretary of State, Dean Acheson, understood the British game, noting that the aim of the British was not to prevent Iran from going communist but to safeguard their only remaining 'bulwark against insolvency'.[40] The extent of the Tudeh influence in the events of 1953 is still vigorously debated, but the Americans were nonetheless spurred into decisive action. The risk of Iran falling into the hands of the Soviets was too great and the CIA was given the green light to engage in its first covert operation to bring down the sovereign government of another country.[41]

De-classified CIA papers show how Langley, in close cooperation with the British Intelligence Service (SIS), concocted the plan to overthrow Mossadegh.[42] Codenamed Operation *Ajax*, it involved attacks on nationalist and religious leaders which were blamed on Mossadegh's office; generous bribes to anti-Mossadegh politicians; mobilisation of street thugs to create the air of popular discontent; and coordination with malcontent senior army officers.[43] The British, in particular, used their network of agents in Iran to sow friction within the National Front and to foment discord between the nationalist camp and the Grand Ayatollah Kashani and his religious followers.[44] Paradoxically, General Zahedi – the man who had organised the pro-German resistance against the Anglo-Russian occupation – now secretly assisted SIS in the overthrow of Iran's democratically-elected government.

Support for Mossadegh splintered as Ayatollah Kashani and the Ulama abandoned him when the prime minister refused to renounce secularism and return to gender segregation. Within the National Front, too, there was increasing criticism of Mossadegh's obdurate anti-imperialist stance with many nationalists urging him to reach a compromise to avert Iran's financial bankruptcy. As the impact of British sanctions chipped away at Mossadegh's popularity, the CIA utilised small arm tactics and propaganda to incite unrest and pro-Shah demonstrations.[45] Sporadic clashes in the streets and anti-government chants created the impression that Mossadegh was losing popular support. Mossadegh called on the army to restore order. However, disaffected generals, angry at the prime minister's earlier purge of the officer corps, rallied behind the putschists. On 19 August 1953 Mossadegh was arrested and a triumphant Shah returned to Iran with General Zahedi appointed as prime minister. In the ensuing weeks, the National Front was dismantled and its leading exponents either imprisoned or executed. The elderly Mossadegh was hauled before the courts in a show trial and then imprisoned. Within a year, Britain had regained some of its oil rights and accompanying concessions.

The rise and fall of Mossadegh underlines how the legacy of World War II converged with the politics of the Cold War to produce a chain of events. Without the abdication of the despotic Reza Shah, who had kept nationalist leaders at bay, and the social-economic turmoil that accompanied Iran's wartime occupation, it is unlikely that the National Front could have emerged with the organisation and popular support that propelled Mossadegh into power. Nor was the oil dispute likely to have assumed the focal point that it did for nationalists determined, on the one hand, to free Iran from British influence and, on the other hand, to use the oil revenue to remedy the deep impoverishment the Allied occupation had inflicted on the country. Britain's response to the Iranian oil dispute was similarly influenced by the legacy of the war: 'Never had so few lost so much so stupidly and so fast', wrote Dean Acheson contemptuously about Britain's management of the crisis.[46]

The Iranian oil saga was to be the deathblow to British hegemony in the Middle East. Far from protecting its prestige, the humiliation Britain suffered at the hands of Mossadegh exacerbated anti-British sentiments across the region and provided the conditions by which the United States soon displaced the old imperial power.[47] Britain even lost out on the substantial control it had hitherto exercised over the AIOC. After Operation *Ajax*, it had no choice but to share the ownership of the company with the Americans who, prior to 1953, had no stake in Iranian oil.[48]

This regional tilt from the British to the Americans had direct repercussions in Iranian political developments. A grateful Shah felt he owed his restoration to the United States and came to view the Americans as the answer to the age-old

Anglo-Russian competition for dominance in his country. Fiercely anti-communist, he also convinced himself that, he alone, could turn Iran into America's steadfast ally in containing Soviet communism around the Persian Gulf; and, in return, he believed the US would help Iran regain its historical role as the region's great power. With this in mind, the Shah began promoting American influence and culture in Iran even while espousing contempt for American-style liberal democracy. As he consolidated his power, he grew increasingly despotic. Political parties were banned, and the Pahlavi dynasty became the only acceptable conduit for any expression of nationalism. Concurrently, the Shah waged a relentless war against Marxists. Aligning himself with the vehemently anti-communist Shia clergy, he unleashed the SAVAK – his notorious secret service – against leftist activists and forced them underground. So it was that of the three great movements that emerged from World War II, only the Shia clerics were permitted to retain their organisation and network and to operate openly across the country.

For Iranians the social-cultural legacy of Operation *Ajax*, and Mossadegh's fall, cannot be overestimated. Among its fallout was the accentuation of existing popular distrust and resentment towards the British, particularly in the form of a uniquely Iranian paranoia known as 'Uncle Napoleonism'.[49] Popular resentment was also now extended to the Americans who, after 1953, began dislodging the British in Iran. While many Iranian nationalists and liberals had expected the worst from the British, they had felt betrayed by the United States' role in the overthrow of the Mossadegh government. This anger reverberated during the 1979 Revolution as Iranians, in their thousands, condemned the United States for hijacking Iran's democracy and replacing it with the tyranny of the Shah.

The Shah and the Americans

The legacy of World War II in Iran cannot be fully appreciated without discussing the man who ruled the country autocratically from 1953 to 1979. Muhammad Reza Pahlavi was deeply affected by his wartime experiences. He had become Shah under inauspicious circumstances when his father had been pressured to abdicate and was then ignominiously banished by the British to never see his family or homeland again. The first four years of the young Shah's reign had unfolded under an occupation regime when he had been agonisingly marginalised in his own country. During the 1943 Tehran Conference neither Churchill nor Roosevelt had even bothered to visit him, their host, as mandated by international protocol. Stalin alone had paid the young monarch a courtesy call, but only after the Red Army had embarrassed the Shah by disarming his bodyguards at the Marble Palace.[50]

The Shah's wartime experience made him mindful of the fate of his father and engendered in him a lifelong fear of being removed from the throne in the same manner. These fears became more pronounced following his brief exile in 1953, with the irony not lost on him that he owed his restoration to foreign intelligence services. For the remainder of his reign, the Shah adopted the public persona of an imposing and all-powerful autocrat to invoke fear and awe in friends and enemies alike. His lavish lifestyle, costly pageantry, and grandiose pretensions were a reaction to the early years of his reign – an overcompensation for his powerlessness during the occupation years and subsequent humiliation by Mossadegh. Deep-down, however, the Shah remained a shy and insecure individual, hesitant to make decisions and self-conscious of his short physical stature.[51]

These personal insecurities, in conjunction with his first-hand experience of defeat and occupation, shaped the Shah's political and military vision. Determined to make Iran the foremost power in the Persian Gulf – a country that could never be bullied again by the Soviets or the British – he asked President Truman for military assistance as early as 1949 when on a state visit to America. Though the Truman administration was unwilling to meet the monarch's demands, the Shah never wavered from his ambition and, in later years, pursued a strategy of making Iran indispensable to American policy in the Middle East. The SAVAK – trained by the CIA and the Mossad – slowly emerged as a useful local network in gathering Cold War intelligence thanks to Iran's territorial proximity to the Soviet Union. While maintaining cordial relations with the Arab world, the Shah fostered close ties with Israel and Turkey; and as oil revenues poured into the country, he provided financial largesse to US allies within and outside the Middle East. His vehemently pro-American tilt secured for the Shah some of the coveted arms and training he desired and allowed him to pursue his regional ambitions with greater confidence and fire power.

Beginning in the 1960s, Iranian expeditionary forces were dispatched to troubled hotspots across the Middle East and Southwest Asia, including the strategically important Dhofar region of Oman. The pro-Soviet regime in Baghdad was routinely harassed as the Shah dispatched covert units into Iraq to arm the Kurds and encourage rebellion; and when the Iraqi dictator Saddam Hussein formally protested, a bellicose Tehran forced him into submission with the threat of war.[52] In tandem with military exertions, the Shah propped-up the pro-western kingdoms of Jordan and Morocco against Nasserite radicalism, and became a powerbroker in the Pakistan-Indian disputes that followed the 1971 South Asian Crisis.[53] By the early 1970s, the Shah had succeeded in turning Iran into one of the 'two pillars' of American policy in the Middle East – an embodiment of the Nixon Doctrine.[54] Indeed, some scholars have argued that far from being its instrument, the Shah was the architect of a doctrine that essentially gave Iran a free reign to act as the regional 'policeman'.[55]

Not satisfied with his country's new regional role, the Shah began harbouring ideas about the resurgence of Persia's 'great civilisation'. His 1967 coronation ceremony was a magnificent affair whose real purpose was to remind the world that Iran was not a mere 'kingdom', but an imperial power with two millennia of history. Such proclivities garnered rebukes of eccentricity or megalomania from critics. But they also betrayed the fact that the Shah was still haunted by the ghosts of 1941. The power he sought for his 'great civilisation' programme was not to come from investment in infrastructure, or the country's economic foundations, or its people – but in the purchase of military hardware and technology. Nor was he content for his military to outdo Third World rivals, such as Iraq. What the Shah aspired was to put Iran on par with the United States so that Iranian armed forces could ward off the Soviet Union on their own. Iran, the Shah insisted, 'must be able to stand alone'.[56] Despite Washington's repeated reassurances about defending Iran in the event of a Soviet invasion, the Shah's procurement policy in the 1970s became more and more extravagant. The Iranian Air Force was a case-in-point: having purchased 80 F-14s in 1972, the Shah placed an order for 160 F-16s in 1976. No sooner had the order been placed that he publicly confirmed an additional order for 140 F-16s, hundreds of F18-Ls, and a fleet of AWACS. The Shah's procurement policy caused such consternation in American political circles that the US Secretary of Defence, James Schlesinger, and members of Congress united to block his more exorbitant orders.[57]

The Shah's obsession with military power was such that he was willing to exploit Cold War politics in order to get what he wanted. This was not simply a matter of uninhibited ambition but a yearning for security: the Shah viewed Iran as an extension of himself and neither were ever again going to be humiliated or subdued.[58] So when in 1965 the Johnson administration refused to meet his weapons demands, the Shah hastily arranged a visit to Moscow to discuss the purchase of $110 million worth of Soviet armaments.[59] It was a bluff on the part of the fervently pro-American Shah, but it caused enough public embarrassment for the Johnson administration that it immediately relented. Similarly, when the Nixon administration vacillated in supporting Iran's aggressions in neighbouring Iraq, the Shah once again demonstrated a shrewd ability to play on Washington's Cold War paranoia to justify his behaviour.[60] Far from allowing Iran to serve as America's 'lackey', the Shah increasingly pursued a 'positive equilibrium' strategy to manipulate the United States and its European allies into giving him what he wanted.[61]

This strategy allowed the Shah to pursue what US Congressman – Gerry E. Studds of Massachusetts – described as 'the most rapid build-up of military power under peacetime conditions of any nation in the history of the world'.[62] The inventory of the Shah's purchases in the 1960s and 70s drew on nearly half of Iran's oil sales to finance the military spending spree.[63] During the first half of the 1970s, Iranian military procurement from the US soared from around $500 million to $4.5 billion. By the late 1970s, the Shah had succeeded in exorcising the demons of World War II by building the Iranian military into one of the most capable and, in some areas, well-trained armed forces in the Third World. With over 150,000 troops, and more Chieftain tanks than the British Army, Iran boasted one of the most advanced and largest air forces in all of Asia.[64] Paradoxically, the more advanced weapons he purchased from the US, the more the Shah's procurement programme made the Iranian military reliant on US technical support.[65]

For all his efforts to secure Iran from invasion, the Shah's downfall was caused not by foreign adversaries but by domestic discontent resulting from economic inequality and corruption. Much of the popular anger was directed at the Shah's autocratic rule and the Pahlavi clan's predilection for treating the country as its personal fiefdom. But some of the anger was also a backlash against the Shah's rampant 'westernisation' policy. This was a top-down programme borne out of the Shah's desire for Iran to be accepted as a western country. If Iran was accepted as a member of this 'exclusive club', then it would never again be threatened by European powers. In assuming the title of *Arayamehr* ('the light of the Aryans'), and in hosting the lavish 2,500 anniversary celebrations of the founding of the Persian Empire, the Shah set out to create the narrative that Iran and its civilisation were ethno-culturally European. In a 1975 speech he affirmed that Iran held no ill-will for the past imperialism of European powers and would be willing to help an economically troubled Britain with a one-billion-dollar loan. After all, the Shah noted, we, too, belong to this European world and do not wish to see it collapse.[66] As it turned out, far from turning Iran into a 'western' country, the Shah's policies led to the emergence of a different Iranian polity.

The long shadow

The 1979 Iranian Revolution that overthrew the Shah was spearheaded by Marxists, nationalists, liberals and the clergy. In the early post-war years, the Marxists and the nationalists had each made a play for power and, having failed, were subsequently suppressed. Now it was the turn of the clergy. As the 1979 revolution unfolded, the clerical movement demonstrated that it had an unrivalled national network. Its activists reached every corner of the country and its passionate followers could be mobilised instantly. In Ayatollah Khomeini they had a charismatic leader whose strong will and single-minded conviction contrasted sharply with the Shah and the fragmented leadership of the left and right. Khomeini's Islamists astutely exploited the broad coalition opposing the monarchy and then ruthlessly moved against their rivals following the seizure of the US Embassy.

If at first glance Khomeini's regime appears detached from the legacy of World War II, closer inspection would suggest otherwise. Having himself lived through the 1941 invasion, Khomeini was to show steadfast resolve in the desperate early days of the Iran-Iraq War. As Saddam's infantry and mechanised units pierced into Iran's oil fields, and with the international community all but abandoning Iran, Khomeini held his nerves. His regime mobilised the masses by appealing not just to Islamism but also to Iranian nationalism in invoking the country's past glories as well as memories of its recent humiliations. The regime's motto of 'neither Eastern, nor

Western, but only an Islamic Republic' was just as much an enunciation of a new Islamist age as it was a declaration of an end to a century and a half of competition between the British, the Russians and the Americans over Iran.

Having also lived through the Allied occupation, Khomeini was not content with expelling 'foreign influence' from Iranian soil: he and his successors set out to rid the entire Middle East of the 'malignance' of foreigners. This was, of course, consistent with Khomeini's Islamist worldview. And yet, alongside allusions to Islam and Shia sectarianism, Iran's clerical leadership frequently has made opaque references to the suffering of the Iranian people at the hands of 'arrogant hegemonists powers'. The Islamic Republic, they insist, has restored 'pride' to an Iranian nation that was once humbled and victimised by the misdeeds of the Russians and westerners. Iran's expansive strategy in the region, they maintain, is a response to three unprovoked invasions in the 20th century. Iran's past victimisation has spurred the Islamic Republic to take its fight to its enemies and to wage its wars on foreign soils – never again allowing adversaries to threaten Iran by amassing unhindered along its borders.

The Islamic Republic regularly boasts that, no matter what the financial, political and human cost, Iran and its people will never again be 'humiliated' or made to feel 'subservient' to foreign powers. But perhaps the singular lesson that the regime has learned from the legacy of World War II and its aftermath is that it cannot afford to bend, be cowed into compromise or intimidated under sanctions or the threat of war. Any sign of weakness, its leadership has concluded, could consign the Islamic Republic to the same fate as Marxist and nationalists, or the Pahlavi Shahs. The long shadow of imperialism and World War II thus linger in the minds of Iranian decision-makers.

Notes

1   The shortened form of *Shahanshah*, or 'King of Kings' – the traditional title of Iran's imperial rulers dating back to 559 BC.
2   The ruling dynasty (1794–1925), widely regarded as the most corrupt and incompetent in Iranian history.
3   Homa Katouzian, *State and Society in Iran: The Eclipse of the Qajars and the Emergence of the Pahlavais* (London: IB Taurus, 2000), 25–54.
4   In 1907 Britain and Russia signed the landmark Anglo-Russian Convention, which formalised Persia's division into spheres of influence.
5   There were persistent rumours that Reza Khan's rise had been engineered by the British. Cyrus Ghani, *Iran and the Rise of Reza Shah: From Qajar Collapse to Pahlavi Power* (London: IB Taurus, 1998), 147–155; and Christopher De Bellaigue, *Patriot of Persia: Muhammad Mossadegh and a Tragic Anglo-American Coup* (London: Harper-Perennial, 2012), 73.
6   Ervand Abrahamian, *Iran between Two Revolutions* (Princeton: Princeton University Press, 1982), 139–142.
7   Jennifer Jenkins, 'Iran in the Nazi New Order, 1933–1941', *Iranian Studies,* Vol. 49, No. 5 (2016): 727–742.

8   David Motadel, 'Iran and the Aryan Myth', in Ali Ansari (ed), *Perceptions of Iran: History, Myths and Nationalism From Medieval Persia to the Islamic Republic* (London: IB Taurus, 2013), 119–145; and De Bellaigue, *Patriot of Persia*, 108.

9   Motadel, 'Iran and the Aryan Myth', 132–133; and Kenneth Pollack, *The Persian Puzzle: The Conflict Between Iran and America* (New York: Random House, 2004), 37–38.

10 Contemporary Iranians were regarded less favourably, with the Nazi hierarchy considering them an example of the perils of inter-breeding. Steven R. Ward, *Immortal: A Military History of Iran and Its Armed Forces* (Washington: GUP, 2009), 151–152; and George Lenczowski, *Russia and the West in Iran 1918–1948* (Ithaca: Cambridge University Press, 1949), 160–161.

11 Nikki R. Keddie, *Modern Iran: Roots and Results of Revolution* (New Haven: Yale University Press, 2006), 101; and Jenkins, 'Iran in the Nazi New Order', 740–742.

12 Whereas the 120,000-strong Red Army had to contend with 37,000 Iranians, the 19,000 British encountered 30,000 and faced stiff but sporadic resistance. Ward, *Immortal*, 155–167.

13 Kaveh Farrokh, *Iran At War 1500–1988* (Oxford: Osprey, 2011), 270–282; and Ward, *Immortal*, 150–180.

14 Thomas H. V. Motter, *The Persian Corridor and Aid To Russia* (Washington: Center of Military History, 1952), 435; and Kaveh, *Iran At War*, 281.

15 Mohammad Gholi Majd, *Iran Under Allied Occupation in World War II: The Bridge To Victory & a Land of Famine* (Lanham: UPA, 2016), 527–562.

16 Abbas Milani, *The Shah* (London: Palgrave-Macmillan, 2012), 106; Keddie, *Modern Iran*, 106–107; Pollack, *The Persian Puzzle*, 43; and Lenczowski, *Russia and the West*, 194–195.

17 Kaveh, *Iran At War*, 281–282. The inspiration for 'Ey Iran' – widely viewed by Iranians as their de facto national anthem – came to lyricist Hossein Gol-e-Golab in 1944 after he allegedly saw a British soldier slap a senior Iranian officer in the face outside the Astarabad military base.

18 Kaveh, *Iran at War*, 282; and Ward, *Immortal*, 177–178.

19 Richard Stewart, *Sunrise At Abadan: The British and Soviet Invasion of Iran, 1941* (New York: Praeger 1988), 194–195; and Ward, *Immortal*, 169–176.

20 Pollack, *The Persian Puzzle*, 48.

21 Keddie, *Modern Iran*, 107–110.

22 Ward, *Immortal*, 179.

23 Milani, *The Shah*, 122.

24 Abrahamian, *Iran*, 282–323.

25 Britain's role in the episode is subject is controversy with claims that it was willing to sacrifice Iranian territorial integrity to reach accommodation with the Russians. Milani, *The Shah*, 118–120.

26 Louise Fawcett, *Iran and the Cold War: The Azerbaijan Crisis of 1946* (Cambridge: Cambridge University Press, 1992); William Eagleton, *The Kurdish Republic of 1946* (Oxford: Oxford University Press, 1963), 44–57; and Ward, *Immortal*, 179.

27 Ali Ansari, *Modern Iran Since 1921* (London: Longman, 2003), 86–93; and Abrahamian, *Iran*, 225–240.

28 Milani, *The Shah*, 128.

29 George Lenczowski, *American Presidents and the Middle East* (London: DUP, 1990), 7–23; and Fred H Lawson, 'The Iranian Crisis of 1945–1946 and the Spiral Model of International Conflict', *Middle East Studies* Vol. 23 (1989): 307–324.

30 See Eagleton, *The Kurdish Republic*; and David McDowall, *A Modern History of the Kurds* (London: IB Taurus, 1997), 231–240.

31 Oliver Harvey, Anthony Eden's Private Secretary, revealed that on the day of Iran's invasion both Churchill and Eden confidentially acknowledged that Britain was committing an act of 'naked

aggression'. Joan Beaumont, 'Great Britain and the Rights of Neutral Countries: The Case of Iran, 1941', *Journal of Contemporary History*, Vol. 16, No. 1 (1981): 226.

32   Ibid., 219–220.

33   Keddie, 'Iranian Power', 11–12; and De Bellaigue, *Patriot of Persia*, 206.

34   Formerly the Anglo-Persian Oil Company and, today, British Petroleum. In 1951, Iran was receiving less than 18 percent of profits from the AIOC. Stephen Kinzer, *All the Shah's Men: An American Coup and the Roots of Middle East Terror* (Hoboken: John Wiley, 2008), 67.

35   De Bellaigue, *Patriot of Persia*, 123.

36   Kinzer, *All the Shah's Men*, 68, 90.

37   Karol Sorby, 'Great Powers and the Middle East After World War II', *Asian and African Studies*, Vol. 10 (2001): 73.

38   Mark Gasiorowski, 'The 1953 Coup d'état in Iran', *International Journal of Middle East Studies*, Vol. 19, No.3 (1987): 262–264.

39   Kinzer, *All the Shah's Men*, 134–166; and Sorby, 'Great Powers', 73.

40   De Bellaigue, *Patriot of Persia*, 184–185.

41   Gasiorowski, 'The 1953 Coup', 274–279; and De Bellaigue, *Patriot of Persia*, 221–224.

42   Malcolm Byrne (ed), 'The Secret CIA History of the Iran Coup, 1953' in the National Security Archive of the George Washington University (29 November 2000).

43   De Bellaigue, *Patriot of Persia*, 217–230; and Kinzer, *All the Shah's Men*, 150–192.

44   Gasiorowski, 'The 1953 Coup', 265.

45   Ward, *Immortal*, 188; Kinzer, *All the Shah's Men*, 210.

46   Kinzer, *All the Shah's Men*, 206.

47   Ibid., 113; and De Bellaigue, *Patriot of Persia*, 274–275.

48   Sorby, 'Great Powers', 73; and Michael A Palmer, *Guardians of the Gulf: A History of America's Expanding Role in the Persian Gulf, 1833–1992* (New York: Free Press, 1992), 20–25.

49   Named after a satirical character and associated with the paranoia that Britain's 'invisible hands' orchestrate and shape every major event experienced by Iranians. See Iraj Pezeshkzad, *My Uncle Napoleon* (New York: Random House, 2000).

50   Milani, *The Shah*, 112.

51   De Bellaigue, *Patriot of Persia*, 110; and Milani, *The Shah*, 35–36, 160, 386.

52   Milani, *The Shah*, 328, 359–360.

53   Roham Alvandi, 'Nixon, Kissinger, and the Shah: The Origins of Iranian Primacy in the Persian Gulf', *Diplomatic History*, Vol. 36, No. 2 (2012): 346–372.

54   When in 1967 Harold Wilson's government announced Britain would be pulling out of the Middle East 'east of the Suez', the *Shah* saw this as an opportunity to re-establish Iran's primacy in the Persian Gulf.

55   Alvandi, 'Nixon', 372.

56   Alvandi, 'Nixon', 370.

57   Stephen McGlinchey, *US Arms Policies Towards the Shah's Iran* (London: Routledge, 2014), 61–120.

58   Pollack, *Persian Puzzle*, 38–39.

59   Ward, *Immortal*, 193; and Efraim Karsh, *Islamic Imperialism: A History* (New Heaven: Yale University Press, 2006), 199.

60   Milani, *The Shah*, 360.

61   Mansur Bonakdarian, 'Great Expectations: US-Iranian Relations, 1911–1951' in Abbas Amanat and Magnus Bernharsson (eds), *US–Middle East Historical Encounters: A Critical Survey* (Tallahassee: University Press of Florida, 2007), 15–16.

62   Michael Klare, *Resource Wars: The New Landscape of Global Conflict* (New York: Henry Colt & Co, 2002), 60.

63 Between 1970 and 1978, alone, the Shah ordered over $20 billion worth of arms.
64 Keddie, *Modern Iran*, 164.
65 Ward, *Immortal*, 195.
66 Marvin Zonis, *Majestic Failure: The Fall of the Shah* (Chicago: Chicago University Press, 1991), 66.

Conclusion: Gathering the Shadows

Andrew Sharpe

On 18 December 1974 the last Axis soldier 'holding out' was arrested by Indonesian soldiers after a search mission conducted at the request of the Japanese government. The discovery by an Indonesian Air Force patrol of a hut and small fenced field a few months earlier, in what was considered to be an uninhabited part of Morotai (a small and remote Pacific island at the northern end of the Maluku Islands chain) had led to speculation about the identity of the owner of the hut. The occupant turned out to be Private Teruo Nakamura (or, rather, Private Attun Palalin) of the Imperial Japanese Army. He had been posted as dead, by the Japanese Army, in November 1945. Nakamura/Palalin was a Taiwanese Amis who had been enlisted (possibly unwillingly) into a 'Takasago' unit of the Japanese Army (made up from indigenous Taiwanese Austronesians) in 1943. Sent to Morotai in 1945 shortly before the end of the war, he was one of several Japanese Army evaders who disappeared into the interior of the island after it fell to the Allies. Disengaging from his fellow soldiers at some time in the 1950s, it would appear that he lived alone and in isolation until his discovery in December 1974. 'Holding out' was probably not a fair description of his existence: he had subsisted, quietly minding his own business, farming a self-made small-holding, and was perhaps better characterised as a castaway than a surviving fighter. He was repatriated with the minimum of publicity directly to Taiwan (at his own request), where he was not particularly well received, being considered a 'Japanese Loyalist' by the Taiwanese Government. He was equally disregarded by Japan as he was not a Japanese national. He died of cancer in 1979 having been supported by public donations from those who felt he had been badly treated by both national governments.

The surrender of Lieutenant Hiro Onada a few months earlier on the Philippines was a stark contrast to the quiet re-emergence of Nakamura/Palalin. As far as Japan was concerned, it was on 11 March 1974 that the last Japanese soldier finally and formally gave up the fight in World War II. He handed over his sword to President Ferdinand Marcos of the Philippines in a ceremony that was attended by a press pack, generating world-wide coverage and holding the nation's full attention in

Japan. Onada was the leader of a small special forces team that had been put ashore on Lubang Island in December 1944. His orders were to fight a disruptive sabotage campaign against the enemy in the event that the island fell, neither surrendering nor committing suicide, but doing all that he could to fight on and interfere with the 'occupying forces'. Lubang fell swiftly to the Americans in March 1945. Onada detached his four-man team from the main forces and disappeared into the jungle to wage his guerrilla campaign. The island, some 100 kilometres out into the South China Sea southwest of the capital Manila, covered roughly 50 square miles, and its dense jungle afforded plenty of places in which a small unit could disappear. Onada's team fought on, killing livestock, burning fields, clashing with police and the Philippine Army, and conducting small acts of sabotage for some 29 years. Figures are hard to verify, but almost certainly at least 30 people, civilian, police and military, were killed by Onada and his men. Messages, leaflets and even letters from home that were dropped into the jungle from the air were considered by the team as being enemy propaganda or tricks to get them to surrender. One of the team (Private Akatsu) 'deserted' in late 1949 and was picked up by the Philippine police in 1950. The other two were shot in clashes with the local security forces (Corporal Shimada dying in 1954, nine years after they had set off into the jungle, and Private Kozuka dying in a shoot-out in 1972 some 27 years after their private war-after-the-war had begun), leaving Onada to soldier on alone for another two years.

The return to Japan of Kozuka's body prompted renewed belief that Onada could still be alive, and further incidents on the island reinforced that belief. An enigmatic character called Norio Suzuki, a self-styled 'explorer', set out to find Onada and located him in February 1974. After a tense stand-off the two spoke, struck up an accord, and Onada eventually agreed that he would turn himself in, but only if he received official orders so to do. Suzuki returned to Japan, announced his 'find' and encouraged Onada's previous commanding officer (Yoshimi Taniguchi – now a bookseller in Tokyo) to accompany him back to Lubang. Taniguchi, recognised by Onada, handed over written orders and Onada finally emerged from the jungle almost exactly 29 years after he had gone in. His return to Japan was feted, he was urged to run for public office, offered back-pay for his entire time in the jungle, received wide publicity and was treated with considerable respect. Discomfort with the attention led to his emigration to Brazil, but he returned shortly afterwards to Japan, splitting his time between the two countries until his death from pneumonia in 2014.

What do these two contrasting stories tell us, as we draw together the threads of the various perspectives of World War II's long shadow? Perhaps the first thing is to reflect that the chapters of this book have largely been impersonal – they have been national, strategic, economic, political and broad-ranging. So it is worth pausing at this concluding point to remember also that global war may well be about strategic muscle movements on a grand scale, but it is also, and at the same time, always an intensely individual and personal experience, leaving unique imprints on every individual. War, Clausewitz reminded us, is first, last and always a human experience. But so is strategy, and politics, and economics – and thus the strategic, political and economic acts of all of those who were involved in shaping events for a lifetime after the end of the war would inevitably be affected by each individual wartime legacy, just as those individual experiences would collect together to form national actions and reactions. The personal experience for Onada resulted in a World War II that lasted for 34 years of unbroken active wartime service (he joined the army in 1940). His war did not 'cast a long shadow' after VJ day – it just kept on going.

The notions of cognitive bias, of personal experience, of learned experience, and of collective and national biases have all been explored throughout the chapters of this book. Each chapter has made it very clear that major strategic decisions have been made as a result of personal experiences or national narratives. While in March 1974 Onada was handing himself in, the world outside was being run by people all of whom were moulded by *their* individual experiences of World War II. In the US, Nixon had seen active duty in the Navy Reserve during the war, and had served as Eisenhower's vice president; in the Soviet Union, Breshnev had served throughout the war as a commissar, leaving the Soviet Army as a Major General, and, despite the political nature of his job, had seen active service in the Ukraine and in Czechoslovakia; in the UK, Edward Heath, the prime minister, had served throughout the war in the Royal Artillery, including coming ashore during the Normandy Landings, being demobilised in 1947 as a lieutenant colonel; in France, Georges Pompidou was still president (he died in office in April that year), having served with distinction early in the war, being decorated with the Croix de Guerre, and later joining de Gaulle's inner circle in 1944 in London, and he subsequently spent eight years as prime minister under de Gaulle; in Germany, Willy Brandt, a marked socialist in the 1920s and 30s, had changed his name (he was born Herbert Frahm) and fled Nazi Germany for Norway in 1933, served in Spain in the civil war as an anti-fascist war reporter, returned to Germany in the late 1930s under a Norwegian pseudonym and reported upon Nazi excesses, and then returned to Norway (where, after the German invasion, he was arrested and released while wearing Norwegian uniform) and then fled again to Sweden. He took Norwegian citizenship, thereby having dual Norwegian and German nationality. And the list goes on – every world leader in 1974 was making decisions, strategic, political, economic, or just personal, all of which would inevitably have been influenced by their own individual wartime experiences. And that personal experience is passed on as related experience which, in its turn, shades the decision-making process of the subsequent generations, both as individual leaders and as national collective influences on those individuals. Michael Neiberg, for example, in his chapter on the US, reflects upon George Bush Senior's wartime experiences on the cognitive frame of George Bush Junior.

Thus war does not just have lasting effects on a collective and grand scale, but so it also does on a singular and personal scale – and where those influences play in the lives of people of little moment in the strategic ebb and flow of events they have little effect, perhaps; but where those influences sit in the back of the minds of strategic decision-makers or in the collective consciences of a nation's shared experience, their effects are much deeper, more palpable and longer-lasting.

But there is also a second point to these stories of Japanese soldiers 'fighting on'. In 1974, after Onada had returned to Japan, there was a popular, but perhaps not that amusing, joke in Japan. Onada had read in the papers as he flew home, the joke went, that Japan had the third largest global economy (after the US and the Soviet Union) and West Germany had the fourth largest (ahead of France and the UK). And now the increasingly bewildered Onada was being driven through the bustling Tokyo traffic for the first time since he left it in 1944, neon lights ablaze and street life thriving. An accompanying government official said: 'Onada-san, this must all be rather overwhelming and you seem confused – can I help by explaining anything?'; and Onada replied: 'Well, it's just that I thought that you said that we *lost* the war …!' A weak joke, perhaps, but it made a strong point.

Lessons from the post-war settlement of World War I had taught decision-makers that, despite the demand for unconditional surrender, it made little or no strategic sense to economically hamstring either West Germany or Japan and hinder their post-war recovery in a lasting bid for vengeful reparation. On the contrary: it made strategic sense in Europe, regardless of the misgivings brought about by the personal experiences of European and American leaders, gradually to help West Germany to play as full a role as possible in keeping the Soviet empire at bay, and it made equal sense in the Pacific for the US to sustain Japanese re-birth after the war as a counter to Chinese expansionism, particularly in light of events in Korea in the 1950s. The Marshal Plan was as much (or more) about building a barrier to Soviet expansionism as it was a philanthropic desire to help West Germans (along with the rest of western Europe) to recover from the ravages (both self-inflicted and Allied-inflicted) of war. The long shadow of World War I and its settlement at Versailles, hung over the resolution of World War II. At the same time, the circumstances of post-war Germany and Japan were such that both nations were able to start their post-war recovery with a clean slate. Germany, in particular, had been laid waste by the bombing campaign and subsequent invasion, especially in its industrial heartlands. Britain, by contrast, began its post-war recovery with its essentially Victorian and Edwardian industrial infrastructure still largely intact. Britain could not afford to knock down and start from scratch. Germany had no choice but to start from scratch. Thus, although Britain started with a head-start in terms of post-war industrial recovery, because it had mostly intact infrastructure, Germany soon caught up and overtook as its by-necessity more modern infrastructure was built up just as the tired British infrastructure waned. The clear-cut conclusions of those who danced in the streets on VE and VJ days were, rapidly and lastingly, to prove neither as clear-cut nor as conclusive as the dancers may have imagined.

Britain, Germany and France

Jonathan Boff, in his chapter on Britain, explores modern strategy-making in a 21st-century Britain still operating amidst the echoes of the 1940s and 1950s. He paints a very strong picture of a wartime nation-at-arms, of a national narrative, of a collective effort, of a country that felt that every member of the war generation had a part to play – whether it was soldiers 'fighting on the beaches' or civilians accepting the Blitz with a fortitude and determination that grew with every affront. Britain, regardless of justification, convinced itself that World War II had been won first by British fighting men standing, alone, when everyone else had failed (or were yet to join in), and then by the whole country, every single citizen, who had shown the world 'what it meant to be British' by refusing with tenacious and stoic stubbornness to blink when the going got tough. For sure, such driven self-belief was required to come through that dark chapter; but self-belief on that scale, once generated, is hard to erase. And such self-belief was also backed up by a long history of imperial dominance and Great Power status, supplemented in World War II by a clear and evident existential threat against which a rallying call could be made. Despite the growth of the so-called woke generation, a trend for apology and regret, and a hard-to-trace tendency to be ashamed of national history, the British people still possess that depth of national self-belief that served Victorian, Edwardian and World War II Britain so well. The Blitz spirit, as Jonathan Boff highlighted, was rolled out to fight COVID-19 as readily as it is to colour the headlines on the sports pages describing an England–Germany football match, as Matthias Strohn points out in our introduction.

For Britain, though, like so many others, the aftermath of World War II brought on the acceleration of change (and arguably decline, certainly in terms of global power and influence) in all sorts of ways. The economy was traumatised, the nation's debt was unprecedented, the myth of the invincibility of the imperial master was shattered and the right to imperial ownership increasingly indefensible. Britain, at home, was on rations, was nursing the physical wounds of war, was re-setting its social pact between state and polity, was re-starting a faltered economy, and was coming to terms with a 'new world order'. Abroad, in that new order, the world map was looking increasingly less confident about its 'pinkness', new lines of confrontation were being drawn as Winston Churchill's 'Iron Curtain descended across Europe' and a new 'rules-based world order' was being established. At the same time, post-war politics, international power-plays and a global strategic re-ordering had given a waning Britain a permanent seat on the UN Security Council, nuclear weapons, NATO membership with significant influence and, in time, the Commonwealth to replace the Empire. Britain, post-war, retained a large measure of its pre-war international standing, but wielded it now with different tools. Significantly for Britain, however, wartime experience had not included defeat and occupation (either by Nazi Germany or by the Soviet Union, or, worst of all, by both) – and only the most superficial of analysts would dismiss that factor when examining the current British population's subconscious undercurrents in their view of Europe and collective international cooperation. The history of British development, both at home and abroad, over the following half-century and far beyond, is therefore deeply coloured by all of those wartime and immediately post-war effects. Thus the long shadow of the war for Britain has been cast in many shades, but, nevertheless, as Jonathan Boff and others have argued, perhaps one of its most significant and lasting effects has been a belief in the effectiveness of 'muddling through' and 'managing events' leading to a hard-to-explain abrogation of the task of serious and initiative-holding strategic thought in the post-war decision-making corridors of that pre-war world-leading power.

Inevitably, however, nowhere do the echoes of war linger more strongly than in 21st-century Germany. Matthias Strohn aptly entitles his chapter on Germany 'This Must Never Happen Again', and that single sentiment sits at the heart of the most populous, economically successful, influential and, arguably, stable state in modern Europe. In Europe, Germany's view matters. 21st-century Germany, just like 1950s West Germany, still stands, before and after everything else, for peaceful co-existence, anti-extremism, anti-nationalism and, particularly, for a tendency for co-operation not for antagonism. Despite considerable domestic pressure to present a more forceful and forthright face to the world, the deep-rooted effects of World War II are likely to continue to constrain Germany's desire to engage more robustly in the ebb and flow of international affairs (unless, possibly, it is to prevent atrocities or persecution). German politics, be they local, national or international, are full of checks and balances to prevent the misuse or abuse of power, as are both German defence and security policy and Germany's still-uneasy relationship with its armed forces. Of course, the first result of the war for Germany was that it has been, since 1945, through a series of post-war evolutions; in over-simple terms: occupation (1945–49); division (Bundesrepublik (West) and Demokratische Republik (East)) (1949); full statehood (East in 1949, West in 1955); occupation of the East by, and then alliance with, the Soviet Union (1955); NATO membership for the West (1955); then reunification (1990), with the restoration of genuine and full sovereignty to a unified Germany finally coming in 1991.

Despite the ties and pulls of the second half of the 20th century, the convolutions of the Cold War, the split personality effects of separation and reunification, and the ambivalent relationship between the German people and their armed forces, 21st-century Germany has established a careful balance of perspectives. As Matthias Strohn has showed us, quoting a 2019 poll, the new generation of Germans may feel no 'moral responsibility' for the events of the 1930s and 40s, but they subscribe entirely to the modern moral responsibility to be palpable standard bearers for the prevention of a repeat of any state of affairs, nationally or internationally, that could lead to a repeat of the events of that period. Thus, regardless of that history, the passage of time, or the striking of that new balance, the core German mantra remains that the best way of ensuring that 'Never Again' is maintained is to sustain internal checks and balances at all sorts of levels, and to foster an underpinning ethos of tolerance and partnership, in which a strong and unified Europe, where cooperation will always trump national self-interest, sets a global example. In that sense, regardless of their inevitably shifting and kaleidoscopic nature, the long shadows that World War II cast upon modern Germany remain as influential as ever.

France's legacy of World War II was (and is) understandably schizophrenic, being one of diverse and disunited memories, as we saw in Olivier Schmitt's chapter. Defeat (rapid, unexpected and confusing); Dunkirk – a 'miracle' for Britain, but 'desertion' for France; resistance (and its multiple interpretations, memories and facets); Vichy; Nazi occupation; collaboration; exiles; deportations and forced work; prisoners of war; Maquisards; Free French Forces; Allied-inflicted casualties (like the sinking of the French fleet at Mers-el-Kebir and the bombing of Caen); liberation; marginalisation by, in particular, the US as the war's end neared; victory; the retributions of aftermath; and the rebirth of the Republic: France's experience of the 1940s had a bit of absolutely everything. Despite the multi-layered schizophrenia, de Gaulle's strong leadership produced a renewed sense of national identity and a spirit of self-reliance that led to a very different cry of 'Never Again!' from the German version thereof. This French rallying cry was about a reinforced belief in France's duty to put France first, and the balancing of self-reliance against alliance membership (leading to a fractured relationship with NATO and a Galapagos-like development of defence policy and the associated military capabilities and doctrine). The possession of a nuclear capability was therefore also an essential off-shoot of such a position. The political structure of modern France, the power of the president, and the mindset of French self-reliance (regardless of alliance membership, be it NATO or the EU), a distrust of US interference in European affairs, and a lasting re-affirmation of the unreliability of 'L'Albion Perfide' are all unchanged fundamental cornerstones from the foundation of the Fifth Republic. France's view of such things as the future of the EU, of the relative importance of the structure and processes of NATO, of the balance between itself and Germany, and of Brexit have as much to do with the lingering aftertaste of World War II as they have to do with present strategic pragmatism and current-day politics.

Wider Europe

Like France, but for very different reasons, Austria's legacy is also one of schizophrenia, but for them, unlike France's new determination to put a self-confident self-reliant nation first, Austria's schizophrenia was, and remains, tempered by a degree of self-doubt. As Lothar Höbelt has shown us, Anschluß and all that that meant during the war itself, followed by ten years of post-war occupation by the Allies and participation in the Marshal Plan, along with strongly anti-communist politics, did not result in NATO membership and full alignment with the western camp in the Cold War. Historical, political and military self-doubt, lasting deep into the 1960s and 70s, resulted in awkward self-denial and neutrality. And unlike the more clear, absolute, established and rather comfortable nature of Swiss neutrality (strengthened by its conduct throughout the war), Austrian neutrality had a more ambiguous and uncomfortable character, fending off the Warsaw pact while rejecting NATO, maintaining a slightly awkward relationship with both organisations and coping with its recent military (and German/Nazi) past with rather less clarity than Germany itself was doing. (Austria did join the NATO Partnership for Peace programme in 1995; but it only did so after Russia had joined.) Even though it now sits at the heart of the nation's self- and international identity, Austria appeared to embrace neutrality by self-conscious necessity rather than by choice.

In wider Europe the shadows are no less deep and lasting. Paul Latawski's chapter on Poland's legacy of 'belated victory' tells a story of allied betrayal and of violent occupation (Nazi and Soviet) etched deep into the mindset of modern Poland. Poland's 20th-century history is one of turmoil, changing borders, changing ownership, and playing the unwilling role of pawn and bargaining chip for others, tempered throughout by a sense of fierce pride and national self-belief. Poles in World War II underwent as fractured an experience as any of the other nations discussed in this book: resistance, violent repression, government through collaboration, government in exile, loyal and heroic service to the Allied cause, and, perhaps above all else, experience as a trampling ground for the ebb and flow of the Nazi and Soviet interplay of war. The end of the war did not bring about the assured Polish independence and self-determination. Broken promises on a number of levels led to personal tragedies, as undertakings to both fighters and political power-brokers were forgotten or conveniently passed over, and, on a national scale, to Polish absorption into the Soviet sphere, all of which put paid to imagined guarantees of self-determination – leaving, instead, Poles reflecting with bitter irony that the pact that held the Soviet security empire together bore the name of their own capital city. For Latawski the underlying message for those casting an eye in the direction of modern Poland is that today's state is as it is because it has, finally, overturned that wartime legacy. But, vitally, it is also clear that if one is to understand the undercurrents of modern Polish politics or Poland's world-view, one first has to understand it's sceptical one-eye-over-the-shoulder approach to friends as well as enemies, or potential enemies; and to understand that that view is as a result of centuries of history, strongly reinforced in vivid and living memory by the events of half a century from 1939 to 1989.

As we have seen in James Corum's chapter, on the Baltic States, much like in Poland, the war had been characterised by the ebb and flow of multiple occupation. Soviet occupation, then German occupation, which seemed rather less harsh than the preceding Soviet experience had thereby resulted in a large number of Lithuanians, Latvians and Estonians fighting, quite understandably, in the Wehrmacht or the Waffen SS, against the Soviet Union. The immediate post-war period involved Soviet re-occupation, re-absorption into the Soviet Empire and the concomitant retribution upon the three states' people for their 'betrayal' of the Soviet ideal during the war. Armed resistance lasted well into the 1950s, with bands of 'Forrest Brothers' waging a partisan war against occupation as brutal repression remained the daily fare of the populations of the three states. The 21st-century septuagenarians and octogenarians lived the best part of their lives under these circumstances, and their children – now the national polity and the decision-makers in all sorts of ways – have had their world-views shaped by the experiences of their parents' and grandparents' generations. It is no surprise therefore that from the 1990s onwards the dominating sentiments in Latvia, Lithuania and Estonia can be characterised as re-birth and youth, tempered by proud nationalism, but, equally, tempered by a wary scepticism and an uncomfortable backward glance over the shoulder towards Russia. A deep history of north European engagement, trade, religious ties and cultural linkages, followed, post-Soviet era, with enthusiastic embracing of NATO and the EU has not been enough to erase the effects of 1939 to 1945 and then to 1991. World War II and its aftermath remain the deep foundation of the dynamics of the modern Baltic States.

For much of the Balkans, at the other end of Europe, World War II allowed the centuries-old issues of east-meets-west, Hapsburg v Ottoman, nationalism, religion, factionalism, racism and narrated national and family histories to surface in open and often vicious hostility. Centuries of 'unresolved business' was being played out in the bloodshed of the war. The war's end, far from solving or salving those issues, simply suppressed them as they reached one of their bloodiest manifestations, thereby heightening the feeling of 'unresolved business', rather than resolving it. Thus, the post-war position delivered a state of suspended animation in which the charismatic leadership of Tito supressed the divisions upon which the war had thrived, but resolved nothing. This, in turn, meant that the death of Tito almost inevitably led to the lid blowing off the pressure cooker as the Balkans descended into bloody neighbour-on-neighbour warfare throughout the 1990s. Many would argue that that state of affairs, suspended again by the UN, then by NATO and ultimately by the Dayton Accords, remains bubbling away under a newly-held-on lid. A visit to the Donja Gradina concentration camp memorial on the Bosnia-Croatia border, an afternoon spent in observing the bombast in the National Assembly chamber of Republica Serpska in Banja Luka, or a short time spent listening to the rhetoric of Hungarian Prime Minister Viktor Orban, would leave students of both modern politics and 20th-century history with a feeling of 'plus ca change, plus c'est la meme chose' across the Balkans. The smouldering embers of World War II's legacy, briefly re-ignited in the 1990s, are smouldering away still.

Indeed, right across Europe the lasting effects of the war continue to shape the populations and politics of the nations that underwent that upheaval. Like those countries' experiences explored above and in the foregoing chapters, all of Europe underwent varying degrees of suffering, of casualties (both human and infrastructure), of armed struggle, of occupation, resistance, victimhood, collaboration, violence, recovery and every other aspect that 'Total War' brings with it, as Jan Hoffenaar explored, for example, in his chapter on the Netherlands' experience. All of those experiences are inevitably tempered by individual nations' histories, characters and cultures, and by the passing of time and of generations, leading to their own nuanced, individual and particular wartime legacy. For the Dutch, their experience, tempered by their history, delivered to them lessons on the unreliability of neutrality and 'strong enough' defence forces as a national guarantee of safety, and therefore of the need for active and meaningful NATO membership alongside bi-lateral defence relationships. For the Danes, as Niels Bo Poulsen relates, wartime experience meant initial acquiescence (1940), then semi-autonomy (to 1943), increasing resistance and subsequent repression, although for a variety of reasons, not least economic and food supply, Denmark was largely spared the worst excesses of the Nazi regime. Nevertheless, modern Danish politics are inevitably shaded by the fact that Denmark must always calibrate its defence and security policies (and, indeed its wider foreign policies) against the fact that its immediate neighbour is Germany, thus Danish/ German history and current German politics will always come into play in Danish decision-making.

For those nations who learned from the war that they were not strong enough to stand alone against a powerful aggressor (and that meant the vast majority of states in Europe) the unifying sentiment was a chorus of France and Germany's very different cries of 'Never Again', nuanced by national narratives to suit not just the specific-to-country events and consequences of the war, but also the shades of individual national histories, identities and cultures. And the logical conclusion from that sentiment was that strength and safety would lie in alliance membership as a cornerstone of defence policy and close cooperation as a cornerstone of foreign policy. From Czechs and Hungarians in the east of Europe, to Belgians and Dutch in the west, and from the Danes and Norwegians in the north to the Portuguese and Italians in the south, the big lesson of the war was to see wisdom in forging a new unity of foreign policy approach that built upon the notion that cooperation and alliance membership form the bedrock of security, stability, safety and strength. It remains this sentiment, deeply rooted in wartime experience, that still sits firmly at the heart of the debate of European international relations, politics, cooperation, integration, strategy and security.

United States and Russia

At first glance Russia and the USA seem like unlikely bedfellows, and their chapters in this book, by Pavel Baev and Michael Neiberg respectively, reflect two very different nations with two very different wartime experiences and legacies. Why bring them together in this concluding chapter? There are two reasons.

First, the re-set international order, as the dust settled over the world, showed a new confrontation line drawn through the heart of Europe, with the United States and the Soviet Union no longer as uneasy allies unified to defeat a greater evil, but now cast in the roles of the two superpowers, nuclear armed and conventionally strong, that held the leadership roles in the two new opposing tectonic plates of international relations, NATO and the Warsaw Pact. The international politics that were to dominate much of the rest of the 20th-century (the Cold War, the rise of the notion of superpowers, nuclear deterrence, Mutually Assured Destruction, powerplays through proxies and 'small wars', and the clash of the ideologies of capitalist democracy and communist autocracy) dominated not just Europe, but the wider world, from 1945 to 1989 and beyond. As the 'old order' of European empires faded with varying degrees of death throe across the globe, the US and the Soviet Union, as a direct knock-on consequence of the effects of World War II, found themselves re-cast in a new role of international counterbalance in every sense – from ideology to material power. Different though their experiences and legacies of the war may have been, the overriding effect on these two nations was the same: superpower status, ideological standard bearer and alliance leader cast against each other in a new confrontation.

Furthermore, as we have seen elsewhere, Cold War leadership, in both superpowers, brought with it significant World War II experience. The nine US presidents from 1945 to 1993 had all had wartime involvement, including, in the shape of Eisenhower for example, significant roles at the highest levels. And the American Chairmen of the Joint Chiefs, up until 1989, were all World War II veterans. So too were the leaders in the Soviet Union: Stalin himself remaining in power for a further eight years after the end of the war; Khrushchev serving throughout the war, including in Stalingrad and at Kursk; Brezhnev similarly serving throughout the war (including under Khrushchev in the Ukraine and Czechoslovakia); Andropov fighting (according to his own account of the war) as a partisan in Finland; and Chernenko's war was spent working in propaganda. The Soviet Union's first leader without wartime experience was, perhaps significantly, the 'great moderniser' Mikhail

Gorbachev. Confirmation and cognitive bias have been explored throughout this book, and there is no doubt that the personal wartime experiences of all of those leaders of the two superpowers played a role in their world view and their subsequent decision-making throughout the face-off of the Cold War.

But it is not just about Cold War dynamics and superpower status, there is a second reason for putting Russia and America alongside each other in this concluding chapter. Interestingly, despite their very different actual experiences and cultural bases, the two nations have some very similar views of their own role in World War II. Whether it is May Day parades in Red Square or a steady diet of consistent film plots from Hollywood, the national overriding sentiment, in both nations, is this was a war that was won by *our* nation (insert here equally the USA or Russia, depending upon the speaker), with minimal help from allies. Forgotten by the Soviet Union and modern Russia are: the Lend-lease programme and $11.3BN in war material, equipment, weapons and food; North Atlantic and Barents Sea convoys; war in the Far East and the Pacific; the North Africa Campaign; the Normandy Landings; or the conclusive effect of the dropping of two atomic bombs. From a Russian perspective the Great Patriotic War was fought on Soviet soil as a result of a treacherous invasion by an evil, fascist regime. And it was won largely by the Soviet Union, and at huge cost in life, suffering and infrastructure; and, irritating like a stone in every Russian shoe, this is something that has never been fully acknowledged by the rest of the world. In America the national core narrative sits comfortably with its own World War II narrative – the land of the brave and the home of the free, champions of the underdog, protectors of the poor, upholders of democracy, America was fiendishly attacked by an 'evil empire' and, stirred by justified outrage, nobly stepped up to the plate and rescued the rest of the world, defeating Japan and launching into Europe through Normandy to defeat Nazi Germany. And, as all of that was happening, America sustained the fight for others through Lend-lease and concluded it through having the know-how to develop, and the courage to use, atomic weapons to end the suffering. And then America put the world back on its feet, magnanimously, with the Marshal Plan when it was all over. This characterisation is not much of an exaggeration (indeed for many Americans it may be an understatement) and remains the underlying plot of a steady stream of Hollywood blockbusters (from *The Sands of Iwo Jima* to *Star Wars*) and thus a major part of the modern American psyche.

In Neiberg and Baev's two very distinct chapters on these two very different nations, their singular war legacies were explored. Yet for both nations a new and similar (even if confrontational) world role had emerged and a similar backstory was (and is still) being told. The two narratives, Russian and American, may be about two entirely distinct experiences, but the moral of their different stories is very similar: 'we were on the side of wronged good fighting against evil, and it may have been a *World* war, but *we* won it.' And, in terms of effects, influences and shadows, it is these two similarities in power and in narrative that have had, and are likely to continue to have, as much effect on the rest of the world as the discrete and separate national shadows described in their own chapters.

Global effect

Kerry Brown opens his chapter on China with the statements that: 'The foundation of the People's Republic of China was due to World War II …' and that: 'The impact of that war has framed the mindset of Chinese political and military leaders ever since.' The war was integral to the foundation of the modern state and stays at the heart of its narrative and its propaganda. This concluding chapter will not seek to repeat the political and strategic implications for China, nor the way in which its legacy is woven into China's regional and global views, and even into the Chinese Communist Party (CCP) core narrative. The key point for our conclusion, as we cast our eyes more globally still, is to pick up that point that for China the war changed everything, and that that change endures now in the shape of the 21st-century state in being. So it was elsewhere across the globe, although the Chinese example serves well as a leading illustration. It serves the purposes of the CCP well to keep the narrative alive, and thus it is used not just to explain the shaping of the birth of the state, but also as a continued explanation (especially internally) of its own policy making. The fact that history for the CCP is a key political tool means that, by pausing to study the Chinese example, as we have done in Kerry Brown's chapter, we have been able to see the legacy as clearly as we have been able to in any of the other chapters.

In his chapter on Africa, Richard Reid explored the effects of the war on an entire continent. From Kenyans and Ethiopians to Congolese and Nigerians, and from Moroccans, Libyans and Algerians to Rhodesians and South Africans, World War II not only found its way into the continent of Africa, across the continent, but it was also responsible thereafter for the end of empires and the shaping of the independent modern states that make up the 21st-century continent. The immediate after-effects of the war brought economic and political impact across Africa. Those twin accelerators of change (that is to say a decline in prosperity and physical wellbeing alongside a questioning of the legitimacy of the status quo), coming on the back of Africans' experiences of the war, either serving globally in the armies of their erstwhile colonial controllers, or providing the battlegrounds for those colonial armies (or both) provided the catalyst for continental transformation. The North African campaign may well have served as a turning point in the fortunes of the war itself, but the effect of the war was to be a new turning point in African continental history.

Not explored in the foregoing chapters, but worthy of consideration, is that those effects that brought about change in Africa echoed to different degrees and in different ways across the globe. In New Zealand, Canada and Australia, for example, a new sense of self-identity had been found. The so-called 'Dominions' decided that they did not much care for that sobriquet. All three nations found that, through their service, sacrifice, martial skill and commitment, be it in North Africa, at Monte Cassino or in Normandy, they had more than earned the right to command themselves and to fight, in their own right, as complete national entities, rather than as adjuncts to British military leadership. And, if they had earned the right to fight for themselves in a military sense, it followed that they had equally earned the right to decide for themselves in a political and national sense. This subsequent world war, coming so hard on the heels of the 1914–18 experience, cemented in the minds of these three nations that their moment of true self-determination had arrived. Thus, across the world, the map was re-coloured and re-set as the births of nations, in multiple different senses, began. The dynamics of so much of the modern world find their roots in the reshuffling of the global pack as a consequence of World War II: the formation and growing power of modern India; the fractious nature of the Indian-Pakistani relationship; the thriving hub that is Singapore, the kaleidoscopic span of modern Indonesia, the list is globally comprehensive. Even in those parts of the world in which the war had least direct effect, like Iran and the wider Middle East as we have seen in Ali Parchami's chapter, the after-effects of the war were formative for the modern states. And, of course, in Israel this is quite literally so as the modern state, and all of its associated tensions and issues, have their roots in post-war resettlement and reshaping.

The big muscle movements

This book has sought to explore the particular echoes, effects and shadows that World War II cast over a range of countries. Euro-centric, but seeking a global perspective (as befits a work on a 'world' war), we have sought to provide for the reader an aid to understanding the viewpoints, influences, mindsets, undercurrents and drivers of a range of modern states and their polities. We have sought to examine why they are as they are and the roots of their policy making. Thus the book has, by necessity, been specific from chapter to chapter in its search for specific-to-nation (or specific-to-continent) nuances, characteristics, effects, structures, constraints or motivators. But it would be wrong to leave the reader without mention of the global effects that, regardless of those individual national effects, inevitably and unavoidably shape and influence the ebb and flow of national and, especially, international affairs.

It has not been our purpose to examine those global changes in detail, but we cannot conclude without making it clear that, regardless of the effects on the individual nations that we have explored, World War II brought about a series of changes that framed, and continue to frame, the modern world. We should therefore not allow this book to close having lost sight of the wood for its examination of individual trees.

The foregoing chapters have variously examined the end of empires and the birth of a new order: of a 'rules-based world order'. The rules to which this over-used phrase refers are most widely accepted to be those laid out in the United Nations Charter. The UN was born as World War II underwent its final awful convulsions: the charter was signed in San Francisco in June 1945 and came into effect in October 1945 (Germany surrendered in May and Japan in September). The United Nations was created out of a desire to put right the failures of the inter-war League of Nations as a world-governing body and to put in place a genuinely global order and code of practice that would, as its core purpose, as stated in paragraph one of Article One of the charter: 'Maintain international peace and security, and to that end: to take effective collective measures for the prevention and removal of threats to the peace, and for the suppression of acts of aggression or other breaches of the peace, and to bring about by peaceful means and in conformity with the principles of justice and international law, adjustment or settlement of international disputes or situations which might lead to a breach of the peace.' The set of 'rules' and the methodology by which those rules should be enforced, that bound all those signatories of the charter, sets the basis of the 'rules-based world order', the preservation of which sits at the heart of many, especially western, states' foreign policies. (The charter was signed in 1945 by 50 countries; now, of the 195 countries recognised by the UN, 193 are member states (the Holy See and Palestine being the exceptions); and observer status is held by those countries still holding a degree of dispute over their statehood: Kosovo, Taiwan, Western Sahara, South Ossetia, Abkhazia and Northern Cyprus). The permanent members of the most significant body in UN decision-making, the Security Council, are the US, Russia, China, the UK and France, and it is no coincidence that these five states were the five principal victors of World War II (and, shortly thereafter the five original nuclear weapon holders).

Beneath the overarching umbrella of the UN we have seen that a wider reliance upon alliance has been a central theme of international affairs since World War II. In military-political terms NATO is perhaps the largest and, arguably, most successful of these international partnerships. As a counter-balance to the Warsaw Pact in the Cold War and, latterly, as a lasting defence and security body relying upon and providing collective decision making and thereby collective security, membership of, and contribution to, NATO sits at the heart of the national defence and security policies of most of the 29 (at the time of writing) member states of the organisation. The size, breadth and longevity of NATO is a reflection of the deep-held belief, in Europe and the United States at least, that alliance membership is a much more effective (and cost-effective) tool in generating security than the pre-war tendency towards less multi-lateral, and often purely bi-lateral, defence agreements and alliances, backed up by heavy domestic defence and security demands on the economy. As we have also seen in our examination of European countries, most of the drivers for the foundation of the EU can be found in the strong echoes of World War II, and the underlying mantra of those who would promote an ever-closer union is that closer union underwrites less division. Individual and national narratives are built upon experience and history – and Europe's history is one of division, competition and, all too often, confrontation and conflict. The EU as an institution, without doubt, has its roots in a desire to put right that centuries-old state of confrontation and uneasy co-existence, with the upheaval of World War II as the last straw and the final catalyst for putting an end to that long-lasting state of international affairs.

Finally, it is worth tipping our hats as we pass to the notion of 'constant competition'. There is a contrast between a western view of a linear progression between peace, competition, confrontation, conflict and war, and a non-western (especially, perhaps, Russian or Chinese) view of a non-linear state of constant competition, in which all tools are equally relevant and a linear rheostat-winding-up-or-down approach is unnecessarily constraining. Many would argue that one of the major impacts of World War II, especially on western thinking, is found in terms of a philosophical approach to the wider notions of war and peace. One of the most useful works in this respect is found in Sir Michael Howard's thoughts in his great little book *The Invention of Peace*[1], especially if we consider his views (and he says so himself) as to be reflecting a particularly western and European view of the matter. Sir Michael takes us though an ever-narrowing lens of two thousand years of history in which he observes that being in conflict with neighbours is a fairly constant state of human inter-existence. 'Peace', as we currently bound it, is largely a 20th-century invention, he suggests, that has much to do with the scale and impact of the two world wars in the first half of the century. This has brought about a mindset that has calibrated a western view of that inevitably permanent state of competition, and led us to set instead an imaginary 'threshold' below which one set of rules applies for international interaction (peace) and above which a different set applies (war). This, he argues, is illusory. Furthermore, it is not a mindset shared by those who oppose the interests of those western states who hold such a constraining view (as stated, Russia and China for example). If western defence and security policy makers in the 21st-century are to enable their actors and instruments to operate within this set of circumstances, they will need to unpack this paradox in order to allow them to prevail.

This concluding chapter began with the prolonged after-effects of the war from a Japanese perspective, with Private Nakamura and Lieutenant Onada hunkered down in the jungle in 1974, still playing out their personal roles in World War II. And it is to Japan that we return for our final observation. The impact of two atomic bombs at Hiroshima and Nagasaki effectively brought the war to an end as humankind confronted for the first time its own ability to destroy itself. Those weapons were invented as a direct product of the war. Their use signalled a whole new approach to international relations and the birth of Deterrence Theory in its modern sense. The stand-off of the Cold War remained a stand-off, arguably, largely because of the likely consequences that came with the use of military force on the continent of Europe. As both sides acquired these ultimate weapons their ability to confront each other directly with other weapons became constrained by concomitant risk. The possession of these weapons, and the power and risk that come with their possession, remains one of the pivotal factors of international power politics and defence and security policies today. The global powerplays on a grand scale still sit largely in the hands of those nations that possess nuclear weapons, but the flash-points that most hold international attention revolve around those places where the possession or aspirant possession of nuclear weapons form part of the undercurrent, but on a less established and well-understood basis: in America's (and Israel's) relationship with Iran; on Iran's relationship with the rest of the Middle East; on India's relationship with Pakistan (and, indeed, with China); and in North Korea's relationship with everybody else, for example. Humankind's ability to damage itself and its planet on such a catastrophic scale, the fragility of the dynamics of human inter-relationship that come with that possibility, along with the fact that these weapons cannot be un-invented and thus will remain a constant, provides, perhaps, the darkest lingering shadow of World War II.

We hope that this book, in its own small way, provides those whose job it is to study or to negotiate their way through that collection of shadows to do so with a little illumination, to help to understand the undercurrents and influences that shape the context, assessments and thought processes of all those who play their individual and national parts in global decision making.

Note

1   Michael Howard, *The Invention of Peace. Reflections on War and International Order* (New Haven: Yale University Press, 2000).

Select Bibliography

Abenheim, Donald and Hartmann, Uwe (eds), *Tradition in der Bundeswehr. Zum Erbe des deutschen Soldaten und zur Umsetzung des neuen Traditionserlasses* (Berlin: Miles, 2018).

Baev, Pavel K., 'Transformation of Russian Strategic Culture: Impacts from Local Wars and Global Confrontation', *Russie.Nei.Visions* Report 118, IFRI, June 2020.

Bergmane, Una 'How Putin is rehabilitating the Nazi-Soviet pact', *Baltic Bulletin*, FPRI, 28 July 2020.

Bloch, Marc, *L'Étrange Défaite* (Paris: Franc-Tireur, 1946).

Bond, Brian, *Britain's Two World Wars against Germany: Myth, Memory and the Distortions of Hindsight* (Cambridge: Cambridge University Press, 2014).

Brands, Hal and Suri, Jeremi (eds), *The Power of the Past. History and Statecraft* (Washington: Brookings Institution Press, 2016).

Buffet, Cyril and Heuser, Beatrice (eds), *Haunted by History. Myths in International Relations* (New York: Berghahn Books, 1998).

Byfield, Judith A., et al. (eds), *Africa and World War II* (Cambridge: Cambridge University Press, 2015).

Calder, Angus, *The Myth of the Blitz* (London: Pimlico, 1992).

Clarke, Peter, *Hope and Glory: Britain 1900–1990* (London: Allen Lane, 1996).

Conelißen, Christoph et al. (eds), *Erinnerungskulturen. Deutschland, Italien und Japan seit 1945*, (Frankfurt a. M.: Fischer, 2004).

Conze, Eckart et al., *Das Amt und die Vergangenheit. Deutsche Diplomaten im Dritten Reich und in der Bundesrepublik* (Munich: Blessing, 2010).

Corum, James, *The Security Concerns of the Baltic States as NATO Allies* (Carlise PA: Strategic Studies Institute, US Army War College, August 2013).

Daddis, Gregory A., *Westmoreland's War: Reassessing American Strategy in Vietnam* (New York: Oxford University Press, 2014).

Davies, Norman, *God's Playground: A History of Poland Volume II 1795–Present* (Oxford: Clarendon Press, 1981).

Englehardt, Tom, *The End of Victory Culture: Cold War America and the Disillusioning of a Generation* (New York: Basic Books, 1995).

Eastman, Lloyd E., *Seeds of Destruction: Nationalist China in War and Revolution, 1937–1949* (Stanford: Stanford University Press, 1984).

Ewa, Ochman, *Post-Communist Poland – Contested Pasts and Future Identities* (London: Routledge, 2013).

Garton Ash, Timothy, *The Polish Revolution: Solidarity 1980–82* (London: Jonathan Cape, 1983).

Gehler, Michael, *From Saint Germain to Lisbon. Austria's Long Road from Disintegrated to United Europe* (Vienna: Österreichische Akademie der Wissenschaften, 2020).

Gholi Majd, Mohammad, *Iran Under Allied Occupation in World War II: The Bridge To Victory & a Land of Famine* (Lanham: UPA, 2016).

Grenier, John, *The First Way of War* (New York: Cambridge University Press, 2005).

Hellema, D. A., *Dutch Foreign Policy. The Role of the Netherlands in World Politics* (Dordrecht: Republiek der Letteren, 2009).

Höbelt, Lothar, *Die Zweite Republik und ihre Besonderheiten* (Vienna: Böhlau 2020)

Hoffenaar, Jan and Teitler, G. (eds), *De Koude Oorlog. Maatschappij en Krijgsmacht in de jaren '50* (The Hague: Sdu Uitgeverij, 1992).

Holbraad, Carsten, *Danish Reactions to German Occupation. History and Historiography* (Chicago: Chicago University Press, 2017).

_____, *Danish Neutrality. A Study of the Foreign Policy of a Small State* (Oxford: Clarendon, 1991).

Honig, Jan Willem, *Defense Policy in the North Atlantic Alliance. The Case of the Netherlands* (Westport: Praeger, 1993).

Howard, Michael, *The Invention of Peace. Reflections on War and International Order* (New Haven: Yale University Press, 2000).

Hyam, Ronald, *Britain's Declining Empire: the road to decolonisation, 1918–1968* (Cambridge: Cambridge University Press, 2006).

Jenkins, Jennifer, 'Iran in the Nazi New Order, 1933–1941', *Iranian Studies,* Vol. 49, No. 5 (2016).

Jonsson, Oscar, *The Russian Understanding of War: Blurring the Lines Between War and Peace* (Washington DC: Georgetown University Press, 2019).

Kampfner, John, *Why the Germans Do it Better. Notes from a Grown-Up Country* (London: Atlantic Books, 2020).

Kasekamp, Andres, *A History of the Baltic States* (London: Palgrave, 2010).

Keddie, Nikki R., *Modern Iran: Roots and Results of Revolution* (New Haven: Yale University Press, 2006).

Kenez, Peter, *Hungary from the Nazis to the Soviets: The Establishment of the Communist Regime in Hungary, 1944–1948* (Cambridge: Cambridge University Press, 2006).

Killingray, David, *Fighting for Britain: African soldiers in the Second World War* (Woodbridge: James Currey, 2010).

MacMillan, Margaret, *Dangerous Games: The Uses and Abuses of History* (London: Modern Library, 2009).

Michnik, Adam, *The Trouble with History: Morality, Revolution and Counterrevolution* (New Haven: Yale University Press, 2014).

Mitter, Rana, *China's War with China, 1937–1945: The Struggle for Survival* (London: Allen Lane, 2013).

Moeller, Robert G., *War Stories: The Search for a usable Past in the Federal Republic of Germany* (Berkeley: University of California Press, 2001).

Neitzel, Sönke, *Deutsche Krieger. Vom Kaiserreich zur Berliner Republik- eine Militärgeschichte* (Berlin: Propyläen, 2020).

Nolan, Cathal J., *The Allure of Battle: A History of How Wars Have Been Won and Lost* (New York: Oxford University Press, 2019).

Pääbo, Heiko, 'War of Memories' Explaining the 'Memorials War' in Estonia', *Baltic Security and Defence Review*, Vol. 10 (2008).

Pannier, Alice and Schmitt, Olivier, *French Defence Policy since the End of the Cold War* (Abingdon: Routledge, 2021).

Pearce, R. D., *The Turning Point in Africa: British Colonial Policy, 1938–1948* (London: Cass, 1982).

Rathbone, R. and Killingray, D. (eds), *Africa and the Second World War* (Basingstoke: Macmillan, 1986).

Ringsmose, Jens and Brøndum, Christian, *Frihedens pris – så lav som mulig. NATO, Danmark og forsvarsbudgetterne* (Denmark: Syddansk Universitetsforlag, 2018).

Roberts, Walter B., *Tito, Mihailovic and the Allies, 1941–1945* (Rutgers: Rutgers University Press, 1973).

Rousso, Henry, *Le Syndrome de Vichy, de 1944 à nos jours* (Paris: Seuil, 1990).

Schivelbusch, Wolfgang, *The Culture of Defeat. On National Trauma, Mourning, and Recovery* (London: Metropolitan Books, 2001).

Teufel, June, *Middle Kingdom and the Land of the Rising Sun: Sino-Japanese Relations Past and Present* (Oxford: Oxford University Press, 2016).

Ward, Steven R., *Immortal: A Military History of Iran and Its Armed Forces* (Washington: Georgetown University Press, 2009).

Wieviorka, Olivier, *La Mémoire Désunie. Le Souvenir Politique des Années Sombres, de la Libération à nos Jours* (Paris: Seuil, 2010).

Index